Tourism Administration

Tourism Administration

Varinder Rana

RANDOM PUBLICATIONS
NEW DELHI (INDIA)

Tourism Administration

ISBN 978-93-5111-943-2

Published in 2016 in India by

RANDOM PUBLICATIONS

4376-A/4B, Gali Murari Lal, Ansari Road
New Delhi-110 002
Phone : +9111-43580356, 011-23289044, 011-43142548
e-mail: sales@randompublications.com,
info@randompublications.com, randomexports@gmail.com

Reprinted 2019

Type Setting by : Friends Media, Delhi-110089
Digitally Printed at: Replika Press Pvt. Ltd.

Preface

Today tourism has flourished as a full fledged industry. It is one of the fastest growing and foreign currency earning industry. Management and administration is also required for this industry. In the present book we have endeavoured to bring everything related to tourism.

Tourism administration is one of the better higher study options for English literature graduates. Good communication skills, proficiency in English and other foreign languages, leadership skills, capacity to work hard and dedication are the prerequisites for a good career in travel and tourism sector. Tourism is the act of travel for predominantly recreational or leisure purposes, and also refers to the provision of services in support of this act. Tourists are people who travel to and stay in places outside their usual environment for not more than one consecutive year for leisure, business and other purposes not related to the exercise of an activity remunerated from within the place visited. The distance between a place of origin and a tourism destination is immaterial to this definition.

This is an essential guide which also explains effective management in relation to current trends in tourism. It incorporates extensive coverage of the characteristics of tourism, making it ideally suited for those studying tourism, travel and business studies. Individual managers and policy decision makers will also find that this book addresses vital management issues and provides practical help.

The book begins with the evolution of tourism and consists all related things like, marketing, administration, a brief description of world and Indian tourist places, factors affecting tourism, development and growth.

– ***Author***

Contents

1

Introduction to Tourism

DEFINING TOURISM

Tourism is the act of travel for predominantly recreational or leisure purposes, and also refers to the provision of services in support of this act. Tourists are people who travel to and stay in places outside their usual environment for not more than one consecutive year for leisure, business and other purposes not related to the exercise of an activity remunerated from within the place visited. The distance between a place of origin and a tourism destination is immaterial to this definition. Tourism has become an extremely popular, global activity.

In 2004, there were over 763 million international tourist arrivals.As a service industry, tourism has numerous tangible and intangible elements. Major tangible elements include transportation, accommodation, and other components of a hospitality industry. Major intangible elements relate to the purpose or motivation for becoming a tourist, such as rest, relaxation, the opportunity to meet new people and experience other cultures, or simply to do something different and have an adventure.

Tourism is vital for many countries, due to the income generated by the consumption of goods and services by tourists, the taxes levied on businesses in the tourism industry, and the opportunity for employment and economic advancement by working in the industry.

For these reasons NGOs and government agencies may sometimes promote a specific region as a tourist destination, and support the development of a tourism industry in that area. The contemporary phenomenon of mass tourism may sometimes result in overdevelopment, however alternative forms of tourism such as ecotourism seek to avoid such outcomes by pursuing tourism in a sustainable way.

The terms tourism and travel are sometimes used interchangeably. In this context travel has a similar definition to tourism, but implies a more purposeful journey. The terms *tourism* and *tourist* are sometimes used pejoratively to imply a shallow interest in the cultures or locations visited by tourists.

Definition, Classification and Prerequisites of International Tourism

One of the earliest definitions of tourism was provided by the Austrian economist Hermann Von Schullard in 1910, who defined it as, "sum total of operators, mainly of an economic nature, which directly relate to the entry, stay and movement of foreigners inside and outside a certain country, city or a region." Hunziker and Krapf, in 1942, defined tourism as "the totality of the relationship and phenomenon arising from the travel and stay of strangers, provided that the stay does not imply the establishment of a permanent residence and is not connected with a remunerative activities". In 1976 Tourism Society of England defined it as "Tourism is the temporary, short-term movement of people to destination outside the places where they normally live and work and their activities during the stay at each destination. It includes movements for all purposes. "In 1981 International Association of Scientific Experts in Tourism defined Tourism in terms of particular activities selected by choice and undertaken outside the home environment.

United Nations classified 3 forms of tourism in 1994 in its Recommendations on Tourism Statistics as follows:

1. Domestic tourism, involving residents of the given country traveling only within this country;
2. Inbound tourism, involving non-residents traveling in the given country;
3. Outbound tourism, involving residents traveling in another country.

UN also derived different categories of tourism by combining the 3 basic forms of tourism:

1. Internal tourism, which comprises domestic tourism and inbound tourism;
2. National tourism, which comprises domestic tourism and outbound tourism;
3. International tourism, which consists of inbound tourism and outbound tourism.

Prerequisites of Tourism

Before people are able to experience tourism they usually need at least:

1. Disposable income, *i.e.* money to spend on non-essentials
2. Leisure time
3. Tourism infrastructure, such as transport and accommodation

Individually, sufficient health is also a condition, and of course the inclination to travel. Furthermore, in some countries there are legal restrictions on travelling, especially abroad.

Certain states with strong governmental control over the lives of citizens (notably established Communist states) may restrict foreign travel only to trustworthy citizens. The United States prohibits its citizens from traveling to some countries, for example, Cuba.

HISTORY OF TOURISM

Wealthy people have always traveled to distant parts of the world, to see great buildings, works of art, learn new languages, experience new cultures and to taste different cuisines. Long ago, at the time of the Roman Republic, places such as Baiae were popular coastal resorts for the rich. The word tourism was used by 1811 and tourist by 1840. In 1936, the League of Nations defined foreign tourist as "someone traveling abroad for at least twenty-four hours". Its successor, the United Nations, amended this definition in 1945, by including a maximum stay of six months.

LEISURE TRAVEL

Leisure travel was associated with the Industrial Revolution in the United Kingdom – the first European country to promote leisure time to the increasing industrial population. Initially, this applied to the owners of the machinery of production, the economic oligarchy, the factory owners and the traders.

These comprised the new middle class. Cox and Kings was the first official travel company to be formed in 1758. The British origin of this new industry is reflected in many place names. In Nice, France, one of the first and best-established holiday resorts on the French Riviera, the long esplanade along the seafront is known to this day as the Promenade des Anglais; in many other historic resorts in continental Europe, old, well-established palace hotels have names like the Hotel Bristol, the Hotel Carlton or the Hotel Majestic – reflecting the dominance of English customers.

Many leisure-oriented tourists travel to the tropics, both in the summer and winter. Places of such nature often visited are: Bali in Indonesia, Brazil, Cuba, the Dominican Republic, Malaysia, Mexico the various Polynesian tropical islands, Queensland in Australia, Thailand, St.Tropez and Cannes in France, Florida, Hawaii and Puerto Rico in the United States, Barbados, St.Marten, St.Kitts, Nevis, Bahamas, Anguilla, Antigua, Aruba, Turks and Caicos and Bermuda.

WINTER TOURISM

Although it is acknowledged that the Swiss were not the inventors of skiing it is well documented that St.Moritz, Graubünden, became the cradle of the developing winter tourism: Since that year of 1865 in St.Moritz, many daring hotel managers choose to risk opening their hotels in winter but it was only in the seventies of the 20th century when winter tourism took over the lead from summer tourism in many of the Swiss ski resorts.

Even in Winter portions of up to one third of all guests consist of non-skiers. Major ski resorts are located mostly in the various European countries, Canada, the United States, New Zealand, Japan, South Korea, Chile, Argentina, Kenya and Tanzania.

MASS TOURISM

Mass tourism could only have developed with the improvements in technology, allowing the transport of large numbers of people in a short space of time to places of leisure interest, so that greater numbers of people could begin to enjoy the benefits of leisure time. In the United States, the first seaside resorts in the European style were at Atlantic City, New Jersey and Long Island, New York. In Continental Europe, early resorts included: Ostend, popularised by the people of Brussels; Boulogne-sur-Mer and Deauville for the Parisians; and Heiligendamm, founded in 1793, as the first seaside resort on the Baltic Sea.

DIFFERENT TYPES OF TOURISM

Wealthy people have always travelled to distant parts of the world to see great buildings or other works of art, to learn new languages, to experience new cultures, or to taste new cuisine. As long ago as the time of the Roman Republic places such as Baiae were popular coastal resorts for the rich.

The terms *tourist* and *tourism* were first used as official terms in 1937 by the League of Nations. Tourism was defined as people travelling abroad for periods of over 24 hours.

The history of European tourism can perhaps be said to originate with the medieval pilgrimage. Although undertaken primarily for religious reasons, the pilgrims in the Canterbury Tales quite clearly saw the experience as a kind of holiday (the term itself being derived from the 'holy day' and its associated leisure activities). Pilgrimages created a variety of tourist aspects that still exist - bringing back souvenirs, obtaining credit with foreign banks (in medieval times utilising international networks established by Jews and Lombards), and making use of space available on existing forms of transport (such as the use of medieval English wine ships bound for Vigo by pilgrims to Santiago De Compostela). Pilgrimages of one sort or another are still important in modern tourism - such as to Lourdes or Knock in Ireland. But there are modern equivalents - Graceland and the grave of Jim Morrison in Pere Lachaise Cemetery.

In the course of the sixteenth century, it became fashionable in England to undertake a Grand Tour. The sons of the nobility and gentry were sent upon an extended tour of Europe as an educational experience. The eighteenth century was the golden age of the Grand Tour, and many of the fashionable visitors were painted at Rome by Pompeo Batoni. The modern equivalent of the Grand Tour is the phenomenon of the backpacker, although cultural holidays, such as those offered by Swann-Hellenic, are also important.

Health tourism has always existed, but it was not until the eighteenth century that it became important. In England, it was associated with spas, places with supposedly health-giving mineral waters, treating diseases from gout to liver disorders and bronchitis. Bath was the most fashionable resort, but Buxton,

Harrogate, and Tunbridge Wells, amongst others, also flourished. Of course, people visited these places for the balls and other entertainments, just as much as 'the waters'. Continental Spas such as Karlsbad attracted many fashionable travellers by the nineteenth century.

It could be argued that Britain was the home of the seaside holiday. In travelling to the coast, the population was following in the steps of Royalty. King George III made regular visits to Weymouth when in poor health. At the time, a number of doctors argued the benefits of bathing in sea water, and sea bathing as a widespread practice was popularised by the Prince Regent (later George IV), who frequented Brighton for this purpose.

Some English travellers, after visiting the warm lands of the south of Europe, decided to stay there either for the cold season or for the rest of their lives. Leisure travel was a British invention due to sociological factors. Britain was the first European country to industrialize, and the industrial society was the first society to offer time for leisure to a growing number of people. Initially, this did not apply to the working masses, but rather to the owners of the machinery of production, the economic oligarchy, the factory owners, and the traders. These comprised the new middle class. Cox and Kings were the first official travel company to be formed in 1758.

The British origin of this new industry is reflected in many place names. At Nice, one of the first and best-established holiday resorts on the French Riviera, the long esplanade along the seafront is known to this day as the Promenade des Anglais; in many other historic resorts in continental Europe, old well-established palace hotels have names like the Hotel Bristol, the Hotel Carlton or the Hotel Majestic - reflecting the dominance of English customers.

Winter Tourism

Winter sports were largely invented by the British leisured classes, initially at the Swiss village of Zermatt (Valais), and St Moritz in 1864. The first packaged winter sports holidays (vacations) followed in 1903, to Adelboden, also in Switzerland. Organized sport was well established in Britain before it reached other countries. The vocabulary of sport bears witness to this: rugby, football, and boxing all originated in Britain, and even Tennis, originally a French sport, was formalized and codified by the British, who hosted the first national championship in the nineteenth century, at Wimbledon. Winter sports were a natural answer for a leisured class looking for amusement during the coldest season.

Mass Travel

Mass travel could not really begin to develop until two things occurred.

- Improvements in technology allowed the transport of large numbers of people in a short space of time to places of leisure interest, and
- Greater numbers of people began to enjoy the benefits of leisure time.

The father of modern mass tourism was Thomas Cook who, on 5 July 1841, organized the first package tour in history. He arranged for the rail company to charge one shilling per person for a group of 570 temperance campaigners from Leicester to a rally in Loughborough, eleven miles away. Cook was paid a share of the fares actually charged to the passengers, as the railway tickets, being legal contracts between company and passenger, could not have been issued at his own price. There had been railway excursions before, but this one included entrance to an entertainment held in private grounds, rail tickets and food for the train journey. Cook immediately saw the potential of a convenient 'off the peg' holiday product in which everything was included in one cost. He organised packages inclusive of accommodation for the Great Exhibition, and afterwards pioneered package holidays in both Britain (particularly in Scotland) and on the European continent (where Paris and the Alps were the most popular destinations).

He was soon followed by others (the Polytechnic Touring Association, Dean and Dawson etc.), with the result that the tourist industry developed rapidly in late Victorian Britain. Initially it was supported by the growing middle classes, who had time off from their work, and who could afford the luxury of travel and possibly even staying for periods of time in boarding houses.

The Bank Holiday Act of 1871 introduced a statutory right for workers to take holidays, even if they were not paid at the time. By the last quarter of the nineteenth century, the tradition of the working class holiday had become firmly established in Britain. These were largely focussed upon the seaside resorts.

The spread of the railway network in the nineteenth century resulted in the growth of Britain's seaside towns by bringing them within easy distance of Britain's urban centres. Blackpool was created by the construction of a line to Fleetwood, and some resorts were promoted by the railway companies themselves - Morecambe by the Midland Railway and Cleethorpes by the Great Central Railway.

Other resorts included Scarborough in Yorkshire, servicing Leeds and Bradford; Weston-super-Mare in Somerset, catering for the inhabitants of Bristol; and Skegness, patronised by the residents of the industrial East Midlands. The cockneys of London flocked to Southend-on-Sea, mainly by Thames Steamer, and the South Coast resorts such as Broadstairs, Brighton, and Eastbourne were only a train ride away, with others further afield such as Bournemouth, Bognor Regis and Weymouth.

For a century, domestic tourism was the norm, with foreign travel being reserved for the rich or the culturally curious. A number of inland destinations, such as the English Lake District, and Snowdonia appealed to those who liked the countryside and fine scenery. The holiday camp began to appear in the 1930s, but this phenomenon really expanded in the post-war period. Butlins and Pontins set this trend, but their popularity waned with the rise of overseas package tours and the increasing comforts to which visitors became accustomed at home. Towards the end of the 20th century this market has been revived by the upmarket inland resorts of Dutch company Center Parcs.

Cox and Co, the forebear of Cox and Kings were in existence from 1758 largely entwined with the travel arrangements for the British Army serving around the Empire. While acting as 'agents' for various regiments, they organised the payment, provision, clothing and travel arrangements for members of the armed forces. In the 19th century their network of offices contained a banking and also travel department. The company became heavily involved with affairs in India and its Shipping Agency had offices in France and the Middle East.

Other phenomena that helped develop the travel industry were paid holidays:

- 1.5 million manual workers in Britain had paid holidays by 1925
- 11 million by 1939 (30 per cent of the population in families with paid holidays)

International Mass Tourism

Increasing speed on railways meant that the tourist industry could develop internationally. To this may be added the development of sea travel. By 1901, the number of people crossing the English Channel from England to France or Belgium had passed 0.5 million per year. Shipping companies were anxious to fill cabin space that was under utilised. For example, PandO found that the majority of their passengers for India and the Far East joined the ship at Marseilles. Consequently, they marketed holidays based upon sea trips from London to Lisbon and Gibraltar. Other companies diverted their older ships to operate cruises in the summer months.

However, the real age of international mass travel began with the growth of air travel after World War Two. In the immediate post-war period, there was a surplus of transport aircraft, such as the popular and reliable Douglas Dakota, and a number of ex military pilots ready to fly them. They were available for charter flights, and tour operators began to use them for European destinations, such as Paris and Ostend.

Vladimir Raitz pioneered modern package tourism when on 20 May 1950 his recently founded company, Horizon, provided arrangements for a two-week holiday in Corsica. For an all inclusive price of £32.10s.-, holiday makers could sleep under canvas, sample local wines and eat a meal containing meat twice a day - this was especially attractive due to the continuing austerity measures in post-war United Kingdom. Within ten years, his company had started mass tourism to Palma (1952), Lourdes (1953), Costa Brava (1954), Sardinia (1954), Minorca (1955), Porto (1956), Costa Blanca (1957) and Costa del Sol (1959).

However it was with cheap air travel in combination with the package tour that international mass tourism developed. The postwar introduction of an international system of airline regulation was another important factor. The bilateral agreements at the heart of the system fixed seat prices, and airlines could not fill blocks of empty seats on underused flights by discounting.

But if they were purchased by a tour operater and hidden within the price of an inclusive holiday package, it would be difficult to prove that discounting had taken place - even though it was obvious that it had! This was the origin of the modern mass package tour.These developments coincided with a significant increase in the standard of living in Britain. At the end of the 1950s, Harold Macmillan could say "you've never had it so good."

Another significant development also happened at the end of this decade. The devaluation of the Spanish peseta made Spain appear a particularly attractive destination. The cheapness of the cost of living attracted increasing numbers of visitors. Mass package tourism has at times been an exploitative process, in which tour operators in a country with a high standard of living make use of development opportunities and low operating costs in a country with a lower standard of living.

However, as witness the development of many tourist areas in previously poor parts of the world, and the concomitant rise in standards of living, when there is equality of bargaining power, both parties can gain economic benefits from this arrangement. Spain and the Balearic Islands became major tourist destinations, and development probably peaked in the 1980s. At the same time, British tour operators developed the Algarve in Portugal. The continuing search for new, cheaper, destinations spread mass tourism to the Greek Islands, Italy, Tunisia, Morocco, parts of the coast of Turkey, and more recently Croatia. For the worker living in greater London, Venice today is almost as accessible as Brighton was 100 years ago. Consequently, the British seaside resort experienced a marked decline from the 1970s onwards. Some, such as New Brighton have disappeared. Others have reinvented themselves, and now cater to daytrippers and the weekend break market.

Recent Developments

There has been a discernible upmarket trend in tourism ovèr the last few decades, especially in Europe where international travel for short breaks is commonplace. Tourists have higher levels of disposable income and greater leisure time. They are also better educated and have more sophisticated tastes. There is now a demand for a better quality product in many quarters. This has resulted in the following trends:-

- The old 'sun, sea, and sand' mass market has fragmented. People want more specialised versions of it, such as 'Club 18-30', quieter resorts with select hotels, self-catering, etc.
- People are taking second holidays in the form of short breaks/city breaks, ranging from British and European cities to country hotels.

- There has been a growth in niche markets catering for special interests or activities, including growth of destination hotels.

The developments in technology and transport infrastructure (particularly the advent of jumbo jets) have placed some types of holiday in the affordable mainstream:-

- The development of a mass cruise holiday market.
- The advent of affordable holidays to long-haul destinations such as Thailand or Kenya.
- The phenomenon of the low budget airline, utilising a new generation of small regional airports.

There have also been changes in lifestyle, which may call into question the current definitions of tourism. Some people (particularly the 45+ and retired) may be adopting a tourism lifestyle, living as a tourist all the year round - eating out several times a week, going to the theatre, daytripping, and indulging in short breaks several times a year.

Much of this results in impulse purchasing. This is facilitated by internet purchasing of tourism products. Some sites have now started to offer dynamic packaging, in which an inclusive price is quoted for a tailor- made package requested by the customer upon impulse.

There have been a few setbacks in tourism, such as the September 11, 2001 attacks and terrorist threats to tourist destinations such as Bali and European cities. Some of the tourist destinations, including the Costa del Sol, the Baleares and Cancún have lost popularity due to shifting tastes. In this context, the excessive building and environmental destruction often associated with traditional "sun and beach" tourism may contribute to a destination's saturation and subsequent decline. This appears to be the case with Spain's Costa Brava, a byword for this kind of tourism in the 1960s and 1970s. With only 11 per cent of the Costa Brava now unblemished by low-quality development (Greenpeace Spain's figure), the destination now faces a crisis in its tourist industry.

Sustainable tourism is becoming more popular as people start to realize the devastating effects tourism can have on communities. Receptive tourism is now growing at a very rapid rate in many developing countries, where it is often the most important economic activity in local GDP.

In recent years, second holidays or vacations have become more popular as people's discretionary income increases. Typical combinations are a package to the typical mass tourist resort, with a winter skiing holiday or weekend break to a city or national park. On December 26, 2004 a tsunami, caused by the 2004 Indian Ocean earthquake hit Asian countries bordering the Indian Ocean, and also the Maldives. Tens of thousands of lives were lost, and many tourists died. This, together with the vast clean-up operation in place, has stopped or severely hampered tourism to the area.

CHANGING FACETS OF TOURISM

From the very inception of life, travel has fascinated man. Travel and tourism have been important social activities of human beings from time immemorial. The urge to explore new places within one's own country or outside and seek a change of environment and experience has been experienced from ancient times. Tourism is one of the world's most rapidly growing industries. Much of its growth is due to higher disposable incomes, increased leisure time and falling costs of travel. As airports become more enjoyable places to pass through, as travel agency services become increasingly automated, and as tourists find it easier to get information on places they want to visit, tourism grows.

The Internet has fuelled the growth of the travel industry by providing on line booking facilities. It has also provided people with the power to explore destinations and cultures from their home personal computers and make informed choices before finalizing travel plans. With its immense information resources, the Internet allows tourists to scrutinise hotels, check weather forecasts, read up on local food and even talk to other tourists around the world about their travel experiences for a chosen destination. This new trend has made the tourism job very challenging. The holiday makers want a good rate of return on their investment. They are to be lured with value additions and improved customer service.

This also put emphasis on the regular flow of manpower with specific skills at the appropriate levels to match and cater to global standards. The success of the hospitality industry comes from provision of quality rooms, food, service and ambience. There is no doubt that fitness has increasingly become a larger part of everyone's life. And business and leisure travellers alike look to maintain their fitness goals while away from home. Awareness should be created about the environment and education.

A collective effort and co-operation with powerful networking are the need of the hour. People should be acting as the watchdogs of the society as far as environmental issues are concerned. Eco-tourists are a growing community and tourism promotions have to adopt such eco-practices which could fit this growing community. Another growing trend in the tourism scene is the Incentive Market and the scope of the destination to attract conferences and convention traffic. Here the prospects are better for those destinations where state of the art infrastructure has been developed along with a safe and clean image. Tourism today is much more than just developing products. It is more about quality, insightful thinking and ability to have global information about technology, partners, contacts and responding quickly to global and regional trends. The fundamental task before tourism promotion is to facilitate integration of the various components in the tourism trade as active participants in the nation's social and cultural life. There is a long road ahead. All must work towards a society where people can work and participate as equal partners. Tourism should be a vehicle for international cooperation and understanding of the various civilizations and a harbinger of peace. From the foregoing we can see how fast the face of tourism is changing and how challenging the job of travel agencies is now. There is therefore a need for proper training of the personnel working in the industry through thorough and a detailed study of the subject A unified approach to the subject is also needed since at present people from different fields have been studying tourism from different perspectives.

DIFFERENT PERSPECTIVES ON THE STUDY OF TOURISM

GEOGRAPHICAL PERSPECTIVE

Geographical Perspective—from a geographer's perspective the main concern of tourism is to look into aspects like the geographical location of a place, the climate, the landscape, the environment, the physical planning and the changes in these emerging from provisioning of tourism facilities and amenities. A geographer feels that it is the climate, landscape or physical attributes which draw the tourist to a destination, for example; if a person from Delhi goes to Shimla in the summer he does so because of the cooler climate which he cannot get in Delhi

SOCIOLOGICAL PERSPECTIVE

From a sociologist's perspective Tourism is a social activity; it is about interaction between different communities—hosts and guests—and encounter between different cultures. This approach studies social classes, habits and customs of both hosts and guests in terms of tourism behaviour of individuals or groups of people and the impact of tourism on society.

HISTORICAL PERSPECTIVE

An historian's perspective tourism is a study of the factors instrumental in the initiation of tourism to a particular destination, the order of happenings leading to tourism development, the reasons for happening of the occurrences in that order, beneficiaries of the tourist activity and an untimely and premature identification of negative effects. For example we all know that a lot of tourists visit Taj Mahal in Agra but a historian would be interested in studying the factors that bring the tourist there, *e.g.* the architecture, the story behind the monument, or something else that draws them there.

MANAGERIAL PERSPECTIVE

The management perspective tourism is an industry, and therefore needs managerial skills in order to be properly managed. As the industry grows we see continuous changes in various organisations and services linked with the industry, the tourism products and so on so this approach concentrates on management activities such as planning, research, pricing, marketing, control etc. as vital to the operation of a tourist establishment.

ECONOMIC PERSPECTIVE

From an economist's perspective tourism is a major source of foreign exchange earnings, a generator of personal and corporate incomes, a creator of employment and a contributor to government earnings. It is a dominant global activity surpassing even trade in oil and manufactured goods. Economists study the effects of tourism industry on the economy. This is a two way process.

THE IMPORTANCE OF MANAGERIAL AND ECONOMIC PERSPECTIVES OF TOURISM

Now due to higher disposable incomes, increased leisure time and falling cost of travel, the Tourism industry has shown a very high growth and since tourism is a service industry it comprises of a number of tangible and intangible components. The tangible elements include transport systems—air, rail, road, water and now, space; hospitality services—accommodation, food and beverage, tours, souvenirs; and related services such as banking, insurance and safety and security. The intangible elements include: rest and relaxation, culture, escape, adventure, new and different experiences. As there are number of bodies involved the need arises for a management of services related to this industry and so the study of Tourism acquires a great practical necessity and usefulness. Tourism industry is very fast growing and this industry involves activities and interests of Transport Undertakings, Owners of Tourist Sites and Attractions, Various tourist Service Providers at the tourist destinations and Central and Local Government, etc. Each of these serves both the resident population and the tourists and their management must reconcile the needs of tourists with the needs of the resident population. So it becomes important to study tourism from the perspective of Management, since the management of various bodies in this industry is invaded.

TOURISM AND DEVELOPMENT

Development can be viewed from various dimensions, however, for the purpose of this current session, we use the following definition of economic development: Economic development is a process of economic transition that involves the structural transformation of an economy and a growth of the real output of an economy over a period of time. It is a long run concept. Structural transformation is achieved through modernization and industrialization and is measured in terms of the relative contribution to gross domestic product of agriculture, industry and service sectors. The potential of tourism to contribute to development is widely recognized in the industrialized countries, with tourism playing an increasingly important role and receiving government support. Tourism along with some other activities like financial services and tele-communications is a major component of economic strategies. Tourism has become a favoured means of addressing the socio- economic problems facing rural areas on one end, while enhancing development of urban areas on the other.

TOURISM AND NATIONAL DEVELOPMENT

Tourism emerged as a global phenomenon in the 1960s and the potential for tourism to generate economic development was widely promoted by national governments. They appreciated that tourism generated foreign exchange earnings, created employment and brought economic benefits to regions with limited options for alternative economic development. National tourism authorities were created to promote tourism and to maximize international arrivals.

However, an awareness of the negative environmental, social and some other impacts also increased. The importance of economic benefits at the local level, environmental and social sustainability was also widely accepted. It was observed that tourism presents excellent opportunities for developing entrepreneurship, for staff training and progression and for the development of transferable skills. Tourism development focuses on national and regional master planning. It also focuses on international promotion, attracting inward investment. The primary concern has been with maximizing foreign exchange earnings. These earnings enable the government to finance debt and also to finance some investment in technology and other imports for economic development.

NO TRADE BARRIERS TO TOURISM

Unlike many other forms of international trade, tourism does not suffer from the imposition of trade barriers, such as quotas or tariffs. Mostly, destination countries have free and equal access to the international tourism market. This position has become strengthened by the inclusion of tourism in the General Agreement on Trade in Services, which became operational in January 1995.

REDISTRIBUTION OF WEALTH

Both internationally and domestically, tourism is seen as an effective means of transferring income, wealth and investment from richer, developed countries or regions to less developed, poorer areas. This redistribution occurs as a result of both tourist expenditures in destination areas and also of investment by the richer, tourist generating countries in tourist facilities. Thus it appears as if, the developed countries support the economic growth and development of less developed countries.

TOURISM AND POVERTY REDUCTION

Tourism can contribute to development and the reduction of poverty in a number of ways. Economic benefits are generally the most important element, but there can be social, environmental and cultural benefits and costs as well. Tourism contributes to poverty reduction by providing employment and various livelihood opportunities. This additional income helps the poor by increasing the range of economic opportunities available to them. Tourism also contributes to poverty alleviation through direct taxation of tourism generated income. Taxes can be used to alleviate poverty through education, health and infrastructure development. Some tourism facilities also improve the recreational and leisure opportunities available for the poor themselves at the local level. Tourism is not very different from other productive sectors but it has four potential advantages for pro-poor economic growth:

- It has higher linkage with other local businesses because customers come to the destination;
- It is relatively labour intensive and employs a large proportion of women workers;
- It has high potential in poor countries and areas with few other competitive exports;
- Tourism products can be built on natural resources and culture, which might sometimes be the only assets that people have.

The contribution of tourism to the local economy is also important to note. It has five kinds of positive economic impacts on livelihood, any or all of which can form part of a poverty reduction strategy:

- Collective income which may include profits from a community run enterprise, land rent, dividends from joint ventures. These incomes can provide significant development capital and provide finance for corngrinding mills, a clinic, teachers housing and school books
- Dividends and profits arising from locally owned firms and business units
- Earnings from selling goods and service or casual labour
- Infrastructure gains, for example, roads, water pipes, electricity and communications.
- Wages from formal employment

At this point it must also be mentioned that there are some disadvantages of tourism as well. For example, leakages and volatility of revenue. These are also common to other economic sectors. However, tourism may involve greater trade-offs with local livelihoods through more competition for natural resources, particularly in coastal areas.

STRATEGY FOR DEVELOPING COUNTRIES

Tourism plays a very important role in the economies of many countries. Earnings from tourism-related activities contribute a considerable portion to their GDPs. Tourism is now being viewed as a significant tool and an important strategy in achieving economic growth in these countries. The WTO is convinced that tourism has considerable potential for growth in many developing countries and Less Developed Countries where it is a significant economic sector and promising high growth rate; and that it has advantages when compared with other economic sectors. This case can be summarized as follows: Comparative Advantages of Tourism as a Development Strategy for Developing Countries.

- Access to international markets is a serious problem for developing countries particularly in traditional sectors like food, agriculture and textiles where they confront tariff and non-tariff barriers. This is not the case for the tourism sector, where barriers would involve visa restrictions and related taxes only. The example of Cuba is instructive in this regard. Whilst Cuba has struggled to find export markets for its sugar and tobacco, it has been much more successful in maintaining a dynamic tourism industry.
- In many developing countries, for example South Africa, China, Philippines and India, domestic tourism is growing rapidly and like international tourism brings relatively wealthy consumers to areas where they constitute an important local market. Domestic tourism can be accessed by people with lower budgets and is often equally valuable to the economy.
- Most export industries depend on financial, productive and human capital. The tourism industry not only depends on these, but also on natural capital and culture, which are sometimes the only assets owned by the poor.
- Tourism has particular potential in many countries with few other competitive exports.
- Tourism is a much more diverse industry than many others and can build upon a wide resource base. This diversity results in wider participation of the informal sector, for example a farming household produces and sells local handicrafts.
- Tourism is consumed at the point of production. This results in great opportunities for individuals and micro-enterprises, in urban or marginal rural areas, to sell additional products or services to the potential consumers.
- Tourism is often reported to be more labour intensive than other productive sectors. Data from six countries with satellite tourism accounts does indicate that it is more labour intensive than non-

agricultural activities, particularly manufacturing, although less labour intensive than agriculture.

- Tourism provides various employment opportunities especially to women as compared to some of the other sectors.

Perceived Disadvantages of Tourism as a Development Strategy:

- Foreign private interests drive tourism and it is difficult to maximize local economic benefits due to the high level of foreign ownership, which means that there are high levels of leakages and few local linkages. But that might not be the case many times.
- Many small enterprises and individual traders sustain themselves around hotels and other tourism facilities and these small companies are not foreign owned. There is often confusion about levels of foreign ownership as local ownership is often masked by franchise agreements and management contracts. WTO is studying this issue in collaboration with UNCTAD as part of its poverty elimination research.
- Tourism can impose substantial non-economic costs on the poor. For example, loss of access to resources, displacement from agricultural land, social and cultural disruption and exploitation.
- Many forms of development bring with them disadvantages that need to be managed. The economic and non-economic negative impact needs to be determined and the issues addressed. It is for this reason that the WTO supports a holistic livelihood approach to assessing the impact of tourism-positive and negative–on the poor. Issues like environmental management and planning at local level need to be addressed through the good governance agenda.
- Tourism is a vulnerable industry. It reacts immediately to factors like changes in economic conditions in the originating markets, levels of economic activity in tourism in the destination markets. Thereby affecting international visitor arrivals. It is also very vulnerable to civil unrest, crime, political instability and natural disasters in destination countries.
- It has been observed that the volatility of export markets for tourism is not significantly greater than other commodities. Many times tourism has the advantage noted that it is not subject to tariff or other non-tariff barriers and that the destination has some control over civil unrest, crime and political instability
- Tourism requires highly sophisticated marketing. International tourism marketing is expensive, although there are more efficient and less costly forms of marketing available today. Many government agencies at the national level, tie ups of domestic hotels and resorts with international participants, word of mouth publicity, target marketing are some of the methods used.

Tourism in many developing countries and many LDCs has been growing strongly in recent years and there are strong reasons to think that these trends will continue. Many developing countries have comparative advantages in tourism where tourism constitutes one of their better opportunities for development.

The disadvantages, which are often identified in relation to international tourism in developing countries, are few when tourism is compared with other sectors of the economy. WTO believes that tourism is considered alongside other industries as a development option and that where tourism presents the best opportunity for local economic development and antipoverty strategies, development banks, bilateral and multilateral development agencies should back it with determination.

LINKAGES AND LEAKAGES

The term leakage in used to refer to the amount spent on importing goods and services to meet the needs of tourists. Leakages take place across national boundaries that can have impact on the balance of payments of the countries. It results from the economic exchange between the two countries. It also occurs when the local economy is unable to provide reliable, continuous, supplies on the basis of competitive prices of the required product or service and of a consistent quality to meet the market demand.

From a tourism and poverty perspective it is generally more productive to focus on the other side of the coin-linkages. When the local economic linkages are weak, the revenue received from tourism in the local economic area leaks out. In order to reduce such leakages, it becomes necessary to deliver consistently at an appropriate quality and at competitive prices, at the same time, engaging the local suppliers who use local capital and resources.

LEAKAGES

From the perspectives of local economic development and poverty reduction, we are not concerned how much a tourist spends outside the country, but how much he is not spending in the local economy, which means, limiting the benefit to local communities and the poor among them.

Leakages, which have negative impact on the development of local tourism, are:

- Advertising and marketing efforts abroad
- Impact skills, expatriate labour
- Imported commodities, goods and services
- Imported technology and capital goods
- Increased oil imports
- Repatriation of profits
- Transporting tourists to the destination country

However developing local sources of supply, encouraging local ownership and enhancing linkages to the local economy can improve this. The last two of these can create more jobs and opportunities for small and medium enterprises at the same time.

LINKAGES

There are many ways in which local communities can be benefitted by these propositions. The best way is to increase the extent of linkages between formal tourism sector and the local economy. By formal tourism sector we mean hotels, restaurants, lodges, and tour and transport agencies. To the extent linkages to the local economy can be increased, the extent of leakages will be reduced.

The increased integration can further develop strong linkages between tourism and other economic sectors. Not only do agriculture, fisheries, manufacturing, construction and domestic industries get integrated, the auxiliary and ancillary industries are also strengthened.

This in turn provides additional revenue and jobs, which reduces the import content and foreign exchange leakages from the tourism industry. Government and development agencies should create local linkages as part of their overall tourism development strategy in the planning, construction and operational phases.

There are three sets of factors, which are important in enhancing the extent of local linkages:

- The creation of employment at all skill levels and particularly where there is existing capacity.
- The Anti-poverty tourism development strategies have suggested 'new attractions'. The tour operators at the ground level should integrate these. The critical areas include creating mutually beneficial business linkages between the formal and informal sectors. Small and emerging entrepreneurs are often neglected. Local government should ensure that microenterprises and emerging entrepreneurs are promoted while taking local tourism marketing initiatives. Visitor attractions, parks, cultural sites and hotels should be encouraged to provide information about local products and services provided by the poor.
- There is need to understand tourist expectations thoroughly. Also, small enterprises to meet the credit needs and marketing needs are also required. Small enterprises sometimes face difficulties in meeting the requirements of health and safety, licensing and other regulatory requirements. There is a need to systematically educate and train the poor in such a way that they are able to integrate themselves with the growing requirements relating to regulations.

The local market should be geared up to deliver qualitatively reliable and competitive goods and services to tourists. The local business community should be actively involved in the process through partnership approaches. This requires continuous efforts, which is possible through long-term partnership to benefit from linkages. Once planning commission concessions are being granted, private sector companies can be asked to make the development of such linkages part of their bid.

Tourism can help in diversifying other sectors of the local economy and can create new ones, offering additional community livelihood opportunities. Local economic benefits and ownership are likely to be greater, if local communities participate in diversified business activities. Now with the growing awareness governments are adopting policies, to encourage and facilitate participation by the local communities. The participation by the poor in the development of tourism projects may result in increasing employment and growth of complementary products. These benefits can further be maximized through partnerships at the destination level. There is a tremendous possibility of bringing about sustainable development for the local economy if Hotels and tour operators work together with local communities, local government and NGOs.

This can help in reducing poverty and can provide a richer experience to domestic and international tourists. Such partnerships will benefit both the host communities and the tourism industry. This will also help them earn more tourism dollars, euros or pounds without any leakages. This can further be utilized for community development. Through affirmative policies, enterprises can contribute significantly to economic development, in both their constructional and operational phases. Some practical strategies for developing local economic linkages.

Market Access and Enclave Tourism

There is practically no link between local people and tourism market. Tourists are not accessible to the local community when they are within their hotels, coaches, and safari vehicles or inside sites and attractions such as museums. These are all enclave forms of tourism. The local community people who wish to sell their products to tourists don't have access to them. They end up hawking and touting at entry points.

The problem is still more difficult in case of Cruise ship passengers and tourist on "all inclusive" hotel or resort packages where local entrepreneurs hardly interact with them. Access to the market plays major role in involving entrepreneurs in the tourism industry. This is particularly true in the case of the informal sector; where the return on local skills and services is often maximized and where the scale of capital investments is low. There is a need to keep this aspect in mind at the time of tourism planning, as access to tourists for the informal sector is often neglected. Some tourists prefer all-inclusive packages, as they do not always feel safe in a new destination and are happier in a protected environment. They feel protected from the poverty and hassle from beggars, touts and hawkers in some destinations. But there is a way to solve this problem. This requires partnership approach between Hotel and informal traders.

This allows informal traders to provide such an environment where tourists feel secure in moving beyond the enclave and to approach "hassle-free" crafts markets. Local guides can also help in establishing contact between tourists and traders by rotation for which they may have agreement among themselves.

This also requires observing certain code of conduct by the local traders and guide. There should be a design to link the informal sector with formal sector so that poor members of community can be helped and tourist market becomes accessible to them. This can help them gain the economic benefit from it. There are a number of strategies that can be used to enhance overall economic benefits and can further reduce poverty.

Growth and Selection

Attracting more of the most appropriate market Segments It has been observed that the tourism sector in the poorest countries is generally highly dependent on international markets, as they do not have significant domestic markets. However, it has also been noted earlier that a significant number of developing countries have strong domestic tourism sectors as well as significant outbound tourists. It becomes imperative that the domestic market should always be considered first by the poorest countries, but in order to maximize foreign exchange revenues, the primary focus continues to be on international arrivals. There is a challenge to attract larger numbers of those international and domestic tourists who are most likely to benefit the poor, those predisposed to visit local markets and to seek first hand experiences of nature, culture and daily life which are most likely to be provided by poor people. It is worth mentioning the importance of intra-regional tourism in this regard; WTO reported intra-regional tourism as growing in most regions of the world. It is significant that 40 per cent of Africa's tourism comes from neighbouring African countries. This opportunity can be grabbed by opening up the roads and improving the modes of transport between countries in Africa, which would greatly enhance the movement of people and contribute in reducing poverty. Intra-regional tourism is especially valuable for pro-poor tourism and local economic development.

This is because of the fact that there is greater likelihood of shared cultural values and familiarity with social systems between the people of neighbouring countries. There is no doubt that there is a case for attracting more visitors in order to increase the economic impact. At the same time we must understand that this strategy will only assist in poverty reduction if the additional tourists can be encouraged to spend in ways that benefit the poor and if it results in overall sustainability.

The World Bank's World Development Report recognized that economic growth does not necessarily result in swift poverty reduction. This requires an explicitly pro-poor strategy. This means that there should be constant growth, which favours poor in a disproportionate way.

Some of the key components of broad-based growth which assist in benefiting the poor include:

- Government commitment and responsiveness to the needs of the poor
- The expansion of employment opportunities for the poor
- Improved productivity for the poor,
- Improved access for the poor to credit, knowledge and infrastructure,
- Investment in the human capital of the poor.

Increasing Tourists' Length of Stay

The economic returns can be increased with the same number of tourist arrivals if efforts can be made to extend their stay for a longer period. This results in the development of the product by increasing the numbers of bed nights and the expenditure of tourists on boarding and lodging.

There will be a poverty reduction impact, if the additional bed nights can create extra employment or create greater opportunities for the poor to sell goods and services to the tourists or to the tourism industry.

Increasing Visitor Expenditure

Now-a-days there is a market trend towards more experiential holidays. Tourists want to learn more about the countries they are visiting: the people, their cultures, traditions, cuisine, etc. It is much more than mere holidaymaking. The trend is towards more active holidays, greater personal involvement and active participation instead of passive relaxation. This again has potential for the diversification and enrichment of the tourism product. There is scope to develop more activities and attractions, with increased demand for interpreters and services of guides and transport necessary for their enjoyment. This increases both expenditure and length of stay. Making more extensive use of natural and cultural heritage, at the same time carefully managing the tourism impacts so as to ensue the conservation of resources, can make an important contribution both to economic development and conservation. This leads to growth in "Special interest tourists" who tend to spend more money on and during their holidays and to stay longer, whether those interests are based on natural, archaeological, historical or cultural heritage, or based on adventure and physical challenge.

Developing Complementary Products

Providing a greater variety and richness of attractions and activities at destination can increase tourists' expenditure. This will increase the propensity of travellers to visit various attractions at the destination and may extend their length of stay and increase their expenditure.

This translates into creating more promising opportunities for the development of complementary products that enable the poor to engage in the industry and to profit from it. The growth in established industry results in stimulating interest in the development of complementary products: tourism services and goods.

This complements the core tourism facilities of transport, excursions and accommodation. The list of complementary effects goes on increasing. These complementary tourism products often provide experiences that are not provided by the tour operators but which enrich their product. Hoteliers and tour operators can encourage local people to develop tourism products and services and to support them in doing so with training and marketing. This will increase the attractiveness of the destination and increase tourist expenditure in the local economy and will also develop the complementary products.

Local communities can often engage in the provision of complementary products because it requires less capital investment and is therefore less risky. Tourism is often best considered as an additional diversification option for the poor, rather than a substitute for their core means of livelihood. As an additional source of income it can play an important part in improving living standards and raising people above the poverty threshold. The poor can maximize their returns by choosing forms of participation, which complement their existing livelihood strategies. It also helps them earn from their cultural and social assets.

Tourists are interested in the "everyday lives" of local communities and there are a host of smallenterprise opportunities for local people. Local guides and cyclerickshaw driver/guides in India's Keoladeo National Park, and guides and charter-boat operators in Indonesia's Komodo National Park are examples of local people diversifying their livelihood strategies. The boat operators also earn their living from fishing and many of the cycle-rickshaw drivers work in town when the tourist season is low.

Spreading the Benefits of Tourism Geographically

Tourism destinations are geographically diverse in nature. There are different geographical sites like beaches, mountains and urban attractions and holidaymakers can be encouraged to travel further, beyond established destinations, which can enhance and diversify their experience of particular environmental, cultural or natural heritage attractions. Heritage Trails and other similar products have been developed to extend length of stay and to spread the advantages of tourism development to new areas and communities.

They can be used as initiatives, which may benefit the poor. National Parks, cultural sites and World heritage sites are often the major attractions, the primary "tourism magnets" in significant parts of the developing world and they often attract people to marginal rural areas. It can be argued that natural and cultural heritage sites as the major attractions should be taking a wider view of their potential to contribute to tourism development and the well-being of local communities. These areas otherwise are of no interest to tourists.

Changing the way in which tourism is organized in and around attractions can increase the economic development impact. For example, at Kamodo National Park in Indonesia, non-local carriers and package tour operators take away a big slice of tourism trip expenditure, *i.e.*, about 85 per cent, which could have otherwise gone to local economy. Estimates for average local expenditure at Komodo per visitor demonstrate the importance of minimizing enclave tourism.

Cruise ship tourists spent on average US $0, 03 in the local economy, package tourists spent US $52.5 and independent travellers US $97.4. The Parks and other major tourism attractions in rural areas can be developed to assist the development of small-scale, locally owned attractions and tourism services. Nature-based tourism and cultural heritage tourism in rural areas can provide significant local markets and economic development opportunities. It contributes to integrated rural development and offers local employment and supplementary income-generating opportunities for poor people. The development of tourism in such areas can significantly improve incomes for local communities and the poor. For this these flagship attractions can be planned and managed so as to maximize the opportunities for local economic development and poverty reduction.

Infrastructure and Planning Gain

The development of infrastructure and tourism development are interrelated. Tourism can contribute to overall socio-economic development through the provision of roads, telephones, and electricity, piped and treated water supplies, waste disposal and recycling and sewage treatment. Roads developed for tourism provide opportunities for trade and new roads opened to improve trade also bring tourism opportunities if they open access to tourism resources. New economic corridor development projects often create tourism development opportunities for local communities in addition to improving trade linkages. These facilities enhance opportunities for other forms of local economic development, but more could be done at the local and national level to maximize those benefits, particularly when new projects are licensed. It is possible to maximize the planning gains through appropriate policies by government and tourism planners. The right policy in the right direction will encourage local economic development and benefit the poor.

Local Management of Tourism and Partnerships

Local communities and the poor amongst them are more likely to benefit from planning gain where they are involved in discussions and decisions about tourism developments. Benefits can be maximized where the complementarities between different forms of tourism development and their livelihood strategies are given due consideration. Appropriate planning structures can facilitate effective community participation in the tourism development process and provide a mechanism for capturing planning gain through infrastructure, employment and economic linkages. A planning process should define carrying capacity and set limits of acceptable change.

This will influence local communities' active participation in tourism development and help in achieving anti-poverty goals. It is through participation by these local community people whose traditional and local knowledge can be utilized for empowering them. This will also help in maintaining the environmental, social and cultural integrity of destinations.

Small and Medium Enterprises Development

The increased interest in local tourism experience results in increased opportunities for the development of new locally owned enterprises. This helps in providing competitive and complementary goods and services. This trend is found in developed country destinations. This can be supported by government policy and SME development strategies. The tourism industry offers viable opportunities for the development of a wide range of SME's. Even in the developed countries they contribute to the largest part of local tourism supply.

In Europe small and medium-sized firms meet 70 per cent of tourist accommodation demand. Some estimates for the developing world put the comparable figure as high as 85 per cent In well-established developing country destinations, like Goa, increasing numbers of international tourists are staying in locally owned accommodation. SME's are very important in the provision of restaurants and bars, handicrafts, the supply of furnishings and other consumables to hotels, the provision of transport, local tour operating, guiding and attractions. All this requires access to capital resources and training in business management for SME's. This requirement is critical in the field of marketing. Providing information, advice and mentoring to small and micro enterprises and emerging entrepreneurs can make a significant contribution to their success.

Reducing Seasonality

Seasonality in tourist arrivals is the major cause of seasonal and casual unemployment. There are a number of strategies that can be employed to extend the tourism season. During festivals arranging melas generates curiosity and helps the development of special interest products. Other strategies include developing places for seminars and conventions, and such pricing policies, which specially address senior citizens who have more flexibility to travel in the low season.

These strategies have an overall impact on the local economy. Strategies that reduce seasonality and successfully attract tourists in significant numbers for a larger part of the year, benefit the hotels and tour operators, their employees and those in the destination who earn all or part of their livelihood by direct or indirect sales to tourists or the tourism industry. Those who benefit from this are most often poor.

EMPLOYMENT LINKAGES

The employment impact of tourism is felt by both direct employment in tourism enterprises and indirect employment in those enterprises and micro-enterprises that supply raw material, goods and services to the tourism industry. The demand of direct employment in tourism is dependent upon the scale and level of tourism development and the extent of tourists' engagement in the local economy and with SME's. This helps in maximizing the employment of locals and nationals in tourism, including managerial grades.

Income is also held within the local and national economies and reduces wage and salary leakages. When wages and salaries are remitted or spent outside the local boundaries, it amounts to leakages from the local economy. However, the success of the tourism enterprise will depend upon the delivery of the appropriate level of service, and in this global industry maintaining high levels of training is an important consideration in the economic sustainability of businesses. One of the ways in which the industry can contribute to poverty reduction is by committing to recruit more local poor people and imparting appropriate training and staff development programmes with the belief that those commitments can be met. Tourism can contribute to poverty alleviation through the creation of employment. Certain changes in existing employment practices can bring desirable developments. Pro-poor employment strategies can be pursued, for example prioritizing the employment of women and youth. Tourism is a relatively labour intensive industry providing direct employment in hotels and tour companies, and indirect employment in taxis, bars, restaurants and other indirect service suppliers, where a proportion of employee time serves the tourism industry and tourists.

Tourism can create jobs, which benefit the poor where specific measures are taken to recruit and train workers from amongst the poor. Where tourism enterprises make these efforts, proper estimates should be made; records should be maintained of its effects on employment to determine to what extent local people, and particularly the poor, benefit and to ensure that their efforts are acknowledged. Beyond the hotels, particular efforts should be made to train and employ local guides, artists, performers and craft workers who are able to interpret their heritage and in the process empower youth and women who have considerable control over it. Entrepreneurship development programmes for tourism SME's do complement these efforts.

These programmes typically include developing business opportunity awareness, business planning including project feasibility analysis and training in management skills. Provision of business advisors and mentoring services may be strengthened for emerging entrepreneurs over several years. Many countries already have small business development and credit programmes and tourism SME development can sometimes be attached to these existing programmes.

MOVING BEYOND "TRICKLEDOWN" EFFECT

It has long been established that tourism development projects, if successful, would attract foreign investment, contribute foreign exchange earnings to the national accounts and generate economic development. Through the process of trickledown, the magnitude of benefits would be amplified. Local communities would benefit through employment and local economic development generated by the additional spending and the new entrepreneurial opportunities which this would create. It must be understood that tourism operations need to be profitable in a competitive world market if they are to survive. There are a number of things, which can benefit the local economy in tourist destinations.

The benefits can arise in the following ways:

- Building and complementing existing livelihood strategies through employment and small enterprise development
- Controlling negative social impacts
- Ensuring the maintenance of natural and cultural assets
- Evaluating tourism projects for their contribution to local economic development not just for their national revenue generation and the increase in international arrivals
- Facilitating local community access to the tourism market
- Maximizing the linkages into the local economy and minimizing leakages

ECONOMIC IMPACT OF TOURISM

EARNER OF FOREIGN EXCHANGE

Tourism has major economic significance for a country. The receipts from international tourism are a valuable source of earning for all countries, particularly, the developing. Visitor-spending generates income for both public and private sectors, besides affecting wages and employment opportunities. Although tourism is sensitive to the level of economic activity in the tourist-generating countries, it provides more fixed earnings than primary products. The income from tourism has increased at a higher rate than primary products. The income from tourism has tended to increase at a higher rate than merchandise export in a number of countries especially in countries having a low industrial base. Now there is practically an assured channel for financial flows from the developed countries to the developing countries raising the latter's export earnings and rate of economic growth. Tourism, therefore, provides a very important source of income for a number of countries, both developed and developing. The figures from World Tourism Organization indicate that, among the world's top 40 tourism earners about 18 were developing countries including India, in the year 1995. Regarding the number of visitor arrivals, in some countries there were more visitor arrivals than the population.

France with a population of 57 million received 74.5 million visitors in the year 2000. Similarly Spain with a population of 37 million received 48.5 million visitors during the same year. Several island countries, like the Caribbean Islands, depend greatly on tourist income resulting from visitor arrivals. These earnings form a major part of the gross domestic product. Even developed countries like Canada which derived over 13 per cent of its gross domestic product from international visitors in the year 1999, rely heavily on income from tourism.

Tourism forms a very important source of foreign exchange, for several countries. Although the quantum contributed in foreign currency per visitor varies from destination to destination, the importance of receipts from tourism in the balance of payment accounts and of tourist activities in the national revenue has become considerable for a number of countries. The major economic benefit in promoting the tourism industry is in the form of earning foreign exchange.

Income from these foreign-exchange earnings adds to the national income and, as an invisible export, may offset a loss of the visible trading account and be of critical importance in the overall financial reckoning. This is truer in the case of developing countries particularly the small countries, which depend heavily upon primary products such as a few basic cash crops where tourism often offers a more reliable form of income. In the case of some European countries, namely Spain, Portugal, Austria, France and Greece, the invisible earnings from tourism are of a major significance and have a very strong positive effect on the balance of payments. Tourism is therefore a very useful means of earning the much-needed foreign currency.

It is almost without a rival as an earning source for many developed as well as developing countries. These earnings assume a great significance in the balance of payment position of many countries. The balance of payments shows the relationship between a country's total payments to all other countries and its total receipts from them. In other words, it may be defined as a statement of income and expenditure on international account.

Payments and receipts on international account are of three kinds:

- The visible balance of trade relating to the import and export of goods
- Invisible items
- Capital transfers.

The receipts from foreign tourism form an 'invisible export', just like other invisibles which come from transportation and shipping, banking and insurance, income on investments, etc. Because most countries at times have serious problems with their international payments, much attention comes to be focused on tourism because of its potentially important contribution to, and also effect upon, the balance of payments. The receipts from international tourism, however, are not always net. Sometimes expenditures are involved which must be set against them.

Net foreign exchange receipts from tourism are reduced principally by the import cost of goods and services used by visitors, foreign exchange costs of capital investment in tourist amenities and promotion and publicity expenditure abroad. Peters, "Certain imports associated with tourist expenditures must be deduced... the importation of material and equipment for constructing hotels and other amenities, and necessary supplies to run them; foreign currency costs of imports for consumption by international tourists; remittances of interests and profits on overseas investment in tourism enterprises, mainly hotel construction; foreign currency costs of conducting a tourism development programme, including marketing expenditure overseas". Reliance on imports to meet the tourist's needs does not, in any way deny developing countries the opportunity of earning foreign exchange in supplying such goods and services. Imports are, to a large extent, essential to the operation of the tourist sector as to that of other sectors. The important question is whether the value added domestically on an item or service in is maximized? Maximization of import substitution without due regard to the effect on overall tourism receipts may be counter-productive.

Also, differences in the pattern and level of reliance on imported goods and services, capital equipment and manpower are very wide, depending upon the level of development of a country. In some cases, this reliance is simply due to a lack of resources that transform into items which are to be sold by the industry. In others, the industry has not yet drawn on such supply potential, for which it may be an important stimulus. There is a general need for careful programmes of positive import substitution.

MULTIPLIER EFFECT

The discussion in earlier paragraphs clearly indicates that earnings from tourism occupy an important place in the national income of any country.

Without taking into account receipts from domestic tourism, international tourism receipts alone contribute to a great extent. The flow of money generated by tourist spending multiplies as it passes through various parts of the economy.

In addition to an important source of income, tourism provides a number of other economic benefits, which vary in importance from one country to another; depending upon the nature and scale of tourism. The benefits from infrastructure investments, justified primarily for tourism such as airports, roads, water supply and other public utilities, may be widely shared by the other sectors of the economy. This enables us to understand how tourism impacts development in the economy. Tourist facilities such as hotels, restaurants, museums, clubs, sports complexes, public transport, and national parks are also used by domestic tourists and visitors, businessmen and residents, but still a significant portion of the costs are sometimes borne by international tourists. Tourists also contribute to tax revenue both directly through sales tax and indirectly through property, profits and income taxes.

Tourism provides employment, develops infrastructural facilities and may also help regional development. Each of these economic aspects can be dealt with separately, but they are all closely related and are many times considered together. Let us first look at the income aspect of tourism. Income from tourism cannot be easily measured with accuracy and precision. This is because of the multiplier effect. The flow of money generated by tourist spending multiplies as it passes through various parts of the economy through the operation of the multiplier effect. The multiplier is an income concept. The Concept: The 'multiplier' measures the impact of extra expenditure introduced into an economy by a person. It is, therefore, concerned with the marginal rather than average changes.

In the case of tourism, this extra expenditure in a particular area can take the following forms:

- Spending on goods and services by tourists visiting the areas
- Investment of external sources in tourism infrastructure or services;
- Government spending
- Exports of goods stimulated by tourism

The expenditure can be analysed as follows:

- *Direct Expenditure*: In the case of tourism, this expenditure is made by tourists on goods and services in hotels and other supplementary accommodation units, restaurants, other tourist facilities like buses, taxis coaches, railways, domestic airlines, and for tourism-generated exports, or by tourism related investment in the area.
- *Indirect Expenditure*: This covers a sum total of inter-business transactions which result from the direct expenditure, such as purchase of goods by hoteliers from local suppliers and purchases by local suppliers from wholesalers.

- *Included Expenditure*: This is the increased consumer spending resulting from the additional personal income generated by the direct expenditure, *e.g.*, hotel workers using their wages for the purchase of goods and services. Indirect and induced expenditure together are called secondary expenditure.

There are several different concepts of the multiplier. Most multipliers in common use incorporate the general principle of the Keynesian model.

The four types of multipliers are intrinsically linked as follows:

- *Sales Multiplier*: This measures the extra business turnover created by an extra unit of tourist expenditure. Output Multiplier: This is similar to the sales multiplier but it also takes into account inventory changes, such as the increase in stock levels by hotels, restaurants and shops because of increased trading activity.
- *Income Multiplier*: This measures the income generated by an extra unit of tourist expenditure. The problem arises over the definition of income. Many researchers define income as disposable income accruing to households within the area, which is available to them to spend. However, although salaries paid to overseas residents are often excluded, a proportion of these salaries may be spent in the local area and should therefore be included.

  Income Multipliers can be expressed in two ways:
  - The ratio method which expresses the direct and indirect incomes generated per unit of direct income;
  - Normal method, which expresses total income generated in the study area per unit increase in final demand created within a particular sector.

Ratio multipliers indicate the internal linkages which exist between various sectors of the economy, but do not relate income generated to extra sales. Hence, on their own, ratio multipliers are valueless as a planning tool. Employment Multiplier:

The employment multiplier can be expressed in one of the two ways:

- As a ratio of the combination of direct and secondary employment generated per additional unit of tourist expenditure;
- Direct employment created by tourism per unit of tourist expenditure. Multipliers can be further categorized by the geographical area which is covered by the research, such as local community, a region within a country or the country as a whole.

The multiplier mechanism has also been applied to tourism and, in particular, to tourist expenditure. The nature of the tourism multiplier and its effect may be described in the example: "The money paid by a tourist in paying his hotel bill will be used by the management of the hotel to provide for the costs which the hotel had incurred in meeting the demands of the visitor, *e.g.*, such goods and services as food, drink, furnishing, laundering, electricity, and entertainment. The recipients, in turn, use the money they have thus received to meet their financial commitments and so on.

Therefore, tourist expenditure not only supports the tourist industry directly but also helps indirectly to support many other industries which supply goods and services to the tourist industry. In this way money spent by tourists is actually used several times and spreads into various sectors of the economy. In sum, the money paid by the tourist, after a long series of transfers over a given period of time, passes through all sectors of the national economy, stimulating each in turn throughout the process".

On each occasion when the money changes hands, it provides 'new' income and these continuing series of exchanges of the money spent by the tourists form what economists term the multiplier effect. The more often the conversion occurs, the greater its beneficial effect on the economy of the recipient country.

However, this transfer of money is not absolute as there are 'leakages' which occur. Such leakages may occur as a result of importing foreign goods, paying interest on foreign investments, etc.

The following are some examples of such leakages:

- Payment for goods and services produced outside, and imported into, the area;
- remittance of incomes outside the area, for example, by foreign workers;
- indirect and direct taxation where the tax proceeds are not re-spent in the area;
- savings out of income received by workers in the area.

Any leakages of these kinds will reduce the stream of expenditure which, in consequence, will limit and reduce the multiplier effect. Income generated by foreign tourist expenditure in countries possessing more advanced economies, which generally are more self-sufficient and less in need of foreign imports which are less self-sufficient and need to support their tourist industries by substantial import. If the developing countries are desirous of gaining maximum economic benefits from tourism, they should strictly control the imported items for tourist consumption and keep foreign investment expenditure at a reasonable level. If the leakages are not controlled then the benefits arising from tourism will be greatly reduced or even cancelled.

The most important leakage would arise from expenditure on import of agricultural products like food and drink. In a primary macro-economic approach to the prospects opened up by tourism establishment in a developing country, it is regarded as advantageous that a good portion of tourist consumption should consist of food products. It is estimated that the major part of these products can be found in those countries, whose economic structure is largely agricultural in character. In this sense tourist consumption, derived from international flow, can offer an assured outlet to a production which is already active within the domestic economy, without raising problems connected with export of such products and could thus be substituted for imported foodstuffs and a significant saving effected thereafter. The host country derives maximum economic benefits from the tourism industry as these savings help in increasing the benefits from the tourism multiplier. This aspect of the question is all the more important as the multiplier effect maintains its efficacy and effectiveness as long as no importation takes place.

It follows that if the national economy is to derive the maximum benefit from the impact of international and national tourism, there is an elementary obligation to find all those products needed for tourist consumption. The dynamics of agricultural production in recent years confirms the ability of developing countries to produce the major part of their agricultural products required for tourist consumption without resorting to massive imports. The tourist economy of any country, if it is to remain healthy, must rely upon local agricultural production and this condition seems today to be on its way to realization in most of the developing countries.

Multiplier of Tourism Income

To sum up, Multipliers are a means of estimating how much extra income is produced in an economy as a result of initial spending or after cash is injected. Every time the money changes hands it provides new income and the continuing series of conversion of money spent by the tourists form the multiplier effect. The more often the conversion occurs, the greater its beneficial effect on the economy of the recipient country.

GROWTH OF INFRASTRUCTURE

A significant benefit of tourism is development and improvement of infrastructure. The benefits from infrastructure investments, justified primarily for tourism–airports, roads, water supply and other public utilities–may be widely shared by the other sectors of the economy. In addition to development of new infrastructure, the improvements in the existing infrastructure which are undertaken in order to attract tourists are also of great importance. These improvements may benefit the resident population by providing them with amenities which they desire. Furthermore, the provision of infrastructure may provide the basis or serve as an encouragement for greater economic diversification. A variety of secondary industries may be promoted which may not directly serve the needs of tourism.

Therefore, it is evident that tourist expenditure is responsible for stimulating other economic activities. One of the characteristics of under development is that of deficiencies in the basic infrastructures, which lie at the root of a series of problems related to the development of tourism. Development of infrastructure requires a certain size of investment. Tourism provides the size of demand which justifies the development of infrastructure. On the basis of this minimum demand for such facilities and for such social capital, the size of such infrastructural services evolves. Construction of primary infrastructures represents the foundation of any future economic growth, even though they are not directly productive. The tourism industry shows the elementary need for basic infrastructure.

It has today the important benefit of being able to profit from the existing infrastructures and thus to make a decisive contribution to the growth of the national economy. The international and national tourist traffic, moreover, represents a reward for the capital invested and can now contribute to the financial efforts required for maintenance. The satisfactory degree of development achieved in this specific sector now permits major tourist progress, while also giving further proof of the complementary character of tourism in relation to other economic sectors. Creation of basic infrastructures for tourist usage will also be of service to the other sectors of the economy such as industry and agriculture. This results in better equilibrium of general economic growth.

TOURISM AND TAXATION

Tourism also results in tax revenues both at national and local levels. Taxes can provide the financial resources for the development of infrastructure, enhancing and maintenance of some types of attractions and other public facilities and services, tourism marketing and training required for developing tourism, as well as to help finance poverty alleviation programmes by governments both at local and national levels.

In addition, tourism-related tax revenues help finance general community improvements and services used by all residents. WTO's 1998 report on tourism taxation emphasizes that taxation policies in a country must be carefully evaluated in an integrated manner to ensure that tourism-related taxes are giving the necessary substantial revenues. However, taxes should not be so high for the country's international competitive position to be counter productive and produce a loss of tourist traffic.

The aim should be to strike a balance between, a level of taxation that maintains a competitive position for the country and reasonable profits for the industry, and, receiving adequate revenues to support investment in and maintenance of the tourism sector, and to contribute towards general community welfare.

BALANCED REGIONAL DEVELOPMENT

Another important domestic effect relates to the regional aspects of tourist expenditure. Such expenditure is of special significance in marginal areas, which are relatively isolated, economically underdeveloped, and have unemployment problems. The United Nations Conference on International Travel and Tourism held in Rome in 1963 stated that tourism was important not only as a source of earning foreign exchange, but also as a factor determining the location of industry and in the development of underdeveloped regions. It further stated that in some cases the development of tourism may be the only means of promoting the economic advancement of less-developed areas lacking in other resources. In fact underdeveloped regions of the country usually greatly benefit from tourism development. Many of the economically backward regions contain areas of high scenic beauty and of cultural attractions. These areas, if developed for use by tourists, can bring in a lot of prosperity to the local people.

Tourism development in these regions accordingly becomes a significant factor in redressing regional imbalances in employment and income. Tourist expenditure at a particular tourist area helps the development of the many areas around it. Many countries both developed as well as developing have realised this aspect of tourism development and are contemplating developing tourist facilities in underdeveloped regions with a view to bringing prosperity there. Khajuraho in India, which is now an internationally famous tourist spot, is an example of one such region.

To show, Khajuraho, a remote and unknown small village about forty years ago, is now on the world tourist map which attracts thousands of tourists, both domestic as well as international. Today, Indian Airlines flies a jet plane between the capital city of New Delhi and Khajuraho and seats are not easy to come by.

Thousands of tourists visit the place by air, rail and road transport every month to see the architectural beauty of temples and erotic sculptures whose creators were the Chandela kings, who ruled in North India from the 9th to the 13th centuries. Today 22 glorious temples remind us of the classic Indian architecture and culture of those times and represent the finest expression of the art of medieval India. The area around Khajuraho is well developed and full of life. The place has provided employment to hundreds of local people in hotels and shops.

There is a thriving clay-model industry devoted to making replicas of the famous temple sculptures and a number of shops dealing with items of presentation, handlooms and handicrafts, have created jobs for many. Tourists love to purchase various souvenirs to take home.

Thus local people are recipients of additional income which has increased the prosperity of the region. Subsequently areas around Khajuraho have also prospered and reaped the benefits from the tourist multiplier. There is no dearth of areas which could, after they are developed for tourism, become great assets to the region in particular and to the country as a whole. The French government has created a series of new resorts particularly to bring prosperity to the areas which traditionally have been underdeveloped. The Italian government is likewise attempting to develop tourism in Southern Italy in order to help redress the economic imbalances which have long existed between the northern and the southern parts of Italy. Tourism is to be regarded not as an area of peripheral investment whose benefits will help in creating employment opportunities and in the regeneration of backward regions. In India a similar approach needs to be adopted to develop areas with great tourism potential.

GENERATION OF EMPLOYMENT

Employment is an important economic effect of tourism. The problems of unemployment and under-employment are more active in the developing countries. Tourism can be looked upon in this light as a major industry which employs manpower on a large scale.

The problems which the industrialized countries face in recruiting manpower for the tourists industry confirm that, in any productive process consisting of services, human labour remains the basic need. If a comparison is to be drawn with the productive sector none of the technological progress achieved has succeeded in rendering the human factor less indispensable than in this sector, and this is true to an absolutely indisputable extent.

The high social impact of the tourist industry is well known, for it has repercussions in every other national economic sector through the multiplier effect, which is particularly marked in those services that are complementary to the tourist accommodation industry. The tourist industry is a highly labour-intensive service industry and hence is a valuable source of employment. It employs a large number of people and provides a wide range of jobs which extend from the unskilled to the highly specialized. In addition to those involved in management there are a large number of specialist personnel required to work as accountants, housekeepers, waiters, cooks and entertainers, who in turn need a large number of semi-skilled workers such as porters, chambermaids, kitchen staff, gardeners, etc. Tourism is also responsible for creating employment outside the industry in its more narrowly defined sense and in this respect those who supply goods and services to those directly involved in tourism are beneficiaries from tourism.

Such indirect employment includes, those involved in the furnishing and equipment industries, souvenir industries and farming and food supply. Construction industry is another very big source of employment. The basic infrastructures-roads, airports, water supply and other public utilities and also construction of hotels and other accommodation units create jobs for thousands of workers, both unskilled and skilled. In many of the developing countries, where chronic unemployment often exists, the promotion of tourism can be a great encouragement to economic development and, especially, employment.

However at this point it is, necessary to consider the seasonal nature of the tourism industry. Where general diversification alternatives are scarce, a combination of heavy dependence on tourism and highly marked seasonality calls for measures to develop off -season traffic. Employment multiplier: This multiplier is similar to the Income Multiplier except that in this case a multiplier impact on employment is observed.

Employment Multiplier can be expressed in the following two ways:

- As a ratio of the combination of direct employment. At the destination, the jobs are directly created in the industry there.
- As a ratio of secondary employment generated per additional unit of tourist expenditure to direct employment. The workers and their families require their own goods and services giving rise to further indirectly created employment in shops, schools, health care institutions, etc.

OTHER DIMENSIONS

The World Tourism conference which was held at Manila, Philippines in October 1980, considered the nature of tourism phenomenon in all its aspects. The role tourism is bound to play in a dynamic and vastly changing world was also identified. Convened by the World Tourism Organization the conference also considered the responsibility of various states for the development and enhancement as more than a purely economic activity of nations and peoples.

The significance of tourism was discussed in during the conference. The participants in the World Tourism Conference attached particular importance to its effects on the developing countries. It stated its conviction "that the world tourism can contribute to the establishment of a new international economic order that will help to eliminate the widening economic gap between developed and developing countries and ensure the steady acceleration of economic and social development and progress in particular of the developing countries."

2

Communication and Sustainable Tourism

COMMUNICATION TECHNOLOGY: SIGNIFICANCE

The communication technology is significant in tourism industry in following ways:

- Allows organizations to use their resources more wisely and profitably.
- Creates a sense of security amongst tourists and also provides a friendly environment.
- Develops new avenues and new tourist spots.
- Enables central control and outsourcing of non-core functions.
- Helps in development of extensive growth between partner organizations and between employees, consumers and organizations.
- Helps in sustaining and promoting the existing ones.
- Information technology devices help in linking and sharing data and processes electronically, to build complementary services, expand, reach and enhance collaboration.
- Most devices result in information power storage and profitability.
- Possibility of handling complex details with increase in speed.
- Results in enhancement of processing capabilities.

Davis and Meyer state "Almost instantaneous communication and computation, for example, are shrinking time and focusing us on speed. Connectivity is putting everybody and everything on line in one way or the other and has led to the "the death of distance", a shrinking of space. Intangible value of all kinds, like services and information is growing explosively reducing the importance of tangible mass". The opinion clearly highlights the importance and impact of emerging communication technologies in this highly dynamic industry.

The concept of "Global Village" would be very appropriate in this scenario because it is growing communication technologies, which have opened doors for tourists and travellers and have made availability of information only with the press of a button, with the help of several new Information Technologies.

NEW INFORMATION TECHNOLOGIES

- Cable Television Technology
- Computer Technology
- Internet and Travel and Tourism
- Satellite Television
- Sky Track Technology
- Telecopy Technology
- Telefax Technology
- Teletex Technology
- Videotex Technology
- Web sites

COMPUTER TECHNOLOGY

Computer is a tool, which is capable of processing a very large amount of data rapidly, or it is any device capable of processing information to produce a desired result. No matter how large or small they are, computers typically perform their work in three well-defined steps:

- Accepting input
- Processing the input just as to predefined rules
- Producing output

Computer is a multi-function electronic device that can execute instructions to perform a task. Therefore an electronic device that performs pre-defined or programmed computations at a high speed and with great accuracy; a machine that is used to store, transfer, and transform information is known as "Computer" to us. It has made its entry in the field of tourism in a big way. In fact, computers are in use in some way or the other in various branches of tourism since the early sixties.

Be it travel agencies, hotels, Airlines or recently even in the Railways, Computers have played a key role in making the task of providers of travel services an easy affair.

Not only this, through home terminals, computers are undertaking, among other jobs, the planning of vacations for an individual and his family.

Computer applications are used in:

- Airlines
- Cargo
- Hotels
- Terminals
- Travel Agency
- Railways

In the year 1983–Thompson Holidays first used computers using online programmes and introduced reservations via Prestel. Several other big tour operators, since then used similar to sell their various programmes.

SATELLITE TELEVISION

Satellite television is television operated by means of orbiting communication satellites located 37,000 km above the earth's surface. The first satellite television signal was relayed from Europe to the Telstar satellite over North America in 1962. The first domestic North American satellite to carry television was Canada's Anik 1, which was launched in 1973. Satellite can also be described as a television system in which the signal is transmitted to an orbiting satellite that receives the signal and amplifies it and transmits it back to earth.

Therefore, it refers to courses that are broadcast, usually live, by an electronic signal sent to a satellite orbiting the earth and then retrieved by a satellite dish. The satellite dish broadcasting the programme is called an "uplink", and the receiving dish is called a "downlink". For Tour operators, as well as Travel agents it serves as a linking device for making available the information of one corner of world to the other corner and Tourists are also, accordingly, benefitted by this linking device.

CABLE TELEVISION TECHNOLOGY

Cable television or Community Antenna Television is a system of providing television, FM radio programming and other services to consumers via radio waves transmitted directly to people's televisions through fixed coaxial cables as opposed to the over-the-air method used in traditional television broadcasting in which a television antenna is required.

Cable system covering defined areas, such as the UK's franchise to install and operate a cable system granted by the Cable Authority and Department of Trade and Industry, offering TV channel output and, increasingly, local loop digital telephony services. The Cable Television Association is the CATV industry's representative organization.

Therefore it is a transmission system that distributes and broadcasts television signals and other services by means of a coaxial cable. Cable Television Technology has also greatly helped in information transfer and information sharing. Therefore, it has brought the tourists, the tour operators and the destinations close. It immensely helps in advertising and marketing of Tourism products.

VIDEOTEX TECHNOLOGY

Videotex is a system for sending of pages of text to a user in computer form, typically to be displayed on a television. It is computer technology of the 1980s that uses ordinary television sets, or similar low-cost monitors, to display computer information.

Videotex systems, such as Canada's Telidon, were a complete commercial failure in North America, but achieved a modicum of success in Europe–*e.g.*

France's Teletel and, to a much lesser degree, the UK's Prestel. Therefore, it is a form of electronic publishing consisting of computer-generated text distributed through telecommunications and received and viewed on home television.

It occupies a special position among the 'new media'. It plays a key role in the link between telecommunication and the computer sciences. Its advantage lies in the possibility it provides for linking computers and also in its interactive dialogue capabilities. Using Videotex, information and communication systems can be converted into interactive systems capable of communicating with one another. In fact, Videotex is a multipurpose instrument with multiplicity of uses.

It serves as:

- An instrument for data processing
- An information medium
- An organizational aid
- A communication system
- A marketing instrument

This relatively new service connects various forms of use of the facilities and at the same time offers some other possibilities. To operate this service, a television set with a decoder and telephone is necessary, without which the service cannot operate. In Europe, nearly all the households have television sets and a telephone and with the help of Vedeotex, separate households can be reached in large areas.

Members of German BTX service as well as Members of France Telecom services can now obtain all kinds of information from external computers or use data bank all through their television sets. In many other European countries and USA, similar systems are in use.

It is being used in a big way in Tourism, also in India because:

- It allows rapid message transmission
- Fast and inexpensive data collection
- Keeps up-to-date information, which is crucial for advertising

It has been found that Videotex is the most advantageous means of Communication, taking into account its low cost and wider range of applications. This technology enables the tour operators and travel agents or hoteliers to send complete pages of information text to the tourist to assist him in deciding and finalizing his tour plans.

Satellite, Cable and Videotex technologies are very important because of their wider coverage and their technical methods of transmission, however, they have one shortcoming that none can be directed to one specific person. In addition, the person receiving information is only partially informed. The receiver of information cannot also start a dialogue or communicate. However, the following gives possibility of direct transmission of information to a single consumer:

TELETEX TECHNOLOGY

Teletex is a text and document communications service that could be provided over telephone lines. Teletex allows for the transmission and outing of Group 4 facsimile documents. It is neither like Telex nor like Teletex. Although it may not be as versatile a technology as some others that have been mentioned earlier in this session, but helps in transmitting information which is required by a tourist from a tour operator, Travel agent or a Hotel.

Computer information and even copies of documents can be transferred to the tourist with efficiency. It is an improvement over telex and has in fact developed from it. The receiver for Teletex is an electronic 'typewriter', which can send electronically enriched 'letters' to owners of ordinary telex equipment.

The transmission of message time is usually shorter in comparison with time taken with telex. Besides, it is also possible to transmit more office typewriters, symbols. A normal electronic typewriter can also be used as a receiver for telefax.

TELEFAX TECHNOLOGY

It is an electronic post office box system. Each member of the system has his or her 'post office box' in the computer, where other members can leave their message. The owner of each box can electronically contact the others. All the means discussed permit the exchange of information electronically through a data 'network'.

The exchange of information between the members with the assistance of electronic transmission is very fast. The data is also available in written form in printouts. 'Network' is a system of transmission linking facilities for automatic data processing. In this way, different computers are connected, permitting data exchange and processing over long distances. Telecommunication is possible only when there is such a network available.

Telephone is the simplest and best communication network. In addition there is also separate clear data network for the exchange of data, which works digitally. In this way, a high transmission speed is achieved and there is a very low ratio of errors during transmission. There are different types of networks, which can be used for telecommunication purposes either separately or combined. In Tourism, in addition to travel agents, tour operators, hoteliers, airlines, travel journalist's etc. use this technology.

TELECOPY

It provides the possibility of exchanging photocopies through a data network. Information, in the form of either written document or technical drawing, is remote copied. This means that two facilities for copying are connected. One at the sender's end and the other at the receiver's end. Transmission time is only a few minutes. Usually the details of packages, booking details or list of itineraries are sent to this tourist by the Tour operator, Travel agent or the Hotel.

INTERNET AND TRAVEL AND TOURISM

So far the information technology dealt with has been of the kind where intermediaries, travel agents, tour operators etc. are an indispensable part in the distribution and marketing of travel and tourism products, and as an important point of sale or product outlets. This is an information technology where the producer and the consumer are directly communicating, by putting the indispensability of travel intermediaries in question.

As has been discussed earlier, the intangibility of the product where risk and uncertainty for the customer is higher, his need for reliable prepurchase information is stronger. Through Internet, which is the latest product of information technology, this need is fulfilled. This interactive information-supplying medium is user friendly and gives enormous information of all kinds related to travel. Apart from supplying information about the world's leading and emerging tourist destination of all kinds, it is now possible to book and buy holidays through Internet using plastic money.

It gives information on all Airlines, Hotels and Car hire companies, which are in its database. Microsoft is a travel agent. Its Internet site branded Expedia is one of the most important examples of the new generation of travel intermediaries. Distribution of travel and tourism products using the Internet has a substantial cost reduction advantage for providers of tourism services. The cost incurred by suppliers in receiving a customer booking is the one, which is costly. So, Internet gives a practical aid both in supplying information and receiving bookings or selling tourism products on the principal's behalf. Marketing tourism products on the Internet is also possible. This is done through the page of the company's Internet site.

Once the company gets access to the Internet, it gets various opportunities. Of these, Electronicmail is one. As a tourism product supplier, especially with business travel as a selected target market, it can communicate with the person through his/her e-mail address wherever the client is. Unlike telephone communication, there is no need for the presence of the receiver of the message during message transmission. It also gives a typed copy of the message. E-mail communication medium is very cheap yet efficient and effective. On the other hand, marketing on the Internet has an advantage of being used by all company's of all sizes as long as they can establish their Web Site on the Internet.

WEB SITES

A web site is a collection of all pages under one domain. Sometimes, the subdirectories of large ISP(s) are also referred to as web sites as they have been designed by different users and with different interests in mind.

BENEFITS OF WEB SITES

No matter how small or large a business is, one can profit enormously from a web site in following ways.

- Reduces advertising costs.
- Information remains on line and always up-to-date.
- Pictures, product description, newly won awards, customer questions and instruction videos are possible on the web-site.
- Announcement of a package, deal, and sale can be promptly updated on the web site.
- Customers find it simpler to surf the net and log-on to the web sites for desired information.
- Web sites almost eliminate waste of time in travelling for the desired information centre.

The tourist can make use of the web sites, sitting back at home for making tour plans. Accordingly enormous web sites are there by tour operators, travel agents, Hotels etc, some of which are given below.

- Luxury Resortsindia.com
- Destinations India.com
- Jaipur JodhpurUdaipur.com
- India Tours and Travels.com
- Asia Tours and Travel.com
- TravelinIndia.com

SKY TRACK

It is an automated airline reservation system, which enables travel agents to make bookings on hundreds of world's airlines using standard Prestel Television set and a keyboard. Possibility of direct transmission between tourists, tour operators and travel agents.

This system invented by British Telecom is a way of providing computerized information terminal. The only requirement is a Telephone line and a standard colour Television set with an Adapter to link it to a decoder and keyboard. The information is transmitted quickly and accurately via ordinary telephone lines. The required information is rapidly transmitted through this technology and is very helpful in providing desired information to tourists.

MODEL OF ECOLOGICAL SUSTAINABLE COMMUNITY TOURISM DEVELOPMENT

The project to set up the Miso Walai Homestay Programme involves four villages in Lower Kinabatangan, Sabah, a state in the eastern part of Malaysia and started in 1998 with funding from the World Wildlife Fund (WWF) of Malaysia and Norway and Discovery Channel Television. The area is within

Malaysia's largest river floodplain, which is the habitat of many rare and endangered wildlife species.

The area was listed as one of the top ten priority sites in the Ecotourism Plan for Malaysia.

The four main objectives of the project are:

- Building community capacity,
- Improving the local economy,
- Conserving the environment and creating greater environmental awareness and
- Cooperation and partnership at both the community and project level.

The project's methodology is based on bottom-up planning with the communities to ensure information transfer to enable local people to fully participate in the planning process and building community capacity to have the necessary skills for sustainable, effective implementation. Awareness about the environment and intensive training for income-generating activities related to ecotourism comprised capacity building of the communities. This included creating skills for handicraft production, training for guides and providing the business fundamentals needed to operate home stay services, boat service and other ecotourism-related activities.

The local economy was improved by providing alternative income-generating activities related to ecotourism. In addition, community tourism associations were set up to operate the home stay, boat service and handicraft product development. Environmental conservation and awareness are part of an ongoing campaign, which involves use of best practice ecotourism codes for all activities, including plans to create an Eco Resort using only natural, renewable resources. The campaign extends to village landscaping and cleaning up litter, rehabilitation of the forest area near the villages and monitoring illegal logging activities. Cooperation and partnership involve a variety of stakeholders, including members of MESCOT (Model of Ecological Sustainable Community Tourism), WWF, the State Department of Tourism (Sabah), the Ministry of Culture, Arts and Tourism (federal government), Sabah Forestry Department, the Community Development Agency, the district office and local and foreign tour operators. The Sabah Forestry Department has highlighted the objectives of the project in relation to forestry issues and made a long-term commitment to support community-based ecotourism.

Reports about the progress of the project have been disseminated and various travel trade enterprises have been interested to pilot similar trial ecotourism programmes. Other local stakeholders have asked for MESCOT to cooperate in efforts at recovering plantations and reforestation. Various interested groups have visited the villages on familiarization tours to give recognition and support to the project. Total revenue earned from the home stay services, the boat service, handicraft sales and relate activities during the first six months of operation have been significant for the communities, given the low economic base before the project. The benefits to the communities have encouraged local people that the project will be able to grow in the future. It is important to keep in mind, however, that community-based tourism must necessarily be a small-scale project designed to benefit local communities while being sustainable and sensitive to the environment. Problems have been encountered at the community level before there was any awareness that sustainable ecotourism development could generate benefits. Greater awareness about the importance of forest conservation and maintaining a commitment to conservation had to be created in a social context that was suspicious of such ideas.

Transparency in all project decisions and activities, maximum efforts to encourage the widest participation and the principle of fair sharing of benefits have helped to overcome local suspicions. It has been reported that the community still needs to develop more skills and experience in order to take over the general community operations of the project.

Social, economic and environmental benefits have been created, but they need to be increased in order to employ a full time coordinator and to operate as a successful, sustainable community ecotourism enterprise. Plans for the future include development of the Eco Resort, ongoing work to strengthen community capacity and continued growth at a steady, sustainable pace.

The process leading to full takeover by the community may involve creation of an umbrella group to act as a cooperative for the community tourism associations. The cooperative could hire a full time coordinator to help oversee development, promotion and marketing of all tourism products offered by the community tourism associations. In this way, a quality ecotourism experience that retains cultural values of the communities and shows a commitment to environmental conservation will help assure the future success of the Miso Walai Homestay programme in Sabah state.

LOCAL COMMUNITIES IN SUSTAINABLE TOURISM DEVELOPMENT

Since 1998, the Republic of Korea has had policies to encourage various efforts to develop tourism. The promotion of tourism has been designed to help overcome the economic difficulties caused by the Asian financial crisis of 1997. Expenditures by foreign tourists are considered to have positive effects on foreign exchange earnings and to improve the employment situation.

For these two main reasons, the government has developed strategies, plans, policies, programmes and projects to increase the positive impact of tourism. The main government agency responsible for tourism matters is the Ministry of Culture and Tourism. Each local government authority in seven cities and nine provinces also has its own bureau or department of tourism.

Other types of enterprises involved in tourism are in the private sector. "Tourism Vision 21" is the main government plan, which aims to attract 7 million international tourists by launching eight categories of activities with 30 projects over a five-year period from 1999 to 2003. Sustainable tourism development is one category of activities under the government's five-year plan. Academic studies and research about sustainable tourism development began in the late 1980s, and the government started its own studies, report and planning in the 1990s. From the beginning of 2000, the central government started to give substantive support and budgets for investment in local ecotourism projects.

Legislation to develop laws and set forth the principles of sustainable tourism development was made at the beginning of the 1990s. The law to cover preservation of the natural environment was passed and projects related to the environment were launched.

From the second half of the 1990s, the government passed a number of laws and regulations to preserve the natural environment from the negative effects of tourism industries. Progress towards sustainable tourism development in the Republic of Korea began in 1999 when projects were selected and the budget was allocated. In 2000, three projects received support. One was a seasonal programme for watching migratory birds in Chulwon-kun, Kangwon Province. A second project was located in a coastal area in Incheon City and designed to promote ecotourism.

The third project in Jeonnam Province was designed to promote tourism to see the effects of tide flows twice a month at a site known as "Mystic Sea Road". By 2001, the government extended support to five projects in one city (Siheung City) and four provinces (Kyungki, Kangwon, Jeonnam and Kyungbuk). There are plans to support 13 projects in one city and six provinces during 2002. Procedures for supporting a project start with the local governments formulating projects with budgets and submitting them to the central government. Then the central government gathers information about projects throughout the country and decides on the priorities in terms of feasibility, equity and sustainability. After projects are selected, the central government decides the level of financial support. Financial support is provided on a 50:50 basis.

Other functions of local governments related to sustainable tourism development include: encouraging cooperation and awareness of citizens, conducting public relations, establishing the system of collaboration with the central government and securing development budgets from various sources. The central government supports 50 per cent of the total budget for each project and the local government covers the other 50 per cent. The central government also functions to keep balanced development among local authorities, urge citizen awareness and understanding, promote international understanding about sustainable tourism development and do research about model forms in order to introduce and encourage industry to develop new models.

A number of issues still have to be addressed in order that sustainable tourism development is carried out successfully and systematically. Among the issues are: concerned policy-makers and officials lack full acceptance of the concept of sustainable tourism development; funds are lacking, especially in view of local financial conditions; misunderstanding exists between central and local government; the central government must consider balance and equity for projects; all local governments request priority for their projects; there is disagreement between those who are for and those who are against sustainable tourism development; and private enterprises oppose government involvement.

Solutions have been proposed that involve a more coordinated approach and special efforts to bring the private sector into the process of sustainable tourism development. Future prospects for sustainable tourism development are good, because the Republic of Korea recognizes its importance and significance as a world trend. During the last three years, the government's financial support and the number of projects increased by 200 per cent.

It is expected that government support for sustainable tourism development will continue and be strengthened. Planning, projects and implementation will be at the provincial and local levels, with political and financial support from the central government. In the future, efforts will be needed at all levels to create public understanding and recognition of the importance of sustainable tourism development. The Republic of Korea also seeks to promote international understanding through sharing of experiences at seminars, workshops and international meetings.

A SYSTEMIC APPROACH TO TOURISM DEVELOPMENT IN ISLAND STATES

Tourism has become more prominent in the Indian Ocean region, because it is viewed as a catalyst for economic growth and a means to alleviate poverty. As a form of development, tourism is relatively human resource intensive and can also address gender issues in employment and equity. However, island states face a situation where the economic benefits tend to be offset by social and environmental costs for host communities.

One of the main issues for islands states is the relationship between tourism development and the natural environment. This can be a conflict relationship because the natural environment is both a factor of production and a source of attraction for tourists. The relationship is also extractive since tourists require good supplies of fresh water, clean air and local produce as basic ingredients, which can be extracted only from the destination.

The relationship is also aesthetic, since most types of tourism depend on the environment to give the tourist a pleasing amenity, such as the marine environment for diving, mountain vistas and other natural settings. This aesthetic relationship could be viewed as non-extractive as long as tourism does not degrade the environmental amenity provided to tourists.

The general interdependent relationship between tourism and the environment indicates the need for a systems approach to the management of economic and environmental resources when deciding development options for island states. By envisioning tourism as a system, it becomes clear that tourism is an open system that responds to changes in the social, economic and natural environment and is evolving towards greater complexity.

Moreover, the tourism system is characterized more by personal interrelations as flows rather than material flows. Once this human element is introduced, there is a clear need for a multidisciplinary approach in order to understand the strength and direction of complex interrelationships. Island states have been the focus of study using the systems approach to consider relationships involving tourism, the economy, the environment and development. The systems approach is also useful to understand the temporal processes of tourism development.

That is, many impacts of tourism are cumulative, such as environmental degradation and over-crowding, and this makes it necessary to understand processes of change in tourism development over time. In addition, a systems approach can be used to understand fundamental interrelationships of tourism development, living standards, community attitudes and environmental conditions, all of which are not well understood for island states.

The issue of biodiversity in coastal and marine environments of island states is characterized by complex interrelationships that need to be understood with a systemic approach. Biodiversity is, in fact, a tourist attraction and any loss of biodiversity could result in reduced tourism. While natural and human forces can cause a decline in biodiversity, programmes to regenerate the environment could offset such declines. However, the positive relationship where greater biodiversity attracts more tourists is finite, which means that overdevelopment could ultimately reduce both biodiversity and tourism.

Policies and programmes about land use, waste generation and fishing will be crucial for making Asian and Pacific island destinations competitive and attractive to tourists. There remains a general lack of understanding about how tourism development is interrelated with the broader economic, social and environmental context of island states. Without this understanding, island states will be less able to address the issues of human and environment resource management, equity in employment and income and poverty eradication.

Where this understanding is missing, there will be uncontrolled tourism and it will create the seeds of its own destruction. For islands in the Indian Ocean region, the systemic approach can give tourism planners and managers a tool and a knowledge base for more complete understanding of how the demand for tourism must be matched by the ability of host communities and the natural environment to meet these needs. In this way, appropriate policies and programmes would help to facilitate tourism development for island states, particularly in the Indian Ocean region.

PUBLIC-PRIVATE PARTNERSHIPS FOR COMMUNITY -BASED TOURISM VENTURES IN INDONESIA

There are several basic characteristics of community-based tourism development that make public-private partnerships a possibility. First, communities may not have the skills and experience in tourism management. Second, community tourism ventures take time to set up and require a process of intensive capacity building.

Third, community tourism ventures may not be profitable when they are initiated. This gives scope for combining private sector capacities with capacities of government agencies in order that both achieve their goals more quickly and efficiently and at lower costs. It is important to keep in mind that public-private partnerships (PPP) can combine the public sector goal of development and the private sector goal of profitability.

There are four criteria that will affect any decision to have a public-private partnership in tourism development:

- Inputs have to be complementary and give advantages to both the public and private partners.
- Project goals should be in line with development priorities, that is, poverty eradication, upgrading skills and providing livelihoods for local people.
- The private company should make a substantial contribution.
- Public inputs target areas (such as training) that would not otherwise get private sector support.

In addition to these general points, it is also important to consider how public-private partnerships can work for community-based tourism. One way to make such partnerships work for community-based tourism is by working with bilateral donor organizations that give priority to this approach. Two examples are the Tourism Challenge Fund (TCF) of the Department for International Development (DFID) of the government of the United Kingdom and the Public Private Partnership Office of the German Agency for Technical Cooperation (GTZ) of the government of Germany.

The central focus of DFID is to reduce by half the proportion of people living in extreme poverty by 2015. The largest share of DFID's assistance is to the poorest countries in Asia and sub-Saharan Africa. The TCF seeks to encourage the private sector to lead tourism initiatives that will benefit the poor. The funds are available to any private sector organization, but a partner from the commercial sector is required. The aim is to have tourism businesses link with small enterprises, provide training to poor people for improved employment opportunities, strengthen the positive social and cultural effects of tourism, reduce the negative environmental impact of tourism and create a policy and planning framework that encourages participation. There are some conditions placed on the financing from the TCF. GTZ has expertise in project management and specializes in consulting for institutional development.

Among the areas for partnership for the German PPP Office of GTZ are: training and education, energy and environmental management, work-place safety, certification, infrastructure and institutional development. GTZ sets conditions on the financing from PPP, including the requirement that the private sector partner should be any German company or its subsidiary, regardless of size or type of business.

One example of a PPP project support by GTZ is the Olango Coral Farm in Cebu, Philippines. In 1998, a community-based coral farm with an ecotourism component received seed funds from GTZ. Private sector contributions were given from resort operators to help rehabilitate the nearby reef. One result of the project was to create a new day-trip destination for resort tourists from Cebu- Mactan. The two examples of bilateral funding agencies show that links between community-based tourism and public-private partnerships have been encouraged as part of donors' support for overall development strategies. Some conditions are attached to the financing component and the projects must have a time frame of three years or less. This type of donor support can serve as a catalyst for local initiatives that combine the goals of the public and private sector in order to overcome some of the development constraints encountered in local communities.

CHALLENGES AND OPPORTUNITIES FOR SUSTAINABLE TOURISM DEVELOPMENT

ECOTOURISM: CHALLENGES AND OPPORTUNITIES

Over the past decade, tourism has become the largest industry worldwide in terms of employment and share of global gross domestic product. The tourism industry has been growing rapidly as well as changing at a fast pace. As more people are interested in spending leisure time in nature, ecotourism has become one of the fastest-growing segments of the tourism industry. This creates opportunities in areas characterized by natural attractions, wildlife and wilderness habitats. Local communities may benefit in economic terms as well as create a commitment to conservation and sustainable development. At the same time, however, increased demands for ecotourism create pressure on carrying capacity. Greater numbers of visitors makes it more likely that habitats will be at risk and the wilderness and cultural heritage could be ruined. It is expected that China will encounter many challenges, because it already ranks sixth worldwide in terms of tourist arrivals. In the next twenty years, China is forecast to be the top tourist destination and the fourth largest source of tourists in the world. This prospect for major tourism growth in China makes it important to quickly consider the environmental and social issues that are part of sustainable tourism development. Careful planning and assessment are important parts of sustainable tourism development.

Officials responsible for national parks and other nature areas will have a major responsibility for handling the challenges and deciding which opportunities for tourism development can be sustained over the long term. Local communities will also have to participate in planning and assessment when culture and heritage are important parts of ecotourism.

It has been noted that the principles for ecotourism have not yet been firmly established in order to guide planning and assessment. However, two basic principles of ecotourism that have been identified are: encourage conservation and provide benefits to the local populations.

However, planners and policy-makers must also keep in mind certain realistic truths about tourism: it consumes resources, creates waste and requires certain kinds of infrastructure; it creates conditions for possible over-consumption of resources; it is dominated by private investment with priority on maximizing profits; its multi-faceted nature makes control difficult; and it may be seen as simply entertainment services consumed by tourists.

The challenge of sustainable tourism development, therefore, is to balance the principles with these truths, and this can be done only through integrated, cooperative approaches involving all stakeholders and related economic activities in the area. There are certain tools that can be used to help achieve balance, such as assessment of carrying capacity, finding the limits of acceptable change and doing cost/benefit analysis.

Tourism policy-makers, planners and managers should consider these tools as helpful only if they take a holistic, coordinated approach, especially since benefits and costs in terms of sustainable tourism development are not easily defined in monetary terms. Furthermore, measuring the success of tourism involving nature and culture should not just be based on number of visitors or amount of income; rather measurement should include the length of stay, quality of the experience and whether natural and cultural resources have been conserved.

Ecotourism can clearly create opportunities for spreading the economic benefits of tourism to villages, remote areas and national parks, as long as the government policy aims to have more tourism in these areas and the local people have participated in the process. Along these lines, policy-makers should be aware that smaller-scale business operators are more appropriate for activities related to ecotourism and government policies need to support this level of tourism services.

The main challenges for policies and activities that develop ecotourism are:

- Ecology and the vulnerability of nature and wildlife;
- Aesthetics in terms of expectations held by the tourists and the local communities;
- Economic benefits, costs (including opportunity costs and externalities) and risks; and
- Social impact involving local communities and cultural heritage.

In China, the wealth of historical and cultural monuments, the vibrant and diverse cultures and the spectacular geographic variety already create a major tourism product. Ecotourism provides a possibility for small-scale, low-impact tourism that can be widely distributed throughout the country. With more than 56 ethnic groups, there is good potential for village-based tourism, especially in areas with natural, cultural and historical resources. The level of investment would not be high, and the returns for villages can be significant to supplement regular incomes. Additional employment could be created through transport services, guide services, handicraft production, lodging and other logistical support. Carefully planned ecotourism, especially if it is village-based and includes local participation, can provide direct benefits that might offset pressures from other, less sustainable uses of natural and cultural resources. In many developing countries, including China, ecotourism can fulfill the need to view the environment and cultural heritage as resources to safeguard for future generations.

SUSTAINABLE TOURISM A FORM OF ETHICAL CONSUMPTION

In recent years, ethical consumption has been a growing phenomenon throughout the West and research into this trend has generated an increasing amount of attention over the past few decades. However, it is widely acknowledged that more extensive engagement with this trend is needed within the field. This object shall critically engage with sustainable tourism and discuss to what extent it might be understood as a form of ethical consumption. The following part shall offer an initial insight into the historical trajectories and key characteristics of both ethical consumption and sustainable tourism, highlighting possible commonalities and inconsistencies between ethical consumption and sustainable tourism.

A SHARED HISTORY

The historical origins of ethical consumption appear somewhat contested with various accounts presented from the activity of the Empire Marketing Board to the co-operative movement in the nineteenth century. Many argue that a key moment for ethical consumption was in 1942 in Britain when the Quakers founded Oxfam.

Oxfam began purchasing goods such as handicrafts from the disadvantaged producers in the developing world at above-market prices. Purchasing products in such a way allowed for an increased income for the producers and the products were sold onto conscientious consumers in the UK wanting to reduce the impact of their consumption.

The concept was adopted across the Atlantic in 1946 in the USA with the retail outlet Ten Thousand Villages established and various faith groups and networks selling handicraft products with the ethos of a fair price for the producers. This growing concern for producers was coupled with an increasing awareness of environmental degradation from the 1960s onwards.

This attention to the environment was strongly influenced by Rachel Carson's book Silent Spring, and a growing concern about the detrimental effects of consumerism on the environment (with a particular focus on pesticides) developed across Europe and North America. It is argued that current levels of consumption in Western societies can be held partly responsible for inequality, environmental degradation, exploitation and socio-economic disparity. This represents a shift in ideology during the latter part of the twentieth century as it previously was production processes which were typically associated with environmental degradation, inequality and exploitation. It was only towards the end of the twentieth century that consumers and mass consumption (in the world's richest nations) began to be identified as major components of the problem.

In response to the growing concern towards the end of the twentieth century, ethical concerns about the exploitation of producers and the environment could now be registered through the purchase of ethical products. For example Cafédirect coffee was launched in 1992 and offered a fairer price (amongst other aspects) for small-scale coffee producers and was sensitive towards the environment in the production process.

Ethical consumption appears to have developed over the latter half of the last century through various movements both in Europe and North America. Further, it appears that ethical consumption has begun to appeal to a broader market with the introduction of fair trade goods in mainstream supermarkets, for example, Cafédirect. The next part shall briefly highlight a few key moments in the history of sustainable tourism and identify any possible similarities and differences with ethical consumption more generally.

Throughout the history of tourism there have been various shifts in tourism practices. From the Grand Tour of the 17th and 18th centuries to the emergence of the package holiday in the later part of the 20th century. More recently a new tourist practice has emerged offering a different outlook on the practices and responsibilities involved in tourism. Initially, tourism was viewed as a clean industry as it did not have such obvious effects on the environment compared to a factory or dock yard.

As Honey highlights '...mass tourism was originally embraced by many countries as a 'smokeless' (non-polluting) industry that could increase employment and gross national product'. However, it has now become apparent that tourism contributes to worldwide pollution, natural resources depletion, and the exploitation of host workers and local cultures.

This shift in understanding of the effects of mass tourism appears to coincide with the broader environmentalist movement in the 1960s. As highlighted above, environmental concerns appeared to expand during the 1960s with consumption practices being examined in relation to the damage they cause to the environment. It would seem that these concerns expanded into the tourism industry and changed the historical perspective that tourism was a non-polluting industry. In addition, the tourism industry was not only coming under pressure from the environmental movement but concerns were raised surrounding the cultural impact of travelling to foreign countries and the treatment of host country natives. Politically, concerns surrounding human rights and the environment were arguably brought to the forefront of global attention by the World Commission on the Environment and Development which is more commonly referred to as the Brundtland Report.

In this report the Commission argued that a developmental paradigm was needed in order to address issues of environmental degradation, preservation of human rights, address economic progress and alleviating poverty, which again reiterate the concerns of ethical consumption more generally. This paradigm is based around the notion of 'development that meets the needs of the present without compromising the ability of future generations to meet their own needs'.

Following on from this the Agenda 21 strategy document was a result of the United Nations Conference on Environment and Development held in Rio de Janeiro in 1992. Agenda 21 was the first document to address issues surrounding tourism and sustainability, however within the report there were only a few incidental references to the social and environmental issues generated by international tourism. Agenda 21 was received with severe criticism as it did not meet the aims of the conference mainly due to its non-binding treaties allowing most of the recommendations surrounding climate change and various other cultural issues to be ignored by the international community. Within academia, the Journal of Sustainable Tourism was first put to print in 1993 aiming 'to advance critical understanding of the relationships between tourism and sustainable development'.

During the same period the WTO pursued the issue of sustainable tourism and in partnership with the World Travel and Trade Council released Agenda 21 for the Travel and Tourism Industry in 1996 which influenced the UN Commission on Sustainable Development in 1999, focusing mainly on issues of sustainable tourism. Following the disappointing impact both Agenda 21 documents had on the implementation of international sustainable development a further UN World Summit on Sustainable Development took place in Johannesburg, South Africa, in 2002.

The discourse employed at the conference appears to highlight similar concerns to the previous summits with the conference concluding:

- 'From the African continent, the cradle of humankind, we solemnly pledge to the peoples of the world and the generations that will surely inherit this Earth that we are determined to ensure that our collective hope for sustainable development is realised

Concerns around implementing these visions have once again arisen surrounding the need for policies to force change on the international community rather than adopting an opt-in system. With this brief history in mind, it is suggested that there appears to be some commonalities between ethical consumption and sustainable tourism: increased awareness regarding the detrimental effects of consumerism on the environment has influenced the growth of ethical products such as Cafédirect coffee from the 1960s onwards.

These concerns are mirrored in relation to the growing acknowledgement of the environmental impact of the tourism industry generating political and academic attention towards the latter part of the twentieth century; in addition, cultural concerns in relation to mass consumerism are at the heart of the development of ethical products and this is also highlighted in the need for culturally sustainable forms of tourism which attempt to reduce the impact of tourism on host communities. Although there appear to be clear commonalities between ethical consumption and sustainable tourism it is not suggested they are exactly the same as they both have their own distinct histories, motivations and practices. The following part shall develop this idea by examining what is meant by ethical consumption and investigate if sustainable tourism shares any of these characteristics.

A COMMON DEFINITION

Ethical consumption is a concept incorporating a number of aspects such as ethical product purchase, boycotts, investment in ethical funds and deposits in ethical banks. When we talk of these different aspects in terms of 'being ethical' a number of key features appear consistently throughout the corpus of definitions. For consumption practices to be defined as ethical they need to incorporate at least one of the key principles surrounding environmental, social concerns/human rights, animal welfare concerns and economic sustainability.

More broadly ethical consumption is defined as '...any practice of consumption in which explicitly registering commitment towards distant or absent others is an important dimension of the meaning of activity to the actors involved'. Cowe and Williams extend the definition of ethical to incorporate 'self-interested health concerns' and use the expansion of organic foods to highlight this as they are not only concerned with the environment through pesticides but also the detrimental effects these chemicals have on the individual's personal wellbeing.

Further, the ethical concept does not simply mark the production process or the values of the consumer, but is also subject to companies acting ethically across the board including their investment strategies. Following this broad definition of ethical consumption, it appears that it represents a complex set of practices addressing different concerns in a variety of different ways. In relation to this definition, initial suggestions regarding the ethical trajectories of sustainable tourism shall be presented in order to examine the possibility of understanding sustainable tourism as an emerging form of ethical consumption.

Sustainable tourism could be understood as an emerging form of ethical consumption as it adopts social, environmental and economic concerns which are also expressed through the form of consumption. Further, within the sustainable tourism domain we have identified four dominant forces as influencing sustainable tourism which may help to show the parallels between it and ethical consumption.

Whilst I also acknowledge there may be additional forces or motivations influencing sustainable tourism in comparison to ethical consumption it would appear that these four forces enable a better understanding of sustainable tourism:

- *Climate change*: Due to the rapid growth in international tourism transport concerns have been raised regarding the environmental impact of such travel. For example, according to the WTO in 1950 there were around 25 million international arrivals compared to 806 million international arrivals in 2005-representing an average annual growth rate of 8.6 per cent. Further, it is now argued that the transport sector of the tourism industry is a major contributor to international greenhouse gas emissions.
- *Impact of mass tourism on landscapes*: Tourist destinations in countries such as Spain and Thailand provide excellent examples of how mass tourism can change the natural landscape, from high-rise hotels to mass backpacker hostels.
- *Growing interest in environmentalism*: Sustainable tourism appears to have grown alongside environmental and conservation concerns with an increasing emphasis on conservation work or environmental tours whilst on holiday.
- *Cultural and human rights*: Cultural sensitivity appears at the forefront of a sustainable holiday. The protection and celebration of indigenous cultures and their traditions appears to have influenced the emergence of sustainable tourism. Further, through cultural projects tourists are able to provide the host communities with the advanced knowledge to develop and enter the post-modern world with the protection of human rights providing the foundations for such values.

Therefore, with a broad definition of ethical consumption presented, followed by forces which have influenced sustainable tourism, similarities between ethical consumption and sustainable tourism will now be discussed. Within the definition of ethical consumption it was noted that the environment or green concerns are a key factor in defining a form of ethical consumption.

From the forces influencing sustainable tourism the first three factors appear to fit within the environmental and green concern paradigm through carbon emission concerns, natural landscape concerns and the conservation of natural environments. The social/human rights concerns of ethical consumption in general appear to be expressed through the fourth force influencing sustainable tourism which addresses issues such as cultural sensitivity, cultural protection, development and the protection of human rights.

Therefore it would appear that the ethical consumption paradigm could provide a useful framework through which to develop a better understanding of sustainable tourism. However, referring back to the definition of ethical consumption offered by Barnett *et al*, it appears that other theories maybe needed to further develop this understanding as there appears to be inconsistencies with the fit.

For example, a key aspect of ethical consumption is the concern with distant or absent others, within the sustainable tourism paradigm it would appear that the others are not distant or absent, at least physically, as the tourists are actually visiting the other. Having established a deeper understanding of ethical consumption and offered suggestions as to how sustainable tourism could be conceptualised as an emerging form of ethical consumption, the paper will challenge and critique some of the fundamental assumptions of sustainable tourism by drawing on current post-colonial critiques.

The following part of this chapter will critically engage with two central themes of sustainable tourism, ecological sustainability and human rights, and apply a post-colonial critique to these concepts.

3

Tourism Planning

TOURISM PLANNING

Tourism is one of many activities in a community or region that requires planning and coordination. This bulletin provides a simple structure and basic guidelines for comprehensive tourism planning at a community or regional level. Planning is the process of identifying objectives and defining and evaluating methods of achieving them. By comprehensive planning we mean planning which considers all of the tourism resources, organizations, markets, and Programme within a region. Comprehensive planning also considers economic, environmental, social, and institutional aspects of tourism development.

Two Sides of Planning

Tourism planning has evolved from two related but distinct sets of planning philosophies and methods. On the one hand, tourism is one of many activities in an area that must be considered as part of physical, environmental, social, and economic planning. Therefore, it is common to find tourism addressed, at least partially, in a regional land use, transportation, recreation, economic development, or comprehensive plan. The degree to which tourism is addressed in such plans depends upon the relative importance of tourism to the community or region and how sensitive the planning authority is to tourism activities.

Tourism may also be viewed as a business in which a community or region chooses to engage. Individual tourism businesses conduct a variety of planning activities including feasibility, marketing, product development, promotion, forecasting, and strategic planning. If tourism is a significant component of an area's economy or development plans, regional or community-wide marketing plans are needed to coordinate the development and marketing activities of different tourism interests in the community.

A comprehensive approach integrates a strategic marketing plan with more traditional public planning activities. This ensures a balance between serving the needs and wants of the tourists versus the needs and wants of local residents. A formal tourism plan provides a vehicle for the various interests within a community to coordinate their activities and work towards common goals. It also is a means of coordinating tourism with other community activities.

Steps in the Planning Process

Like any planning, tourism planning is goal-oriented, striving to achieve certain objectives by matching available resources and Programme with the needs and wants of people. Comprehensive planning requires a systematic approach, usually involving a series of steps. The process is best viewed as an iterative and on-going one, with each step subject to modification and refinement at any stage of the planning process.

There are six steps in the planning process:

1. Define goals and objectives.
2. Identify the tourism system.
   (a) Resources
   (b) Organizations
   (c) Markets
3. Generate alternatives.
4. Evaluate alternatives.
5. Select and implement.
6. Monitor and evaluate.

Step one: Defining Goals and objectives. Obtaining clear statements of goals and objectives is difficult, but important. Ideally, tourism development goals should flow from more general community goals and objectives. It is important to understand how a tourism plan serves these broader purposes. Is the community seeking a broader tax base, increased employment opportunities, expanded recreation facilities, better educational Programme, a higher quality of life? How can tourism contribute to these objectives?

If tourism is identified as a means of serving broader community goals, it makes sense to develop plans with more specific tourism development objectives. These are generally defined through a continuing process in which various groups and organizations in a community work together towards common goals. A local planning authority, chamber of commerce, visitor's bureau, or similar group should assume a leadership role to develop an initial plan and obtain broad involvement of tourism interests in the community. Public support for the planning process and plan is also important.

Having a good understanding of tourism and the tourism system in your community is the first step towards defining goals and objectives for tourism development. The types of goals that are appropriate and the precision with which you are able to define them will depend upon how long your community has been involved in tourism and tourism planning.

In the early stages of tourism development, goals may involve establishing organizational structures and collecting information to better identify the tourism system in the community. Later, more precise objectives can be formulated and more specific development and marketing strategies evaluated.

Step two: Identifying Your Tourism System When planning for any type of activity, it is important to first define its scope and characteristics. Be clear about exactly what your plan encompasses. A good initial question is, "What do you mean by tourism?" Tourism is defined in many ways. Generally, tourism involves people traveling outside of their community for pleasure. Definitions differ on the specifics of how far people must travel, whether or not they must stay overnight, for how long, and what exactly is included under traveling for "pleasure". Do you want your tourism plan to include day visitors, conventioneers, business travellers, people visiting friends and relatives, people passing through, or seasonal residents?

Which community resources and organizations serve tourists or could serve tourists? Generally, tourists share community resources with local residents and businesses. Many organizations serve both tourists and locals. This complicates tourism planning and argues for a clear idea of what your tourism plan entails. You can begin to clarify the tourism system by breaking it down into three subsystems:

1. Tourism resources,
2. Tourism organizations, and
3. Tourism markets.

An initial task in developing a tourism plan is to identify, inventory, and classify the objects within each of these subsystems. Tourism Resources are any (1) natural, (2) cultural, (3) human, or (4) capital resources that either are used or can be used to attract or serve tourists. A tourism resource inventory identifies and classifies the resources available that provide opportunities for tourism development. Conduct an objective and realistic assessment of the quality and quantity of resources you have to work with.

Tourism organizations combine resources in various proportions to provide products and services for the tourist. It is important to recognize the diverse array of public and private organizations involved with tourism. The most difficult part of tourism planning is to get these groups to work towards common goals. You should develop a list of these organizations within your own community and obtain their input and cooperation in your tourism planning efforts. Setting up appropriate communication systems and institutional arrangements is a key part of community tourism planning.

TERRITORIAL PLANNING IN TOURISM

Environmental quality is often a key success factor for tourism. At the same time, tourism makes extensive use of natural resources thereby jeopardizing its long-term viability. To address such a dilemma, from the general notion of sustainable development (SD) tourism scholars have coined the term 'sustainable tourism' (ST) that encompasses a set of principles, business methods and policy prescriptions relevant to the tourist industry (Sinclair and Stabler, 1997). However, recent research has advocated the need to reconcile the concept of ST with that of SD, by making the concerns of the former adhere more strictly to the tenets of the latter (Collins, 1999; Hunter, 1997). This paper looks at the issues of tourism development and environmental conservation through the lens of SD principles and assesses the pivotal role that local governments can play in designing policies that make the two perspectives compatible.

A common denominator in the literature on SD is the Bruntland Commission's definition that "SD is development that meets the need of the present without compromising the ability of future generations to meet their own needs". Such a mandate affirms the importance of intragenerational and intergenerational equity issues. As far as the former is concerned, "SD places emphasis on providing for the needs of the least advantaged in society". This is particularly relevant in developing countries, where the need to generate income is more likely to lead to a rapid exploitation of the resource base and an uneven distribution of the related profits between foreign investors and host populations. To prevent this, it is generally recommended that local populations and governments be directly involved in the shaping of development activities in association with foreign developers, because locals can better assess the short and the long-term effects of growth.

As far as the latter is concerned, intergenerational fairness implies that future generations should receive a fair share of the net benefits generated by the development. The fact that development is sustainable only as long as future generations are fairly treated led to the view that "...we in the present generation are but the present tenants of the earth, not its absolute owners. As present tenants we have the right to make use of its productivity, but not the right to impair its productivity for its later tenants the future generations".

In theory, future generations are entitled to just compensation for the current generation's actions that lead to a depletion of natural resource. In practice, doing so requires making difficult judgements about the substitutability of natural capital with physical capital. This is a crucial point in the case of tourism, whose activity relies extensively on the transformation of natural capital into accommodation and service facilities. Thus, the tourism industry faces the particularly difficult challenge to "develop tourism capacity and the quality of its products without adversely affecting the physical and human environment that sustains and nurtures them".

It is argued, however, that the WCED definition is too vague to use as a working tool, and often results in ambiguous admonition for policymakers (Norton and Toman 1997). Indeed, the requirement that the needs of the present generation be met without compromising the ability of future generations to meet their needs, could be satisfied simply by allowing constant consumption over time at no more than a subsistence level. Although such a policy would achieve equity among different generations, it could hardly be accepted as a reasonable target for public policy, as it may fail to incorporate a notion of dynamic efficiency. In the following analysis, efficiency implies a notion of "non-wastefulness", that is, the possibility that inputs are transformed in a way that leads to an increase in individuals' well-being in a sustainable manner, *e.g.*, consumption above the subsistence level for every generation.

Such an increase in individuals' welfare entails a decision on the optimal allocation of scarce resources (*e.g.* natural assets) among alternative uses (*e.g.*, development or preservation). Because tourism can never be totally without environmental impacts, the real challenge is to indicate sustainable policies that combine intra-generational and intergenerational equity with efficiency considerations in a mutually compatible manner (Page, 1997). As far as intergenerational equity and efficiency considerations are concerned, assessing under what circumstances turning natural resources into capital stock (*e.g.* a hotel) leads to an increase in the well-being of the present and future generations, is central.

Furthermore, the notion of efficiency is closely linked with that of intragenerational equity when the local populations of the tourist areas are allowed to appropriate a fair share of the net benefits generated by tourism. The theoretical analysis in this article presents a policy measure that enables local governments to retain the surplus from tourism activities when these are run by foreign organizations. The existing literature has refined the definition of sustainable development - from very weak to very strong depending on the importance given to such notions as reversibility and substitutability between physical and natural capital.

Unfortunately, the interpretation of such concepts varies, depending on the disciplinary approach being adopted. For instance, economists and ecologists assign different meanings to the notions of substitutability and reversibility. For economists, substitutability refers to the possibility of maintaining a desired level of production using different combinations of inputs, while reversibility indicates the extent to which a given resource becomes scarce as a consequence of human actions. For ecologists, these two factors determine such ecosystems' physical properties as, for instance, resilience. In this sense, a more resilient ecosystem is one that is more likely to revert to its original condition after a perturbation and/or to find other substitutes in the event that one of the ecosystem attributes is diminished.

Applying the notion of weak sustainability is possible if we assume that natural and physical capitals are substitutable, or when changes to the natural asset base are reversible. This implies that under the weak sustainability paradigm, intra-generational equity is obtained through the distribution of the efficiency gains arising from the implementation of development projects, while future generations are compensated for the loss of natural assets by inheriting a greater stock of physical capital. However, even advocates of weak sustainability acknowledge that under certain circumstances, *e.g.* when physical capital is a poor substitute for the natural resource, efficiency considerations ought not to occupy a central role. For instance, it has been argued that one generation might set aside special places and features such as the Grand Canyon or the Reef Barrier for future generations because of their intrinsic qualities.

The uncertainty surrounding both the effects of human intervention on the environment and the likelihood of finding feasible technological solutions to environmental problems provides an important argument for strong sustainability. By this it is meant that the opportunities of future generations can be secured only if natural resources and environmental quality are specifically conserved for their benefit. Thus, within the strong sustainability paradigm, conservation concerns are paramount.

Combining Conservation and Efficiency

The foregoing discussion has illustrated that intragenerational/efficiency and intergenerational equity goals are less likely to be in conflict when considered from within a weak sustainability perspective, while supporters of strong sustainability are inclined to reject any trade-off between conservation and efficiency. In line with the latter view, it has become abundantly clear that tourism cannot continue to be the killer of the "goose laying golden eggs".

However, it has been argued that strong sustainability, with its emphasis on intergenerational fairness, can conflict with the efficient use of resources that may engender beneficial effects for both the present and the future generations. That is, the strong sustainability approach is often associated with an anti-economic growth position that appears to deny the world's poor the opportunity of meeting basic needs, both in the short and the long run.

Therefore, this article takes the Centre ground stance indicated in Hunter (1997) by arguing that the essential role of ecological conservation in the implementation of sustainable tourism strategies should, depending on the circumstances, be complemented by efficiency considerations. This is in line with many methodological contributions aimed at bringing together efficiency and intergenerational equity.

The combination of a conservation criterion with an efficiency criterion constitutes the central element of the two-tier method advocated by Page (1977). Using this approach, problems are categorized as being intragenerational or intergenerational in their effects, in the sense specified above. That is, when intergenerational issues figure prominently, more attention is given to conservation, with possible applications of the 'safe minimum standard of conservation principle', which places the burden of proof on today's resource allocators to demonstrate that their behaviour is consistent with intergenerational fairness (Howarth, 1997). In practice, this approach recognizes the fundamental right of future generations to inherit an intact stock of natural resources, unless the costs of foregoing the resource exploitation, that is, the loss of the efficiency gains from development, are unbearably high.

Page (1997) provides a list of inter-related issues that need to be addressed to achieve a satisfactory combination of efficiency and equity. First, instruments need to be identified. He suggests that "shifting the tax base towards virgin material taxes and taxes on environmental harms would work towards sustainability". Second, intergenerational equity should always come first when the resource is essential. He cites the U.S. Drinking Water Regulation as an example of public intervention based on equity grounds, as future generations are entitled to a safe supply of drinking water.

The example that comes to mind in the case of tourism, is the establishment of parks or natural reserves, where regulatory measures are taken towards environmental protection so that the functional integrity of essential, and possibly unique, natural ecosystems is preserved as far as is possible, for the benefit of future generations. Indeed, once a law attributes the status of park or of natural reserve to a given geographical area, heavy restrictions are imposed on the possibility to develop the area, that curtail or impede tourist activity.

More importantly, to guarantee that the resource base remains intact, and can be bequeathed to future generations, the status of park cannot be abolished and remains associated with the area indefinitely. Third, and related to the latter point, the role of the legal framework in which the decision-makers operate is crucial. Practically, this entails that the environmental decisions associated with important equity and efficiency considerations should be dealt with in a manner similar to that used to preserve a system of constitutional law.

This is because the "framers of a constitution are expected to abstract themselves from their own narrow self-interest and establish the rules of the game that are sustainable indefinitely".It is essential for modern societal institutions to maintain the constitutional system: to protect it from myopic opportunism triggered by short-term benefits, it is commonplace to have special procedures to modify constitutional dictates. By the same token, environmental problems with important intergenerational equity aspects should be dealt with like constitutional issues whereby the future generations' entitlement to an intact resource base has paramount importance.

Three points that are central in this study may be inferred from the previous discussion:

1. The importance of natural resources,
2. The identification of appropriate policy instruments and
3. The legislative framework. This article aims to clarify some of the relationships among these issues. At the same time it develops a

conceptual framework encompassing all the basic elements that are taken into account in the public assessment of tourism development projects. To this purpose, a theoretical economic model of land taxation is illustrated. Its results show the crucial role played by a tax on land development for the joint achievement of conservation and economic efficiency goals. In addition, its cost-benefit approach clearly indicates that in environmentally sensitive areas - where the resource is essential - the tax should be set at a level that deters development. This result is thus equivalent to the creation of a park or a reserve that remains as close to its original form as possible.

The importance of the legislative framework is investigated using the case study of the so-called "Master Plan" in North Sardinia (Italy). The evidence presented, together with considerations from the theoretical model, are used to shed light on the Sardinian government's refusal to grant a developer special exemptions from existing territorial planning legislation. Indeed, the Sardinian government decided to forego the short-term benefits of a large tourism development because the development allowed the possibility of construction within 300 meters of the coastline, a practice that is prohibited by Sardinian law. The local government recognized that the Defence of the conservation principle embodied in the regional law could not be a matter of bargaining, even though this would have entailed, as it actually did, the withdrawal of the project by the developer.

Regardless of the merit of the specific project and the good reputation of the developer for quality tourism, the Sardinian government's stance on the project aimed to ensure that other developments might not be created unless sustainable principles were applied.

Sustainability and Public Intervention

To our knowledge, there is no formal economic model explicitly linking tourism and sustainable development. There exists, however, a growing literature aimed at integrating sustainability and formal economic analysis. Faucheux et al. (1996) classified the existing analytical approaches to sustainability using four categories of models: 1) neo-classical, 2) evolutionary, 3) ecological economic and 4) neo-ricardian.

The model presented in the next subsection falls within the first category but departs from existing models by adopting a game theoretic approach where different incentives faced by public and private institutions are taken into account. For a technical presentation of the model, the reader is referred to Piga (1999). The emphasis here will be the description of the assumptions used in this model, and the policy recommendations that can be drawn. The second part of the section consists of a case study that complements and supports the theoretical analysis.

Sustainability and Taxation

The model under analysis is dynamic; that is, it considers a sequence of time periods and how decisions taken in early periods influence the outcomes of subsequent periods. A dynamic approach allows a better identification of the development's long-term effects, notably on land, which is the natural resource under study.

This is particularly relevant for tourism because territorial planning, environmental design and land use, are crucial factors that create and sustain a tourist resort competitive advantage. This is because tourists increasingly expect a picturesque landscape to be integral to the holiday experience. Moreover, land development is associated with various forms of environmental costs. Both these aspects are captured in the following analysis.

The first economic agent taken into account is a private tourism developer who owns a territory of size L For instance; L could represent the size of an island. The developer chooses the rate of land exploitation, that is, the portion of the site on which tourist facilities will be erected. Denoting with B(t) the stock of developed land at time t and with the size of territory on which the developer decides to build in period t, we postulate that these two variables are linked by this simple law of variation over time. t). Such an expression indicates that in every period t a portion of land sð(t) is used to build accommodations. Thus, what is built this year is added to what was built in previous years, thereby increasing the stock of buildings that constitute the site's capacity.

The discussion so far highlights the well known impact of tourism development on environmental quality: "In reality, it is impossible to imagine any kind of tourism activity being developed and then operating without in some way reducing the quantity and/or quality of natural resources somewhere". In this particular case, for tourism activity to take place, it is impossible to maintain the resource base intact (*i.e.*, not to exploit land). It follows that a satisfactory combination of efficiency and conservation hinges around the identification of both the private and public benefits engendered by the development, of its environmental costs and of the appropriate policy instruments that induce an optimal level of use of the natural resource.

The first type of private benefit that we consider is the revenue deriving from selling to tourists. Revenues depend on the price of the holiday and on the site's capacity, B (t). In turn, it is assumed that the tourists' willingness to pay for a holiday (which represents the highest price they would pay for a holiday) is positively influenced by the environmental quality of the site, which is measured by the amount of land that is left unused.

More importantly, the previous analytical expression indicates that the more the place is developed (*i.e.*, the greater B (t) relative to L), the lower the price the developer can charge for a holiday. Therefore, the developer, when deciding to expand (*i.e.*, increase the size of B(t) through the choice of ó(t)), has to take into account that the revenue increase, due to the possibility of accommodating more tourists, may be more than offset by the reduction in price that is triggered by the deterioration in the environmental quality.

Such a novel representation of the links between tourists' demand and environmental quality captures a peculiar feature of the tourist industry that is supported by empirical evidence. Font (2000) presents evidence supporting the notion that environmental considerations are important drivers of tourism demand. Huybers and Bennett (2000) reach a similar conclusion in an analysis of changes in environmental quality and other features that affect demand.

The local government is the second economic agent taken into consideration. The instrument used to achieve sustainability is a tax on each unit of newly built territory.

This clarifies the crucial role of the public sector: the tax is a cost to the developer and can be used by the government to appropriate some of the profits generated by the development. As discussed below, the tax guarantees the achievement of intragenerational equity objectives, as the tax revenues in each year can be deployed to ameliorate the local public infrastructure which is then inherited by future generations.

In line with the real-world situation where the legislative framework and the taxing policy is often a given for the developers, the economic model assumes that the local government has a first-mover advantage, that is, the government sets the tax level before the developer decides the expansion size. In the economic literature the player that moves first is defined as a "Stackelberg leader". In each period, the local government obtains tax receipts given by the tax multiplied by the size of the expanded capacity.

The second part of the government's objective function consists of the net value derivable from the use of the land. Such a value is the net outcome of the government's evaluation of the public benefits from development against its environmental costs. On the one hand, public benefits are generated by tourism development through a multiplier effect on the local economy arising because a local workforce is used in construction, in operating the tourist facilities and because tourists consume local products.

For more examples of the relationship between tourism and the local multiplier. On the other hand, land development engenders environmental costs for the local population both in terms of congestion and exhaustion of the natural resource and in the form of loss of non-market benefits such as bequest, option and existence values (Pearce et al., 1989). The bequest value is the willingness to pay to preserve the environment for the benefit of future generations.

The option value identifies an expression of preference for the preservation of an environment against some probability that a community will make use of it at a later date. The existence value is represented by the utility that individuals enjoy when the risk to an endangered species has been reduced. Development implies the loss of all these values for the local population, the sum of which constitutes the non-market environmental costs.

These are particularly high in areas where the ecosystem is less resilient, that is, less likely to fully recover from exogenous shocks, and where, therefore, development may engender irreversible degradation to the environment. Finally, land development engenders another form of environmental costs to the local population, that is, the lack of access to natural resources (*e.g.*, beaches) due to congestion arising from having an intensively developed destination occupied by tourists.

The foregoing analysis of the local government's pay-off function has highlighted that the development engenders benefits in the form of private profits and public income multiplier effects, and environmental costs whose size depends on the characteristics of the area's ecosystem. The difference between these benefits and costs gives rise to a net value function, W(B(t)), that depends on the size of the development. A realistic analytical expression for the net value function W(B(t)) is one that allows, at an early stage of development, growth benefits, and the related efficiency gains, to be greater than environmental costs, which become predominant as the development increases in size.

A quadratic function such as $W(t)=B(t)-\tilde{a}B^2(t)$, exhibits this property: the minus sign attached to the quadratic value of the total development size, denoted by B(t), implies that the environmental costs associated with development, increase at a faster rate than growth benefits, captured by the linear part of B(t). Furthermore, this effect is reinforced depending on the value of ã, that is, the larger ã, the larger the environmental costs relative to the growth benefits. Note, however, that when ã is sufficiently large (*e.g.*, when the loss of existence, option and bequest values is conspicuous) W(t) may be negative even for small levels of development.

This is made up of the pecuniary tax take and of the external effects of the development, namely the growth benefits and the environmental costs. When ã is large enough, environmental costs exceed the monetary value of tax receipts and income multiplier effects even for small values of B(t) that correspond to an early stage of development. In this case, given that $E\ (t)<0$, the local government should not allow any development in the territory. However, in more general cases, the tax receipts may be used to improve the site's infrastructures - schools, hospitals, roads etc. - whose creation thus compensates future generations for inheriting a smaller stock of natural resource.

The foregoing discussion highlights the different objectives pursued by the developer and the local government, because the taxation policy creates a benefit for the latter and a cost for the former. However, without the tax, the external (*i.e.*, income multiplier and non-market environmental) effects that the tourist development engenders do not affect the developer's pay-off. Thus, the tax constitutes an instrument that induces the internalization of these external effects in the developer's decision concerning the amount of land to develop.

Furthermore, we have noted that the local government can use taxation to appropriate some of the private profits. This guarantees the participation of the local population in the sharing of the tourist development's benefits and, hence, intragenerational equity. It has also been argued that tourism developments are unable to transfer an intact stock of natural resources to future generations. It follows that the analysis of intergenerational equity, and the related issues of conservation and efficiency, should be carried out by studying how the development tax presented above should be set depending on the environmental characteristics of the territory.

Results: The following results are derived assuming that both the developer and the government choose, respectively, the size of newly developed land and the land tax in each period so as to maximize the discounted flow of profits over an infinite time horizon. The optimal tax is such that the local government's inter-temporal pay-off E(t) is maximized. The technical analysis used to derive the solution to this maximization problem is beyond the scope of this article.

To analyze how the tax affects the equilibrium value of land use, it is customary to derive the socially optimal result and use it as a benchmark against which the model's results are compared. The best outcome, from a social viewpoint, is one in which both parties mutually agree on the size of the territory that is developed in every period. Such a decision entails that all types of benefits and costs identified above are taken into account. Hence, there is no need for the tax, as both parties understand the impact of development on the environment, to the extent that no development is carried out if the environmental costs are greater than the private and public benefits. If development is undertaken, then a lump-sum transfer from the developer to the local government is sufficient to obtain intragenerational equity.

We denote such a benchmark case as the "cooperative case", to emphasize the fact that the parties behave as a single entity: this implies that all the external effects associated with the development are internalized and properly accounted for in the decision regarding the project's size. In the remainder of the paper, the equilibrium level of land use in the perfectly cooperative scenario is denoted as B (t). Such a case is equivalent to the partnerships model advocated in Middleton (1998: 128-9), where a collaborative process is established between the private and the public institutions for dealing with tourism planning and management for a destination.

However, it is very unlikely that the developer and the government have perfectly aligned objectives. While the cooperative case can be used as a benchmark, in a more realistic case the government and the developer behave non-cooperatively as two distinct entities pursuing conflicting goals. Indeed, it is reasonable to expect that the developer wants to maximize the development's private benefits without considering the social costs that it entails, while the government may be particularly concerned with its social costs and the loss of environmental values.

From a strategic viewpoint, the government can exploit its 'first-mover advantage' by imposing a development tax, in order to induce the optimal level of land use which is equivalent to that in the cooperative case. Indeed, if the developer were left free to operate without any form of public intervention, the development size would exceed that in the cooperative case, as the environmental costs would not be taken into account. However, even in the non-cooperative scenario, obtaining.the socially optimal level of land use is possible when the government behaves like a Stackelberg leader.

Another advantage of the non-cooperative scenario is that it allows analyzing the effects that different weights used by the parties to discount future benefits and costs have on the resource use. Such weights are represented by the discount factors that capture the extent to which different individuals presently value a gain or a loss that will occur in the future. Those who prefer to make a lower gain today rather than a higher gain tomorrow have a greater discount factor. The length of the planning horizon over which investments are evaluated also influences the discount factor. Traditionally, private developers are more concerned about the short-term implications of their strategies, and therefore discount the future more heavily. When evaluating the impacts of human activity on the environment, governments are, at least in theory, more likely to consider the related long-term costs.

Hence, more concern by the government for the intergenerational effects of development is represented by a lower discount rate. The results from the theoretical model reported below are obtained assuming that the developer's discount rate, denoted by ñD, is greater than the government's rate, denoted by ñG. However, the results are reversed if the local government discounts the future more than the developer, a situation that is more likely to occur in a certain phase of the political cycle, namely before an election. Having defined the model's components, we now describe the qualitative features characterizing the model's solution.

First, a result common to the cooperative and the non-cooperative setting is that the largest portion of space is developed at the beginning of the development. The rationale behind such a choice is clear: it is optimal to build as much capacity as possible at the beginning of a project because an extra unit of capacity generates revenues forever. Thereby, the developer can more quickly recoup the large initial capital investment used to finance the high start-up costs associated with the development.

It would therefore seem that the two settings generate the same outcome with regard to the conservation issue. However, in the non-cooperative setting the two institutions usually value future benefits and costs differently. This has profound bearings on the development size in equilibrium. Indeed, as assumed before, if the private developer is fewer patients, then the model clearly shows that in the non-cooperative case less land will be used in total relative to the benchmark. The rationale of such a result is intuitive. A government that places a great weight on the environmental costs that future generations will incur, can set the development tax high enough to deter development beyond B^{nc}(t,ñD, ñG).

It can be shown that the rate of exploitation of the natural resource occurs at a slower pace in the non-cooperative case, that is, less land is used in every period. It follows that less environmental costs are also incurred. The results that in the non-cooperative case less land is used in total and that the development occurs at a slower pace, cast some doubts on the recommendation that the private and the public sector should seek more collaborative forms of organization of the tourism activity. While it can be argued that the same outcome could be achieved without the tax by having the government setting the limits of development, and the developer agreeing to comply with these limits, such a command-and-control arrangement presents, relative to the market instrument of taxation, at least two drawbacks.

First, it carries high bureaucratic costs for monitoring and enforcement. Second, and most importantly, it may be easier for the parties to renegotiate the terms of the initial agreement because of changes in socio-economic and/or political conditions, while changes in the tax legislation have to undergo a lengthy parliamentary scrutiny. We then conclude that a better outcome is obtained when the local government regulates the activity of the private developer by imposing a development tax, relative to a situation where a mutual agreement between the parties is created.

The model indicates how public policy adjusts according to the relative size of environmental costs and public benefits in the cost-benefit analysis. First of all, regardless of whether the environmental costs are greater than the benefits from development or not, it is always optimal for the local government to impose a positive tax on the use of the natural resource at the outset of planning. Obviously, the tax remains positive whenever the environmental costs are greater than the public benefits due to endogenous growth and income multiplier effects.

However, when the public benefits are larger than the environmental costs at any level of development, the optimal tax's time profile exhibits an interesting behaviour: at the outset of planning, the tax is positive but at some point in time it is turned into a subsidy, which corresponds to a negative tax. Traditional economic literature suggests the use of a subsidy to attract investments that determine beneficial effects for the host community (*e.g.*, jobs creation, higher local firms' birth rate etc). An important difference in the present case is that it is optimal for the policymaker to introduce the subsidy only after an appropriate time period, and not at the outset. The rationale can be found in the ability of the tax to extract some of private benefits engendered by the development which otherwise would be totally appropriated by the firm.

Finally, the analysis implicitly allows geographic areas to be taxed differently depending on the sensitiveness of the natural environment. Low environmental costs are associated with non-sensitive areas. The government therefore initially imposes a low tax for development in such areas, which may then become a subsidy if public benefits are greater than environmental negative effects.

On the other hand, when concerns for the resilience of the natural environment exist, the tax is set at such a high level that no development is economically profitable for the developer. This is tantamount to one of the four sustainable tourism approaches proposed by Hunter, that of "Neotenous Tourism", which corresponds to a "very strong sustainability approach predicated upon the belief that there are circumstances in which tourism should be actively and continuously discouraged on ecological grounds".

Furthermore, Hunter (1997: 862) argues that "In some places, including national reserves of national or international importance, tourism growth should be sacrificed for the greater good". Such a recommendation is equivalent to the case of no development due to the high tax that arises as an equilibrium outcome in the model.

To summarize, the results from the economic model of taxation show that it is possible to pursue conservation objectives without hindering the implementation of viable economic projects that impact the environment. The results crucially hinge on the assumption that the government has a concern for conservation, which in practice is identified by the government's willingness to give proper weight to environmental damages that may occur in the distant future. As argued in the Introduction, such willingness can be expressed by the creation of a legislation that has constitutional value. The following case study illustrates the crucial role that regional planning legislation plays for the establishment of a government's stance towards conservation.

An Application: The Case of Costa Smeralda in Sardinia.

The previous analysis is based on the properties of a normative model that encompasses a set of economic issues. We now test its predictions by considering a case study involving a local government and a tourist developer. The evidence presented suggests that the recommendations derivable from the model's results provide a set of principles that local governments apply - or should begin to apply - in their evaluation of tourist projects.

In 1997 a multinational company, Ciga Immobiliare, prepared a development scheme for a part of Costa Smeralda on the Northeast coast of Sardinia in the Mediterranean Sea. The project was literally called Master Plan in the Sardinian and national press, and this is how it will be referred to in the remainder of this article. The following are taken from the executive summary released by the developer when the project was presented to the press. The entire project was to cover an area of 24 km^2, 85 per cent of which is located in the territory of the Arzachena municipality and the remainder 15 per cent in the Olbia municipality territory.

The total volume of the 11 hotels, 2,000 villas and 1,900 apartments included in the project was estimated to be 2,550,000 m^3 (14 per cent in hotels, 9 per cent in ancillary services and 77 per cent in residential dwellings). The planned capacity of hotels and residential dwellings was, respectively, 4,000 and 16,000 beds.

The cost of the total investment was calculated to be US$1.45 billion and the related increase in local income to be $2.375 billion, with an investment multiplier of 1.72. Although the project was to cover a time span of 25 years, most construction would be completed within the first 5-10 years.

The yearly demand, measured in bednights, was evaluated at 504,000 units in hotels and 960,000 units in residential dwellings, the total being almost three times higher than the average of 560,000 units recorded during the 1990's in the already existing hotels owned by the developer in Costa Smeralda. The expenditure by tourists in hotel accommodation and dwellings was expected to total, respectively, $151 and $240 millions and generate an increase in local production of around $500 millions. Finally, the developer's study estimated the overall increment in employment in Sardinia to be 12,200 jobs: 4,800 new jobs in hotels and restaurants, 2,000 in trade and retailing, 4,200 in the services and 1,200 in manufacturing.

Given these figures, the project should certainly have appeared enticing to a local government operating in a region characterized by an extremely high unemployment rate and a much lower per capita income than the Italian average. How was it, then, that the parties did not find a satisfactory agreement and eventually the developer withdrew the project? An answer can be found by analyzing the political stance of the Sardinian government with respect to the magnitude of the social and environmental costs associated with the project.

The Sardinian government had made it clear that the "safeguard of the environmental quality is a factor for economic development". Moreover, as far as the Master Plan was concerned, the position of the Sardinian government was that "a better balance between the use of the territory, the socio-economic effects and the developer's profit has to be found". The Sardinian government seemed inclined to grant the building permission, subject to a few changes in the project, including:

1. A significant reduction in the number of residential dwellings, and possibly an increase in the number of hotels;
2. Priority to the building of hotels and tourism facilities; and
3. Respect for the norm that prohibits the construction of any building within 300 metres of the coastline.

Finally, the local government expressed concern about the number of "scattered dwellings" presumably villas - which "consume land and make access to the sea more difficult". The Sardinian government's preference for hotels, as expressed by requirement (b) and the request to increase the number of hotels can be found in the regional government's belief that hotels and related facilities would extend the tourist season well beyond the peak months of July and August. The Sardinian government's remark that villas and apartment use more land than hotels is consistent with the theoretical approach and indicate the government's awareness of the environmental costs associated with the development.

The first part of requirement (a) is directly linked to the theoretical analysis. The number of dwellings increased sharply thereby suggesting that intensive building activity took place during the decade in the municipalities of Olbia and Arzachena. A similar phenomenon occurred also in the remaining part of the North Sardinian Province, which includes many other seaside resorts. A first consideration is the obvious positive correlation between the change in the number of resident population and the increase in the number of occupied dwellings. However, more relevant to the present analysis is the drastic increase in the number of holiday dwellings, whose number more than doubled in Arzachena and almost doubled in Olbia.

Row (5) reports the ratio of holiday dwellings over occupied dwellings. It shows that, relative to the rest of the province, the two municipalities are characterized to a great extent by the so-called "second homes" phenomenon (*i.e.*, holiday houses which are left unoccupied for most of the year). In terms of the theoretical analysis, the extensive use of land associated with this type of accommodation entails high environmental costs, deriving for example, from loss of flora and fauna, beach erosion, and degradation of water quality. Other environmental problems relate to the fact that second homes are used mainly during the period of peak demand. Moreover, self-catering accommodations, such as second homes, do not generate as high multiplier effects as hotels. The Master Plan might have exacerbated the overcrowding and congestion.

Indeed, the dwelling density for the Master Plan –3900/24=162.5 dwellings per Km^2 (3900 is the sum of 2000 villas plus 1900 apartments, 24 Km^2 is the size of the territory) —is well above the averages of the territories concerned. This is indicative of how intensively some parts of the space would have been used by the developer. As many of the Master Plan's buildings would have occupied areas characterized by high environmental sensitivity, it can be inferred that the social costs deriving from the loss of the "hidden environmental values" would have been conspicuous.

The variables are the volumes built for residential and non-residential purposes, the number of new residential dwellings and the related number of rooms. Volumes are used in the following analysis for various reasons. First, in Italy planning regulations dictate the maximum allowable volume of a building erected in a territory of given size. Statistics are collected accordingly. Second, volume is a good indicator of building activity because territorial planning imposes restrictions on the total height of buildings. Therefore, volumes are highly correlated with the size of the territory occupied by buildings.

First, notice that the volume of residential buildings completed over the period in the two municipalities is less than the amount planned by the Master Plan's developer (row

The comparison and the size is made even more striking by the consideration that only 15 per cent of the project was planned in the Olbia municipality. This implies that 85 per cent of the residential volumes intended in the Master Plan (totaling 1668975 m^3) would have been built in the Arzachena's territory. This exceeds the total volumes built there for residential and non-residential purposes over the period 1982-1996.

Second, an inspection of rows (4) and (5) reveals that the number of residential dwellings and rooms intended in the Master Plan is greater than the number of residential dwellings and rooms actually built in each single municipality over the period 1982-1996.

Hence, had the project been allowed to progress as originally planned, many future development options in the area would have been foreclosed, thereby engendering further social costs in territories where building activity for tourism has been particularly intensive over the last two decades.

The rationale for condition (c) (*i.e.*, respect for the norm that prohibits construction with 300 meters of the coastline) lends support to the choice in the theoretical model of considering the local government as endowed with a first-mover advantage enabling them to pursue long-term conservationist policies.

By stating in the law that no building permit would be granted within 300 meters from the coastline, the Sardinian government had declared its commitment towards the safeguarding of the coastal environmental quality. The exception granted to the Master Plan's developer could easily have become the rule, and led to greater environmental costs from over-exploitation.

When it became clear that the project had to be changed substantially in its residential component and that condition (c) was not negotiable, the developer decided not to exercise the option to buy the territories from the current owner (the American multinational Starwood) and abandoned the project.

To summarize, the analysis of the case study highlighted the following points that are consistent with the theoretical predictions from the model discussed in the previous section. Firstly, the concern of a local government for the preservation of environmental quality may lead to no development. Secondly, the local government's behaviour emphasizes the importance of maintaining existing legislation aimed at conservation, thereby giving it the status of constitutional dictate. Finally, and more generally, the study also shows how the variables considered in the theoretical analysis are normally taken into account in the blueprint of any investment project in the tourism industry.

This study argues that a limitation of the strong sustainability approach is the lack of emphasis given to efficiency considerations. It suggests the application of the two-tier approach outlined in Page (1997) as a conceptual framework to tackle the issues of intergenerational equity and economic efficiency simultaneously. Such a two-tier method conceives the importance of the natural resource, the identification of the appropriate instruments and the legislative framework as crucial elements. To provide further support to Page's recommendations for the case of tourism, this study has presented a theoretical economic model of taxation and a case study involving a local government and a private developer.

When economic efficiency considerations are paramount, the theoretical model suggests the use of a land tax at the beginning of the development followed by the possible introduction of a subsidy at a later stage. The tax guarantees that local communities can extract some of the rents created by the development that otherwise would entirely accrue to the developer. At the other extreme, when the development endangers the existence of an essential resource or ecosystem, the theoretical model suggests the prevention of any form of development. In intermediate cases, the tax on land use combines efficiency and conservation goals, as the tax curtails, but does not prevent, the development. This situation is represented in the case study where emphasis is given to the crucial role of territorial planning legislation for the reduction of negative impacts of tourism development.

Indeed, in the two municipalities of Arzachena and Olbia the number of holiday homes has grown dramatically over the last two decades, thus suggesting the economic viability of such developments. At the same time, the norm prohibiting constructions within 300 meters of the coastline has prevented the irreversible damage that building on the coast entails, and has forced developers to locate their sites in less sensitive areas. The fact that the Sardinian government chose not to create a precedent by allowing special treatment for the Master Plan's developer, suggests that the norm regulates issues that deserve to be treated within a constitutional framework, in line with Page's recommendations. Unfortunately, the norm above does not have a legal constitutional status, and could therefore be changed using the process applicable to any ordinary law. This is indeed the intention of the new Sardinian government elected in the year 2000, that is, to modify legislation on territorial planning to accommodate the possibility of buildings near the coastline.

Both the model of taxation and the Sardinian case study provide support for the argument in Middleton (1998) that governments do not need to introduce new policy instruments but rather, they should gear the existing ones towards the achievement of sustainable objectives. Thus territorial planning, building regulation, provision of.infrastructure, fiscal incentives and disincentives, ecological labeling assessment and management of carrying capacity (Collins, 1999), information and education of tourists (Filho, 1996) can all be used effectively and play a central role in a public strategy for sustainable tourism.

However, the view advocated by Middleton (1998) that the public and the private sector should seek more integrated forms of organization in the management of tourism does not necessarily follow. The theoretical analysis of taxation clearly indicates that the best outcome, both in terms of conservation and overall efficiency, is obtained when the public sector takes advantage of its ability to set the rules of the game.

The "Master Plan" example shows that negotiations with the private sector may turn out to be unbeneficial in the long run, especially if the private developer requests special exemptions from the existing legislation, which is aimed at limiting the environmental impact of development. Whenever the government and the private developer have conflicting views regarding the development of an environmentally sensitive area, the analysis of the theoretical model, and the support it has received from the case study, suggest that the government should exploit its first-mover advantage, which is incompatible with Middleton's bargaining approach. As a corollary to the analysis, we may conclude that private-public partnership may be Favoured whenever intergenerational equity issues are not a crucial concern.

THE IMPORTANCE OF PLANNING TOURISM

Planning tourism at all levels is essential for achieving successful tourism development and management. The experience of many tourism areas in the world has demonstrated that, on a long-term basis, the planned approach to developing tourism can bring benefits without significant problems, and maintain satisfied tourist markets.

Places that have allowed tourism to develop without the benefit of planning are often suffering from environmental and social problems. These are detrimental to residents and unpleasant for many tourists, resulting in marketing difficulties and decreasing economic benefits. These uncontrolled tourism areas cannot effectively compete with planned tourist destinations elsewhere. They usually can be redeveloped, based on a planned approach, but that requires much time and financial investment.

Tourism is a rather complicated activity that overlaps several different sectors of the society and economy. Without planning, it may create unexpected and unwanted impacts. Tourism is also still a relatively new type of activity in many countries. Some governments and often the private sector have little or no experience in how to develop tourism properly. For countries that do not yet have much tourism, planning can provide the necessary guidance for its development. For those places that already have some tourism, planning is often needed to revitalize this sector and maintain its future viability.

First, tourism should be planned at the national and regional levels. At these levels, planning is concerned with tourism development policies, structure plans, facility standards, institutional factors and all the other elements necessary to develop and manage tourism. Then, within the framework of national and regional planning, more detailed plans for tourist attractions, resorts, urban, rural and other forms of tourism development can be prepared.

There are several important specific benefits of undertaking national and regional tourism planning.

These advantages include:

- Establishing the overall tourism development objectives and policies -what is tourism aiming to accomplish and how can these aims be achieved.
- Developing tourism so that its natural and cultural resources are indefinitely maintained and conserved for future, as well as present, use.
- Integrating tourism into the overall development policies and patterns of the country or region, and establishing dose linkages between tourism and other economic sectors.
- Providing a rational basis for decision-making by both the public and private sectors on tourism development.
- Making possible the coordinated development of all the many elements of the tourism sector. This includes inter-relating the tourist attractions, activities, facilities and services and the various and increasingly fragmented tourist markets.
- Optimizing and balancing the economic, environmental and social benefits of tourism, with equitable distribution of these benefits to the society, while minimizing possible problems of tourism.
- Providing a physical structure which guides the location, types and extent of tourism development of attractions, facilities, services and infrastructure.
- Establishing the guidelines and standards for preparing detailed plans of specific tourism development areas that are consistent with, and reinforce, one another, and for the appropriate design of tourist facilities.

- Laying the foundation for effective implementation of the tourism development policy and plan and continuous management of the tourism sector, by providing the necessary organizational and other institutional framework.
- Providing the framework for effective coordination of the public and private sector efforts and investment in developing tourism.
- Offering a baseline for the continuous monitoring of the progress of tourism development and keeping it on track.

The planned approach to developing tourism at the national and regional levels is now widely adopted as a principle, although implementation of the policies and plans is still weak in some places. Many countries and regions of countries have had tourism plans prepared. Other places do not yet have plans, but should consider undertaking planning in the near future.

In some countries, plans had previously been prepared but these are now outdated. They need to be revised based on present day circumstances and likely future trends. Founded on accumulated experience, the approaches and techniques of tourism planning are now reasonably well understood. There is considerable assurance that, if implemented, planning will bring substantial benefits to an area.

DECISION BASIS IN TOURISM PLANNING

Currently, information gains more and more importance, leading legitimately to the development of a fourth economic sector – the information sector. Information also plays a vital role in tourism for entrepreneurs and managers who spend the whole day involved in information processing. In the tourism industry there is no lack of market research data, on the contrary, there is a rather uncontrolled growth of various data sources, each having different survey purposes and survey designs. Tourism surveys of national and international market research institutes are published in ever shorter intervals and the level of itemization of market data increases rapidly. Information collected by these means has indicated data which can be organized into the following groups:

1. Information on markets and environment,
2. Information on customer behaviour,
3. Information on competition in the industry, and
4. Internal information for executive boards.

The first three information groups are predominantly non-discretionary from a manager's point of view as the information can very rarely be directly influenced by an individual company. Information from these groups are similar in nature and scope for most sectors represented in the tourism industry (hotel trade, restaurant trade, tour operators, travel agents, common carriers, pressure groups, etc.). In the fourth group however, there is a larger scope for variety. Due to high costs for primary market research many tourism managers abandon market research in general. Even the larger businesses and tourism organizations lack market research departments and employees rarely work exclusively on market research items. This results again in an inconsistent development of marketing aims and strategies, as businesses as often as not grope in the dark for their direction.

In Europe the most frequent or highly recognized of the commissioned tourism studies are either publicly financed, directly by national or local authorities, or indirectly by government agencies. This method of procuring market research, is important and often a condition for its development, as the expensive primary studies cannot be financed by the numerous small or medium-scale businesses. The resulting obligation to pass on information, created by the above mentioned research financing, has lead to a wider search-inregional tourism organizations, and other bodies representing tourism-to find means of successfully sharing and communicating information.

Traditional data resources in tourism market research are reports, records and statistics which may be presented either in printed format or are electronically driven (CD-ROM). Computer-based information systems (databases) are currently a rarity, but usually can be found either in connection with the official statistical data of a country or a region or international institutions.

The in- formation available by this method is rarely used since it ignores the special information requirements of the end-user (managers), or is simply inaccessible due to high fees, complicated application procedures or is simply not user friendly. The lack of practical relevance, of these information systems, can be explained by their bias towards representing the economic interest of the sponsors and data collectors and/or by the universal requirements the systems have to meet in the collection, storage and search of statistical data from other industries. Market research results are mainly available in print and they can be obtained either in bookshops, online or directly from the author. From the consumer's perspective this way of passing on secondary information has a number of dis- advantages:

- Due to the complex design of market research reports the surveyed data is not up to date any more.
- Data from different sources cannot be easily compared especially if it has been surveyed for different purposes.
- Information contained in reports is often of limited relevance for the particular problem.
- Presentation of data is either not detailed enough, not significant enough, or supplementary information is missing which prevents a faultless interpretation of results.
- Often only very specific data from a more comprehensive study is required and thus the cost-benefit-ratio becomes unattractive.

There is usually an overabundance of available information leaving managers to cope with determining which is the best source. Often the entrepreneur has to rely on external consultants and market research specialists resulting in additional costs.

PROCEDURAL KNOWLEDGE

"The big problem with management science models is that managers practically never used them." More than 20 years ago John Little described the discrepancy between the scientific development of planning instruments, models, level of itemization and the fact that, when available, the knowledge gathered is rarely put into practice. This is caused by the numerous, often poorly documented assumptions of model architects, which was denoted as model plutonism by Hans Albert. As a response to this problem Little suggested that the manager is included in the model. He postulated in his article on the Decision Calculus, aniline models with the following features: robustness, ease of control, simplicity, completeness of relevant detail and suitability for communication.

The communication problem is of vital importance in the every day life of managers' daily events. It is still common practice to employ various levels of change rather than continue- ally observe the changes in market share and volume. Many entrepreneurs do not even know terms such as market segmentation or market positioning and they do not regard them as essential. They keep on looking for measures to expand seasonal business but lack knowledge of methods that will measure their success. Corporate planning only takes place if external financing is required and supporting documents have to be submitted to the lender. Heuristic forecasting methods are hardly ever used, accordingly quantitative methods are never used. Models of strategic market plan- ningportfolio analyses and analyses of the lifestyle of a product-employed in other in- dustries are hardly ever used in tourism management. The grounds for the poor employment of methodological processes in tourism management can be divided into two groups; technological development and insufficient training. Issues related to the technological development of existing information processing and transmission systems are:

- Data required for the application of tourism models is either not up-to-date or unsuitable.
- Standard software is not able to support the relatively complex tasks in tourism management.
- Specially developed software is too expensive for single tourism businesses. Issues related to the insufficient training of tourism managers are:
- Managers have little knowledge of existing methods or available data.
- Managers are confronted with various data sources and different results and they do not know how to cope with this situation.

PLANNING TOURISM AS AN INTEGRATED SYSTEM

An underlying concept in planning tourism is that tourism should be viewed as an inter-related system of demand and supply factors. The demand factors are international and domestic tourist markets and local 'residents who use the tourist attractions, facilities and services.

The supply factors comprise tourist attractions and activities, accommodation and other tourist facilities and services. Attractions include natural, cultural and special types of features - such as theme parks, zoos, botanic gardens and aquariums - and the activities related to these attractions. Accommodation includes hotels, motels, guest houses and other types of places where tourists stay overnight.

The category of other tourist facilities and services includes tour and travel operations, restaurants, shopping, banking and money exchange, and medical and postal facilities and services.

These supply factors are called the tourism product. Other elements also relate to supply factors. In order to make the facilities and services usable, infrastructure is required. Tourism infrastructure particularly includes transportation (air, road, rail, water, etc.), water supply, electric power, sewage and solid waste disposal, and telecommunications.

Demand Factors

- International tourist markets
- Domestic tourist markets
- Residents' use of tourist attractions, facilities and services

Supply Factors

- Attractions and activities Ïper cent Accommodation
- Other tourist facilities and services Ïper cent Transportation
- Other infrastructure
- Institutional elements

Provision of adequate infrastructure is also important to protect the environment. It helps maintain a high level of environmental quality that is so necessary for successful tourism and desirable for residents.

The effective development, operation and management of tourism requires certain institutional elements.

These elements include:

- Organizational structures, especially government tourism offices and private sector tourism associations such as hotel associations.
- Tourism-related legislation and regulations, such as standards and licensing requirements for hotels and tour and travel agencies.
- Education and training programmes, and training institutions to prepare persons to work effectively in tourism.

- Availability of financial capital to develop tourist attractions, facilities, services and infrastructure, and mechanisms to attract capital investment.
- Marketing strategies and promotion programmes to inform tourists about the country or region, and induce them to visit it, and tourist information facilities and services in the destination areas.
- Travel facilitation of immigration (including visa arrangements), customs and other facilities and services at the entry and exit points of tourists.

The institutional elements also include consideration of how to enhance and distribute the economic benefits of tourism, environmental protection measures, reducing adverse social impacts, and conservation of the cultural heritage of people living in the tourism areas.

As an inter-related system, it is important that tourism planning aim for integrated development of all these parts of the system, both the demand and supply factors and the physical and institutional elements. The system will function much more effectively and bring the desired benefits if it is planned in an integrated manner, with coordinated development of all the components of the system. Sometimes, this integrated system approach is also called the comprehensive approach to tourism planning because all the elements of tourism are considered in the planning and development process.

Just as important as planning for integration within the tourism system is planning for integration of tourism into the overall development policies, plans and patterns of a country or region. Planning for this overall integration will, for example, resolve any potential conflicts over use of certain resources or locations for various types of development. It also provides for the multi-use of expensive infrastructure to serve general community needs as well as tourism.

Emphasis is given to formulating and adopting tourism development policies and plans for an area in order to guide decision-making on development actions. The planning of tourism, however, should also be recognized as a continuous and flexible process. Within the framework of the policy and plan recommendations, there must be flexibility to allow for adapting to changing circumstances. Planning that is too rigid may not allow development to be responsive to changes. There may be advancements in transportation technology, evolution of new forms of tourism and changes in market trends. Even though allowed to be flexible, the basic objectives of the plan should not be abrogated although the specific development patterns may be changed. Sustainable development must still be maintained.

Planning for tourism development should make recommendations that are imaginative and innovative, but they must also be feasible to implement. The various techniques of implementation should be considered throughout the planning process. This approach ensures that the recommendations can be accomplished, and provides the basis for specifying the implementation techniques that should be applied. Implementation techniques can also be imaginative and not only rely on established approaches. It is common practice for a tourism plan to include specification of implementation techniques, and sometimes a separate manual on how to achieve the plan recommendations.

STAKEHOLDER INVOLVEMENT IN TOURISM MANAGEMENT PLANNING

When leading management institutions want to facilitate the participation of a local population, they do this by using the concept of stakeholder involvement. That doesn't mean that there are no planning processes in which really the whole population can take part. In most cases, however, individuals from societal groups will represent their groups and their interests.

These representatives form a smaller group of stakeholders, which is generally easier to manage. Stakeholders in sustainable tourism management planning are all the individuals who are interested in and/or affected by tourism development and biodiversity conservation.

They should participate in the planning process from the early stage. Sustainable tourism development emphasises in particular the importance of considering and respecting the wishes and needs of the local population of the tourism destination.Tourism development is usually not a primary subject of public administration, and therefore can only be managed effectively if all the stakeholders participate in the decision-making process. The goals of sustainable tourism development can only be achieved if the people involved in tourism in the area act just as to the tourism management plan and commit themselves to the vision of sustainable tourism development.

Reasons for stakeholder involvement when developing a tourism management plan:

- They live within the BR and are affected by tourism and conservation measures.
- They are engaged in the tourism industry and therefore influence tourism development.
- Their businesses usually benefit from the natural resources and services in the area.
- They may be required to carry out certain tasks to achieve the sustainable tourism development goals.
- They can also cause major degradation and depletion of natural resources.
- They may utilise it to such a degree that they threaten biodiversity.
- They constitute part of future generations for whom the natural and cultural heritage should be maintained.

The development of a tourism management plan takes place within the framework of the national and regional conservation strategies and the designation of the Biosphere Reserve. For this reason, all stakeholders in the development area are also asked to act in accordance with these regional specifications. It will then be the task of the manager to create a common goal, which all stakeholders are committed to, and which is based on the principles of sustainable tourism development and the conservation of biological diversity. This means that stakeholders cannot seek any outcomes they please, especially not ones which may have too negative impacts on the natural environment.

Who are the Stakeholders in Tourism Management Planning?

The tourism sector includes a great variety of products and services and influences the local economy as well as the culture and living-conditions of the tourism destination. This means that there is a wide range of people involved in tourism, such as local tourism service providers, retailers, hoteliers, etc. Furthermore, the whole local population is affected by tourism development.

The preparation of the tourism management plan means also, deciding on which of these different stakeholder groups are important for the process. Care should be taken not to exclude parts of the local population which are not directly involved in tourism. There are various methods which can be used to identify and group stakeholders. One of these is the division of all stakeholders into smaller more cohesive groups or "key stakeholders".

Stakeholders come from governmental, nongovernmental and private sectors and from indigenous and local communities and can be grouped just as to their background, *e.g.* whether they are primarily political, economical, social, technological, legislative or environmental. Another way would be to divide them into the professional public and the general public.

The professional public:

- Individuals, groups and organisations that are involved in tourism and/ or the spatial development of the project region
- *In addition:* professionals – experts in various fields
- *General public*: individuals, groups and organisations that are neither directly involved in tourism sector nor immediately affected by tourism
- Their participation in the process is extremely important. As tourism is an important economic and social tool for guaranteeing or even increasing the living standard of the people, communication with the public and their consultancy with issues of tourism development in "their" region are of great importance.

It is important that, in the preparation phase, managers of tourism management planning know something about the stakeholders in the region, before they begin to identify those who are the most important for the development of the tourism management plan. It is, however, normally the case that the management of the BR and/or the protected area is already familiar with the stakeholders and can quickly identify those who are vital to the success of the tourism management plan. The list of stakeholders will vary just as to the size and characteristics of the BR and the actual situation of tourism development within the BR. The list of participating stakeholders may also change during the tourism management planning process.

Stakeholders in tourism management planning:

- Neighbours and residents
- Farmers, foresters, hunters and fishermen
- Tourism providers such as hoteliers, restaurant owners, tourist guides, etc.
- Tours operators and tourism agencies
- Local business men, *e.g.* retailers
- Local authorities: local municipalities, local administration
- Local NGOs
- Educational institutions, research centres
- Visitors
- Media

It is important not to exclude those who are opposed to or sceptical about the tourism management plan and the BR or national park. They may be vital for the development of an effective tourism management plan, though they may present counterproductive facts that need to be faced.

It is important to control the size and scale of stakeholder involvement so that the tourism management plan preparation process does not get out of hand. A difficult problem that might occur during the process of identifying key stakeholders is how to ensure that stakeholders represent their group well.

HOW TO WORK WITH STAKEHOLDERS

Stakeholder involvement requires careful preparation and thought, about:

- How to identify stakeholders
- How to encourage their participation
- Who should facilitate the work with stakeholders
- What the basic objectives of tourism development and biodiversity conservation are.

Tourism management planning process managers should be prepared for the fact that the first steps of preparation for stakeholder involvement will be time consuming. Stakeholders should be involved into every step of tourism management planning. The participation of stakeholders is firstly part of the capacitybuilding process, and secondly, it creates a "common issue of concern" which then leads to a common vision. That can help the stakeholders to understand why biodiversity and the ecosystems of their BR are valuable, why they are important and why their loss or degradation should be avoided. Stakeholders can contribute with their special knowledge and are therefore a useful source of information. This ensures the inclusion of all relevant information and it also reinforces the credibility and reliability of the information. In the steps of visioning, creation of goals and objectives as well as during the steps of impact management, monitoring and approval, stakeholders have the opportunity to develop their own ideas of and decide upon tourism development in the region. This fosters the ownership of the tourism management by stakeholders and facilitates their commitment to implement the plan.

METHODS OF PARTICIPATION

There are different methods of stakeholder involvement that will be applied at the different stages of plan development. Providing information to all stakeholders about the tourism management planning process is one precondition of stakeholder involvement. Another requirement for effective participation is to enable the stakeholders to take part in the planning process through capacity building, awareness raising and education.

Information and Consultation

Firstly, comprehensive information has to be provided to the public so that the aim of, the reasons for and the intentions of tourism management planning are well communicated and understood.

Information and consultation:

- *Providing information:* presenting significant documents and plans, providing reports about important activities, sharing experiences and findings, consulting proposals and conclusions, etc.
- Motivating local people to get involved in the process, to increase their interest in the process, etc.
- Guiding through an intricate process of tourism development, informing about achievements and things that yet need to be done, background information and implementation measures, etc.
- Promoting tourism and its development, explaining its importance to local people in order to include it among other activities and tasks that exist in the region and/or are considered important

Information on the topics, methods and outcomes of the management planning process should be provided to all stakeholders as well as to the general public in a timely manner, throughout the whole planning process. This consultative process at all stages of management plan development tries to create "ongoing and effective dialogue and information sharing with stakeholders".

Constantly informing the stakeholders not only enables stakeholders to participate, it is also useful for preventing conflicts, because people affected by the outcomes of the tourism management plan are informed about these and can communicate their opinion on them at an early stage of the process.

Capacity Building, Awareness Raising and Education

The second precondition for making stakeholder participation effective is to ensure that local communities are equipped with the necessary decision-making abilities as well as with the skills and knowledge necessary for undertaking tourism management. First of all stakeholders and the general public need to be educated about the impacts of tourism on biological diversity, good management practices in sustainable tourism development and the necessity and benefits of tourism management planning.

This stage of awareness-raising and education can be realised through different methods such as media campaigns, public lectures and seminars, exhibitions, etc. Stakeholders should be informed about and become interested in the aims of tourism management and should be encouraged to participate in the planning process by making the potential benefits of tourism management clear to them. Capacity-building activities help to develop and strengthen the capacities of all stakeholders for participating in the management planning process.

Subjects of capacity-building:

- Accessing, analysing and interpreting baseline information
- Undertaking impact assessments and evaluations
- Impact management, decision-making, monitoring and adaptive management
- Sustainable tourism development
- Mechanisms for approval of goals and objectives
- Training of tourism professionals in conservation and biodiversity issues
- Information exchange and collaboration regarding sustainable tourism implementation through networking and partnerships between all stakeholders

Capacity-building and education measures require sufficient time and adequate human, financial and technical resources. It is important that capacity-building is carried out by experts who have knowledge in public education and training and also experience in participative processes.

Notification

Notification is, in most countries, a legal requirement for the approval of tourism investments. Detailed information on the proposed tourism developments must be accessible to everybody who is affected by it. The information must be presented clearly, and written in way which all stakeholders understand. Enough time should be given to the stakeholders to enable them to read and process this information and to express their opinions about the proposals. For the process of tourism management planning, this becomes especially important around the phase concerning impact assessment of and decision-making about the proposals for tourism development and activities at particular locations. There is the information which has to be provided in the notification process.

Participation Techniques

There is a variety of participation techniques which can be useful at various stages of the planning process. Establishing a multistakeholder group, whose members participate in the whole process of plan development is, however, the most important participation technique and should get the most attention. For individual tasks the managing body can also establish subgroups, workshops etc.

Round tables and panel discussions:

- Round tables and panel discussions are opportunities to form networks between organisations, institutions and local stakeholders. Each round table or panel discussion should address a specific topic. The main advantage of this method is that a variety of different perspectives and opinions will be heard and should be taken into account.

Workshops and seminars:

- Workshops and seminars – either for participants with special invitations and/or open to the general public - are an efficient way to a) inform about the actual state of the project, and b) for those involved to decide on and to develop further steps together, incorporating all local standpoints.

Advisory committees/boards:

- The purpose of an advisory committee is to provide advice or recommendations which will help to facilitate cooperation between affected/involved groups at the local level.

The Multi-stakeholder Group

The multi-stakeholder group should include all relevant stakeholders interested in participating in the management planning process. Some of the stakeholders may only take part in special workshops and not in every part of the process. Those managing the planning process should make sure that as many stakeholders as possible participate in the multistakeholder group and that they represent their groups well. Stakeholders should commit themselves to different parts of planning and implementation and should also take over different tasks involved in the work programme. They should, however, agree all together on the vision, goals and objectives of the tourism management plan. The process of stakeholder involvement starts with one or several informal meetings, in which the rules for discussions should be established and work which needs to be carried out in the future should be discussed and decided. It is often more effective if a "neutral" moderator, who isn't directly involved in the managing institution of the tourism management plan leads these meetings. It is better to present tourism management planning as an attractive opportunity for stakeholders, who can use it to have their say on development in the region and who can therefore eventually benefit from it. Discussion in the first meetings should be open and used as an opportunity to share different points of view and to begin to establish some common objectives for sustainable tourism management. The first informal meetings should include opportunities for the participants to get to know each other even if the participants feel that they already know each other well. This will bring uncertainties and suspicions to the forefront and relationships and existing conflicts among participants can be seen.

During these informal conversations common perceptions and visions of conservation and tourism development can be identified. To reduce fears of "territoriality" the venue for these meetings should be "neutral". After the initial meeting, a group of people should form the multistakeholder group. They should be prepared to commit themselves to a series of meetings which will involve organising and developing the next steps of the management plan.

4

World Tourism

WORLD TOURISM ORGANIZATION

The World Tourism Organization predicts 21st century tourism will be the antidote to high-tech living. WTO Secretary General Francesco Frangialli discusses their new report Tourism: 2020 Vision. The year 2020 will *see* the penetration of technology into all aspects of life. It will become possible to live one's days without exposure to other people, according to WTO's latest look into the future. But this bleak prognosis has a silver lining for the tourism sector. People in the high-tech future will crave the human touch and tourism will be the principal means to achieve this.

Tourism companies that manage to provide "high-touch" products will prosper. Upscale, luxury services that pamper and spoil their customers have a bright future in the upcoming century. But WTO's report also predicts good prospects for low-budget destinations and packages. Self-catering holiday facilities, for example, which offer plenty of opportunities for socialising among families and friends. Opportunities abound at both ends of the spectrum and there will be plenty of them.

WTO's study Tourism: 2020 Vision predicts 1.5 billion tourists will be visiting foreign countries annually by the year 2020, spending more that US$2 trillion or US$5 billion every day. These forecasts represent nearly three times more international tourists than the 663 million recorded in 1999 and nearly five times more tourism spending, which last year topped US$453 billion. Tourist arrivals are predicted to grow by an average 4.3 per cent a year over the next two decades, while receipts from international tourism will climb by 6.7 per cent a year.

To factor in domestic tourism, WTO multiplies arrivals by 10 and quadruples receipts, which brings us to the grand totals of 16 billion tourists spending US$8 trillion in 2020. Tourism in the 21st century will not only be the world's biggest industry, it will be the largest by far that the world has ever seen. Along with its phenomenal growth and size, the tourism industry will also have to take on more responsibility for its extensive impacts. Not only its economic impact, but also its impact on the environment, on societies and on cultural sites, all of which will be increasingly scrutinised by governments, consumer groups and the travelling public. We hope that Tourism: 2020 Vision will be more than a useful marketing tool, that ft will act as a warning signal for destinations-helping them recognise the need to 'prepare for the pressures of growth. WTO is advising destinations to implement long-term, strategic planning and to strengthen the partnerships, both strategically and at the operational level, between the public and private sectors.

Tourism: 2020 Vision indicates that tourists of the 21st century will be travelling further afield on their holidays, often to China and even to outer space. The percentage of long-haul travel is predicted to increase from 18 per cent in 1995 to 24 per cent by 2020. Tourism companies looking to cash in on this booming sector are advised to look towards Asia. China will be the world's number one destination by the year 2020 and it will also become the fourth most important generating market. Currently it does not even figure among the world's top twenty generating countries.

Other destinations predicted to make great strides in the tourism industry are Russia, Hong Kong, Thailand, Singapore, Indonesia and South Africa. Short pleasure voyages to outer space will become a reality by 2004 or 2005, according to the study carried out by WTO Statistics Chief Enzo Paci in consultation with 85 governments and 50 tourism visionaries. It is expected space trips will last up to four days and cost on average US $100,000. NASA, the US space agency, has recently surveyed the travel industry for interest in space tourism and some US companies are already taking reservations and deposits from private citizens hoping to become the first tourists in outer space. But while some travellers may be suiting up for space voyages, the vast majority of the world's population will never leave their own countries, not even by the year 2020. The study concludes that only 7 per cent of the world's population will be travelling internationally by the year 2020, up from 3.5 per cent in 1996-but still just the tip of the iceberg.

"Tourism: 2020 Vision" predicts that Europe will remain by far the leading inbound tourism region as well as the main generator of international tourists. International arrivals in Europe will reach 717 million by 2020? more than twice as many as last year. Overall, tourism to Europe is predicted to grow more slowly than the world average; at a rate of 3.1 per cent annually, though some countries will fare better than others. Central and Eastern European countries will become the new motor for Europe, feeding and being fed by other European and long-haul generating markets. Tourism to Central and Eastern Europe will grow by 4.8 per cent a year and the former Soviet Bloc countries will surpass 200 million arrivals by 2016-a doubling in just 15 years. The Eastern Mediterranean countries of Cyprus, Turkey and Israel are also expected to show good growth of 4.6 per cent a year. Tourism to the United Kingdom is forecast to grow by 4 per cent annually, just under the world average. Reflecting world patterns and increasing air travel, Europeans will be taking trips more frequently and further from home. Total outbound travel from European countries is predicted to reach 771 million trips a year by 2010, again more than twice as many as last year.

TOURISM MEGATRENDS FOR THE 21ST CENTURY

- Globalisation versus Localisation
- Electronic technology will become all powerful in influencing destination choice and distribution.
- Fast track travel—emphasis will be placed on facilitation and the speeding up of the travel process.
- Customers will "call the shots" through technology such as CD ROM atlases, Internet inspection of hotels and other facilities, brokers offering discounted rooms of Web sites, last minute e-mail low fares, etc.
- Polarisation of tourist tastes: The comfort-based and the adventure-oriented.
- The tourist "shrinking world" more tourists to off-the-beaten track places and the advent of near space tourism.
- Destination as a "fashion accessory".
- Targeted product market development (especially theme based) oriented to one or a combination of the three Es-enterainment, excitement and education.
- More destination focus on image as a rerequisite for diversification and expansion of drawing power.
- Everyone chasing the Asian tourist.
- Growing impact of consumer led campaigns for sustainable tourism development and "fair trade" in tourism.
- Conflict socio-environmental consciousness versus the urge for travel consumption.

Long-haul travel to countries outside of Europe will grow by 6.1 per cent a year in the upcoming decades to reach 15 per cent of all trips taken by Europeans or 115,600,000 departures. Long-haul currently accounts for 12 per cent of European outbound travel or about 42 million trips a year. Since the typical European tourist who spends his holiday at the beach will be more frequently choosing Asian or Caribbean resorts, European beach destinations are advised to orientate their product development and marketing increasingly to new tourist sources, especially Japan, the newly industrialised countries of Asia and the Americas. Mature European destinations will have continually to strive to seek product and market differentiation to avoid a tired or stale image in major generating markets. While growth of the tourism industry will be unstoppable in the 21st century, increased benefits cannot be taken for granted. Competition among destinations will also become increasingly fierce. The study Tourism: 2020 Vision outlines a series of 12 megatrends that will shape the sector and offers advice on how to better compete. No destination or tourism operator can afford to sit back and wait for more tourists to arrive. They have to be won and there will be winners and losers. To be a winner, there are a number of imperatives:

- Development focused on quality and sustainability.
- Value-for-money.
- Full utilisation of information technology to identify and communicate effectively with market segments and niches.

Product development and marketing will need to match each other more closely, based on the main travel motivators of the 21st century. Tourism: 2020 vision calls these motivating factors the Three E's-Entertainment, Excitement and Education. The study also highlights the importance of image in a tourists' selection of a holiday destination in the future. While an image of safety and security is already an important deciding factor for tourists, holiday makers of the 21st century will be looking for places with a trendy image. As 2020 Vision points out, the next century will mark the emergence the tourism destinations as 'a fashion accessory'. The choice of holiday destination will help define the identity of the traveller and, in an increasingly homogeneous world, set him apart from the hordes of other tourists. Boutique destinations and space agencies beware! You are on the threshold of meeting the 21st century tourist. Tourism is the world's largest industry, with over 10 per cent of GDP globally directly related to tourism activities. Rising standards of living in the countries of the North, declining long-haul travel costs, increasing holiday entitlements, changing demographics and strong consumer demand for exotic international travel have resulted in significant tourism growth to developing countries. Tourism is the principal export for one third of developing countries. Tourism brings relatively powerful consumers to Southern countries, potentially an important market for local entrepreneurs and an engine for local sustainable economic development.

There is no reliable data on domestic tourism but it is growing rapidly in South America and in China and South East Asia; it represents a very significant economic opportunity for many local communities. Multilateral and bilateral aid agencies are wary of involving themselves in the tourism sector. In 1969 the World Bank created a Tourism Projects Department recognising that in the Mediterranean and Adriatic countries, and in Mexico, tourism had been a significant generator of foreign exchange and of direct and indirect employment. Internationally in the late nineteen sixties, there was considerable concern about high rates of unemployment and the ability of developing countries to service debt. Tourism sector studies were completed in some 31 countries and tourism staff regularly participated in World Bank macro-economic missions their reports focussed on the potential for growth in tax revenues, foreign exchange earnings and direct and indirect employment effects. The primary emphasis was on national economic impact. By 1978 when the World Bank closed its Tourism Projects Department the Bank had provided loans and credits for 18 projects in 14 countries and it was the major source of funds and technical assistance for tourism development.

The Bank withdrew from tourism development for a range of reasons amongst which were anxieties about the role of the Bank in funding projects to develop luxury hotels designed to attract wealthy travellers from the developed countries. This strategy was seen as inconsistent with new policy objectives which prioritised the bottom 40 per cent, the Bank's priorities were shifting towards the poor, a group which was gaining relatively little from tourism development. There was a growing literature that focussed on the negative economic, social and cultural impacts of unmanaged tourism on local communities. The fuel crises of the nineteen seventies also undermined some of the forecasts that had been made for the strength of the market and the Bank withdrew from the sector in parallel with most other multilateral and bilateral agencies.

Tourism is the world's largest industry with an enormous potential for further growth. While the bulk of tourist arrivals are still in industrial states, developing countries are also increasingly sharing in the tourism boom. But do the poor in these countries also benefit? This study outlines strategies for promoting pro-poor tourism. The international agencies followed a macro-economic tourism agenda in the nineteen seventies and eighties focussing on tax and foreign exchange revenues at the national level, major hotel and resort development, international promotion and national and regional master planning all attracted funding.

In the nineties the' adoption of the new poverty elimination target of halving the number of people living on less than 1 US$ per day by 2015 has refocused development assistance on pro-poor growth. Multilateral and bilateral aid agency agendas are shifting towards a microeconomic focus on local sustainable economic growth strategies which benefit local communities, and in particular those below the poverty threshold. With poverty elimination now at the heart of decision-making about international develop aid, the potential for using tourism to generate pro-poor economic growth is being reassessed. Since the mid-1980s, interest in 'green' tourism, ecotourism and community tourism has grown rapidly among tour operators, policymakers, advocates and researchers. All of these focus on the need to ensure that tourism does not erode the environmental and cultural base on which it depends. The emphasis has been on minimising social, cultural and environmental impacts; rather than on positively affecting the livelihoods of the poor.

There are a number of reasons to look again at tourism and to assess its potential to generate pro-poor growth. 80 per cent of the world's poor live in just 12 countries and tourism is significant or growing in all but one of them. Tourism is a very large sector, it is growing rapidly, and there is some evidence that it is relatively labour intensive. The consumer travels to the destination, creating additional-local-opportunities for the sale of additional goods and services ranging from local pottery to a guided walk. Tourism can be used to diversify local economies, it can often be developed in remote and marginal areas with few other diversification or export opportunities. These areas often attract tourists because of their high landscape, cultural and wildlife values. These natural resources and the local culture are amongst the few assets of the poor. Pro-poor tourism generates net benefits for the poor. It can be defined as forms of tourism where the benefits to the poor are greater than costs which tourism brings them.

Economic costs and benefits are clearly important, but social, environmental and cultural costs and benefits, also need to be taken into account. Pro-poor tourism aims to expand opportunities for those living on less than 1US$ per day. Whilst it will also need to be sustainable preserving local culture, minimising environmental impacts, it will be driven by the poverty agenda.

Community-based tourism seeks to promote initiatives by local communities or individuals within them, much has been learnt from these projects. Maximising the poverty elimination effect requires that the emphasis is placed on involving those people who are living on less than 1US$ per day and creating economic opportunities for them. Not all community tourism is pro-poor in this sense. Assessing the livelihood impacts of tourism is not simply a matter of counting jobs or wage income. Participatory poverty assessments demonstrate great variety in the priorities of the poor and factors affecting livelihood security and sustainability. Tourism can affect many of these, positively and negatively, often indirectly. It is important to assess these impacts and their distribution.

Tourism can generate four different types of local cash income generally involving different categories of people:

- Wages from formal employment;
- Earnings from selling goods, services/or casual labour (*e.g.* food, crafts, building materials, guide services);
- And profits arising from locally-owned enterprises;
- Income: this may include profits from a community run enterprise, dividends from a private sector partnership and land rental paid by an investor.

Waged employment can be sufficient to lift a household from insecure to secure. But it may only be available to a minority, and not to the poor. Casual earnings per person may be very small, but much more widely spread and may be enough, for instance, to cover school fees for one or more children. Work as a tourist guide, although casual, is often of high status and relatively well paid. There are relatively few examples of successful and sustainable collective income from tourism. Examples from Kenya, Namibia and Zimbabwe illustrate that it can match wage income in scale and that in principle it can benefit all residents, although it can be difficult to manage. Negative economic impacts include inflation, dominance by outsiders in land markets and in-migration which erodes economic opportunities for the local poor. Impacts differ between men and women. Women can be the first to suffer from loss of natural resources (*e.g.* access to fuel-wood) and cultural/sexual exploitation, but may benefit most from physical infrastructure improvements (*e.g.* piped water or a grinding mill) where this is a by-product of tourism.

On the positive side, tourism can generate funds for investment in health, education and other assets, provide infrastructure, stimulate development of social capital, strengthen sustainable management of natural resources, and create a demand for improved assets (especially education). On the negative side, tourism can reduce local access to natural resources, draw heavily upon local infrastructure, and disrupt social networks. Tourism affects the livelihoods of the poor by changing their access to assets.

In several cases, tourism's impact on people's access to natural resources or physical infrastructure has been identified as the most important benefit or concern. For example, the Ngwesi lodge in Kenya was developed by members of the Ngwesi group ranch (a registered group of around 500 pastoral households with collective tenure rights over their land). A recent participatory assessment of livelihood impacts revealed that impacts on natural capital, particularly grasing resources, and access to physical infrastructure are more important to most members than the nearly 50 new jobs. The wildlife/wilderness area around the lodge provides emergency drought grasing. The lodge's physical presence, radio, and vehicle help to keep others out and provide emergency access to a hospital, which was previously lacking.

However, there are more numerous examples where local residents lose access to local natural resources. A comparative study by Shah and Gupta provides a range of examples.

On Boracay Island in the Philippines, one quarter of the island has been bought by outside corporations, generating a crisis in water supply and only limited infrastructure benefits for residents. Similarly in Ball, Indonesia, prime agricultural land and water supplies have been diverted for large hotels and golf courses while at Pangandaran (Java, Indonesia) village beach land, traditionally used for grasing, repairing boats and nets, and festivals, was sold to entrepreneurs for a 5-star hotel. Local residents often highlight the way tourism affects other livelihood goals whether positively or negatively-such as cultural pride, a sense of control, good health, and reduced vulnerability.

Socio-cultural intrusion by tourists is often cited as a negative impact. Certainly sexual exploitation particularly affects the poorest women, girls and young men. The poor themselves may view other types of cultural change as positive. Tourism can also increase the value attributed to minority cultures by national policy-makers. Overall, the cultural impacts of tourism are hard to disentangle from wider processes of development.

The overall balance of positive and negative livelihood impacts will vary enormously between situations, among people and over time, and particularly in the extent to which local priorities are able to influence the planning process. The application of a 'sustainable livelihoods framework' is essential to developing pro-poor approaches. The distribution of livelihood impacts has to be considered.

The poor are far from being a homogenous group. The positive and negative impacts of tourism will inevitably be distributed unevenly among poor groups, reflecting different patterns of assets, activities, opportunities and choices.

The most substantial benefits, particularly jobs, may be concentrated among few. Net benefits are likely to be smallest, or negative, for the poorest. A recent review, by Shah and Gupta, of two dozen case studies in Asia indicates economic gains for all sections of the community, but with those already better off gaining most.

Despite innumerable case studies of tourism development, there is relatively little assessment of practical experience in strategies to make tourism more pro-poor. Nevertheless, lessons can be drawn from a wealth of small initiatives (many from 'community tourism' or 'conservation and development' programmes), supplemented by expanding knowledge on 'pro-poor growth strategies', several policy implications clearly emerge.

1. *Put poverty issues on the tourism agenda* A first step is to recognise that enhancing the poverty impacts of tourism is different from commercial, environmental, or ethical concerns. PPT can be incorporated as an additional objective, but this requires pro-active and strategic intervention. There may well be trade-offs to make for example between attracting all-inclusive operators and maximising informal sector opportunities, or between faster growth through outside investment, and slower growth building on local capacity. These trade-offs need to be addressed.
2. *Enhance economic opportunities and a wide range of impacts* Two approaches need to be combined:
   - Expand poor people's economic participation by addressing the barriers they face, and maximising a wide range of employment, self-employment and informal sector opportunities;
   - Incorporate wider concerns of the poor into decision-making. Reducing competition for natural resources, minimising trade-offs

with other livelihood activities, using tourism to create physical infrastructure that benefits the poor and addressing cultural disruption will often be particularly important.

3. *A multi-level approach* Pro-poor interventions can and should be taken at three different levels:
   - This is where pro-active practical partnerships can be developed between operators, residents, NGOs, and local authorities, to maximise benefits;
   - National policy level—policy reform may be needed on a range of tourism issues (planning, licensing, training) and non-tourism issues (land tenure, business incentives, infrastructure, land-use planning);
   - International level—to encourage responsible consumer and business behaviour, and to enhance commercial codes of conduct.
4. *Work through partnerships, including business and tourists* National and local governments, private enterprises, industry associations, NGOs, community organizations, consumers, and donors all have a role to play. It is particularly important to engage businesses, and to ensure that initiatives are commercially realistic and integrated into mainstream operations. Private operators will not be able to devote substantial time and resources to developing pro-poor actions. NGOs and donors can help in reducing the transaction costs of changing commercial practice-for example, facilitating the training, organization, and communication that would enable businesses to use more local suppliers. Changing the attitudes of tourists (at both international and national levels) is also essential if pro-poor tourism is to be commercially viable and sustainable.
5. *Incorporate pro-poor tourism approaches into mainstream tourism* Pro-poor tourism should not just be pursued in niche markets (such as eco-tourism or community tourism). It is even more important that mass tourism is developed in ways that benefit the poor. It is also important to assess which tourism segments are particularly relevant to the poor. Domestic tourists are likely to be important customers.
6. *Reform decision-making systems* It is impossible to prescribe exactly how each tourism enterprise should develop in ways that best fit with livelihoods. The most important principle is to enhance the participation of the poor. Three different ways of doing this can be identified:
   - Strengthen rights at local level (*e.g.* tenure over tourism assets), so that local people have market power and make their own decisions over developments.
   - Develop more participatory planning.

– Use planning gain and other incentives to encourage private investors to enhance local benefits. These approaches require implementation capacity among governmental and non-governmental institutions within the destination, and require a supportive national policy framework.

It is time to reconsider the role of tourism in contributing to pro-poor development. Tourism should be judged against other possible strategies and where it offers the best opportunities for pro-poor growth, or where it can make a useful contribution by increasing the diversity of opportunities for the poor, tourism it should be considered. However, careful and effective local management will be essential if it is to contribute to meeting poverty targets and if tourism dependency is to be avoided.

GLOBAL TOURISM GROWTH AND THE NEED FOR ADJUSTMENT IN TOURISM INDUSTRY

In the last decade, global environmental policies have made substantial progress in institutional development, international cooperation, public participation and private sector action. National governments and the private sector have developed stronger legal frameworks, market-based environmental incentive instruments, environmentally sound technologies, and cleaner production processes. Consequently, several countries report significant progress in controlling environmental pollution and slowing the rate of resource degradation as well as reducing the intensity of resource use (UNEP 1997).

The tourism industry, arguably the world's largest, bears a great responsibility in the effort to move towards sustainable development. The economic importance of tourism is undeniable. A study sponsored by the World Travel and Tourism Council (WTTC) and conducted by Wharton Econometric Forecasting Associates (WEFA) found that the tourism industry generates 11.7 per cent of global gross domestic product (GDP) and nearly 200 million jobs worldwide. These figures are forecast to total 11.7 per cent global GDP and 255 million jobs in 2010 (United Nations Economic and Social Council 1999). While the economic development potential of tourism is substantial, there is also strong evidence of the negative environmental impact of tourism development. Nevertheless, tourism may be a more sustainable option for economic development because, unlike other natural resource based industries, it is based on enjoyment and appreciation of local culture, built heritage, and the natural environment which provides a powerful economic incentive to conserve these valuable assets (United Nations Economic and Social Council 1999).

The potential for tourism development to be a sustainable - that is for it to *meet the needs of the present without compromising the ability of future generations to meet their own needs* - has resulted in support for environmentally sustainable tourism development from both the public and private sectors at the national and international levels.The United Nations and its associated organisations, the World Bank, and regional development banks are attempting to 'green' their loan programmes and assistance mechanisms. They are also supporting the development of environmentally sustainable tourism directly and indirectly through a variety of means, including sustainable tourism product identification, infrastructure development, environmentally sound hotel financing, and ecotourism development in protected areas.

The Commission on Sustainable Development (CSD) - an intergovernmental forum to coordinate and monitor the progress of Agenda 21's implementation - has produced a number of policy recommendations for stakeholders involved in the sustainable tourism development following their annual meetings in 1999. These recommendations were broken down into private sector, public sector, non-governmental organisation, and international community policy challenges. The following section summarises these recommendations (United Nations Economic and Social Council 1999).

PRIVATE SECTOR POLICY CHALLENGES

The key challenges facing the tourism industry are to:

- Promote wider implementation of environmental management, particularly in the many small and medium enterprises that form the backbone of the tourism industry, and spread initiatives to all sectors of the tourism industry;
- Use more widely environmentally sound technologies, in particular to reduce emissions of CO and other greenhouse gases and ozone-depleting substances, as set out in two international agreements;
- Address the key issues of siting and more eco-efficient design of tourism facilities;
- Raise the awareness of tourism clients of the environment and social implications of their holidays, and of opportunities for their responsible behaviour;
- Develop a better dialogue with the local communities in travel destinations, and promote the involvement of local stakeholders in tourism ventures;
- Work with governments and other stakeholders to improve the overall environmental quality of destinations; and
- Report publicly on environmental performance.

Public sector policy challenges:

Governments need to further develop and implement the legislative and policy frameworks for sustainable development. In particular, they need to:

- Ratify, if they have not already done so, and work towards the effective implementation of, international and regional environmental conventions;

- Integrate more fully tourism development into the overall plans for sustainable development and develop participatory approaches;
- Develop more widely land use planning, and protect the coastline through building restrictions (for example, legislation in France, Spain, Denmark and Egypt forbids building within a defined distance from the coast);
- Identify and adopt the most appropriate mix of regulation and economic instruments, and, in many cases develop economic instruments to address environmental issues; and
- Work towards the effective enforcement of regulations and standards.

Governments need to raise awareness, build capacity and promote effective action for sustainable tourism.

This requires that they strive to:

- Improve the understanding of the benefits and burdens of tourism in environmental, social and economic terms, for the areas under their jurisdiction;
- Strengthen capacity for the management and control of tourism in their sphere of responsibility, and establish and maintain procedures for cooperation and coordination with neighbouring authorities, and with relevant state authorities;
- Provide support through pilot projects and capacity development programmes, including capacity development at the local government level;
- Ensure the participation of all stakeholders affected by or involved in tourism and its development, especially indigenous and local communities;
- Ensure that tourism makes a positive contribution to economic development, and that the economic benefits of tourism are equitably shared;
- Encourage and catalyse industry initiatives for sustainable tourism across all sectors of tourism, including accommodation, land, air and sea transportation, tour operators, travel agents, attractions sectors, etc.; and
- Promote changes in consumer behaviour in both tourist-originating countries and destinations towards more sustainable forms of tourism.

Governments will also need to develop monitoring of progress towards sustainable tourism. It is important to develop activities to monitor, control and mitigate adverse effects that may arise from tourism activities and development.

NON-GOVERNMENTAL ORGANISATIONS POLICY CHALLENGES

The key environmental policy challenges that face non-governmental organisations are to:

- More specifically voice their views in tourism policies and strategies;
- Contribute to the development and implementation of environmental standards for tourism;
- Develop or participate in raising awareness and education activities for sensitising tourists towards improving guest consumption patterns; and
- Assist in monitoring tourism activities and development and progress towards more sustainable tourism.

INTERNATIONAL COMMUNITY POLICY CHALLENGES

The key challenges facing the international community are to:

- Assist and support governments in the development of national strategies or master plans for the sustainable development of tourism, and of environmental land use and building regulations and standards for tourism;
- Raise awareness and build capacity of all stakeholders by providing information on best practices for sustainable tourism;
- Encourage the private sector to develop and apply codes and guidelines, and environmental management systems, and promote the development of the use of environmental reporting by companies in the various branches of the tourism sector;
- Assist in assessing the environmental effectiveness of existing voluntary initiatives in the various branches of the tourism sector, and make recommendations accordingly;
- Promote the transfer of environmentally sound technologies (ESTs), practices and management tools adapted for the tourism sector, and disseminate information on ESTs to governments and the tourism industry;
- Work with other stakeholders to establish and disseminate lessons from best practices projects on sustainable tourism;
- Provide support through provision of information and capacity development programmes, particularly on the costs and benefits of tourism development, the use of economic incentives to promote sustainable tourism, and on destination management; and

THE ROLE OF THE INTERNATIONAL COMMUNITY AND GLOBAL ENVIRONMENTAL INITIATIVES

Some other notable international environmental institutions that support sustainable tourism initiatives include:

- *The world bank group*: Despite its formal distancing from the tourism sector in the 1970s, the Bank's focus on economic development and its private sector capacity, particularly in the International Finance

Corporation, makes it technically well placed to address the pressures of a global tourism industry. Its now strong environmental capacity also makes it well placed to address the impacts of the tourism sector on biodiversity.

- *The united nations development programme* (UNDP): A United Nations organisation whose mission is to help countries in their efforts to achieve sustainable human development by assisting them to build their capacity to design and carry out development programmes in poverty eradication, employment creation and sustainable livelihoods, the empowerment of women and the protection and regeneration of the environment, giving first priority to poverty eradication.
- *The united nations environmental programme* (UNEP): The environmental voice of the United Nations, responsible for environmental policy development, scientific analysis, monitoring, and assessment.
- *The global environment facility* (GEF): A financial mechanism that addresses the incremental costs that developing countries face in responding to selected global environmental problems. The World Bank, UNEP and UNDP implement GEF projects.

New international environmental conventions and agreements are being adopted, older treaties are being improved, and new approaches to international policy are being developed and implemented. Four important international environmental conventions and treaties that are particularly relevant to the tourism industry include the following:

RIO DECLARATION ON ENVIRONMENT AND DEVELOPMENT (AGENDA 21)

The plan of action adopted by governments in 1992 in Rio de Janeiro provides the global consensus on the road map towards sustainable development. Agenda 21 is grouped around a series of themes - comprising 40 chapters and 115 separate programme areas, each of which represents an important component in the overall strategy towards global sustainable development.

The Agenda identifies three core tools to be used in achieving sustainable development goals:

1. Introduction of new, or strengthening of existing, regulations to ensure the protection of human health and the environment.
2. Use of free market mechanisms through which the prices of goods and services will reflect the environmental costs of resource inputs and process outputs.
3. Industry-led voluntary programmes that deliver environmentally responsible products and services.

In 1996, WTTC, the World Tourism Organisation and the Earth Council joined together to launch 'Agenda 21 for the Travel and Tourism Industry: Towards Environmentally Sustainable Development', making the tourism industry the first industrial sector to develop an industry specific action plan based on Agenda 21.

WTTC has now introduced an addition to this programme - The Alliance for Sustainable Tourism - which invites public and private sector tourism organisations to record their Agenda 21 based activities on a central Internet site and encourage cooperation with other local partners.

THE CONVENTION ON INTERNATIONAL TRADE IN ENDANGEREDSPECIES OF WILD FAUNA AND FLORA (CITES)

CITES is an international convention banning commercial international trade in an agreed list of endangered species and by regulating and monitoring trade in others that might become endangered. The international wildlife trade, worth billions of dollars annually, has caused massive declines in the numbers of many species of animals and plants.

The scale of overexploitation for trade aroused such concern for the survival of species that an international treaty was drawn up in 1973 to protect wildlife against such over-exploitation and to prevent international trade from threatening species with extinction (World Conservation Monitoring 1998).

THE UNITED NATIONS FRAMEWORK CONVENTION ON CLIMATE CHANGE

In the 1992 United Nations Framework Convention on Climate Change (UNFCCC), finalised for the Earth Summit in Rio de Janeiro, Brazil, the world's nations agreed on voluntary actions to reduce greenhouse gas emissions. Negotiations on the Kyoto Protocol to the UNFCCC were completed on 11 December 1997, committing the industrialised nations to specified legally binding reductions in emissions of six 'greenhouse gases'.

During negotiations that preceded the December 1997 meeting in Kyoto, Japan, little progress was made, and the most difficult issues were not resolved until the final days - and hours - of the Conference.

There was wide disparity among key players especially on three items:

- The amount of binding reductions in greenhouse gases to be required, and the gases to be included in these requirements.
- Whether developing countries should be part of the requirements for greenhouse gas limitations.
- Whether to allow emissions trading and joint implementation, which allow credit to be given for emissions reductions to a country that provides funding or investments in other countries that bring about the actual reductions in those other countries or locations where they may be cheaper to attain.

The convention on biological diversity:

A convention adopted as part of the 1992 UN Conference on the Environment and Development with the goals of:

- Maintaining biodiversity;
- Using its elements sustainably; and
- Sharing in a balanced and fair way the advantages springing from the exploitation of genetic resources.

The Convention on Biological Diversity (CBD) is the major and most visionary global biodiversity agreement. Now ratified by almost all the countries in the world - with the notable exception of the United States, the CBD is attempting to develop a global framework for the management of biodiversity.

It is striving to meet the trinity of biodiversity objectives - conservation, sustainable use and equitable benefit sharing - through globally agreed policies and procedures for managing biodiversity. These policies and procedures are also intended to support the overall goal of sustainable development and the corollary objective of poverty alleviation. But given the tradition of biodiversity management, the CBD has understandably yet to address the pressures of globalise commerce directly.

There is, however, an increasing recognition that the private sector must be an active player in managing biodiversity, but this recognition has yet to be articulated into clear roles and responsibilities for the private sector and global market processes.

CRITICAL WEAKNESSES IN THE GLOBAL ENVIRONMENTAL POLICY STRUCTURE

While global policy structures and international environmental solidarity are growing in strength, they remain too weak to make significant progress a worldwide reality. As a result, the gap between what has been done thus far and what is needed is widening. From a global perspective, the environment has continued to degrade during the past decade, significant environmental problems remain, and the outlook is, unfortunately, pessimistic. Internationally and nationally, the funds and political situation are not sufficient to halt continuing global environmental degradation or address the most pressing environmental issues, even though the technologies and knowledge are available to do so. The recognition of environmental issues as necessarily long-term and cumulative, with serious global and security implications, exists but the will to act remains limited. The continued preoccupation with immediate local and national issues and a general lack of sustained interest in global and long-term environmental issues remain major impediments to environmental progress internationally.

*According to the CSD's report on:*Tourism and the Environment, there are several important emerging issues with regard to tourism and environmental

protection that must be addressed in order to overcome these impediments. These include:

- *Developing partnership*: For sustainable tourism, the involvement and commitment of all stakeholders is essential. However, public, private and academic sector partnerships are still underdeveloped and therefore need to be encouraged.
- *Involvement of the banking and insurance sectors*: Banks and insurance companies could greatly expedite the progress of sustainable tourism by incorporating environmental and social criteria into assessment procedures for loans, investments, and insurance. They could help to finance environmentally sound technologies and provide incentives for sustainable tourism. This approach has worked well in other contexts. Widespread involvement of the banking and insurance sectors should be sought.
- *Use of economic instruments*: The tourism industry consumes increasingly scarce natural resources. The costing of energy and water in particular could expedite greatly eco-efficiency in the tourism industry and raise revenue for the improved management of those resources. Governments should consider the development and widespread use of economic instruments for sustainable tourism.
- *Involvement of tourism boards*: Often, marketing strategies and messages are not in line with the principles of sustainable tourism. There is a need to better involve tourism boards in sustainable tourism efforts.
- *Capacity-building of local government*: In many countries, local governments have important responsibilities regarding tourism development. Capacity-building programmes should be implemented to help them understand those responsibilities, develop integrated and participatory approaches, and define and implement policies for sustainable tourism.
- *Greater focus on transport*: There is a continued development of long-haul travel. Economic, technological and management approaches should be developed to reduce emissions, waste and pollution resulting from tourism transportation. Changing consumption patterns should also be considered.
- *Emerging types of tourism*: Tourism is rapidly diversifying. Emerging forms of tourism should also develop according to sustainability criteria. The increase of cruises and the current trend towards mega-ships necessitate that the cruise ship industry develop a socially and environmentally responsible approach.
- *Improve monitoring*: Careful monitoring of impacts and results, as well as the adoption of corrective measures, are conditions for sustainable tourism. All stakeholders at all levels should thus develop monitoring

programmes. As previously stated, the private sector should develop monitoring and public reporting of its activities. Local and central governments should develop monitoring tools, such as indicators, and should incorporate the results into their decision-making process.

Where appropriate, participatory approaches should be used. Monitoring is currently uncommon and that should be made a priority (United Nations Economic and Social Council 1999).

SUSTAINABLE TOURISM AT THE NATIONAL AND REGIONAL LEVEL

While the global policies and international donor organisation priorities discussed above are important because they tend to act as positive drivers towards environmental sustainability, particularly in the developing world, it is the national and regional policies within individual countries that are the key to sustainable tourism development strategies.

ENVIRONMENTAL MANAGEMENT SYSTEMS AND THE TOURISM INDUSTRY

Within the last two decades the concept of quality management systems emerged in an effort to gain consistent performance in meeting specified standards (initially in military equipment procurement and operations). The best-known QMS in the commercial world is the ISO 9000 standards of the International Standards Organisation. The implementation of a QMS is intended to provide consumers with an assurance that a company's products and services will be of consistent quality.

As the importance of environmentally-friendly private sector operations grew (as reflected generally in the industry sponsored sustainable development principles described previously), the conceptual model of QMS was applied to industry operations that impacted on the environment. (An EMS can be defined as a management system that incorporates management commitment, organisational structure, operational practices and procedures, and resources into a documented and implemented environmental policy.)

The implementation of an EMS represents the basis by which an organisation can exercise control over its impact on the environment by systematically gathering and coordinating knowledge about those impacts. Implementing an EMS demonstrates a strong commitment to Agenda 21 principles. Typically, a private sector EMS most often conforms with the International Standards Organisation ISO 14001 standard, although the European Union's Eco-Management and Audit Scheme (EMAS) is a valuable reference because of its rigourous parameters. It is important to note that all of the preceding material regarding QMS/EMS and ISO14001 is actually intended for use by private businesses or perhaps certain public sector agencies.

It is not designed for use with a tourism destination that comprises many different types of organisations from the public and private sector; but it does lay a foundation of terminology and processes that will be used in discussing EMS for tourism destinations.

The application of the EMS process to tourism destinations is an emerging area of interest, and while there is not yet a substantial amount of direct anecdotal or documentary evidence to examine we can look to recent work by groups like the World Travel and Tourism Council's Green Globe Alliance and others for case studies that illustrate the potentials and pitfalls of the destination-based EMS process. The rationale behind applying the EMS process to tourism destinations is simple and logical.

The natural environment is an extremely valuable resource for most tourism destinations and the aggregate impact from many different sectors of the travel and tourism industry - transportation, accommodations, and tour operations - tends to have a negative environmental effect. Coupled with this assumption is the fact that the public sector is responsible for many functions that should minimise negative environmental impacts - waste management, land use planning, transportation infrastructure, biodiversity conservation, etc. - but often fails to meet this challenge adequately.

Proponents of the destination-based EMS believe that truly sustainable destination management requires a public/private sector partnership in the form of a cooperative management structure that deals proactively with environmental issues. With this in mind, we will be looking closely at methodologies and processes that can be used in the creation of a strategically designed EMS with broad public/private stakeholder support.

The benefits of such an EMS will include:

- Providing a systematic framework for public and private sector cooperation on environmental issues;
- Improving compliance with regulatory requirements and industry codes of conduct;
- Reducing public and private sector operation costs as greater energy/resource savings are achieved;
- Increasing competitive advantage in the market for 'green' tourism destinations; and
- Creating a practical mechanism for pursuing the Agenda 21 principles of sustainable development.

PROPERTY-BASED ENVIRONMENTAL MANAGEMENT SYSTEMS

The creation of property-based EMSs to guide site audits and monitoring processes and in which to anchor certification processes is a new phenomenon in the hospitality industry and, to date, one without a defined standard. This is generating a mounting confusion within the industry over what environmental

standards, which criteria, and whose certification programme to use. The advent of EMSs into tourism is based on the success of EMS operations in other industries, the perceived market benefits of independent certification of environmental standards for individual tourism enterprises, and a demonstrated growth in demand for environmentally friendly or 'green' tourism destinations in major outbound markets.

EMSs are desirable because their adoption can reduce operation costs through energy and resource savings, improve internal management methods, reduce liability/risk from environmental deterioration, improve a property's image in the area of environmental performance and compliance with regulatory requirements, and open opportunities for profit in the emerging market for 'green' tourism destinations.

The overall benefit of a properly designed and administered EMS, then, is its ability to provide credible and objective assurance to inbound markets that the environmental conditions in a particular property or destination are of a higher quality than those of competing locations.

5

Marketing for Tourism

TOURISM MARKETS

Tourists makeup the third, and perhaps most important subsystem. Successful tourism Programme require a strong market orientation. The needs and wants of the tourists you choose to attract and serve must be the focus of much of your marketing and development activity.

Therefore, it is important to clearly understand which tourism market segments you wish to attract and serve. Tourists fall into a very diverse set of categories with quite distinct needs and wants. You should identify the different types of tourists, or market segments that you presently serve or would like to serve. This may involve one or more tourism market surveys.

A visitor survey identifies the size and nature of the existing market and asks the following questions:

- What are the primary market segments you presently attract?
- Where do they come from?
- What local businesses and facilities do they use?
- What attracted them to the community?
- How did they find out about your community?
- How satisfied are they with your offerings?

A market survey (usually a telephone survey) also can be conducted among households in regions from which you wish to attract tourists. This type of study helps identify potential markets, and means of attracting tourists to your area.

TOURISM MARKET SEGMENTS

In a general tourism plan, some clear target tourism market segments should be identified. You might begin by defining the market area from which you will draw most of your visitors. The size of your market area depends upon the uniqueness and quality of your "product", transportation systems, tastes and preferences of surrounding populations, and your competition. Identifying the market area will help target information and promotion and

define transportation routes and modes, competition, and characteristics of your market.

Next, divide your travel market into the following trip length categories:

- Day trips from a 50 mile radius,
- Day trips from 50 to 200 miles away,
- Pass-through travellers,
- Overnight trips of 1 or 2 nights (most likely weekends), and
- Extended overnight vacation trips.

After you have an idea of your market area and kinds of trips you will be serving, begin defining more specific market segments like vehicle campers, downhill skiers, sightseers, family vacationers, single weekenders, and the like. These segments can be more clearly tied to particular resources, businesses, and facilities in your community.

What kinds of products and services are likely to attract each of these groups? Tourist needs as well as their impact on the local community are quite different for day tourists versus overnight tourists. Areas catering primarily to weekend traffic will experience large fluctuations in use. In deciding the relative importance of these different segments, communities need to assess both their ability to provide required services (do you have enough rooms?), as well as the demand for different types of trips relative to the supply and your competition.

THE ENVIRONMENT

A tourism plan is significantly affected by many factors in the broader environment. Indeed, one of the complexities of tourism planning is the number of variables that are outside of the control of an individual tourism business or community. These include such things as tourism offerings and prices at competing destinations, federal and state policy and legislation, currency exchange rates, the state of the economy, and weather. These factors are discussed more fully in Extension bulletin E-1959 as part of the market environment analysis.

Local populations also must be considered in tourism planning. As they compete with tourists for resources, they can be significantly affected by tourism activity, and they are an important source of support in getting tourism plans implemented. A survey of local residents can be conducted to assess community attitudes towards tourism development, identify impacts of tourism on the community, and obtain local input into tourism plans. Public hearings, workshops, and advisory boards are other ways to obtain public involvement in tourism planning. Local support and cooperation is important to the success of tourism Programme and should not be overlooked.

Step three: Generating Alternatives. Generating alternative development and marketing options to meet your goals requires some creative thinking and

brainstorming. The errors made at this stage are usually thinking too narrowly or screening out alternatives prematurely. It is wise to solicit a wide range of options from a diverse group of people. If tourism expertise is lacking in your community, seek help and advice outside the community.

Tourism planning involves a wide range of interrelated development and marketing decisions.

The following development questions will get you started:

- How much importance should be assigned to tourism within a community or region?
- Which general community goals is tourism development designed to serve?
- Which organization(s) will provide the leadership and coordination necessary for community tourism planning? What are the relative roles of public and private sectors?

TOURISM MARKETING DECISION QUESTIONS INCLUDE

- *Segments*: Which market segments should be pursued; geographic markets, trip types, activity or demographic subgroups?
- *Product*: What kinds of tourism products and services should be provided? Who should provide what?
- *Place*: Where should tourism facilities be located?
- *Promotion*: What kinds of promotion should be used, by whom, in which media, how much, when? What community tourism theme or image should be established?
- *Price*: What prices should be charged for which products and services. Who should capture the revenue?

Step four: Evaluating Alternatives. Tourism development and marketing options are evaluated by assessing the degree to which each option will be able to meet the stated goals and objectives.

There are usually two parts to a systematic evaluation of tourism development and marketing alternatives: (1) Feasibility analysis, and (2) Impact assessment. These two tasks are interrelated, but think of them as trying to answer two basic questions: (1) Can it be done?, and (2) What are the consequences? A decision to take a specific action must be based both on feasibility and desirability.

FEASIBILITY ANALYSIS

First, screen alternatives and eliminate those that are not feasible due to economic, environmental, political, legal, or other factors. Evaluate the remaining set of alternatives in more detail, paying particular attention to the market potential and financial plan. Make a realistic assessment of your community's ability to attract and serve a market segment or segments. This

requires a clear understanding of the tourism market in your area and how this market is changing. Also carefully identify your competition and evaluate your advantages and disadvantages compared to the competition. Plan towards the future because it takes time to implement decisions and for your actions to take effect.

Therefore, look at the likely market and competition for several years to come. Review forecasts for the travel market in your area, if available. Careful tracking of tourism trends in your own community can help identify changes in the market that you will have to adapt to.

IMPACT ASSESSMENT

When evaluating alternative development and marketing strategies it is important to understand the impacts, both positive and negative, of proposed actions. The types of impacts and their importance vary across different communities and proposed actions.

Generally, the size, extent, and nature of tourism impacts depend upon:

- Volume of tourist activity relative to local activity
- Length and nature of tourist contacts with the community
- Degree of concentration/dispersal of tourist activity in the area
- Similarities or differences between local populations and tourists
- Stability/sensitivity of local economy, environment, and social structure
- How well tourism is planned, controlled, and managed.

Look at both the benefits and costs of any proposed actions. While tourism development can increase income, revenues, and employment, it also involves costs. Evaluate benefits and costs of tourism development from the perspectives of local government, businesses, and residents.

IMPACTS ON LOCAL GOVERNMENT

Local government provides most of the infrastructure and many of the services essential to tourism development, including highways, public parks, law enforcement, water and sewer, garbage collection and disposal. Evaluate tourism decisions with a clear understanding of the capacity of the local infrastructure and services relative to anticipated needs, and take into account both the needs of local populations and tourists.

A fiscal impact analysis evaluates the impact of tourism on the community's tax base and local government costs. It entails predicting the additional infrastructure and service requirements of tourism development, estimating their costs, deciding who will pay for/provide them, and how. Will tourism generate increased local government revenue through fees and charges, local sales or use taxes, increased property values or property tax rates, or larger local shares of federal and state tax revenues?

IMPACTS ON BUSINESS AND INDUSTRY

Businesses that are directly serving tourists benefit from sales to tourists. Through secondary impacts, tourism activity also benefits a wide range of businesses in a community. For example, a local textile industry may sell to a linen supply firm that serves hotels and motels catering primarily to tourists. A local forest products industry sells to a lumberyard where local woodcarvers or furniture makers buy their supplies. They in turn sell to tourists through various retail outlets. All of these businesses benefit from tourism.

If most products and services for tourists are bought outside of the local area, much of the tourist spending "leaks" out of the local economy. The more a community is "self-sufficient" in serving tourists, the larger the local impact.

IMPACTS ON RESIDENTS

Local residents may experience a broad range of both positive and negative impacts from tourism development. Tourism development may provide increased employment and income for the community. Although tourism jobs are primarily in the service sectors and are often seasonal, part time, and low-paying, these characteristics, are neither universal nor always undesirable. Residents may value opportunities for part time and seasonal work. In particular, employment opportunities and work experiences for students or retirees may be desired.

Residents may also benefit from local services that otherwise would not be available. Tourism development may mean a wider variety of retailers and restaurants, or a better community library. It may also mean more traffic, higher prices, and increases in property values and local taxes. The general quality of the environment and life in the community may go up or down due to tourism development. This depends on the nature of tourism development, the preferences and desires of local residents, and how well tourism is planned and managed.

Steps five and six: Implementation, and Monitoring and Evaluation. We will not attempt a complete discussion of decisionmaking, plan implementation, and monitoring, but these are critical steps in the success of a tourism plan. A set of specific actions should be prescribed with clearly defined responsibilities and timetables.

Monitor progress in implementing the plan and evaluate the success of the plan in meeting its goals and objectives on a regular basis. Plans generally need to be adjusted over time due to changing goals, changing market conditions, and unanticipated impacts. It is a good idea to build monitoring and evaluation systems into your planning efforts.

Successful tourism planning and development means serving both tourists and local residents. The bulletins in this series stress the importance of a market orientation for attracting and serving tourists.

This market orientation must be balanced with a clear view of how tourism serves the broader community interest and an understanding of the positive and negative impacts of tourism development. Remember, tourism should serve the community first and the tourist second. Tourism development must be compatible with other activities in the area and be supported by the local population. Therefore, the tourism plan should be closely coordinated with other local and regional planning efforts, if not an integral part of them.

SEGMENTATION ANALYSIS

Segmentation analysis refers to the way in which organizations identify and categorize customers into groups defined by similar characteristics and similar needs or desires. The Global Spotlight above showed how the owner of Freedom Paradise spent three years researching the plus-size community to determine both the needs and concerns of his target market. The concept of segmentation is widely adopted in tourism marketing, as few companies in the industry attempt to appeal to an entire market.

The core advantage of segmentation is that customers will be more satisfied with the product because it has been designed with their needs in mind. Their social needs are also satisfied because they will be mixing with people like themselves and avoiding incompatible types.

If an organization knows exactly which segments it wishes to reach, it can select the media most likely to be read, heard, or seen by those consumers, and so spend less on general mass-market advertising. If it knows the lifestyles and attitudes of that segment and the benefits they are seeking from the product, the advertising message can be made more persuasive. It shows the major European customer travel segments, their characteristics, and the tour operators that serve each segment.

The practice of dividing total markets up into groups on the basis of similar characteristics

The criteria used most often by tourism and hospitality suppliers to segment the market are as follows:

1. Demographic segmentation uses the primary variables of age, gender, family life cycle, and ethnicity to segment the markets. Club 18–30, for example, uses age and lifestyle stage variables to attract young singles interested in a vibrant night life.
2. Psychographic segmentation divides buyers into different groups based on social class, lifestyle and personality characteristics. Psychographics and lifestyle segmentation are based on personality traits, attitudes, motivations, and activities. People in the same demographic group can have very different psychographic profiles.
3. Geographic segmentation is the division of markets according to geographical boundaries, such as countries, provinces/states, regions,

cities, or neighbourhoods. In the past, for most destination marketing organizations (DMOs), market segmentation was often limited to understanding the more lucrative international tourist market. However, since the terrorist attacks of 11 September 2001, destination marketers have recognized the significance of local and provincial residents and the impact that they have on tourism receipts (Hudson and Ritchie, 2002).

4. Benefit segmentation divides customers based on the benefits they desire, such as education, entertainment, luxury, or low cost. Customers weigh different features of a service, and these are evaluated to form the basis of benefit segmentation. Customers of Freedom Paradise would value benefits such as large walking spaces and large dinner portions, whereas for most sport tourists these services would be irrelevant.
5. Behaviour segmentation divides the market into groups based on the various types of buying behaviour. Common bases include usage rate (light, medium, and heavy), user status (former users, non-users, potential users, first-time users, and regular users of a product), loyalty status (many people stay in five-star hotels as much for the status it confers on them as for the additional comfort), buyer-readiness stage, and occasions. On special occasions, people are prepared to pay more for special treatment, so many restaurants now have deals for children's birthday parties, while hotels and cruise lines have special honeymoon suites.
6. In sum, the heart of any marketing plan is careful analysis of available market segments and the selection of the appropriate target markets. A common mistake within tourism and hospitality is the selection of inappropriate segments. Las Vegas tried unsuccessfully to rebrand itself as a family destination, providing pirate- and circus-themed hotels, funfairs, rides, amusement and games arcades, and animal attractions. They have since reverted to attracting more appropriate market segments, with the help of their 'What Happens in Vegas, Stays in Vegas' advertising campaign. When developing a marketing plan, marketers can gather information concerning market segments from two sources. Internal data can be analysed by looking at business cards, guest registrations, credit card receipts, customer surveys, direct observations and staff perceptions. External data can be gathered from published industry information, marketing research, or by making guesstimates after talking with competitors, vendors, and others in the industry.

Market segmentation is a dynamic process because customer trends are not static. It is thus important to carry out regular – preferably continuous –

tracking studies to monitor changes happening in the market. One of the most recent trends in tourism and hospitality has been a 'demassification' of the market, in which a greater number of niche markets are replacing the mass ones of the past.

As a result, niche marketing is increasing, whereby products are tailored to meet the needs and wants of narrowly defined geographic, demographic, or psychographic segments. The Snapshot below highlights how an Australian wine tourism company has successfully targeted the Generation X market.

SWOT ANALYSIS

SWOT is an acronym for strengths, weaknesses, opportunities and threats. A SWOT analysis provides scope for an organization to list all its strengths (those things it does best and its positive product features) and its weaknesses (problems that affect its success).

These factors are always internally focused. For hotels and visitor attractions, location may be a major strength, or the strength may lie in the skills of certain staff members. Strength may also lie in historical artifacts or architectural style, or having a particularly favourable consumer image. Once identified, strengths are the basis of corporate positions and can be promoted to potential customers, enhanced through product augmentation, or developed within a strategic framework. In the Snapshot profiling Four Seasons in this chapter, several strengths of the Four Seasons Hotels and Resorts can be identified, including their reputation, brand equity and global positioning.

Weaknesses, ranging from aging products and declining markets to surly customer contact staff, must also be identified. Once identified, they may be subject to management action designed to minimize their impact or to remove them where possible. Weaknesses and strengths are often matters of perception rather than 'fact', and may be recognized only through consumer research. Again, using Four Seasons as an example, weaknesses could include not being diversified enough and therefore being vulnerable to negative external environmental impacts.

Opportunities are events that can affect a business, either through its reaction to external forces or through its addressing of its own weaknesses. An opportunity identified recently by Four Seasons Hotels and Resorts is in private charters and general cruises, a move that may improve the group's weakness of not being diversified enough.

Threats are those elements, both internal and external, that could have a serious detrimental effect on a business. After 11 September 2001, the subsequent downturn in the economy had a devastating impact on tourism and by the end of 2002, Four Seasons had not recovered. The subsequent Iraq war and concerns about sudden acute respiratory syndrome (SARS) led to a huge number of cancelled trips to North America and to thousands of dollars in lost tourism revenue for all hotels, including Four Seasons. A SWOT analysis is usually best undertaken early in the planning process, and in large organizations a SWOT is often carried out for each division. For example, a convention hotel would conduct a SWOT on the property as a whole, but might also undertake a separate exercise for the functions area, restaurants, retail outlets and recreation facilities. To enhance their own foresight and bring to bear an independent, fresh vision, it is common practice in large market-oriented businesses for managers to commission consultants to carry out regular audits of all aspects of their business, including a SWOT analysis.

FORECASTING

Because information is never perfect and the future is always unknown, no one right conclusion can ever be drawn from the evidence gathered in the SWOT process. As a result, forecasting becomes an important stage in the planning process to support a SWOT. Forecasting is market research based but future oriented, and it relies on expectations, vision, judgement, and projections for factors such as sales volume and revenue trends, consumer profiles, product profiles, price trends, and trends in the external environment.

The Snapshot below provides forecasts for the growing Chinese travel market based on reports by several market research companies. Because the future for tourism and hospitality products is subject to volatile, unpredictable factors and competitors' decisions, the goal of forecasting is not accuracy but careful and continuous assessment of probabilities and options, with a focus on future choices. Forecasting recognizes that most marketing-mix expenditure is invested months ahead of targeted revenue flows. Since marketing planning is focused on future revenue achievement, it is necessarily dependent upon skill, judgement, foresight and realism in the forecasting process. There are two main sets of forecasting techniques: qualitative and quantitative. Qualitative techniques are those that seek to estimate future levels of demand, based on detailed subjective analysis. They include sales staff estimates, senior management opinions and buyers' intention surveys. Two more sophisticated qualitative techniques are the Delphi technique and scenario planning.

The Delphi technique involves obtaining expert opinions about the future prospects for a particular market without the experts actually meeting or necessarily knowing at any stage the composition of the panel. Long-term scenario planning is undertaken by larger organizations such as hotel or airline companies. This is a systematic attempt to predict the composition of the future market environment in 10–25 years' time, and the likely impacts on the company.

Quantitative techniques rely on analysis of past and current data. In some instances this implies the simple projecting of future demand in terms of past trends; in other instances, unravelling causal determinants needs to be considered. A number of well-tested methods are used, but most require a degree of statistical ability.

Time-series (non-causal) techniques involve the forecasting of future demand on the basis of past trends. Causal methods attempt to show, by using regression analysis, how some measure of tourism demand is influenced by selected variables other than time. Finally, computer simulations are becoming more popular – trend-curve analysis and multiple regressions are combined mathematically to generate a computer model that simulates tourism demand.

RECREATION AND TOURISM MARKETING

Earlier it was mentioned that a product can be "ideas, goods, or services." Since tourism is primarily a service based industry, the principal products provided by recreation/tourism (R/T) businesses are recreational experiences and hospitality. These are intangible products and more difficult to market than tangible products such as automobiles.

The intangible nature of services makes quality control difficult but crucial. It also makes it more difficult for potential customers to evaluate and compare service offerings. In addition, instead of moving the product to the customer, the customer must travel to the product (area/community).

Travel is a significant portion of the time and money spent in association with recreational and tourism experiences and is a major factor in people's decisions on whether or not to visit your business or community. As an industry, tourism has many components comprising the overall "travel experience." Along with transportation, it includes such things as accommodations, food and beverage services, shops, entertainment, aesthetics and special events. It is rare for one business to provide the variety of activities or facilities tourists need or desire. This adds to the difficulty of maintaining and controlling the quality of the experience. To overcome this hurdle, tourism related businesses, agencies, and organizations need to work together to package and promote tourism opportunities in their areas and align their efforts to assure consistency in product quality.

THE MARKETING PLAN

One of the most important steps a business or community can take to improve the effectiveness and efficiency of their marketing efforts is to develop a written marketing plan. This plan will guide their marketing decisions and assist them in allocating marketing resources such as money and personnel time.

The plan should include:

- The overall business objectives—what you want to accomplish;
- An assessment of the market environment—what factors may affect your marketing efforts;

- A business/community profile—what resources are available,
- Market identification (segmentation)—the specific groups or clientele most interested in your product;
- The marketing objectives for each segment;
- The marketing strategies (or mixes) for different markets you target—the best combination of the 4 Ps (product, price, place, promotion) for each segment;
- An implementation plan—how to "make it work;"
- The marketing budget-how much you have to spend; and
- A method for evaluation and change.

A framework which can be used to develop a marketing plan. Each component will be briefly discussed in the remainder of the bulletin. For more information regarding different components of the plan be sure to consult other bulletins in this series.

OVERALL BUSINESS OBJECTIVES

Businesses, agencies, and communities should develop overall objectives and regularly monitor their progress. The objectives should provide guidance for all decisions including finances, personnel and marketing. They should be quantitative and measurable statements of what the business or community wants to accomplish over a specified period of time.

Business objectives are often stated in terms of sales, profits, market shares and/or occupancy rates. Communities frequently establish objectives relating to such things as increasing the number of tourists, developing or changing their image, facility and activity development, cooperation among tourism related businesses and increasing length of stay and local expenditures.

It is important that the objectives be reasonable given the market conditions and the firm's or organization's resources. Establish a few reasonable objectives instead of a long, unrealistic "wish list." This is especially true for new businesses or communities which do not have much experience in tourism development and/or marketing.

MARKET ENVIRONMENT ANALYSIS

The next step in developing a marketing plan is to assess the impact of environmental factors (such as economic, social and political) on present and future markets. Changes in these factors can create marketing opportunities as well as problems.

DEMOGRAPHIC AND LIFESTYLE TRENDS

Changing demographics and lifestyles are having a major impact on R/T participation. An assessment of these trends is important to understand how they will likely affect your business or community.

Some of the important trends that bear watching:

- Population growth and movement;
- Rural community growth compared to metropolitan areas;
- Number of adult women employed outside the home;
- The number of households is growing, especially non- family and single parent households, but family size is decreasing;
- The impact of two wage earner households on real family income;
- The number of retired persons with the financial ability to travel;
- Better health to an older age; and
- Continued aging of the population (we are becoming a middle aged society).

ECONOMIC CONDITIONS

Overall economic conditions can have significant impacts on recreation and tourism markets. A marketing strategy that is effective during periods of low unemployment rates may have to be significantly adjusted if unemployment increases.

Businesses and communities should monitor and assess the likely impact of factors such as unemployment rates, real family income, rate of inflation, credit availability, terms and interest rates. Consideration should also be given to the prices of complementary products, such as lodging, gasoline and recreation equipment.

LAWS AND GOVERNMENT ACTIONS

As a complex industry, tourism is significantly affected both positively and negatively by laws and by actions of governmental agencies. For instance, rulings on such things as liability issues or decisions regarding building and health codes may change or possibly prevent the construction of a proposed facility. If a public facility changes the prices of its services, this could affect the service offerings of associated private businesses. These actions may have both positive and negative effects on the marketing efforts of the business and community. To avoid wasting valuable resources it is important that R/T businesses, agencies, and communities continually monitor and evaluate governmental actions.

TECHNOLOGY

Technological developments are increasing rapidly. New recreation products, such as all-terrain vehicles and wind surfers, provide new ways for people to satisfy their recreational preferences.

New production technologies and materials offer recreation and tourism businesses ways to reduce costs and improve the quality of their products/ services. Advances in telecommuni-cations have and will continue to create new promotional opportunities. Technological innovations, in relation to jobs and the home, have resulted in increased leisure time for many people.

COMPETITION

Businesses and communities must identify and analyse existing and potential competitors. The objective of the analysis is to determine the strengths and weaknesses of the competition's marketing strategies. The analysis should include the competition's:

- Product/service features and quality;
- Location relative to different geographic markets;
- Promotional themes and messages;
- Prices; and
- Type of customer they are attracting.

BUSINESS AND COMMUNITY PROFILES

Too many communities attempt to market themselves as tourist destinations without accurate information about their resources (facilities, services, staff), image (projected vs. Actual), and how well their customers are satisfied. Without this information, it is difficult to make other decisions in the planning process.

Included should be such things as recreational and entertainment facilities, cultural and historic sites, overnight accommodations, restaurants, shopping opportunities, special events and activities, staff size, and transportation. Each item of the "inventory" should also be assessed in terms of quality and availability.

MARKET SEGMENTATION (IDENTIFICATION)

Recreation and tourism businesses and communities often make the mistake of attempting to be all things to all people. It is difficult, and risky, to develop marketing strategies for the mass market. Strategies designed for the "average" customer often result in unappealing products, prices, and promotional messages. For example, it would be difficult to develop a campground that would be equally attractive to recreational vehicle campers and backpackers or promote a property to serve both snow mobilers and nature oriented cross country skiers.

Marketing is strongly based on market segmentation and target marketing. Market segmentation is the process of:

- Taking existing and/or potential customers/visitors (market) and categorizing them into groups with similar preferences referred to as "market segments;"
- Selecting the most promising segments as "target markets;" and
- Designing "marketing mixes," or strategies (combination of the 4

Ps), which satisfy the special needs, desires and behaviour of the target markets.

There is no unique or best way to segment markets, but ways in which customers can be grouped are:

- Location of residence—instate, out-of-state, local;
- Demographics—age, income, family status, education;
- Equipment ownership/use—RV's, sailboats, canoes, tents, snowmobiles;
- Important product attributes—price, quality, quantity; and
- Lifestyle attributes—activities, interests, opinions.

To be useful, the segment identification process should result in segments that suggest marketing efforts that will be effective in attracting them and at least one segment large enough to justify specialized marketing efforts. After segments have been identified, the business or community must select the "target markets," those segments which offer them the greatest opportunity.

When determining target markets, consideration should be given to:

- Existing and future sales potential of each segment;
- The amount and strength of competition for each segment;
- The ability to offer a marketing mix which will be successful in attracting each segment;
- The cost of servicing each segment; and
- Each segment's contribution to accomplishing overall business/community objectives. It is often wiser to target smaller segments that are presently not being served, or served inadequately, than to go after larger segments for which there is a great deal of competition.

MARKETING OBJECTIVES FOR EACH SEGMENT

Marketing objectives which contribute to the accomplishment of the overall business objectives should be established for each target market.

Objectives serve a number of functions including:

- Guidance for developing marketing mixes for different target markets;
- Information for allocating the marketing budget between target markets;
- A basis for objectively evaluating the effectiveness of the marketing mixes (setting standards); and
- A framework for integrating the different marketing mixes into the overall marketing plan.

The target market objectives should:

- Be expressed in quantitative terms;
- Be measurable;
- Specify the target market; and
- Indicate the time period in which the objective is to be accomplished.

For example, increase the number of overnight stays by people from the Chicago market over the next two years by five per cent. Remember, rank objectives by priority and carefully evaluate them to ensure that they are reasonable given the strength of the competition and resources available for marketing.

MARKET FAILURE IN TOURISM

The market failures are part of the rationale for government intervention to facilitate tourism investment. The Guide provides further detail about what form that facilitation should take.

POSITIVE SPILLOVERS

Spillovers are a market failure because they lead to under investment in tourism. This happens because the full benefit of the investment is not captured by the investor.

Recognising this provides a basis for tourism investment facilitation — because the returns from investment in tourism are distributed to other businesses and regions frequented by tourists as well as the investor.

This results in economic benefits to the wider community. While these spillover benefits are difficult to quantify, TTF and Urbis (2010) estimate that on average, every ten hotel rooms create 18.2 jobs.

About five of these jobs are in accommodation, and the rest are elsewhere. Arriving at reliable estimates of spillover effects over time, which account for economic, social and environmental benefits, is a significant yet important challenge for governments undertaking tourism investment facilitation. These estimates will provide a basis for cost benefit analysis of facilitation efforts, which the Guide recommends as a feature of good practice.

PUBLIC GOODS

Public goods warrant public investment because the investment benefits the community as a whole. Furthermore, if left to the market there would not be a sufficient incentive to invest in these goods because the return to the investor cannot be captured.

In a tourism context, there are features of public goods both in natural assets and in certain types of infrastructure:

- Certain tourism assets such as heritage sites, public parks and gardens and natural landscapes such as beaches display features of public goods because they are assets that benefit the wider community.
- Public infrastructure (such as convention centres, cruise ship terminals and airports) that also benefits the whole community, but which has a greater commercial imperative due to the capacity to generate significant income.

Regarding natural assets, tourism investment can be thought of in two ways:

- The provision of maintenance, conservation and access — which do not have explicit commercial objectives and are likely to be undertaken by government in keeping with their statutory responsibilities. While these investments may benefit tourism, they are less suited to joint investment with industry.
- Developments which leverage the attraction of those locations as places to visit — which have commercial objectives as a major objective and are therefore more suited to private sector investment. These investments will also be done in a way that supports statutory requirements.

Regarding public infrastructure, these assets may be privatised to obtain an optimal allocation of risks and rewards or to allow more efficient management of the asset (due to the specialised skills and capacity of the private entity). However, they are still essentially assets utilised by the public and generate economy-wide benefits.

Public Private Partnerships (PPPs) may be a good fit for these projects. The *Natural Tourism Partnerships Action Plan* (2007) emphasised that successful public-private partnerships are based on good planning, commitment and 'effective monitoring, regulation and enforcement by government'. Government provision of maintenance, conservation and access can also be used as part of PPP arrangements.

COORDINATION FAILURE

The OECD (2010) has referred to the 'fragmented SME-based structure' of tourism giving rise to various market failures, which governments have a role in reducing. Tourism consists of numerous businesses across various industries, and the majority of tourism businesses are SMEs.

For example, an investor may wish to build a luxury hotel in a beautiful location, but if there is inadequate transport infrastructure in place tourists will be unlikely to visit. In addition, having a mix of attractions (museums, diving facilities, nature walks, etc.) leads to a destination being fully developed. The individual developer is not in a position to improve the transport infrastructure or to influence other attractions.

This presents an investment challenge, which may be described as the 'indivisibility problem', where effective investment is hindered due the structural features of the industry. Government is uniquely placed to coordinate effective responses that address this problem. A lack of effective coordination within and between governments can introduce uncertainty or delay the supply of infrastructure that supports tourism.

The Jackson Report called for greater coordination across government and industry. Urbis (2010) noted that effective coordination allows the industry and other parties to provide meaningful input into the tourism plan-making process. Government has a role to play in assisting with coordination and in some cases, funding infrastructure for access, so that tourism is viable for other businesses. With effective coordination, a location can reach its tourism potential.

INFORMATION ASYMMETRY

Investment in tourism assets is hindered due to imbalances in information about the tourism industry and associated investment opportunities.

Investors need sufficient information in a number of important areas to inform investment decisions:

- *Research on risk/return attractiveness compared to comparable assets* — tourism projects may be unique or unusual, meaning the viability of proposals cannot be assessed based on precedent projects. The uniqueness may be because a region may not have had notable tourism investment previously, or the business offering itself has not been tried previously. The latter could particularly be the case for a tourist attraction proposal. As a consequence, investors may have difficulty in developing detailed business plans. This makes it difficult to attract finance, particularly for larger scale, more innovative investments.
- *Investment opportunities* — investors may not know about the range of tourism investment opportunities that are on offer. Investment opportunities may not be labelled as being potential tourist developments because that has not been the previous use of the site, or a tourism use may be only one proposed element of a development.
- *Approval processes* — all steps and requirements in an approval process for a tourism development may not be clear to the investor. There may not be one place where the investor can get this information. Rather, there are elements of approval processes that belong to different levels of government and departments. Other regulatory and tax issues may pose similar problems. This issue has been examined recently in Victoria. On the basis of submissions, reports, and research, the VCEC concluded that elements of Victoria's land-use planning system are impeding the development of the tourism industry in parts of regional Victoria and in Green Wedge Zone areas. The Commission also found that the administration of land-use planning regulation is imposing unnecessary uncertainty, time delays and costs on Victorian tourism businesses. Our research and consultations indicate that these problems are not limited to Victoria.

Further to these areas where information gaps exist, while macro-level statistical information on the tourism industry is available in Australia, substantial information gaps exist at the regional level. This is further worsened by small sample sizes at the regional level, which reduces the accuracy of statistical information. The Tourism Satellite Account provides macro-level statistics on tourism, but the multi-industry nature of tourism means that gaps still exist in other areas. There is also a lack of information on performance benchmarks and cost structures, both of which are necessary to benchmark tourism productivity. There is a need for timelier information and supply forecasting and benchmarking tools for investors and tourism businesses.

Government is well placed to both develop and disseminate data and information to overcome information asymmetry in each of areas outlined above. The OECD (2010) has observed that providing research-based intelligence to the tourism industry is an effective area for policy intervention.

NATURAL OR INDUCED MONOPOLIES

Some tourist assets may have monopoly features. In particular, major transport hubs such as airports and seaports may have a monopoly in the market for interstate and international passenger transit. To ensure that airport owners are not engaging in monopolistic pricing, the ACCC regularly collected financial information from some major Australian airports up until 2007.

A new price monitoring regime at the five most important airports (Adelaide, Brisbane, Melbourne-Tullamarine, Perth and Sydney-Kingsford-Smith airports) commenced on 1 July 2007. While price regulation may address monopolistic behaviour to an extent, there are other aspects not addressed by price regulation. For instance, price regulation will not address poor customer service (due to lack of competitors) or out-dated infrastructure (due to lack of incentives to undertake capital upgrades).

The level of monopolisation depends on how the market for tourist attractions or facilities is defined. For instance, natural or heritage assets may be unique but this does not make them a monopoly.

This is because the site is still subject to competition in terms of the service that it offers (for example, a culturally significant theatre competes with other providers of performance space). To take the example of casinos, while the casino may be the only one of its kind in that city to offer the range of casino games, they compete with other gambling and leisure service providers.

There is growing recognition that government needs to take a lead role in facilitating tourism investment. In the industry survey undertaken for this project, 91 per cent of respondents agreed that tourism investment required specialised investment facilitation.

This marks a change in the role governments have historically played. As the TRA (2010) notes, the main interventions taken by governments for the tourism industry are direct support for marketing through Tourism Australia and state/territory tourism offices.

Investment facilitation cannot overcome major shortcomings in approval processes or fix projects that are fundamentally unprofitable. However, investors consulted have emphasised that the government can provide information for investors to make an informed decision, coordinate their facilitation efforts with state/territory governments to make tourism investment more feasible. Governments can also be more proactive in working closely with investors during a project as a way of raising investor confidence and attracting further investment. As the OECD (2006) stated:

Investment promotion and facilitation measures, including incentives, can be effective instruments to attract investment provided they aim to correct for market failures and are developed in a way that can leverage the strong points of a country's investment environment. As this chapter has shown, there is a clear and compelling case for government facilitation of investment in tourism. The case for government facilitation is based on the following findings.

- Tourism is of key importance to the Australian economy and tourism investment offers significant benefits.
- Leaving tourism investment to the market will not achieve optimal investment outcomes. The level of investment will be inadequate and the investment that does occur will not be directed to the areas of best use and greatest overall benefit.
- Government at all levels has a role but it needs to be the right role, focussed on facilitating private investment, albeit with government as a partner and sometimes as a direct investor. Government facilitation needs to be based on sound guiding principles so as to achieve an overall benefit compared to what would have occurred without the facilitation.
- The Guide is designed to help governments to do this. It provides advice on what type of facilitation is appropriate in different circumstances and the principles that should guide facilitation efforts.
- The Guide is based on a good practice framework, the good practices respond to the market failures and investment barriers described in this chapter, so the benefits of tourism investment facilitation can be realised.

TOURISM MARKETING INFORMATION SYSTEM

The major aim of Tour MIS is an optimal information supply and decision support for the tourism industry. The first step is to provide aniline tourism survey data, as well as evaluation programmes to transform data into precious management information. Tour-MIS predominantly comprises:

1. A database containing tourism market research data (declarative knowledge),
2. Various programme modules (method-base, procedural knowledge) converting acknowledged methods/models into simple surfaces, and
3. Various administrative programmes which assist the maintenance of

the data- base and track and control the information search behaviour of users.

The internet supports the transport and presentation of animated and unanimated pictures, sound and video recordings and text and numerical data and is expandable. A high- performance SQL-database and a functionally designed user interface for Tour MIS based on hypertext and Perl permits the development of interactive applications. The programme modules contained in the method-base are developed according to the specific requirements of tourism managers. The internet offers a number of advantages against the old PC-solution. Since changes in the database have immediate worldwide effect the speed of information transmission can be reduced to the availability of the information source.

For example, Tour MIS makes the monthly projections of Statistics Austria available within only a few seconds to all regional managers of the Austrian National Tourist Office regardless of whether they are located in New York, Sydney, Tokyo or Madrid. Anybody provided with access to the internet and entitled to use Tour MIS may access data and information, make calculations or simulations send or receive data – without tiresome postal procedures, danger of loss, delays and costs. All these advantages have led to a significan expansion in the number of users.

Conditions for the use of the System

In the beginning Tour MIS was provided with strict access control and used to be only accessible to certain users. In this respect the application did differ from traditional internet offers. However, the present concept is also not an Intranet.

Unlike the Intranet which supports internal information management systems Tour MIS is not owned by a certain organization but is open to all authorized tourism organizations, societies, tourism consult- ants, companies, tourism training centres, pressure groups, etc. in Austria and abroad. By covering the maintenance costs, a consortium of 12 of the most important initiators of market research projects in Austria (Austrian National Tourist Office, nine provincial tour- ism organizations, the two special interest associations for Hotel Trade and Restaurant

Trade of the Federal Chamber of Commerce, Federal Ministry for Economic Affairs and Labour Tourism and Recreational Commerce Section) guarantee the continuous updating of the comprehensive database. Since 2000 this initiative has provided the Austrian tourism industry with free access to overall data and functions (with some exceptions) of Tour MIS. The necessary hardware resources are situated at the Institute for Tourism and Leisure Studies at the University of Economics and Business Administration in Vienna where a major part of the necessary maintenance work is carried out.

The Tour MIS Database

In the beginning Tour MIS contained data that was strongly influenced by the internal interests of its commissioner, the Austrian National Tourist Office. In this respect international tourism statistical data, empirical tourism studies and economic indicators for the most important markets of origin for the Austrian tourism industry have been collected in Tour MIS. The PC-version, developed in the early nineties, contained more than 10,000 time series. The periodicity of information was generally based on annual data, however the most significant time series have also been recorded for periods of less than a year.

Over the years the database has continually expanded. Due to the increasing importance of overseas markets further information has been required. Unequal needs of provincial tour- ism organizations led to additional statistics regarding the federal provinces and Vienna, being city and federal province at the same time, acquired an exceptional position. Furthermore data on the Austrian and international city tourism has been added. This information was collected at the branch offices of the Austrian National Tourist Office, transmitted by fax and data was entered manually into the marketing information system in order to be available to users.

Later based on international cooperation (European Cities' Tourism, European Travel Commission) the first online maintenance agreements with local tourism organizations were initiated. The most important available data sources of Tour MIS are indicated in. Besides the basic information search functions the method-base has also been continually upgraded. In this respect the system more and more meets the requirements of an efficient decision support tool. In the next paragraphs the most important data sources and the facilities for analysis and reporting are discussed.

National Tourism Statistics Austria

One of the first data sources which was installed in Tour MIS was the official tourism statistics in Austria. Data generated from the registration with accommodation suppliers is one of the fundamental supports of the official inbound tourism statistics in Austria. Accommodation statistics are divided into two different kinds of survey: the accommodation for inbound travel and the accommodation capacity. The data on arrivals and over nights are surveyed for 50 generating countries related to 13 different accommodation types and 1,600 municipalities (= report communities) on a monthly basis.

Thus the official travel survey offers 25 million data points per annum which can be transformed into precious information for tourism managers. From the data material important information on tourism development, trends in markets of origin and accommodation types, evaluation of the competing situation can be derived. For example, for each of the 1,600 municipalities the database allows the user to regularly monitor the development of the average duration of stay, the seasonality, market shares, guest-mix structure, and, in connection with the capacity statistics, the occupancy rate. Tour MIS presently offers official tourism statistics only at the provincial basis which nevertheless requires maintenance work of 11,700 data sets per month. The necessary data transfer from the host system of Statistic Austria (ISIS) to Tour MIS takes place automatically each time after the arrival of new data segments and in accordance with various maintenance routines.

The information supply of Tour MIS users takes place by means of predominate tables and reports created for the user in real time operations. The content and design of tables or reports plays an important role in the user's perception of the system's usefulness and usability. Only if the information supply meets the users' needs will the system achieve its aim of providing a high-performance usage of market data and improve the information supply in tourism management.

NATURAL TOURISM PRODUCTS

These include natural resources such as areas, climate and its setting, landscape and natural environment. Natural resources are frequently the key elements in a destination's attraction.

Let us look at some examples:

- Countryside
- Climate- temperature, rains, snowfall, days of sunshine
- Natural Beauty- landforms, hills, rocks, gorges, terrain
- Water- lakes, ponds, rivers, waterfalls, springs
- Flora and Fauna
- Wildlife
- Beaches
- Islands
- Spas
- Scenic Attractions

The climate of a tourist destination is often an important attraction. Good weather plays an important role in making a holiday. Millions of tourists from countries with extreme climates visit beaches in search of fine weather and sunshine. The sunshine and clear sea breeze at the beaches have attracted many people for a very long time. In fact, development of spas and resorts along the sea coasts in many countries were a result of the travellers. urge to enjoy good weather and sunshine. In Europe, countries like France, Italy, Spain and Greece have developed beautiful beach resorts. North Europeans visit the Mediterranean coast searching for older resorts like Monte Carlo, Nice and Cannes on the Riviera and new resorts in Spain and Italy.

Beautiful beaches of India, Sri Lanka, and Thailand, Indonesia and Australia and some other new destinations are more examples of how good weather can attract tourists. All these areas capitalise on good weather. Destinations with attractive winter climates, winter warmth and sunshine are also important centres of tourist attraction. Many areas have become important winter holiday resorts attracting a large number of tourists. Around these winter resorts, winter sport facilities have been installed to cater to the increasing needs of tourists. People from warm climates travel especially to see snowfall and enjoy the cold climate. In countries with tropical climates, many upland cool areas have been developed as 'hill stations'. Hence climate is of great significance as a tourism product. The scenery and natural beauty of places has always attracted tourists.

Tourists enjoy nature in all its various forms. There are land forms like mountains, canyons, coral reefs, cliffs, etc. One of the great all time favourite tourist destination is the Grand Canyon, Arizona. Mountain ranges like the Himalayas, Kilimanjaro, and Swiss Alps, etc. There are water forms like rivers, lakes waterfalls, geysers, glaciers, etc. The Niagara Falls shared by Canada and the United States is an example of how scenic waterfalls attract tourists. Lake Tahoe in California and the, deserts of Egypt are other examples of great tourist products.

Other great natural wonders that attract tourists are the Giants Causeway of Northern Ireland, the Geysers of Iceland, the glaciers of the Alps, the forests of Africa etc. Vegetation like forests, grasslands, moors deserts, etc. has all been developed as tourist products. Flora and Fauna attract many a tourist. Tourists like to know the various types of plants and trees that they see and which trees are seen in which seasons. There are many plants which are specific to certain regions and many times students and travellers visit those areas especially to see those varieties of plants.

Thick forest covers, attract tourists who enjoy trekking and hunting activities. Fauna attracts tourists who like to watch birds, wild mammals, reptiles and other exotic and rare animals. Countries in South East Asia have crocodile gardens, bird sanctuaries, and other tourist products that display the fauna of their region. Spas are gaining popularity as modern tourism products all over the world.

While most parts of the world have their own therapies and treatments that are effective in restoring the wellness and beauty of people. New kinds of health tours that are gaining popularity are spa tours. Spas offer the unique advantages of taking the best from the West and the East, combining them with the indigenous system and offering best of the two worlds. For example Swedish massages work well with the Javanese Mandy, lulur, aromatherapy, reflexology and traditional ayurvedic procedures. Now various spa products are being combined with yoga, meditation, and pranayama, giving a holistic experience to tourists. Spa treatments are now combined with other medical treatments to treat blood pressure, insomnia, depression, paralysis and some other diseases. People are now travelling to spas and clinics for curative baths and medical treatment. In some countries like Italy, Austria and Germany, great importance is given to spa treatments. In Russia along the Black Sea coast and in the foothills of the Caucasus Mountains, there are many world famous sanatoria where millions of Russians and international tourists throng every year. Beach tourism is very popular among the tourists today. Tourists of all age groups, backgrounds, cultures and countries enjoy this tourism product. Besides attraction and saleability, beach holidaying has lead to overall development of tourism in many parts of the world.

The basic importance of beaches is that they provide aesthetic and environmental value of the beach such as beautiful natural scenery with golden sands, lush green vegetation and bright blue sky. The water should be clear, free of currents and underwater rocks. Beach tourism activities include water and land resource use. The water usage involves swimming, surfing, sailing, wind surfing, water scootering, Para- sailing, motorboat rides, etc.

The land use has multifacets like sunbathing, recreational areas for tourists (parks, playgrounds, clubs, theatre, amusement parks, casinos, cultural museums, etc.), accommodation facilities (hotels, cottages, villas, camping sites, etc.), car and bus parking areas, entertainment and shopping complexes, access roads and transportation network. Due to its multidimensional requirements the beach product needs special care. A beach resort needs to be developed as an integrated complex to function as a self-contained community. Environmental management should also ensure the availability of necessary infrastructure in the immediate hinterland to the coastal region in support of the development on the coast to maintain its ecosystem. Islands abound with natural beauty, with the rare flora and fauna and tribes. This makes islands an ideal place for adventure, nature and culture lovers to visit.

This tourist product has great scope as these islands are being developed as tourist paradises. For example, Hawaii, Maldives, Mauritius, Tahiti, Andaman and Nicobar Islands, etc. has developed with tourism activity over the past few decades. The topography is generally undulating and they offer natural scenic beauty with exotic flora and fauna. Most of these islands have places of worship like churches, temples, etc. As an added attraction some of these islands have developed as tax havens thereby encouraging commercial development of these economies.

They offer social and cultural attractions as tourists can experience the local lifestyle, local food, fairs and festivals, etc. Scenic attractions, like good weather, are very important factors in the development of tourism. Breath-taking mountain scenery and the coastal stretches exert a strong fascination on the tourist the magnificent mountain ranges provide an atmosphere of peace and tranquillity. Tourists visiting the northern slopes of the Alps in Switzerland and Austria and the southern slopes in Italy and also the Himalayan slopes of

India and Nepal for the first time, cannot but be charmed by their physical magnificence.

MAN- MADE TOURISM PRODUCTS

Man- made tourism products are created by man for pleasure, leisure or business.

Man- made tourism products include:

CULTURE

- Sites and areas of archaeological interest
- Historical buildings and monuments
- Places of historical significance
- Museums and art galleries
- Political and educational institutions
- Religious institutions

Cultural tourism is based on the mosaic of places, traditions, art forms, celebrations and experiences that portray the nation and its people, reflecting the diversity and character of a country. Garrison Keillor, in an address to the 1995 White House Conference on Travel and Tourism, best described cultural tourism by saying, "We need to think about cultural tourism because really there is no other kind of tourism. It's what tourism is...People don't come to America for our airports, people don't come to America for our hotels, or the recreation facilities....They come for our culture: high culture, low culture, middle culture, right, left, real or imagined—they come here to see America." Two significant travel trends will dominate the tourism market in the next decade.

- Mass marketing is giving way to one-to-one marketing with travel being tailored to the interests of the individual consumer.
- A growing number of visitors are becoming special interest travellers who rank the arts, heritage and/or other cultural activities as one of the top five reasons for travelling.

The combination of these two trends is being fuelled by technology, through the proliferation of online services and tools, making it easier for the traveller to choose destinations and customise their itineraries based on their interests. Today we can witness large masses of people travelling to foreign countries to become acquainted with the usages and customs, to visit the museums and to admire works of art. One way of hastening the beneficial effects resulting from tourism is to bring the cultural heritage into the economic circuit, thus justifying the investments made at the cost of the national community, for its preservation.

Taking an economic view of the cultural heritage of a nation may not altogether be justified, considering that the preservation of its culture is one of the basic responsibilities of any community.

But considering the financial obstacles especially for the developing countries, this may appear to be a rational approach. Hence mass tourism can contribute unique benefits to the exploiting of the cultural heritage of a nation and can serve indirectly to improve the individual cultural levels of both citizens and travellers. Cultural resources have another specific characteristic, which many tourists want to experience the exotic.

There will be a great urge on the part of the tourist to visit and become acquainted with the ancient civilization in their quest for novel human knowledge. Culture means the prospect of contact with other civilizations, their original and varied customs and tradition with their distinct characteristics. This entire process creates a powerful motivator towards travel. Various Museums also attract tourists like Madame Tussauds Museum in London, the Louvre Museum in Paris, Smithsonian Washington Museum, Museums of famous painters like Salvador Dali, Pablo Picasso, Natural History Museum, British Museum, Museum of Modern Art are also popular tourist products. Sites of archeological interest like remains of Mohenjodaro and Harrapan civilizations, museums for fossils and dinosaurs. Sites for historical interest like city of Hiroshima and Nagasaki, sites of holocaust in Germany, tombs of various leaders and emperors. Historical buildings like Warwick Castle, Tower of London, Stratford-on-Avon which is Shakespeare's birthplace, the Roman Baths are all popular with tourists. Even historical cities like Varanasi in India get a lot of tourists due to its status as one of the oldest cities of the world. Stonehenge in United Kingdom, The White House, Buckingham Palace and other places of political significance, are also great tourist draws.

TRADITIONS

- Pilgrimages
- Fairs and festivals
- Arts and handicrafts
- Dance
- Music
- Folklore
- Native life and customs

A pilgrimage is a term primarily used for a journey or a search of great moral significance. Sometimes, it is a journey to a sacred place or shrine of importance to a person's beliefs and faith. Members of every religion participate in pilgrimages. A person who makes such a journey is called a pilgrim. Secular and civic pilgrimages are also practiced, without regard for religion but rather of importance to a particular society. For example, many people throughout the world travel to the City of Washington in the United States for a pilgrimage to see the Declaration of Independence and the Constitution of the United States. British people often make pilgrimages to London to witness the public appearances of the monarch of the United Kingdom. A large number of people have been making pilgrimages to sacred religious places or holy places. This practice is widespread in many parts of the world. In the Christian world, for instance, a visit to Jerusalem or the Vatican is considered auspicious. Among Muslims, a pilgrimage to Mecca is considered a great act of faith. In India there are many pilgrimage centres and holy places belonging to all major religions of the world. India is among the richest countries in the world as far as the field of art and craft is concerned. Tourists like to visit and see the creative and artistic treasures of various countries.

Every country has certain traditional arts like soap sculptures and batik of Thailand; gems and jewellery, tie and dye works, wood and marble carving in Indonesia; ivory, glasswork, hand block printing, sandalwood, inlay work; are some of the examples of traditional art that attract tourists. There are many forms of dance in the world like Salsa, Hip- Hop, Jazz, Flamingo, Ballet and Traditional Dances. People who travel like to watch these dance performances and sometimes even take some introductory classes.

Music can be either traditional or modern. Traditional music like folk music and classical and country music is specific to every region and country. Modern forms include Blues, Rock, Pop, Jazz, Rap, Techno and Hip- Hop. Music also adds to the attraction of a destination. Fairs and Festivals capture the fun loving side and bring out the joyous celebrations of the community. Festivals like Christmas, Easter, Thanksgiving, Eid, Ramadan, Diwali, and Holi and so on, also bring people to destinations where the celebration can be enjoyed. Some popular Fairs which cater to fun and work are Pushkar Mela in Rajasthan, Prêt fair in Paris, Magic Fair in Vegas for garments, Hong Kong Fashion Week and various job fairs where people are recruited.

ENTERTAINMENT

- Amusement and recreation parks
- Sporting events
- Zoos and oceanariums
- Cinemas and theatre
- Night life
- Cuisine

Tourist products that have entertainment as their main characteristic are many. Just to name a few there are amusement and recreational parks like Disneyworld in United States, Hong Kong, Paris, Singapore and theme parks in various countries and cities like Appu Ghar and Fun and Food Village in Delhi, Essel World in Mumbai and so on. Tourists may come to attend sports events and it is also an opportunity to explore the country. The fundamental concept is that all tourist activities have an influence on providing economic benefits and have a powerful influence in some definite locality, like the

Olympics in Athens has given immense benefit to all in tourism business in Athens in particular and Greece in general.

Many countries organise year round sports events like swimming meets, athletic meets, weight lifting events, cricket matches, baseball and football events and many more such events which encourage tourism. India will be hosting the Common-Wealth Games on 2010 and it is anticipated to give the tourism industry a big boost. Night Life is one of the prime attractions in a holiday. Tourists like to especially visit areas in cities where the night life activity is promoted. These areas are usually lit up with street stalls like flea markets and food areas. Bars, night clubs, casinos and very often open air bands attract and add to the psychological satisfaction and experience of tourists.

Cuisine is very often an understated but highly important part of any holiday. Now-a-days there is cuisine from all areas of the world which is found at most tourist destinations. Specialty restaurants serve Indian, Continental, Chinese, Italian, Japanese, Thai, Indonesian, Fast food, Mexican, Mediterranean, and Arabic and so on. However, tourists usually like to eat the local food of the areas they visit.

BUSINESS

- Conventions
- Conferences

People who travel in relation to their work come under the category of business tourism. However such travel for business purposes is also linked with tourist activity like visiting places of tourist attraction at the destination, sight seeing and excursion trips. Business travel is also related to what is termed today as convention business, which is a rapidly growing industry in hospitality and tourism. A business traveller is important to the tourism industry as it involves the usage of all the components of tourism. He travels because of different business reasons- attending conventions and conferences, meetings, workshops etc. Participants have a lot of leisure time at their disposal.

The conference organisers make this leisure time very rewarding for participants by organising many activities for their pleasure and relaxation. The spouses and families accompanying the participants are also well looked after by the organisers. The organisers plan sight seeing tours and shopping tours for the participants and their families. In India, cooking classes for learning Indian food cooking from the various states, visits to the craft bazaars where tourists see how artisans make clay pots and other handicrafts, they visit tie and dye units to see Indian printing eg. Batik printing etc. Women tourists enjoy henna demonstrations. Conferences are events which require meticulous planning and efficient implementation, co-coordinating various activities so that the right things happen at the right time. There are a number of players in the convention business. On one hand are the customers or the consumers and on the other hand are the principle suppliers like hotels, transporters, convention centres, tour operators and travel agencies, tourism departments, exhibition organisers, sponsors etc.

SYMBIOTIC TOURISM PRODUCTS

Wildlife sanctuary, Marine parks, Aero products and Water sports, Flower festivals are the example of tourism products which are a blending of nature and man. Nature has provided the resource and man has converted them into a tourism product by managing them. National parks for example, are left in their natural state of beauty as far as possible, but still need to be managed, through provision of access, parking facilities, limited accommodation, litter bins etc.

Yet the core attraction is still nature in this category of product. These products are symbiosis of nature and man. In case of adventure sports tourists can be participants. The basic element of adventure is the satisfaction of having complete command over one's body, a sense of risk in the process, an awareness of beauty and the exploration of the unknown. Adventure tourism can be classified into aerial, water based and land based.

Aerial adventure sports include the following activities:

- Parachuting, which involves jumping off from an aircraft or balloon and descending by means of a parachute. The infrastructure required, includes an aircraft, parachutes and large landing zones
- Sky Diving, which involves a sky diver jumping off an aircraft or balloon at a much greater height without deploying his parachute initially and opening it after some interval at a pre determined height.
- Hang Gliding, which involves running off a mountain or being towed by a winch and essentially flying like a glider where the directional control is achieved by a shift in his own weight by the pilot.
- Para Gliding, is the latest aero-sport which has taken the world by storm. A Para Glider is a specially designed square parachute, along with a harness attached by lines.
- Para Sailing is a simple sport that involves towing a parachutist to a height of a few hundred feet in the air and then descending by means of a parachute. As a year round activity, Para sailing can be done on land and water.
- Bungee Jumping, which requires no equipment except a 'bungee cord' made of nylon fibre of enough elasticity to be able to absorb the shock at the end of the jump. The jumper makes a headlong jump into empty space and the resultant rush of adrenalin makes the experience very exhilarating.
- Ballooning, where a balloon is attached to a basket by steel wire ropes. By regulating hot and cold air, the pilot can steer the balloon along any charted course.

Water based adventure sports include the following:

- White water rafting which is one of the most important and exciting water sports, which involves riding down water rapids in an inflatable raft which is used to negotiate fast flowing rivers.
- Canoeing and Kayaking are adventure sports which begin upstream where the water is wild and white. The gradient best suited for canoeing is the stage near the river's entry into the plains where the trip can be combined with a natural holiday in a forest. Kayaking is appealing as it enables innovation on the river by one or two oarsman seated in tandem.
- Adventure sports in the waters of the sea like wind surfing, scuba diving, snorkeling, yachting, water skiing, etc. also offer thrilling activities to the tourists.

Land based adventure tourist products include the following:

- Rock climbing which originated as a means of practicing techniques for ascending high mountains. It was earlier provided as training to mountaineers but has now evolved into a highly developed sport. The climber moves up, using knowledge of rope handling, climbing, securing one to another, etc. Very sophisticated techniques and equipments are used nowadays to ascend or descend on very steep terrain.
- Mountaineering requires trained physical ability and suitable equipment. The higher peaks need better equipment which is also costly. The challenges which mountains like the Indian Himalayas pose attract mountaineers from various countries.
- Trekking the mighty Himalayas which spread across five Indian states form a sweeping arc and compress in its expanse a wide geographical variety and contrasting cultures.
- Skiing is the practice of sliding over snow on runners, called skis, attached to each foot. There are three types of ski resorts, the first are large towns, second type are alpine villages and the third resorts built for skiing.
- Heli skiing is a type of alpine skiing where the skier is dropped to the top of a mountain by a helicopter and then he slides down on his own.
- Motor Rally is a sport that tests the navigational skills of man and his endurance with the machine. Motor rallies, grand prix racing, hill climbing rallies, vintage car rallies, sports car racing, etc. are some forms of this tourism product.
- Safaris were earlier taken on camel, horse and elephants as an excursion for hunting or a journey. As a modern tourist product now safaris are taken on jeeps and in the form of caravans. Viewing and

enjoying nature, meeting the local villagers, seeing their traditions, customs and lifestyle, entertainment and camp fires are some of the characteristics of modern safaris. Eg, Egypt desert safaris. Horse and elephant safaris are arranged in most of the national parks and wildlife sanctuaries.

EVENT BASED TOURISM PRODUCTS

Where an event is an attraction, it as an event based tourist product. Events attract tourists as spectators and also as participants in the events, sometimes for both. The Ocktoberfest organised in Germany, Dubai and Singapore shopping festivals, the camel polo at Jaisalmer, Kite flying in Ahmedabad attracts tourists, both as spectators and participants.

Whereas in case of the Snake Boat race of Kerala can be enjoyed witnessing it. Event attractions are temporary, and are often mounted in order to increase the number of tourists to a particular destination. Some events have a short time scale, such as the Republic Day Parade, others may last for many days, for example Khajuraho Dance Festival or even months like the Kumbh Mela. A destination which may have little to commend it to the tourist can nevertheless succeed in drawing tourists by mounting an event such as an unusual exhibition.

SITE BASED TOURISM PRODUCTS

When an attraction is a place or site then it is called a site based tourist product. Site attractions are permanent by nature, for example Taj Mahal, The Great Wall of China, The Grand Canyon in Arizona, Eiffel Tower, Statue of Liberty, Temples of Khajuraho, etc. A site destination can extend its season by mounting an off season event or festival. A large number of tourists are attracted every year by the great drawing power of Stratford on Avon in England because of its association with Shakespeare, the city of Agra in India with its famous Taj Mahal, Pisa in Italy for its famous Leaning Tower. Some new features have been added to the same product to keep the tourist interest alive in the products. For example now visitors can see Taj by night, music shows have been organised with Taj as the backdrop so that there are repeat tourists.

6

Airport Tourism: Handling and Ticketing Management

AIR TRANSPORTATION IN INDIA

Air transportation in India is under the purview of the Department of Civil Aviation, a part of the India's Ministry of Civil Aviation and Tourism. In 1995 the Indian government owned two airlines and one helicopter service, and private companies owned six airlines. The government-owned airlines dominated India's air transportation in the mid-1990s. Air India is the international carrier; it carried more than 2.2 million passengers in FY 1992. Indian Airlines is the major domestic carrier and also runs international flights to nearby countries.

It carried 9.8 million passengers in FY 1989, when it had a load factor of more than 80 per cent in its fifty-nine airplanes. Analysts, however, attributed this high load factor to a shortage of capacity rather than efficiency of operation. A major expansion was planned for the 1990s, but an airplane crash in 1990 and a pilots' strike in 1991 damaged the airline, which carried only 7.8 million passengers in FY 1992. Two other accidents in 1993, plus several hijackings, put constraints on the growth of both airlines.

A third government-owned airline, Vayudoot, was also a domestic carrier in the early 1990s. It provided feeder service between smaller cities and the larger places served by Air India and Indian Airlines. By 1994 Indian Airlines had taken over Vayudoot. Another publicly owned company, Pawan Hans, runs helicopter service, mostly to offshore locations and other areas that cannot be served by fixed-wing aircraft. In 1995 India's six private airlines accounted for more than 10 per cent of domestic air traffic. Both the number of carriers and their market share are expected to rise in the mid-1990s. The four major private airlines are East West Airlines, Jagsons Airlines, Continental Aviation, and Damania Airways. In addition to the Indian-owned airlines, many foreign airlines provide international service. In 1995 forty-two airlines operated air services to, from, and through India. In the mid-1990s, India had 288 usable airports. Of these, 208 had permanent-surface runways and two had runways of more than 3,659 meters, fifty-nine had runways of between 2,400 and 3,659 meters, and ninety-two had runways between 1,200 and 2,439 meters. There are major international airports at Bombay, Delhi, Calcutta, Madras, and Thiruvananthapuram under the management of the International Airport Authority of India.

International service also operates from Marmagao, Bangalore, and Hyderabad. A consortium of Indian and British companies signed a memorandum of understanding with the state government of Maharashtra in June 1995 to build a new international airport for Bombay, across the harbour from the main city and to be linked by a cross-harbour roadway. Major regional airports are located at Ahmadabad, Allahabad, Pune, Srinagar, Chandigarh, Kochi, and Nagpur.

AVIATION POLICIES IN INDIA

REGULATORY FRAMEWORK

- In the context of a multiplicity of airlines, airport operators and the possibility of oligopolistic practices, there is need for an autonomous regulatory authority which could work as a watchdog, as well as a facilitator for the sector, prescribe and enforce minimum standards for all agencies, settle disputes with regard to abuse of monopoly and ensure level playing field for all agencies. Therefore, a statutory autonomous Civil Aviation Authority will be constituted. The basic objectives of setting up of the Authority will be to ensure aviation safety, security and effective regulation of air transport in the country in the liberalised environment.
- *The functions of the CAA will be as under*:
  - Ensure level playing field for all agencies and
  - Ensure that there are no unfair trade practices and market dominance through encouragement of entry and fostering of competition in accordance with Competition Policy of the Government;
  - Ensure that these agencies and personnel continuously fulfil the standards;
  - Issue license to these agencies and personnel;
  - Regulate tariff;
  - Set the standards for various agencies and personnel of civil aviation sector;
  - Study and analyse the trends in international and domestic civil aviation, project likely future scenario and publish periodical reports.

  - Take appropriate preventive/corrective/punitive action against the agencies and personnel for violations of set standards;
- The agencies include airport, airport-operators, passenger aircraft operators, cargo aircraft operators, helicopters, private aircraft operators, flying clubs, aero-sports clubs, security agency, training institute, air-travel operators or any other agency having role in civil aviation sector.
  - The personnel include pilots, flight engineers, navigators, cabin crew, flight despatchers, aircraft maintenance engineers/ technicians, air traffic controllers and personnel engaged in the maintenance of communication, navigation, surveillance/air traffic management systems and other ground aids.
- A comprehensive Indian Aviation Law will be framed to replace the existing Acts relating to aviation and security which will be in tune with the present day civil aviation scenario, and would also put the proposed CAA in place.
- Civil Aviation Authority will also be required to make available information regarding passenger and cargo traffic including regular analysis in an appropriate consolidated format on a commercial basis.
- Civil Aviation Authority will be required to publish Annual Report on the Air Safety and Security Environment in the country.
- Civil Aviation Authority will conduct safety and security audit including flight inspections of the concerned agencies to ensure that they are meeting the prescribed standards.

PERSONAL SECTOR PARTICIPATION

- Private sector participation will be a major thrust area in the civil aviation sector for promoting investment, improving quality and efficiency and increasing competition.
- Competitive regulatory framework with minimal controls will be created to encourage entry and operation of private airlines/airports.
- Private sector investment in the construction/upgradations/operation of new as well as existing airports including cargo related infrastructure will be encouraged.
- Rationalization of various charges and price of ATF/AVGas will be undertaken to render operation of smaller aircraft viable so as to encourage major investment in feeder and regional air services by the private sector.
- Training Institutes for pilots, flight engineers, maintenance personnel, air-traffic controller, security will be encouraged in private sector.
- Private sector investment in non-aeronautical activities like shopping complex, golf course, entertainment park, aero-sports etc. near

airports will be encouraged to increase revenue, improve viability of airports and to promote tourism. CAA will ensure that this is not at the cost of primary aeronautical functions, and is consistent with the security requirements.

- Government will gradually reduce its equity in PSUs in the sector.
- Government will encourage employee participation through issue of shares and ESOP.

AIRPORT ROAD AND RAIL NETWORK

- The Government will aim at ensuring adequate world class airport infrastructure capacity in accordance with demand, ensuring maximum utilization of available capacities and efficiently managing the airport infrastructure by increasing involvement of private sector.
- Greenfield airport will be permitted by the Government where
  - The existing airport is unable to meet the projected requirement of traffic or
  - A new focal point of traffic emerges with sufficient viability and
  - The new location is normally not within an aerial distance of 150 kilometers of an existing airport
- Encouragement will be given to development/construction in private sector of small airstrips/helipads/heliports, which are smaller and cheaper to construct. These will be particularly suitable in remote hilly or island areas, large business, city centres, factory locations and at other important nodal points. This will also facilitate increase in small aircraft operations
- Private sector participation
  - Private sector will be free to undertake
    a. Construction and operation of new airports/airstrips/helipads/ heliports including cargo complexes, express cargo terminals, cargo satellite cities and cargo handling facilities
    b. Upgradation and operation of existing airports/airstrips/ helipads/heliports in consultation with the existing operator including cargo complexes, Express cargo terminals, cargo satellite cities and cargo handling facilities
  - Foreign equity participation will be permitted up to 74 per cent with automatic approval and 100 per cent with special permission of government
  - Private sector participation will include participation of state government, urban local bodies, private companies, individuals and joint ventures on Build-Own-Operate basis or any other pattern of ownership and management depending on the circumstances.

- Restructuring of major airports of Airports Authority of India will be undertaken through long-term lease to private investors for efficient management, improvement of standards of services/ facilities and attracting private investment
- At privately managed airports, air traffic control and aviation security will continue to be provided by the Airports Authority of India and customs and immigration facilities by respective Government departments.
- The equipment needed for any service would normally be provided by the agency responsible for the service and an equitable system would be established for sharing of revenue between different agencies. Keeping in view their respective investments and responsibilities.

- All airports/airstrips/helipads/heliports used for scheduled air-transport services will be licensed by Civil Aviation Authority.
- Airport/airstrip/heliport/helipad operators will follow ICAO guidelines for levying airport/airstrip/heliport/helipad charges based on cost recovery principle. The CAA would put in a place a regulatory mechanism to prevent abuse of monopolistic nature of such infrastructure.
- An objective and well-defined transparent mechanism for allocation of slots at airports will be ensued at all times.
- CAA will ensure fair play between different airport/airstrip/heliport/ helipad operators and user agencies so that no airport/airstrip/heliport/ helipad operator is accused of discriminating against any particular airline or any other user. Similarly, Government will ensure that no airport-operator is discriminated against with regard to allotment as point of call, if there is demand for air services from such airport.
- More international gateways shall be provided. It would be ensured that there is at least one international airport in every region of the country in order to give a boost to trade and tourism and adequate capacity in all the routes.
- Major thrust will be given for increasing the share of commercial revenue from non-aeronautical sources by giving total freedom to airport/airstrip/ heliport/helipad operators in the matter of raising non-aeronautical revenue
- New Ground Handling regulations with following broad particulars envisage:
  - At airports managed by AAI, new private investors have been allowed by AAI to undertake ground handling besides national carriers and self-handling by carriers which will increase competition resulting in improvement in services and reduction in costs.

  - At private airports, at least limited competition will be mandatory.
- A rationalized dynamic system for airport charges for AAI airports will be introduced for
  - Optimum utilization of airport by using peak and off-peak time charges,
  - Increasing revenue of airport operators
  - Promoting airports in far-flung regions by having varying airport charges from airport to airport depending upon the facilities available at the airport.
  - Promoting use of small aircraft
- A new Directorate of Lands shall be established in AAI and land use guidelines will be formulated for utilizing vacant land.
  - Vacant land at airports will be evaluated for construction of aviation related activities.
  - For optimal exploitation of airport land for civil aviation purposes, private-sector/State Government participation would be welcome.
  - Land at such airports where there is no likelihood of future use for civil aviation purposes will be utilized for other commercial purposes like gold courses, tennis, etc. either by AAI itself or in joint venture.
  - Effective steps will be taken for removing encroachments from AAI land and if necessary, comprehensive rehabilitation package will be formulated.
- Cargo handling
  - Infrastructure like satellite freight cities with multi-modal transport, cargo terminals, cold storage centres, automatic storage and retrieval systems, mechanized transport of cargo, dedicated express cargo terminals with airside and city side openings, computerization and automation etc. will be set up on priority basis.
  - Private sector participation in cargo handling will be encouraged.
  - Efficient Electronic Data Interchange systems will be developed and linked amongst all stakeholders in the trade.
  - Air cargo complexes and dedicated express cargo terminals will be integral part of all major airports.
- Operation of airports would be in accordance with the provisions relating to prevention of air, water and noise pollution.
- Guidelines for naming of airports will be formulated to ensure that the airports are named after the cities they are situated in as per international norms.
- Air Traffic services
  - Air Traffic controllers will be licensed by CAA.

- AAI will continue to provide Air Traffic Services over the Indian air Space as per standards set by CAA in accordance with ICAO norms.
- Approach and aerodrome control services may be provided by licensed ATCs engaged by the airport operators
- New satellite based CNS/ATM systems will be introduced as per ICAO's Regional Plan
- India to have a significant say in the provision of new satellite based CNS/ATM services in Asia- pacific/SAARC regional airspace
- Fresh Air traffic Services and Controlling procedures will be evolved for helicopters and small aircraft to exploit their inherent advantages and to reduce the cost of their operations and efficient use of airspace without compromising safety. This will also give boost to Flying Clubs.
- Efforts will be made for Civil-Military co-ordination for
  a. Greater sharing of civil and military airspace for unidirectional air-corridors and straightening of air-routes to save fuel and time,
  b. Uniform air-traffic procedures,
  c. Additional slots for civilian flights at military airports,
  d. Sharing of revenues at civil enclaves

DOMESTIC PASSENGER AND CARGO AIR TRANSPORT

- ATF will be taken out from administered price mechanism for petroleum prices. The price of ATF for domestic airline will, therefore, be governed by market and customs duty. Airlines will also be permitted import of ATF.
- Capacity induction will be regulated with a view to ensuring safety, security and preventing unhealthy levels of capacity.
- Flying clubs, Aerosports like hang-gliding, ballooning, heli-skiing, para-jumping etc. will be promoted by encouraging private investment and formulating liberalized guidelines in consultation with users. This will include rationalized Avgas prices and liberalized air space control.
- Foreign equity up to 25 per cent and Non-Resident Indian investment up to 100 per cent will be permitted for domestic passenger transport services. However, participation from foreign airlines either directly or indirectly will not be permitted. Substantive ownership and effective control by Indians will be a pre-requisite.
- Government and CAA will ensure that there is no discrimination between different passenger and cargo air-operators.
- Helicopter operations will be given a new boost by a total change in

outlook. At present, fixed wing norms with minor changes are broadly applied to rotary wing aircraft. Fresh guidelines will be formulated in consultation with user industry from the point of view of rotary wing aircraft. Fresh Air Traffic Services and controlling procedures, which exploit the inherent advantages of helicopter without compromising safety, will be evolved. This will also reduce the cost of operations of helicopters and efficient use of airspace. Encouragement will be given to use of helicopters in the areas of heli-tourism, adventure sports, mountaineering/trekking, point-to-point heli-services to bypass traffic congestion on the road, connecting remote areas and islands in Northeast, Andaman and Nicobar and Lakshdweep, religious places, sky crane for construction/laying of transmission lines etc.

- It is necessary that both airline operations as well as airport infrastructure be treated as mutually dependent and complementary and given similar concessions to promote a balanced growth of the sector. Therefore, airline operations and acquisition of aircraft should be given the status of "infrastructure ".
- Permission to start scheduled passenger and cargo air transport service would be given by government on demonstration of competency, minimum capital requirement and viability of the company to provide a safe and reliable service. CAA may also fix a minimum number of aircraft for scheduled operators permit.
- Private sector participation in providing domestic passengers and cargo air transport services will be encouraged.
- Special consideration will also be given to Private operators and Corporate operators by way of rationalized Avgas prices, encouragement for construction of smaller airstrips/helipad et. in private sector.
- The government will encourage provision of safe passenger and cargo air transport services to every region of the country at economic prices.
- There will be freedom to operate non-revenue and passenger charter and cargo flights to any foreign destinations. Indian passport holders will also be allowed to travel on these flights.
- Wet leasing of foreign registered aircraft by operators will be permitted only in special circumstances like grounding of aircraft, augmentation of capacity for short term, to meet the capacity requirements for handling natural calamities, etc.

PROMOTION OF COMMON AVIATION AND PETITE AIRCRAFT OPERATION

- Single engine aircraft of seating capacity upto 10 seats can be permitted for passenger charter and cargo flights. Such operations shall be in accordance with the single engine operation guidelines and over land areas having no hilly terrain or other obstructions.

- There is a need to change the traditional concept of airport development, ownership and operations in view of the economics of small aircraft/charters operations. Participation of state Government, urban local bodies, airline/aircraft operators, other private investors will be encouraged in development, upgradation and management of small airports/airstrips. These airports will be distinct from traditional airport and will be bare-bone type with no frills. Such airports need not be mandatorily manned and onus of ensuring security and safety of operations will rest on the aircraft operator in conjunction with the local administration/bodies, etc. This will encourage the operation of small aircraft/air taxis, as operators themselves or in collaboration with State Government/Urban local bodies/residents of a specific locality, factory, nearby factories, tourist operators will be able to manage such airports/airstrip flexibly and efficiency at reduced cost. This will boost passenger transport and tourism
- There is need to open up the country and tap the latent demand for air services in many parts of the country currently not on the air map. However, the traffic profile in these areas does not permit viable operations of jet. Even smaller aircraft operations are not viable because of the high cost of operation and high break-even factor.
- Therefore, Aviation Turbine Fuel for turbo prop aircraft operations will be provided at par with price for international air services, with a cap of 4 per cent on sales tax. Operation of smaller aircraft/charters will be further encouraged through rationalization of airport charges, Inland Air Travel Tax and Avgas prices. For the North-East region, IATT has been fully exempted on all routes. Government will consider extending similar facilities to other category II areas.
- While Route-Dispersal Guidelines do help in providing air services in the remote and inaccessible areas, further measures are required to encourage widespread air-connectivity. Passenger and cargo air transport services to many regions will not be possible unless operation of small aircraft is made economically viable either on stand alone basis or in conjunction with major trunk routes.

WORLDWIDE AIR TRANSPORT

- Air India and Indian Airlines would be guaranteed the use of traffic rights actually being utilised by them for five years following privatisation.
- Efforts will be made by national carriers to join global alliances in their own commercial interest and in the interest of travelling

passengers through code-sharing, exchange of frequent- flier programmes etc.

- Government will also establish, in the long run, an objective and well-defined mechanism for sharing of international traffic rights amongst all airlines in a transparent manner.
- Government will ensure that there will be no discrimination between different airport operators in allotting capacity to foreign carriers as per bilateral agreements if demand exists.
- Government will ensure that traffic rights are utilized to the maximum extent possible through direct operations, creation of virtual equipment by way of joint flights, code sharing arrangements etc. by the two national carriers *i.e.* Air India and Indian Airlines. Other domestic carriers who fulfill the minimum criteria for designation as Indian carrier to operate international passenger flights will also be permitted to meet this objective. Initially, they may be permitted to fly to neighbouring countries against unutilised rights subject to right of first refusal by national carriers. The requirement of substantial ownership and effective control of the airlines by Indians would continue to be operative.
- Liberal bilateral rights will be given for promoting international operations to less developed regions of the country as well as to ill-connected far away countries to promote trade and tourism in those regions.
- The Government will aim at ensuring adequate capacity to fully meet the requirement of international trade and tourism.
- There will be freedom to international tourist Charter operation to different custom airports.
- There will be no restriction on international cargo flights. However, they will not be allowed to carry domestic cargo on their flights within the country.
- Tourist charters from domestic airports to foreign destinations will also be permitted subject to safeguards for scheduled operations.

TOURISM AND TRADE PROMOTION

- Tourism and trade sectors are closely linked to civil aviation sector. Therefore it is important that airport infrastructure and air services are planned keeping in view the requirement and promotion of these sectors. Multi-modal approach will be used for planning to ensure better connectivity.
- A thrust for international tourism in India will be given by
  - Providing freedom to International Tourist Charters to all airports linking places of tourist interest

  - Declaring additional airports as international airports resulting in easy connectivity and better services,
  - Upgradation of airports at places of Tourist interest like Buddhist circuit, sanctuaries, beach resorts etc.
  - Encouraging private sector participation in building tourist infrastructure near airports like transport services from airports to nearby cities, golf courses, amusement park, business centres, duty free shopping complexes of international class, aviation recreation activities, adventure aviation, hang-gliding, microlight aircraft, parachuting etc
  - Efforts will be made to issue visa on arrival at the airport in larger number of cases.
  - Improvement in passenger facilitation and sensitisation of personnel of immigration, customs, security and AAI at airport to make them more courteous and passenger friendly.
- For promotion to trade and industries, following steps will be undertaken:
  - Abolition of On-Board Courier Scheme to facilitate courier trade
  - Introduction of "Known Shipper "scheme for reducing dwell time in exports by doing away with "cooling off" requirement
  - Introduction of Electronic Data Interchange interlinking trade agencies, customs, immigration for faster efficient trade transactions
  - Private sector participation in cargo handling for increasing competition and improved services.

AIRLINE TICKET

An airline ticket is a document, issued by an airline or a travel agency, to confirm that an individual has purchased a seat on a flight on an aircraft. This document is then used to obtain a boarding pass, at the airport. Then with the boarding pass and the attached ticket, the passenger is allowed to board the aircraft. There are two sorts of airline tickets - the older style with coupons now referred to as a paper ticket, and the now more common electronic ticket usually referred to as an e-ticket.

Regardless of the type, all tickets contain details of the following information:

- The passenger's name.
- The issuing airline.
- A ticket number, including the airline's 3 digit code at the start of the number.
- The cities the ticket is valid for travel between.
- Flights that the ticket is valid for. (Unless the ticket is "open")
- Baggage allowance.

- Taxes. (It is normally a legal requirement to show taxes, even if the fare is not shown).
- The "Fare Basis", an alpha-numeric code that identifies the fare.
- Restrictions on changes and refunds. (Not always shown in detail, but referred to).
- Dates that the ticket is valid for.
- "Form of payment" ie, details of how the ticket was paid for, which will in turn affect how it would be refunded.

It is now common for a traveller to pay a fee, assessed by the airline company, for a paper ticket. In fact, many airlines no longer issue paper tickets. IATA has announced, that as of June 1, 2008, IATA-member airlines will no longer issue any paper tickets. A ticket is generally only good on the airline for which it was purchased.

However, an airline can endorse the ticket, so that it may be accepted by other airlines, sometimes on standby basis or with a confirmed seat. Usually the ticket is for a specific flight. It is also possible to purchase an 'open' ticket, which allows travel on any flight between the destinations listed on the ticket. The cost for doing this is greater than a ticket for a specific flight. Some tickets are refundable. However, the lower cost tickets are usually not refundable and may carry many additional restrictions. A ticket is made up of one or more flight coupons. In the old paper ticket system, these flight coupons were the actual tickets that were used for travel. One flight coupon was used for each leg of the flight. The carrier is represented by a standardized 2-letter code. Thai Airways is TG. The departure and destination cities are represented by International Air Transport Association airport codes. Munich is MUC and Bangkok is BKK. The International Air Transport Association is the standard setting organization. Only one person can use a ticket.

If multiple people are traveling together, the tickets are linked together by the same record locator or reservation number, which are assigned, if the tickets were purchased at the same time. If not, most airlines can connect the tickets together in their reservation systems.

This allows all members in a party to be processed in a group, allowing seat assignments to be together (if available at the time of the assignment) When paper tickets were still frequently used, a practice existed by travellers to get rid of their tickets (which are person-specific), when they decided to alter the course of their trips. This practice consisted of selling the ticket to other travellers (often at discount prices), after which the seller accompanied the buyer at the time of departure to the airport.

Here, the original owner checked in under his name and provided the airline with the buyer's baggage. After this, the buyer boarded the airplane at the moment of departure. However, since most airlines check identification on boarding, this procedure is rarely functional.

AIRLINE TIMETABLE

Airline timetables are booklets that many airlines worldwide use to inform passengers of several different things, such as schedules, fleet, security, in-flight entertainment, food menu, restriction and phone contact information. Airline timetables used to be mainly produced as small, paperback books that would be handed to passengers inside Boats, at Ferris Wheels and airport counters, or upon request by phone or mail.

On January 16, 1928, Pan Am published one of their first books. It read The air-way to Havana, Pan American Airways, Pershing Square Building, New York. Airline timetable books are famous for their diversity: Many had colourful covers, such as the ones produced by many Latin American airlines. Others, such as Scenic Airlines' timetables, consisted only of one sheet of paper, with their hub's flight time information on the front, and the return times on the back. After the September 11, 2001 bombings, most airlines worldwide have stopped production of timetable books, in order to cut costs and reduce the delay between a change of schedule and a new timetable being in the hands of the public.

As a consequence, most airlines now post their timetables only online (the larger airlines often offering a stand-alone application, while others provide just a downloadable document such as a PDF), and the value of many airline timetable books has risen among collectors.

BEREAVEMENT FLIGHT

A bereavement flight is an airline ticket purchased when a close relative has died or is dying. Bereavement fares are offered by many airlines. While a bereavement flight may have flexible rules, it may be at either a reduced or a higher cost to the consumer, depending on the airline.

While airlines often charge much more for a flight that is booked less than 7 days beforehand than one that is booked farther in advance, customers may be able to obtain a bereavement fare in such last-minute flights that is comparable to that of a regular fare purchased far in advance.

In recent years, many airlines have been cutting back on bereavement fares or changing fare structures to accommodate them in other ways. In 2004, U.S. Congress approved language that required airlines to offer bereavement fares.

POLICIES OF VARIOUS AIRLINES

Airlines have varying policies pertaining to bereavement flights. This may include the relatives for which one is eligible to obtain such a ticket, the proof that is required, and the price that is charged in comparison with other fares.

The most common discount is 50 per cent off the original fare:

- United Airlines offers bereavement fares of 10 per cent off the ticket price in the event of the death or grave illness of a family member or for individuals seeking medical treatment for tickets sold within six days of travel.

- Continental Airlines offers varying percentages off fares of different prices, and allows such bookings to be made on its web site.
- Delta Airlines allows discounts for death or imminent death for those who call in advance for reservations.
- Air Canada offers bereavement fares within 7 days of a funeral and for stays of up to 30 days with a copy of a death certificate, a letter from a funeral director, or a certificate from an attending physician. The airline will also refund the difference between the regular and the bereavement fare if one is these is presented after travel.
- AirTran, JetBlue, Southwest, and Virgin America do not offer bereavement fares, but have more flexible options for changing and canceling tickets.

OTHER ISSUES

Various other issues have been applied to bereavement flights. One concerns which family members to whom the fare can be applied. Some airlines offer the fares only for immediate family members. Others offer it to a longer list, including foster relatives, half relatives, and step relatives.

Other airlines have taken up the issue over whether those involved in domestic partnerships that are not legal marriages, and those involved in gay and lesbian relationships can be included. It has also been questioned as to whether the bereavement fares are really the best on the market.

OTHER WAYS AROUND BEREAVEMENT FARES

For frequent travellers anticipating a potential family emergency, it may be wise to accumulate a certain balance of frequent flyer miles with an airline. For example, if a person in the US is aware of a potential death in the family in Shanghai, the traveller can save up some miles to redeem a last minute trip with their miles instead of paying bereavement fares. Most carriers offer mileage award tickets with last seat availability (usually at 2x the usual cost), which can still be a great value financially.

BOARDING PASS

A boarding pass is a document provided by an airline during check-in, giving a passenger the authority to board an aircraft. As a minimum, it identifies the passenger, the flight number, and the date and scheduled time for departure. In some cases, flyers can check in "on-line" and print the boarding passes themselves. Generally a passenger with an electronic ticket will only need a boarding pass. If a passenger has a paper airline ticket, that ticket (or flight coupon) may be required to be attached to the boarding pass for him or her to board the aircraft.

The paper boarding pass (and ticket, if any), or portions, are sometimes collected and counted for cross-check of passenger counts by gate agents, but more frequently are scanned (via barcode or magnetic stripe). The standards for bar codes and magnetic stripes on boarding passes are published by IATA.

The bar code standard (BCBP) defines the 2D bar code printed on paper boarding passes or sent to mobile phones for electronic boarding passes. The magnetic stripe standard (ATB2) will expire in 2010. For "connecting flights" there will be a boarding pass needed for each new flight (distinguished by a different flight number) regardless of whether a different aircraft is boarded.

Most airports and airlines have automatic readers that will verify the validity of the boarding pass at the jetway door or boarding gate. This also automatically updates the airline's database that shows the passenger has boarded and the seat is used, and that the checked baggage for that passenger may stay aboard.

This speeds up the paperwork process at the gate, but requires passengers with paper tickets to check in, surrender the ticket and receive the digitized boarding pass. Many airlines have moved to issuing electronic boarding passes, whereby the passenger checks in either online or on a mobile device, and the boarding pass is then sent to the mobile device as a SMS or e-mail; airlines that issue electronic boarding passes include United Airlines, AirAsia (The first airline to introduce SMS boarding passes), Singapore Airlines, Air Canada, WestJet (the first in North America to do so), Cathay Pacific Airways, Delta Airlines, JetBlue Airways, American Airlines, Lufthansa, Scandinavian Airlines, Jetstar Airways, Iberia and KLM (selected destinations only).

CODESHARE AGREEMENT

A codeshare agreement, sometimes simply codeshare, is an aviation business arrangement where two airlines share the same flight. A seat can be purchased on one airline but is actually operated by a cooperating airline under a different flight number or code. The term "code" refers to the identifier used in flight schedule, generally the 2-character IATA airline designator code and flight number. Thus, XX123, flight 123 operated by the airline XX, might also be sold by airline YY as YY456 and by ZZ as ZZ9876. It allows greater access to cities through a given airline's network without having to offer extra flights, and makes connections simpler by allowing single bookings across multiple planes. Most major airlines today have code sharing partnerships with other airlines and code sharing is a key feature of the major airline alliances. Under a code sharing agreement, the airline that actually operates the flight (the one providing the plane, the crew and the ground handling services) is called the operating carrier.

The company or companies that sell tickets for that flight but do not actually operate it are called marketing carriers or validating carriers. In 1967, Richard

A. Henson joined with US Airways predecessor, Allegheny Airlines, in the nation's first codeshare relationship. The term "code sharing" or "codeshare" was coined in 1989 by Qantas Airways and American Airlines (Financial Review—November 21, 1989), and 1990 the two firms provided their first codeshare flights between an array of U.S. domestic cities and Australian cities. Code sharing has become widespread in the airline industry since that time, particularly in the wake of the formation of large airline 'alliances.'

These alliances have extensive codesharing and networked frequent flyer programmes. Under a code sharing agreement, participating airlines can present a common flight number for several reasons, including:

For passengers:

- *Connecting flights*: This provides clearer routing for the customer, allowing a customer to book travel from point A to C through point B under one carrier's code, instead of a customer booking from point A to B under one code, and from point B to C under another code. This is not only a superficial addition as cooperating airlines also strive to synchronize their schedules and coordinate luggage handling, which makes transfers between connecting flights less time-consuming.
- *Shared responsibility between the carriers*: When flying between two cities without a single-airline connection, the passenger can pick a codeshared flight over two airlines or two flights booked separately. If the flights are not codeshared, then the second airline has no responsibility if the passenger or luggage misses the second flight due to a delay with the first. Under a codeshared flight, the second airline is unlikely to charge extra fees or deny boarding should the first, cooperating airline cause a delay.

For airlines:

- *Flights from both airlines that fly the same route*: This provides an apparent increase in the frequency of service on the route by one airline
- *Perceived service to unserved markets*: This provides a method for carriers who do not operate their own aircraft on a given route to gain exposure in the market through display of their flight numbers.
- When an airline sacrifices its capacity to other airlines as a code share partner, its operational cost will generally be reduced to nil.

In Global Distribution Systems, such as Amadeus, Galileo, Worldspan, or Sabre, this results in the same flight details, except for the flight number, being excessively displayed on computer screens, forcing other airlines flights to be displayed on following where they may be missed by passengers searching for required flights. Much competition in the airline industry revolves around ticket sales (also known as "seat booking") strategies (revenue management, variable pricing, and geo-marketing). Most passengers and travel agents have a preference for flights that provide a direct connection.

Code sharing achieves this. Computer reservations systems (CRS) also often do not discriminate between direct flights and code sharing flights and present both before options that involve several isolated stretches run by different companies. Criticism has been levelled against code sharing by consumer organizations and national departments of trade since it is claimed it is confusing and not transparent to passengers. There are also code sharing agreements between airlines and rail lines also known as Rail and Fly systems. They involve some integration of both types of transport, *e.g.*, in finding out the fastest connection, allowing exchange between an air ticket and a train ticket, or a step further, the air ticket being valid on the train, etc.

In Europe these Rail and Fly systems are used to divide markets by selling these combination tickets abroad for a lower price to attract more customers. The systems also prevent local customers from buying these much cheaper tickets as the customer is only allowed to board the plane with a valid train stamp from a station outside the country.

CONTINENT PASS

A continent pass (usually called something like Europe (air)pass, Pacific (air)pass or American (air)pass) is a product and service of an airline alliance. For a relatively low price the traveller can travel freely using all (intra)continental flights the airline alliance offers on that continent. There are restrictions on the number of miles and/or the number of flights as well as the number of stops the traveller can make. Travellers can benefit from the extensive networks airline alliances offer and can be rewarded for each mile they fly by participating in the alliance's frequent flyer programme.

ELECTRONIC TICKET

An electronic ticket or e-ticket is used to represent the purchase of a seat on a passenger airline, usually through a web site or by telephone, or sometimes through airline ticket offices or travel agencies. This form of airline ticket rapidly replaced the older multi-layered paper tickets (from close to zero to 100 per cent in about 10 years) and became mandatory for IATA members as from June 1, 2008. During the last few years, where paper tickets were still available, airlines frequently charged extra for issuing them.

E-tickets are also available for some entertainment venues. Once a reservation is made, an e-ticket exists only as a digital record in the airline computers. Customers usually print out a copy of their receipt which contains the record locator or reservation number and the e-ticket number. The critical acclaim, Joel R. Goheen is recognized as the Inventor of Electronic Ticketing in the Airline Industry, an industry where global electronic ticket sales (the industry standard) accounts for over US$400 billion a year (2007). Electronic tickets have been introduced in road, urban or rail public transport as well.

CHECKING IN WITH AN E-TICKET

To check in with an e-ticket, the passenger usually goes to the check-in counter and presents the e-ticket itinerary receipt which contains a confirmation or reservation code. In some airports and airlines it is not even necessary to present this document or quote the confirmation code or e-ticket number as the reservation is confirmed solely on the basis of the passenger's identity, which may be proven by a passport or the matching credit card.

The rest of the check-in process remains the same as when paper tickets were the norm, that is, the passenger checks-in his/her luggage. The e-ticket is not a substitute for the boarding pass which must still be issued at the end of the check-in process.

SELF-SERVICE AND REMOTE CHECK-IN

E-tickets are very popular because they allow extra services like:

- Online access to a passenger's reservation which makes amendments to flight plans (such as change of flight date and refunds) possible (subject to ticket restrictions)
- Online/telephone/self-service kiosk check-in (if the airline makes this option available)
- Early check-in
- Printing boarding passes at airport kiosks and at locations other than an airport

It is also possible to have many copies of an e-ticket, hence the "loss" of an airline ticket becomes impossible. Several web sites exist to help people holding e-tickets accomplish online check-ins in advance of the twenty-four-hour airline restriction. These sites store a passenger's flight information and then when the airline opens up for online check-in the data is transferred to the airline and the boarding pass is e-mailed back to the customer.

E-TICKET LIMITATIONS

E-tickets are sometimes not available for some flights from an airline which usually offers them. This can be due to a number of reasons, the most common being software incompatibility. If an airline issues tickets for a codeshare flight with another company, and there is no e-ticket interlining agreement, the operating carrier would not be able to see the issuing carrier's ticket. Therefore, the carrier that books the flight needs to provide hard copy versions of the tickets so that the ticket can be processed. Similarly, if the destination airport does not have access to the airline who booked the flight, a paper ticket needs to be issued. Currently the ticketing systems of most airlines are only able to produce e-tickets for itineraries of no more than 16 segments, including surface segments.

IATA MANDATED TRANSITION

As part of the IATA Simplifying the Business initiative, the association instituted a programme to switch the industry to 100 per cent electronic ticketing. The programme concluded on June 1, 2008, with the association saying that the resulting industry savings were approximately US$3 billion. In 2004, IATA Board of Governors set the end of 2007 as the deadline for airlines to make the transition to 100 per cent electronic ticketing for tickets processed through the IATA billing and settlement plan; in June 2007, the deadline was extended to May 31, 2008.

As of June 1, 2008 paper tickets can no longer be issued on neutral stock by agencies reporting to their local BSP. Agents reporting to the ARC using company-provided stock or issuing tickets on behalf of an airline (GSAs and ticketing offices) are not subject to that restriction. The industry was unable to comply with the IATA mandate and paper tickets remain in circulation as of February 2009.

FLIGHT CANCELLATION

Flight cancellation occurs when an airline cancels a scheduled flight for a certain reason. When flights are canceled, passengers may be entitled to compensation due to rules obeyed by every flight company, usually Rule 240, or Rule 218 in certain locations. This rule usually specifies that passengers may be entitled to certain reimbursements, including a free room if the next flight is the day after the canceled one, a choice of reimbursement, rerouting, phone calls, and refreshments.

TRACKING TRANSACTION

An advanced computer-based electronic security management system is instrumental in making the Mirage Resort Hotel a progressive facility. Security has assumed an increasingly important role in the hotel business. The larger the facility and the more diverse the features, services, and amenities, the more demanding the need for comprehensive security management.

Nowhere is this more evident than at a 100-acre entertainment complex like the Mirage Resort Hotel in Las Vegas, where security concerns are heightened by the cash-intensive casino operation. The creation of a fully integrated security environment at the Mirage represents an exciting new dimension in security management.

Opened in 1989, the desert resort is among the most progressive facilities of its type. The Mirage has three 30-story towers and more than 3,000 rooms, including suites, villas, and bungalows with private pools. Two ballrooms, at 20,000- and 40,000-square feet, are available for special events, and meeting rooms can handle groups up to 5,000 people. The complex includes waterfalls, an erupting volcano, a tropical plant atrium, and an artificial coral reef aquarium with sharks and tropical fish. Also available for the enjoyment of guests and visitors are natural animal habitats: one for a pair of rare Royal White tigers, the other for six Atlantic Bottlenose dolphins.

An array of entertainment, recreational, and shopping opportunities are featured, including a 1,500-seat theater and around-the-clock casino operations. Guests can find restaurants, health and fitness centres, interconnected lagoon-shaped swimming pools, boutiques, and lounges. Special events such as prize fights and boat and auto shows compound the importance of security.

Security control in a gaming resort as large and complex as the Mirage is a demanding and never-ending challenge. Sophisticated security controls are in force in the casino, where millions of dollars are transacted every hour in games, including slot machines, video poker, keno, craps, blackjack, baccarat, and poker.

Strict compliance with gaming laws and established casino procedures is controlled by close supervision, surveillance, and carefully monitored audits. An advanced computer-based electronic security management system, the Polaroid ID-2000 Plus, plays a central role in supporting the Mirage's integrated security environment. The system has proven to be a formidable management tool. Designed for expansion, the modular system is a core component in the recording and payroll programme.

The system combines advanced data base, computer, and electronic imaging technologies. It provides, for example, a streamlined ID card and badge production capability and a responsive, economical way to manage employee-related security information.

The system also serves as an auditing aid to track activities, such as the number of meals served to employees in the cafeteria each day. Swipe readers at cash registers in the cafeteria make the process fast and efficient.

Specific information about the resort's 7,000 employees is input, stored, and retrieved by the digital electronic security management system. It captures image data, including colour portraits and signatures; generates photo ID cards and management reports; and communicates with other data bases. Report-generating capabilities simplify the tracking of ID cards that have been issued for active and former employees. The system also facilitates the monitoring of staff levels.

The electronic production and data base system is connected to a file server in the computer centre. Several sites are now on-line by means of a local area network using standard Ethernet connections and Novell network software. Additional terminals or systems can be added for expansion. One of the locations integrated by the LAN is the ID card and badge production centre in the human resources department. New employees are processed and badged at this location; other areas on the network use the system to validate employee security information.

Verification terminals are installed in the security and finance departments, casino surveillance, and the casino cash cage. Authorized individuals can validate, on-screen, employee photos, signatures, and related data. Although verification information is easily obtained by entering an employee number, access to the complete data base is limited to supervisory personnel.

Information available for access includes the employee's full name, signature sample, colour portrait, ID number, job title, work location, and date of hire or termination. The individual's affiliation as a Mirage employee or corporate employee is shown. Powering the system is a high-speed 386 CPU using special workstation software, which incorporates password authorization and an internal audit trail to prevent system abuse.

Using an optional 180 megabyte magnetic disk, the Mirage system can store approximately 14,000 full-colour portraits or 11,500 portraits and signatures. Optional storage modules, including larger capacity magnetic disk drives and optical disk drives, are available.

Active files, including signatures, colour portraits, and related textual information, are safely stored in digital format on the hard disk. Safety backups of the complete system are made on magnetic tape by the computer centre at least three times a week. If an employee is terminated or quits, the photo and signature files are deleted to save storage space. Text files, however, are stored indefinitely.

Information systems helped define the requirements and objectives of the departments involved. The system has improved productivity on several operating levels. Working closely with Polaroid engineers, information systems developed a maintenance strategy with flexible service levels and contingency provisions for priority service in designated areas. If emergency maintenance service is required, downtime in critical operations will be minimized.

Producing more than 6,000 ID CARDS a year could be an expensive, time-consuming operation. For the Mirage's human resources department, however, it is merely routine. Human resources is responsible for processing new employees, issuing new ID cards and badges, replacing damaged or lost badges, and responding to the continuing need for special events badges. To handle the challenges of ID card production the company relies on the production speed and efficiency of the computer-based security management system.

"Compared to the marathon effort involved in producing new ID cards when the Mirage first opened," reflects Monalee Stockner, human resources supervisor, "normal day-to-day activities are calm." ID cards were produced for more than 7,000 employees by the human resources team, with assistance from several temporary employees and a few of the management system devices on loan from Polaroid.

Employee processing and imaging activities were completed during a five-day whirlwind operation involving 10- to 12-hour shifts. Cards were assembled at night. According to Stockner, "Without the speed and automated features of the computerized production system, the job could not have been done as quickly, economically, or efficiently."

The electronic production workstation includes an operator console consisting of a colour video camera, electronic flash lighting, portrait and text monitors, keyboard, and a signature capture device. A colour film recorder, film cutter, laminator, and print development timers are included in the output unit. Information acquisition for an ID card, including text entries and video imaging of the subject's portrait and signature, takes less than five minutes per person. The badge is given to the employee the same day. Temporary special event IDs are produced for employees assigned to such activities as large parties, banquets, conventions, and prize fights. Since the Mirage was opened, more than 50,000 employee ID cards have been produced.

An operator can enter employee information and capture, digitally store, and retrieve high-fidelity colour portraits and signatures or access data from existing computer data bases. A freeze-frame feature allows the operator to preview and freeze the subject's video portrait before the card is made. A built-in signature capture camera stores signatures from a signed signature card.

At the touch of a button the system electronically merges the digitized video portrait, signature, text, and multicolour Mirage logo contained in the software package. Information entered is contained on a new-hire document prepared by the employee's department. It includes pertinent information about the employee, his or her job title, and where he or she works.

ID cards can be produced in many of visual formats. More than a dozen variations are used by the Mirage to distinguish between different personnel classifications and affiliations. These include Mirage employees, corporate staff, and contractors. Special formats have also been developed for restricted areas or for temporary use at special events. Although the electronic security management system can automatically assign sequential employee numbers, human resources prefers to control this function.

In this way, blocks of numbers can be reserved for special applications in the system. When the employee number is entered, a bar code representing the number is automatically generated and printed on an adhesive-back label by a printer. Inexpensive, hard-copy, black-and-white thermal reference images can also be produced in seconds by a printer at the production station.

With a single keystroke, electronically assembled images for two separate employee badges are exposed on a sheet of instant colour print film. Development takes about a minute. Prints are then die-cut and inserted into a special laminate sandwich with a printed insert containing card use guidelines and the bar code label. The envelope is then permanently sealed. The finished card is attractive, durable, and virtually tamperproof. After lamination the bar code is verified with a test device, which displays the employee number.

REMOTELY LOCATED VERICATION

Terminals integrated through the LAN facilitate employee recognition, signature validation, and confirmation of employment status. In addition to the information verification capabilities of the production workstation, data verification terminals on the network provide valuable information for security and management-related functions.

Security staff. Responsible for the safety of patrons and protection of the Mirage's physical assets, the security staff also plays an active role in maintaining guest relations and providing emergency services. The 275-person security staff, larger than the police departments of many small cities, operates around the clock.

Security's responsibilities include controlling access in restricted areas, knowing the location of employees in emergencies, and monitoring property removal. "The ability to access an employee's security records in seconds, to determine where they can be located, saves valuable time in an emergency," says Jennifer Keeney, security coordinator.

"We can locate an employee quickly, for example, should there be an emergency at home, without having to make lots of phone calls and be faced with unnecessary delays. We can see what the person looks like and even get fast thermal prints to help our staff recognize the person. In emergencies, visual recognition is extremely important, especially with a workforce involving thousands of people." Photo ID badges need not be worn in most areas. Employees can carry the ID card in a wallet or purse. In instances where individuals are not recognized by security personnel at employee entrances or in restricted areas, they will be asked to show their ID card.

ID information for new hires or terminated employees is available at all verification terminals on a same-day basis. In yet another important function, the ability to compare signatures with samples stored in the security management system's digital memory has streamlined the Mirage's property removal procedures. Because signatures of people authorized to approve property passes can be easily validated, it is now easier to control the removal of property. Thermal prints of authorized signatures for property removal forms are kept on file and current at various security stations.

Casino surveillance. Rapid information verification is critical for the casino surveillance group. Operating around the clock, 365 days a year, a team of trained observers keeps a watchful eye on cash transactions, operational procedures, and dealer interactions with patrons. Patricia Cipolla, director of surveillance, is emphatic about the importance of security control. "Our job," she states, "is to protect the Mirage's assets and its patrons. We watch the money and the way the games are run. Any deviation in established procedures signals that something may be wrong."

Ceiling-mounted video cameras can record the activities at any game in the casino. Videotapes of randomly selected games or those being monitored are available for review on video monitors located in the surveillance area. Should a transaction involving markers, redemption slips, bills, and credits, or a dealer's performance deviate from established guidelines, information about the dealer can be accessed instantly.

Since the videotape can be seen in normal or close-up modes, surveillance specialists start the process by zooming in on the dealer's name badge. By entering the name at the verification terminal, employee information is instantly displayed, including a colour portrait and signature sample.

If irregularities are observed, other than what appears to be an honest mistake, the surveillance team may continue monitoring the dealer. A random check of a particular table could, for example, reveal a disparity between the dealer's photo and the name shown on thc badge. This disparity would be checked out immediately with a casino supervisor. In other instances, the dealer's name may not appear on the casino schedule for the shift.

The disparity could be attributed to a last-minute schedule change, which can be easily verified by calling the floor supervisor. Occasionally, casino accounting is advised that an audit of documents pertaining to a particular game may be warranted. "Instant access to employee information, especially ID pictures, makes our job a lot easier," says Cipolla. "It often took hours or days to scour through computer printouts to pinpoint the person involved in a specific transaction. The task can now be done in minutes.

The search process, which also involved phone calls to casino supervisors, wasted valuable time, was cumbersome, and expensive." Casino accounting. Casino accounting operates two shifts a day and is responsible for important audit functions for the Mirage's gaming activities. The department is responsible for maintaining the casino's operational integrity and for strict compliance with established procedures. Timely information about gaming activities and people who authorize transactions is necessary for effective management. "The most important piece of information available," comments Robert Galvin, casino accounting manager, "is an employee's ID number.

For us, it provides the means to access a key piece of data, employee signature samples." The accounting department's data verification terminal provides instant access to information needed for transaction audits. Matching photos to names or comparing signature samples with those appearing on documents is extremely helpful.

Cash cage. Because of the large amounts of money involved, the casino cash cage may require complete ID verification, including signatures and photos of unfamiliar people. In the past, matching signatures on cash disbursement forms or receipts to signature cards took hours or even days to accomplish. It now takes minutes.

Performing rapid searches of information with specific parameters, such as name, employee number, title, department, and job description, has resulted in significant productivity improvement.

"Immediate access to essential information," says Galvin, "has resulted in better control, increased audit speed, and reduced labour hours. Since we've been linked to the security management system, productivity has improved dramatically." The verification terminal, also used by internal auditing and gaming control board personnel, allows greater audit frequency and improved monitoring of money flow. An innovative time and attendance system, to be fully implemented by early 1993, is being phased into the Mirage's operations on a controlled schedule. The ambitious undertaking is expected to produce enormous cost savings and efficiency improvements while providing significant benefits for both employees and management.

As an integral part of a comprehensive management control system, badges provide the media for time clock entries. According to Ernie Pearce, director of information systems, "The new time and attendance system, now in use by several departments, is one of the most progressive programmes to be introduced at the Mirage.

The sophisticated, computerized time-keeping and payroll system improves the interaction between supervisors and the workforce. It also eliminates many of the payroll-related transaction errors that inconvenienced employees and wasted valuable company time.

"The ability to use the benefits of the security management system's large data base, along with the photo ID badge as a clock entry system," continues Pearce, "provides important functional and economic advantages." Using sophisticated computer-based time clocks with bar code readers, the new system integrates employee work-time and payroll information with the security management data base. In this way, a long-standing information gap has been bridged. The new, high-tech computer-based clocks—to be located at every work location—will allow employees to use their ID cards to log in and out in a virtually error-free system.

The "smart" clocks are programmed with all the necessary operating parameters. These include authorized clock locations for different departments, employees' normal start and stop times, and overtime pay scales, including holidays, IRS regulations, and applicable union rules. The new system will improve efficiency and minimize transaction discrepancies, such as illegible manual entries.

It will also eliminate time-keeping problems for people working at remote locations or whose work locations vary. In the past, bar codes have been used only to track the number of meals served in the cafeteria. With the new time-keeping system, however, they will play a more significant role in overall efficiency.

An opaque strip covering the bar code prevents tampering and reduces the likelihood that copies could be used to fool the clocks. Appearing opaque to the eye and to copy machines, the protected bar code is scanned without difficulty by bar code readers. Applied to the inside of the laminate envelope, the strip is considered tamperproof.

The Mirage's electronic security management system, which has been in operation for more than two years, has provided cost-effective solutions for a variety of problems. Software-driven and modular, important upgrades can be achieved simply by replacing a disk or a module. The combined data base, management, and electronic imaging system is easy to use, requires minimal training, and is inexpensive to operate. During its first 18 months of operation the system was on-line 24 hours a day, seven days a week, with virtually trouble-free performance.

An international company was preparing to evacuate 15 expatriate employees and dependents from a country that had suffered an earthquake. When it came time to meet at the departure point, 25 people showed up. Those arranging for the evacuation had not known that two technical teams were in the country supporting clients at the time.

The additional evacuees, who had heard of the evacuation informally from individuals at the local office, disrupted the company's plan. There were not enough vehicles to get everyone to the airport in one trip, and there were not enough seats on the airplane that had been reserved.

The other employees had made their way to the departure point hoping to get a seat because the local office employee did not tell them of the limited transportation or inform them that it would be safer to wait in the hotel until other transportation could be arranged.

The company evacuated the 15 people originally expected at that time, and the additional 10 employees were flown out two days later. This meant that an evacuation that should have been completed in approximately 12 hours—from when the employees and dependents arrived at the rendezvous point until they actually departed—ended up lasting 60 hours. Fortunately, everyone was able to get out safely, but the delay could have been disastrous.

As companies seek new business in far-flung markets, their employees increasingly need to travel and work around the globe. Companies must be prepared to help these employees through any contingencies, including earthquakes, civil unrest, and other crises.

While some risks are greater in developing countries, emergency situations requiring evacuation can arise anywhere. For instance, Singapore, a relatively safe and natural-disaster-free city, suffered from severe smog in 1999 as the result of forest fires that were raging in nearby Indonesia. The conditions made the city unbearable and forced many foreign personnel to evacuate. Other examples of such incidents include an earthquake in Taiwan, civil unrest in Indonesia, a coup in Fiji, and the invasion of Kuwait—all of which necessitated the evacuation of international personnel. Most companies with international operations have detailed plans in place for evacuating their expatriate personnel should the local security situation deteriorate or in case of a natural disaster. But as the case highlighted at the beginning of this article illustrates, these plans often fail to address the evacuation of another category of employees; Those who are visiting on a business trip when a disaster strikes.

The evacuation of international travellers often falls between the travel advisory service, which provides employees with information on areas where it might be dangerous to travel, and evacuation planning efforts, which focus on expatriate personnel based in the country. Many companies do not even know how many employees are visiting a particular international location.

In the event of an emergency, they might spend hours, if not days, trying to determine which employees are there. This problem especially affects companies that are organized along functional lines rather than geographically. It is not uncommon for an in-country office to report to a certain department, such as marketing. Personnel from other departments might travel in and out of the country without ever contacting the local office.

To avoid confusion, companies must coordinate their travel security and international evacuation programmes. Corporate security should serve as a central point for activity and information related to evacuation planning, coordinating the role of other players in the travel process, such as internal departments, travel service providers, employees, host country offices, and hotels.

How travel information is collected, maintained, and distributed will vary among companies. Generally, however, security should not bother with routine tracking of employee travel plans. Instead, the security department can enlist the help of various internal departments to ensure that it is able to locate employees on travel in an emergency. For example, security should ask human resources or travel service providers to collect the data on employee travel.

In an emergency, security will know that it can turn to this resource for the information. Security may want to ask the company's public relations department to communicate the details of the travel and evacuation plan to staff as part of the internal communications programme.

TRAVEL SERVICE PROVIDER

A company's travel service provider, whether a company employee or outside firm, can play an important role in gathering information about employees traveling abroad. Generally, these firms keep detailed records for billing purposes, and those records can help the security department to determine the location of employees when needed. The travel service company could also provide weekly or daily reports of which employees are traveling and to where. In addition to regular reports, the travel service provider should be able to give the company access to its staffs travel records 24 hours a day in case of an emergency. Many companies have erroneously assumed that they could get the necessary staff location information from travel service providers in an emergency.

The provider can also be required to book only designated hotels, perhaps ones where corporate security has verified the safety and security of the facility. In addition, because travel itineraries often change while employees are on the road, if the travel service provider has an office in a host country, employees can contact it to change hotel and flight reservations rather than going directly to the hotel or airline. This means that the changes will immediately be keyed into the system, and the information can be distributed to the corporate security department or another internal point of contact, such as human resources.

In addition, the provider can be asked to include emergency telephone numbers and procedures with each airline ticket issued to employees. The security department should periodically audit the programme for tracking employee travel to make sure that the records are being kept and that the contact telephone numbers and other information are all up to date. It also might be useful to test the programme under simulated conditions.

At the same time, security needs to keep the travel agent advised of any high-risk areas so that he or she can caution current or future travellers or, in serious cases, refer them back to security. In companies where there is an approval system for travel, those responsible for approving travel requests must be brought into the system so that they don't approve travel to "no-go" areas.

EMPLOYEES

In many cases, employees make their own travel changes by contacting the airline or hotel directly, or they use the hotel concierge or business centre. Employees should be required to advise a designated corporate contact or the travel service provider of these changes.

Some companies now require employees to submit weekly movement sheets listing travel destinations and contact details for the week to come. It is generally advisable to include these schedules with some other form of business report, such as the employees' weekly progress or sales reports, to increase the level of compliance.

One multinational telecommunications company, which has employees traveling to more than 20 countries every day of the year, implemented a Web-based itinerary tracking system to allow employees to update their travel schedules online. Employees can use any computer with Internet access to enter the password-protected site and update their information.

HOST COUNTRY OFFICES

The company's offices abroad are also important players in the security process. Though it would be difficult for international offices to report all of the internal travel movements of visiting employees, they should at least be required to track which employees are visiting their countries and where they are staying. This task can be made easier by requiring the traveling employees to check in with the local office or to go there to connect to the computer network or access their corporate e-mail account. If the local offices will be responsible for making in-country travel and accommodation arrangements for visiting employees, they should be required to use only designated hotels and they should be asked to provide contact information for hotels and transportation providers as well as other reservation details to headquarters.

One company with several international offices encouraged travellers to check in with the local offices by setting up workstations specifically for travellers and providing technical support to help them connect to the corporate -mail system. This approach worked well, especially in the countries where local communications were unreliable.

However, the company neglected to put in place a system for the local office to report to headquarters about the travellers in the country. When an earthquake struck, the main office did not know how many employees were in the vicinity of the earthquake or how to locate them. The information was available at the local office, but it was unreachable. At a minimum, international offices should be required to monitor the internal travel of visitors if a situation shows signs of deteriorating, even if they do not track which employees are visiting their country during normal times. They should also be able to locate and provide assistance, including evacuation, for visiting employees.

Similarly, headquarters or travel vice providers should notify the host country office when employees plan to travel there, though in practice this depends on the company. For instance, if another division of the company runs the host country office, the traveller's division might not even have the contact details for the host country office. Also intra-office politics plays a role.

HOST COUNTRY HOTELS

The hotels that employees use while traveling play an important part in the security process. A strong business relationship between a company and the hotel can be key. The more nights per year that the company contracts for, the more willing a hotel will be to comply with additional security demands. For instance, contracts with hotels can require them to report to a designated corporate contact when employees are staying there and to provide assistance to the employees in case of an emergency. Also, hotels can be expected to provide basic medical care through a contracted doctor as well as emergency cash.

Larger hotels that employ a full-time security manager are preferable. The hotel security manager can be given procedures to follow for corporate employees if an evacuation is necessary. These procedures should provide detailed instructions on how and to where employees should be evacuated.

Any reporting procedures and phone numbers for relevant contacts should also be given to the hotel's security manager. Obviously, there will be costs associated with services such as evacuating employees, and arrangements for payment must be made with the hotel.

NONRESIDENT SITUATIONS

An international non-profit organization was holding a conference with 150 delegates in a country where it did not have a representative office. The organization had been meticulous with its evacuation planning for all the countries where it had offices, but it failed to draw up a plan for the conference locale. As a result, when civil unrest suddenly erupted, the organization struggled to get everyone out of the area safely.

All the delegates had come from different parts of the world on many different airlines, and they were staying at hotels scattered around the city. When the company tried to get the delegates out, gathering them together and trying to book 150 people on about 20 different airlines initially proved to be an impossible task.

Later, the organization decided to prioritize the flights to four airlines, choosing the most available and reliable and issuing new tickets for the delegates who were not originally scheduled to depart on those flights. The delegates should have been required to travel on certain airlines and they should have been booked into fewer hotels that were closer together. Also, arrangements could have been made with the airlines to assist with an evacuation.

If security had done a risk assessment, the organization would have known that the potential for civil unrest was high. In such a case, even if the group did not change the venue, it could have required that delegates fly into a neighbouring country so that everyone could then take the same charter flight to the conference city, which would have made evacuation much easier.

As this case illustrates, special plans are needed for countries where the company does not have a permanent presence but to which company employees travel regularly or in large numbers. When problems occur in such areas, employees will have no support from a local office that, even without prior notice, typically has some vehicles, houses, cash, and local employees who know their way around.

A traveller to a country without a company office would have to rely on the embassy, if there is one, the hotel, and in some cases, the client he or she was visiting. But the company can smooth the way by providing contact information to authorities, such as the embassy, and by making prior arrangements with hotels and other resources. Plan preparation. Though it is nearly impossible to draw up separate plans for every country to which company employees travel, a basic threat assessment will determine which of these countries are a high risk. Plans should be created for these countries first. Then, more generic plans should be written and distributed.

The plans should provide instructions for what to do in case of an emergency, factors to consider when trying to leave the country, and resources where employees can seek assistance. Appropriate actions might include traveling in groups, keeping small denominations of cash to give away at roadblocks for the purpose of extortion, traveling in two vehicles in case one breaks down, getting to the airport early, and repeatedly checking that an airplane seat has not been "mistakenly" given to someone else.

In addition, evacuees should carry only limited luggage, keeping documents and valuables in a hand-carried bag in case they lose or have to abandon their luggage. Telephone numbers for the police, embassies, airlines, the travel service provider, and other sources of assistance should also be included.

LOCAL CONTACTS

Corporate security might consider contracting with local security companies in international locations to provide assistance in an emergency. An agreement can be made with a local security company whereby it will locate, secure, and, if necessary, evacuate the company's employees in the host country for a set fee or agreed upon hourly rate. These companies can also provide assistance to the traveling employee for minor emergencies, such as a lost passport or traffic accident. While this might also he done in locations where the company has a permanent facility, it is especially useful if the company does not maintain an office in the country.

COMMUNICATIONS

Some local security companies with strong emergency response capabilities may also have satellite communications, which means they might be among the few groups reachable immediately following a disaster. Being able to speak with someone in the country to get firsthand information about local conditions and the well-being of employees is key. Not being able to reach traveling staff or a local office after receiving news of a disaster can often result in the company activating its crisis management team and spending hours working on numerous scenarios and outcomes, only to find out that employees have escaped unscathed.

TRAVEL CLAIMS

Back at company headquarters or the employee's home office, the department responsible for reimbursing travel expenses is in the position to assist with the enforcement of travel security policies. One obvious option is for the company to refuse to reimburse employees for accommodations other than those approved by security. The department can also ensure that employees use the company's travel service provider and not their own travel agent by paying the travel service provider directly.

One U.S.-based multinational firm was able to increase employee use of designated international hotels by contracting with the hotel chain to pay the employees their per diem allowances. The company did not reimburse general travel expenses for accommodation, meals, and incidentals but instead paid a daily allowance via the hotels. The choice was simple. If employees wanted the money, they would have to use the designated hotel.

The system achieved almost 100 per cent compliance. It will often be necessary, however, for traveling employees to pay for a number of expenses themselves. Typically, the best approach is to issue the employee a corporate credit card with sufficient limits to pay for several air tickets, rent vehicles, and so forth. But in countries with deteriorating security situations, cash is king.

After an earthquake or other natural disaster, there may not be electrical power to run ATM machines or the point-of-sales machines required to process credit card transactions. Telephone lines may be down or congested, making telephone authorization for a credit card transaction impossible. During civil unrest, merchants may be reluctant to accept credit cards for fear of not being reimbursed by local banks for the transactions. Traveling employees should, therefore, be required to carry enough cash with them at all times to pay for meals, taxis, and "exit taxes," which are often collected by groups that set up roadblocks on the roads leading to international airports.

The best approach is for the traveller to keep a small "mugger's toll" where it can be quickly accessed and to hide the rest on one's person. Cash should be both in local currency and U.s. dollars and should be in small denominations. Corporate travel is unavoidable. And in a world where both natural and man-made disasters are increasing in number, close encounters with crises are also inevitable. But security can ensure that those situations do not result in loss of life by coordinating the company's travel and emergency response plans and getting all parties to understand the importance of compliance.

In 1998, governments and international organizations continued their active efforts to increase regulatory and criminal enforcement of various laws to stem the tide of transnational crime. These efforts were reflected in the criminalization of various business and financial transactions, the imposition of new due diligence measures on the private sector and the concomitant weakening of privacy and confidentiality laws, strengthened penalties for non-compliance with regulatory efforts, and new law enforcement techniques, such as undercover sting operations, wiretapping, expanded powers to search homes and businesses, and controlled deliveries. So obtrusive are many of the law enforcement techniques and the privatization of law enforcement, whereby governments transfer their responsibilities to the private sector, that many professionals engaged in international transfer of wealth counseling analogized the trends to those in Aldous Huxley's A Brave New World. This discussion outlines the trends in six areas and draws some practice pointers from the trends. Section II will discuss the activities of international organizations that are driving much of the strategy, framework, and minimum standards for the development of an international anti-money laundering regime. Increasingly, international organizations, both of a universal and a more regional level, are consciously trying to build alliances and networks with each other and the private sector. In Section III, selective elements of the substantive law of anti-money laundering are considered in the context of recent developments, such as the continued erosion of secrecy and the imposition of increased due diligence requirements. Section IV discusses major case and miscellaneous developments, such as the failure of Russian offshore banks in Antigua.

Section V highlights the growth of international tax enforcement, the increased reporting requirements and unilateral extraterritorial application of the law, the increasing bilateral and multilateral cooperation, and the new traps for the wary due to tax enforcement developments.

In Section VI, international asset forfeiture trends are highlighted. These activities pose a much graver threat to the ability of clients to do business internationally than ten years ago. The goal of immobilizing the assets of transnational criminals has become increasingly the watchword. While the rights of innocent third parties are protected in principle, it sometimes takes a lot of money and professional acumen for such persons to obtain due process. Section VII focuses on criminal cooperation mechanisms. Section VIII discusses the use of international human rights provisions as a shield for defendants, fiduciaries, and intermediaries in the context of international anti-money laundering and financial crime cases. As an introductory matter, the life cycle of money laundering is important to grasp.

It has three cycles:

- Placement, whereby the criminal has enormous amounts of dirty money in the form usually of cash that he needs to place or initiate in a way that neither law enforcement nor the private sector will identify as the proceeds of crime;
- Layering, which involves the creation of many layers between the dirty money and the ultimately cleaned money through the use of offshore vehicles, such as trusts in secrecy jurisdictions, in tandem with multiple, entitles, such as companies, and secrecy mechanisms, such as nominees, stamen, bearer shares, and sophisticated structuring; and

- Integration is achieved when the criminal has transformed the dirty money through enough layers of the laundering cycle that a legitimate banker, lawyer, or fiduciary, even one with cutting edge due diligence, would never suspect the criminal source of the money.

Integration means that, in 1999, the money of the many heirs of Joseph Kennedy, the famous former bootlegger during the prohibition days, now is not questioned. Indeed, the money even finances federal elections. In Colombia, the money of the Cali cartel has been integrated for two or three decades into the leading pharmaceutical companies, soccer teams, and also the financing of political elections.

Much of the emphasis of the politics of international anti-money laundering is to try to deprive criminals—especially transnational criminals—and organized crime of the fruits of the crimes and the means of their committing more crimes. Another goal is to allocate the seized proceeds to governments and law enforcement. Hence, the economics and politics of anti-money laundering are to redistribute economics and power of crime. To help with the fight, governments and international organizations have solicited the collaboration of the private sector to prevent money laundering through know-your-customer and identifying and reporting to law enforcement suspicious transactions.

7

Indian Tourism

AN OVERVIEW

Tourism is the largest service industry in India, with a contribution of 6.23 per cent to the national GDP and 8.78 per cent of the total employment in India. India witnesses more than 5 million annual foreign tourist arrivals and 562 million domestic tourism visits. The tourism industry in India generated about US$100 billion in 2008 and that is expected to increase to US$275.5 billion by 2018 at a 9.4 per cent annual growth rate.

The Ministry of Tourism is the nodal agency for the development and promotion of tourism in India and maintains the "Incredible India" campaign. World Travel and Tourism Council, India will be a tourism hotspot from 2009-2018, having the highest 10-year growth potential. The Travel and Tourism Competitiveness Report 2007 ranked tourism in India 6th in terms of price competitiveness and 39th in terms of safety and security. Despite short- and medium-term setbacks, such as shortage of hotel rooms, tourism revenues are expected to surge by 42 per cent from 2007 to 2017. India has a growing medical tourism sector. The 2010 Commonwealth Games in Delhi are expected to significantly boost tourism in India.

TOURISM IN INDIA: MISSED OPPORTUNITIES

Internationally, tourism occupies a very important place in the economies of several countries. Among the world's largest industry, it is forecasted to grow 4 per cent annually till 2010. It currently contributes about 11.6 per cent to the global GDP and employs about 9.4 per cent of the global labour force.

However, in India, the industry has largely remained ignored, performing well below its potential, despite the fact that India has a unique heritage and culture and a wide gamut of tourism attraction it has to offer to the world. Surprisingly, despite the winds of liberalization blowing across the country, tourism seems to have been the least affected. Even now, setting up a resort means getting as many as 72 clearances from different authorities! Will the tourism industry in this country be yet another victim of missed opportunities?

Will the tremendous potential, and the resultant benefits to the economy that it has to offer, go unexplored? And just what is the potential like? According to figures put up by Confederation of Indian Industries (CII), an apex body representing Indian industry, by the year 2020 India could have 40 million tourist arrivals, constituting 4 per cent of the world travel. Currently, the country gets 2.4 million international arrivals or 0.4 per cent of the world travel. The report goes on to state that the industry could end up employing about 50 million people, as against 20 million now — 10 million directly and another 10 million indirectly. At today's prices the travel and tourism economy could grow as big as Rs.10 lakh crore or 7 per cent of the GDP, as against Rs 6 lakh crore now or 5.6 per cent of GDP. Foreign exchange earnings could grow ten times, from the current US $ 3 billion to about US $ 30 billion!

Speaking to domain-B, Mr. Ravi Bhoothalingam, president the Oberoi Group and head of the tourism committee at the CII said, "Looking at the tremendous potential the tourism industry offers, it is time the government pays some attention to the needs of the industry, lest it may turn out to be another case of "opportunity lost", which will be very sad." According to him, the travel and tourism economy in India accounts for 5.6 per cent of the GDP, supports 5.8 per cent of the total employment in the country and generates 10.8 per cent of the total exports from the country.

In spite of this, the capital investment that goes into the industry is a paltry 6.4 per cent of the GDP compared to the world average of 11.8 per cent. The government's support to the industry has fallen well short of expectations and budgetary and other allocations to the sector have been 1 per cent of public spending, as against global average of 6.8 per cent. Despite this partisan approach on the part of the government, tourism in the country has registered a fairly impressive growth rate over the last few years. Says Mr. Bhoothalingam, "We, at CII, have come out with a 17 point agenda, which needs to be incorporated into the new tourism policy on the anvil if the country wants to avail the benefits the sector offers."

One of the most vociferous demands is to declare tourism an "infrastructure industry", which will help it attract low cost funds, so important to keep any industry globally competitive. Despite being the largest net foreign exchange earner and the second largest gross foreign exchange earner, after the IT industry, tourism as a segment continues to find itself ignored by the government. Insufficient aviation seating capacity, pathetic road and airport conditions, poor rail infrastructure, inadequate economical hotel accommodation and relatively high level of taxation continue to be the bane of an average international traveller. According to the World Travel and Tourism Council, an international association of the tourism industry, "Tax paid by tourists in India, is the highest in the world. Indian hotels charge about 40 per cent tax compared to other Asian countries where the tax rate varies between 3 per cent and 6 per cent." It is not surprising therefore that repeat visits of international travellers to India are few and far in between. The Indian government however stays unmoved. Strange and very criminal considering that India, as a nation, remains starved of foreign exchange and an adequate support to tourism could go a long way in bolstering its forex reserves. Needless to say that forex "Earned" in this fashion is "India's own" and not borrowed!

Procedural hassles in getting visas and poor infrastructure (including roads which are pot-holed, dusty and narrow to say the least) are some of the major problems that need to be attended to. Against present requirement of about 130,000 hotel rooms, India offers just about 60,000. Says Mr. Bhoothalingam, "The biggest shortfall is in the three star category. Our archaic land laws, which make land acquisition a very cumbersome process, are doing precious little to solve this problem. They render the cost of putting up a hotel very high. There is a big gap between five star and lower categories of hotels. The government needs to create separate zones and then give liberal floor space index or FSIs for setting up two and three star hotels. This will dramatically and drastically change the economics of the hotel industry."

The industry is also worried about airline seat capacity. Against a demand of 10 million seats in the international segment the supply is just about 5.3 million and in the domestic segment against a demand of 19 million supply is just about 9.79 million. According to Mr. Bhoothalingam, the demand-supply gap will get compounded with the outbound traffic growing so fast. He adds, "Our airports are bursting at the seams. We not only need more airports, but also mush better roads. The Cochin airport is a fine example of private enterprise. Privatisation is the only answer and we have to move towards open skies. The government must accept that aviation is no longer a luxury — it is the basic need of a growing economy."

Visa facilitation is yet another process, which needs to be rationalized urgently. Stringent eligibility requirements and cumbersome procedure put off many visitors from visiting India. One of our major policy restrictive to the growth of tourism is "reciprocity", under which we give visas to citizens of only those countries which give to Indians. Countries like Bhutan, Nepal, Singapore, Seychelles, Maldives, Thailand, Turkey, Taiwan and Indonesia give visas on arrival without reciprocity as a condition.

Thailand has a visa-on-arrival policy for over 140 countries and there is no reciprocity in every case. Suggests Mr. Bhoothalingam, "We should abolish visa requirements for main source markets such as USA, European Union and Japan. For other countries it should be visa-on-arrival. Finally we could have a third list of countries which could qualify for strict visa requirements." The government may however cite security concerns as prime reason for very strict visa requirements. Advantages of tourism are plenty. It remains confined not just to urban agglomerations, but spreads its benefits deep and wide into the rural countryside providing significant gains for the economy. Further, by its very nature tourism is conducive to protecting the environment.

According to figures provided by the CII, an additional 1 million visitors can help generate revenues of Rs. 4,300 crore annually. For every Rs. 1 million of investment, tourism can help create 47.5 jobs, manufacturing 12.6 jobs and agriculture 44.7 jobs. With just 2.4 million arrivals (0.4 per cent of the world list of international arrivals) in fiscal 2000, India finds itself ranked a poor 43rd in the world list of international arrivals, despite the fact that it boasts of some of the most exquisite sites and locales, with some of the best monuments to see. Countries far smaller in size such as France (62 million arrivals — ranked 1st), Spain (41 million arrivals — ranked 3rd), Hungary (21 million arrivals — ranked 8th) and Poland (19 million arrivals— ranked 9th) are way ahead of India. Even a country as small as Sri Lanka, despite the ethnic conflicts plaguing it for the last 12 years, is ahead of India with about 4 million international arrivals.

It is time therefore that the government pulls up its socks and pushed tourism ahead. Else, it will be one more case of missed opportunities.

THE BOOMING TOURISM INDUSTRY

The year 2004-05 saw tourism emerging as one of the major sectors for growth of Indian economy, the foreign exchange earnings increased from Rs. 16,429 crore to 21,828 crore up to December. Similarly in the last year, tourism industry registered a growth rate of 17.3 per cent in foreign tourist arrivals, which has been the highest in last 10 years. Foreign exchange earnings grew at an even higher rate 30.2 per cent.

India's tourism industry is thriving due to an increase in foreign tourists arrivals and greater than before travel by Indians to domestic and abroad destinations. The visitors are pouring in from all over the world: Europe, Africa, Southeast Asia and Australia. At the same time, the number of Indians travelling has also increased. Some tourists come from Middle East countries to witness the drenching monsoon rains in India, a phenomenon never seen in desert climates. Domestic tourists are also fueling the industry's revival. Many of them escape from the summer heat on the plains to resorts in the Himalayan Mountains. One of the major beneficiaries this year is Kashmir, where a cease-fire between India and Pakistan has reduced violence, if not completely, at least enough to help revive the state's sagging tourism industry.

Among the most favoured tourist destinations in India, Kerala for its scenic beauty, Agra for Taj Mahal, Khujraho for its sculptures and temples, Goa for its beaches and some pilgrimages are the most important. Interesting feature of this growth is that it has come even as global tourism has dropped, due to the September 11 terrorist attacks in the United States, the outbreak of Severe Acute Respiratory Syndrome in East Asia, and the Iraq war. Even the disastrous tsunami didn't affect India's tourism industry, as tourist arrivals in India rose

23.5 percent in Dec 2004 and tourist arrivals crossed 3 million mark for the first time in 2004.. The disaster was expected to have a negative impact on India's tourism in terms of large-scale cancellations of tourists to India but nothing of that sort was seen.

Reasons for this Boom

There could be several reasons for the buoyancy in the Indian tourism industry. First, the upward trend observed in the growth rate of Indian economy has raised middle class incomes, prompting more people to spend money on vacations abroad or at home. Also, India is booming in the information technology industry and has become the IT centre. Aggressive advertising campaign " Incredible India" by the government has also had contribution in changing India's image from that of a land of snake charmers, and sparking new interest among overseas travellers.

Tourism Contribution to the Indian Economy

It is not hidden that tourism is among India's important export industries. Even with comparatively low levels of international tourist traffic, tourism has already emerged as an important segment of the Indian economy. Tourism also contributed to the economy indirectly through its linkages with other sectors like horticulture, agriculture, poultry, handicrafts and construction. Foreign exchange earnings from tourism during 2003-04 were US $ 3,533 million (Rs 16,429 crore). Besides being an important foreign exchange earner, tourism industry also provides employment to millions of people in India both directly and indirectly (through its linkage with other sectors of the economy.) It is estimated that total direct employment in the tourism sector is around 20 million.

Measures Taken for Tourism Promotion

Recently, Indian government adopted a multi-pronged approach for promotion of tourism, which includes new mechanism for speedy implementation of tourism projects, development of integrated tourism circuits and rural destinations, special capacity building in the unorganized hospitality sector and new marketing strategy.

A nation wide campaign, for creating awareness about the effects of tourism and preservation of our rich heritage and culture, cleanliness and warm hospitality through a process of training and orientation was launched during 2004-05. The aim was to rebuild that sense of responsibility towards tourists among Indians and re-enforces the confidence of foreign tourist towards India as a preferred holiday destination. More than 6500 taxi drivers, restaurant owners and guides trained under the programme. Government also took several other initiatives to promote Indian tourism industry and increased the plan allocation for tourism *i.e.* from Rs 325 crore in 2003-04 to Rs. 500 crore in 2004-05. Road shows in key source markets of Europe, Incredible India campaign on prominent TV channels and in magazines across the world were among the few steps taken to advertise Indian tourism. In addition a task force was set up to promote India as prominent health tourism destination. However, in order to attract more visitors, India still needs to upgrade its airports, roads and other infrastructure to global standards. Even with the recent surge, tourist arrivals are just a mere percentage of those in such popular Asian destinations like Bangkok and Thailand.

Recent Development in Tourism Industry

India Tourism office at Tokyo won two International Awards in Tour Expo held at Daegu in Korea for excellent tourism promotion. Indian Pavilion won the Best Booth Design Award as well as Best Folklore Performance Award competing with major players in tourism such as China, Japan, Thailand, Malaysia and Canada. The theme of pavilion was the Buddhist pilgrimage in India. Multi promotional activities undertaken by Tokyo office drew a large crowd to India Pavilion, which added colours to the entire travel show. The Korea's leading newspapers published on the front page the Incredible India booth's photographs highlighting various aspects. The live Yoga performance and Indian traditional snacks at the pavilion were enjoyed very much by the visitors.

CURRENT STATUS AND FUTURE POTENTIAL

Tourism as an activity or as a phenomenon has been existing since the olden days. The quest travel often quoted as the "travel bug" is apart of human psyche. A result of this psyche is the birth and growth of the all encompassing "tourism industry". Goa has long been identified as a major tourism destination in India and the world over. The "flower children" of the 1960's ended up at the pristine and virgin beaches of Goa thus giving the first indications of what was to become of Goa as a tourist destination. Last year *i.e.*, 2004-05 season witnessed a tourist inflow of the magnitude of 2.4 million (Tourism Statistics: Govt. Of Goa) which included more than 300,000 international tourists and 2,100,000 domestic tourists. These figures are being seen in the last few years with the growth in the immediate past three years being in the range of 9 per cent to 27 per cent. This kind of phenomenal growth in a short span is certainly not without its share of issues as far as tourism is concerned. Growth is an essential part of life and tourism industry is no exception. However planning for growth is a prudent activity if one desires to harness its full potential.

Many people have researched destination growth and Miossec(1976) identifies a five-stage pattern in the growth of a destination. The destination witnesses these stages slowly and each stage is indicative of the changes that occur both in the tourists' perception of the destination as well as in the nature of the reaction of the local community to tourism activities at the destination.

Britton (1982) has argued that the international tourism industry, due to the commercial power held by the foreign enterprises, imposes on peripheral destinations a development mode that reinforces dependency on and vulnerability to, developed nations. This would be seen in different intensities at different stages of the destination's growth path.

Pearce (1989) observes that tourism is encouraged as a means of increasing the inflow of foreign funds into the economy or pursued for political purposes and not as an end in itself. It is perhaps this focus on tourism as a means that is creating the myopia that destination development activity is suffering from.

HONEY-POT AREAS IN TOURISM IN GOA

Tourists like to travel and explore different places, people, cultures, traditions etc., and experience them. This penchant for travel in fact is the backbone of tourism so much so that Smith (1995) calls it "geography in action". Given this nature of tourism it is but natural that most destinations try to showcase their products and product potentials for the tourists so that visitation can be increased. In most resource-intensive destinations where the natural resources of the destination are the most visited attractions, the development takes place rapidly in the early stages of destination development. In fact Butler (1980) identifies the stage as the stage of involvement wherein the local and outside investment is seen for the growth of the destination. Further stage of development witnesses the loss of local control on investment n tourism as larger investment needs are felt by the destination to accommodate a larger inflow of tourists. In such a situation investments generally find their way to areas that have high resource interactive attractions, thus creating a honey-pot situation where the attraction is the main reason for which tourists come and related activities are planned around it.

Over a period of time this leads to either haphazard growth due to ad-hoc decision-making and ad-hoc development or saturation or both. In all the above cases destination resources get depleted in terms of quality as there is tremendous pressure on their capacity to service the tourists. In fact Jeffries (1971) indicates that resources by themselves are not products at a destination but need to be developed in quite different ways in answer to the needs of quite different markets.

This shows that one needs to showcase the tourism resources at a destination in a manner that is conducive to tourists form a viewpoint of creating a good experience for them. This is possible only when there is an optimum utilization of the resource base. With honey-pot areas this rarely happens as the resource gets degenerated and results in a negative experience for the tourists. Though honey-pot areas at a tourism destination generate higher revenues the concomitant depletion of the natural resources around the area negate the economic benefits arising out of it.

Tourism Experience Development

Creating tourism experiences for tourists is the central theme of any tourism destination stakeholder. This has to be borne in mind when the developmental platform of tourism is debated. The need for proper planning as far as tourism product development or tourism attraction development could never have been more emphasized than in the process of creating experiences for tourists.

One of the most desired experiences for tourists is to get the feel of being welcomed at a place, which she visits. If such experiences are designed then the tourist would certainly involve herself with the experience and create a better tourism experience for herself as well as for others around her. Currently Goa has seen a huge rise in the tourist inflows in the past three years and this is a good indication for the economic benefits to the industry in particular and to the general public at large. However one needs to look more deeply at this issue because there is more to economic benefits than meets the eye.

One needs to look as to who benefits and how the benefit percolates in society. Foster (1985) says that "the search for, and developing and launching of new products is essential for the long term survival in tourism. The slow rate of change in demand for tourism products disguises this necessity". This statement indicates that there is a dynamic activity that is necessary, which can look at the product development process effectively throughout the destination.

The Future

The increase in tourism arrivals heralds with it the imminent need for increased resource usage. This is evident from the requirement of increased beds per tourist in terms of hotels in all categories. At the current level of Tourist arrivals in Goa in 2004 of 24,48,959 the total bed requirement is 39,183 beds. If we fit a trend to the tourist arrivals then the tourist arrivals for the year 2016 are projected at 42,80,000, which needs a phenomenal increase in bed requirement of 69,400, which is almost twice the amount for 2004. This is only one area of resource development need and one can imagine what kind of resources are needed in terms of basic resources such as water, electricity, garbage disposal, land, roads etc.

Furthermore one needs to look at the kind of resources on the primary demand side of tourism such as increased demand on attractions, natural as well as man-made. Viewed from this point one is compelled to take a hard look at the honey-pot areas such as Calangute, Baga, Candolim, Palolem etc., and then incorporate the tourism attraction demand from tourists in future. This would certainly lead to the development of hinterland areas of Goa and most of this would be in the realms of Heritage and Culture. This is where the destination managers and stakeholders need to come together to create strong policies that are conducive to better tourism experience creation.

Till recently tourism has been viewed as an economic activity that creates and distributes wealth at the destination. One needs to look deeply into this phenomenon and realize what impacts this has on the phenomenon of tourism itself. Most people call the traditional approach as the demand side approach in the sense that tourism is looked at from the benefits of demand for tourism. However the supply-side aspect is not taken with equal vigour. There are many organizations and stakeholders who are eager to market their product to the tourists but not many of them would get together and spend time, efforts and money in designing the tourism products that are offered to the tourists. The future of Tourism in Goa will certainly depend on how this is created. Economic benefit dispersion and resource generation, maintenance and dynamic evaluation alone will help Goa retain its pristine nature and benefit both the hosts as well as the guests.

Tourism dependent economies generally create products and services keeping in mind the tourists. However it would be prudent to view the local economy and population as the main demand sector and tourism as an add-on economy. The reason for this is the involvement of all sections of the local economy.

Tourism products created and distributed to the tourists have a built in risk factor of competition, market backlash by way of tourism activities not occurring in the region due to exogenous factors. If the tourism products are a part of the local economy then there is lesser fluctuation as far as the demand is concerned and hence price stability is relatively ensured. This in itself is a great relief for investors who seek a stable business environment to enable them to take better investment decisions. This in turn would lead to a sense of stability for investors thus boosting their confidence in terms of bringing in new investments to bolster the supply side of a destination.

Robustness of a Tourism Destination

A tourism destination is as robust as its weakest link or weakest spot. As such creating a destination growth path that includes growth and stability of resource utilization is the need of the hour. At current levels of resource strength Goa will reach saturation point in terms of Carrying Capacity in the year 2018. This is indicative of how fast the tourism scenario is growing in comparison with the resource development process. Unless priority is given to the development of resources there is no hope for Goa to keep creating better tourism experiences for the tourists. The level of resources needed for tourism development is large and individual organizations may not be able to marshal them. Since most of the firms that are functioning at a tourism destination are small and medium enterprises it becomes all the more imperative that larger investments come in from the state itself or are outsourced through other means such as joint ventures, alliances, specifically created organizations that have access to larger funds, etc,. In terms of creating an image for the destination and in terms of ensuring that the effects of tourism are spread throughout the destination strong cooperative environment needs to be created. Co-operation can exist in the form of alliances, joint ventures, Co-operatives for specific purposes etc,. Most resource specific activities could use these forms to foster the growth and development of tourism as well as that of the resource.

One such example is of the heritage tourism in Portugal, which is created out of a strong co-operative organization to rejuvenate the hinterland tourism. Rural tourism is fostered through this Co-operative organization caller TURIHAB and its success in restoring cultural and heritage tourism is quite astounding. One can safely say that the future of tourism in Goa will depend a lot on how the different stakeholders of the destination will co-operate and build a significantly strong Goa from the viewpoint of tourism.

TOURISM BY STATE

ANDHRA PRADESH

Andhra Pradesh has a rich cultural heritage and a variety of tourist attractions. The state of Andhra Pradesh comprises scenic hills, forests, beaches and temples. Also known as The City of Nizams and The City of Pearls, Hyderabad is today one of the most developed cities in the country and a modern hub of information technology, ITES, and biotechnology. Hyderabad is known for its rich history, culture and architecture representing its unique character as a meeting point for North and South India, and also its multilingual culture. Andhra Pradesh is the home of many religious pilgrim centres. Tirupati, the abode of Lord Venkateswara, is the richest and most visited religious centre in the world.

Srisailam, the abode of Sri Mallikarjuna, is one of twelve Jyothirlingalu in India, Amaravati's Siva temple is one of the Pancharamams, and Yadagirigutta, the abode of an avatara of Vishnu, Sri Lakshmi Narasimha.

The Ramappa temple and Thousand Pillars temple in Warangal are famous for some fine temple carvings. The state has numerous Buddhist centres at Amaravati, Nagarjuna Konda, Bhattiprolu, Ghantasala, Nelakondapalli, Dhulikatta, Bavikonda, Thotlakonda, Shalihundam, Pavuralakonda, Sankaram, Phanigiri and Kolanpaka.

The golden beaches at Visakhapatnam, the one-million-year old limestone caves at Borra, picturesque Araku Valley, hill resorts of Horsley Hills, river

Godavari racing through a narrow gorge at Papi Kondalu, waterfalls at Ettipotala, Kuntala and rich bio-diversity at Talakona, are some of the natural attractions of the state. Visakhapatnam is home to many tourist attactions such as the INS Karasura Submarine museum, Yarada Beach, Araku Valley, VUDA Park, Indira Gandhi Zoological Gardens. The weather in Andhra Pradesh is mostly tropical and the best time to visit is in November through to January. The monsoon season commences in June and ends in September, so travel would not be advisable during this period. Also worth visiting, the only Indian Buddhism Based Theme Park and Resorts on the Vijayawada-Guntur Highway-Agrigold Haailand.

ARUNACHAL PRADESH

Arunachal Pradesh attracts tourists from many parts of the world. Tourist attractions include Tawang, a beautiful town famous for its Buddhist monastery, Ziro, famous for cultural festivals, the Namdapha tiger project in Changlang district and Sela lake near Bomdila with its bamboo bridges overhanging the river. Religious places of interest include Malinithan in Lekhabali, Rukhmininagar near Roing and Parshuram Kund in Lohit district. Rafting and trekking are common activities. A visitor's permit from the tourism department is required. Places like Tuting have wonderful, undiscovered scenic beauty.

ASSAM

Assam is the central state in the North-East Region of India and serves as the gateway to the rest of the Seven Sister States. Assam boasts of famous wildlife preserves - the Kaziranga National Park, which is home to the Great Indian One-Horned Rhinoceros and the Manas National Park, the largest river island Majuli, historic Sivasagar, famous for the ancient monuments of Ahom Kingdom, the city of eternal romance, Tezpur and tea-estates dating back to time of British Raj. The weather is mostly sub-tropical. Assam experiences the Indian monsoon and has one of the highest forest densities in India.

The winter months are the best time to visit. Assam has a rich cultural heritage going back to the Ahom Kingdom, which governed the region for many centuries before the British occupation. Other notable features include the Brahmaputra River, the mystery of the bird suicides in Jatinga, numerous temples including Kamakhya of Tantric sect. 'Gurdwara Sri Guru Tegh Bahadur also known as Damdama Sahib at Dhubri '. This famous Gurudwara is situated in the heart of the Dhubri Town on the bank of the mighty Brahmaputra river in far north-east India.

Guru Nanak the first Sikh Guru visited this place in 1505 and met Srimanta Sankardeva as the Guru travelled from Dhaka to Assam, ruins of palaces, etc. Guwahati, the capital city of Assam, boasts many bazaars, temples, and wildlife sanctuaries.

BIHAR

Bihar is one of the oldest continuously inhabited places in the world with history of 3000 years. The rich culture and heritage of Bihar is evident from the innumerable ancient monuments that are dotted all over this state in eastern India. This is the Place of Aryabhata, Great Ashoka, Chanakya and many more. Bihar is one of the most sacred places of various religions such as Hinduism, Buddhism, Jainism, Sikhism and Islam. Famous Attraction includes Mahabodhi Temple, a Buddhist shrine and UNESCO World Heritage Site is also situated in Bihar, Barabar Caves the oldest rockcut caves in India, Khuda Bakhsh Oriental Library the Oldest Library of India.

DELHI

Delhi is the capital city of India. A fine blend of old and new, ancient and modern, Delhi is a melting pot of cultures, religions. Delhi has been the capital of numerous empires that ruled India, making it rich in history. The rulers left behind their trademark architectural styles. Delhi currently has many renowned historic monuments and landmarks such as the Tughlaqabad fort, Qutub Minar, Purana Quila, Lodhi Gardens, Jama Masjid, Humayun's tomb, Red Fort, and Safdarjung's Tomb.

Modern monuments include Jantar Mantar, India Gate, Rashtrapati Bhavan, Laxminarayan Temple, Lotus temple and Akshardham Temple. New Delhi is famous for its British colonial architecture, wide roads, and tree-lined boulevards. Delhi is home to numerous political landmarks, national museums, Islamic shrines, Hindu temples, green parks, and trendy malls.

GOA

Goa is one of the most famous tourist destinations in India. A former colony of Portugal, Goa is famous for its excellent beaches, Portuguese churches, Hindu temples, and wildlife sanctuaries. The Basilica of Bom Jesus, Mangueshi Temple, Dudhsagar Falls, and Shantadurga are famous attractions in Goa. Recently a Wax Museum has also opened in Old Goa housing a number of wax personalities of Indian history, culture and heritage. The Goa Carnival is a world famous event, with colourful masks and floats, drums and reverberating music, and dance performances. The celebrations run three days culminating in a carnival parade on fat Tuesday.

HIMACHAL PRADESH

Himachal Pradesh is famous for its Himalayan landscapes and popular hill-stations. Many outdoor activities such as rock climbing, mountain biking, paragliding, ice-skating, and heli-skiing are popular tourist attractions in Himachal Pradesh. Shimla, the state capital, is very popular among tourists. The Kalka-Shimla Railway is a Mountain railway which is a UNESCO World

Heritage Site. Shimla is also a famous skiing attraction in India. Other popular hill stations include Manali and Kasauli. Dharamshala, home of the Dalai Lama, is known for its Tibetan monasteries and Buddhist temples. Many trekking expeditions also begin here.

JAMMU AND KASHMIR

Jammu and Kashmir is the northernmost state of India. Jammu is noted for its scenic landscape, ancient temples, Hindu shrines, castles, gardens and forts. The Hindu holy shrines of Amarnath in kashmir attracts about. 4 million Hindu devotees every year. Vaishno Devi alsoattract tens of thousands of Hindu devotees every year.

Jammu's historic monuments feature a unique blend of Islamic and Hindu architecture styles. Tourism forms an integral part of the Kashmiri economy. Often dubbed "Paradise on Earth", Kashmir's mountainous landscape has attracted tourists for centuries. Notable places are Dal Lake, Srinagar Phalagam, Gulmarg, Yeusmarg and Mughal Gardens etc. Kashmir's natural landscape has made it one of the popular destinations for adventure tourism in South Asia.

Marked by four distinct seasons, Ski enthusiasts can enjoy the exotic himalayan powder during winters. 7000000 tourists arrived in kashmir in the months of April,May and June alone In recent years, Ladakh has emerged as a major hub for adventure tourism. This part of Greater Himalaya called "moon on earth" comprising of naked peaks and deep gorges was once known for the silk route to High Asia from the subcontinent. Leh is also a growing tourist spot.

KARNATAKA

Karnataka has been ranked as fourth most popular destination for tourism among states of India. It has the second highest number of protected monuments in India, at 507. Kannada dynasties like Kadambas, Western Gangas, Chalukyas, Rashtrakutas, Hoysalas and Vijayanagaras, ruled Karnataka particularly North Karnataka. They built great monuments to Buddhism, Jainism, Shaivism.

The monuments are still present at Badami, Aihole, Pattadakal, Hampi, Lakshmeshwar, Sudi, Hooli, Mahadeva Temple, Dambal, Lakkundi, Gadag, Hangal, Halasi, Galaganatha, Chaudayyadanapura, Banavasi, Belur, Halebidu, Shravanabelagola, Sannati and many more. Notable Islamic monuments are present at Bijapur, Bidar, Gulbarga, Raichur and other part of the state.

Gol Gumbaz at Bijapur, has the second largest pre-modern dome in the world after the Byzantine Hagia Sophia. Karnataka has two World heritage sites, at Hampi and Pattadakal, both are in North Karnataka. Karnataka is famous for its waterfalls.

Jog falls of Shimoga District is one of the highest waterfalls in Asia. This state has 21 wildlife sanctuaries and five National parks and is home to more than 500 species of birds. Karnataka has many beaches at Karwar, Gokarna,

Murdeshwara, Surathkal. Karnataka is a rock climbers paradise. Yana in Uttara Kannada, Fort in Chitradurga, Ramnagara near Bangalore district, Shivagange in Tumkur district and tekal in Kolar district are a rock climbers heaven.

KERALA

Kerala is a state on the tropical Malabar Coast of southwestern India. Nicknamed as one of the "10 paradises of the world" by National Geographic, Kerala is famous especially for its ecotourism initiatives. Its unique culture and traditions, coupled with its varied demography, has made it one of the most popular tourist destinations in India. Growing at a rate of 13.31 per cent, the tourism industry significantly contributes to the state's economy. Kerala is known for its tropical backwaters and pristine beaches such as Kovalam.

MADHYA PRADESH

Madhya Pradesh is called the "Heart of India" because of its location in the centre of the country. It has been home to the cultural heritage of Hinduism, Islam, Buddhism, Sikhism, Jainism. Innumerable monuments, exquisitely carved temples, stupas, forts and palaces are dotted all over the State. The temples of Khajuraho are world-famous for their erotic sculptures, and are a UNESCO World Heritage Site.

Gwalior is famous for its forts, the Tomb of Rani Lakshmibai, and the Palace of Tansen. Madhya Pradesh is also known as Tiger State because of the tiger population. Famous national parks like Kanha, Bandhavgadh, Shivpuri, Sanjay, Pench are located in MP. Spectacular mountain ranges, meandering rivers and miles and miles of dense forests offering a unique and exciting panorama of wildlife in sylvan surroundings.

MAHARASHTRA

Maharashtra is the second most visited state in India by foreign tourists, with more than 2 million foreign tourists arrivals annually. Maharashtra boasts of a large number of popular and revered religious venues that are heavily frequented by locals as well as out-of-state visitors.

Ajanta Caves, Ellora Caves and Chhatrapati Shivaji Terminus are the three UNESCO World Heritage sites in Maharashtra and are highly responsible for the development of Tourism in the state. Mumbai is the most cosmopolitan city in India, and a great place to experience modern India.

Mumbai famous for Bollywood, the world's largest film industry. In addition, Mumbai is famous for its clubs, shopping, and upscale gastronomy. The city is known for its architecture, from the ancient Elephanta Caves, to the Islamic Haji Ali Mosque, to the colonial architecture of Bombay High Court and Chhatrapati Shivaji Terminus. Maharashtra also has numerous adventure tourism destinations, including paragliding, rock climbing, canoeing, kayaking, snorkeling, and scuba diving in places like Kolad, Tarkarli, Koyna, Manor. Maharashtra also has several pristine national parks and reserves, some of the best ones are Tadoba with excellent accommodation and safari experiences besides little known by amazing wildlife destinations like Koyna, Nagzira, Melghat, Dajipur, Radhanagari and of course the only national park within metropolic city limits in the world-Sanjay Gandhi National Park.

The Bibi Ka Maqbara at Aurangabad the Mahalakshmi temple at Kolhapur, the cities of Nashik, Trimbak famous for religious importance and the city of Pune the seat of the Maratha Empire and the fantastic Ganesh Chaturthi celebrations together contribute for the Tourism sector of Mahrashtra.

MANIPUR

Manipur as the name suggest is a land of jewels. Its rich culture excels in every aspects as in martial arts, dance, theater and sculpture. The charm of the place is the greenery with the moderate climate making it a tourists' heaven. The beautiful and seasonal Shirui Lily at Ukhrul, Sangai and the floating islands at Loktak Lake are few of the rare things found in Manipur. Polo, which can be called a royal game, also originated from Manipur.

MEGHALAYA

Meghalaya has some of the thickest surviving forests in the country and therefore constitutes one of the most important ecotourism circuits in the country today. The Meghalayan subtropical forests support a vast variety of flora and fauna. Meghalaya has 2 National Parks and 3 Wildlife Sanctuaries. Meghalaya also offers many adventure tourism opportunities in the form of mountaineering, rock climbing, trekking and hiking, water sports etc.

The state offers several trekking routes some of which also afford and opportunity to encounter some rare animals such as the slow loris, assorted deer and bear. The Umiam Lake has a water sports complex with facilities such as rowboats, paddleboats, sailing boats, cruise-boats, water-scooters and speedboats. Cherrapunjee is one of the most popular tourist spots in North East of India. It lies to the south of the capital Shillong. The town is very well known and needs little publicity. A rather scenic, 50 kilometer long road, connects Cherrapunjee with Shillong. The popular waterfalls in the state are the Elephant Falls, Shadthum Falls, Weinia falls, Bishop Falls, Nohkalikai Falls, Langshiang Falls and Sweet Falls. The hot springs at Jakrem near Mawsynram are believed to have curative and medicinal properties.

ORISSA

Orissa has been a preferred destination from ancient days for people who have an interest in spirituality, religion, culture, art and natural beauty. Ancient and medieval architecture, pristine sea beaches, the classical and ethnic dance forms and a variety of festivals. Orissa has kept the religion of Buddhism alive. Rock-edicts that have challenged time stand huge and over-powering by the banks of the river Daya.

The torch of Buddhism is still ablaze in the sublime triangle at Udayagiri, Lalitagiri and Ratnagiri, on the banks of river Birupa. Precious fragments of a glorious past come alive in the shape of stupas, rock-cut caves, rock-edicts, excavated monasteries, viharas, chaityas and sacred relics in caskets and the Rock-edicts of Ashoka.

Orissa is also famous for its well-preserved Hindu Temples, especially the Konark Sun Temple and The Leaning Temple of Huma. Orissa is the home for various tribal communities who have contributed uniquely to the multicultural and multilingual character of the state. Their handicrafts, different dance forms, jungle products and their unique life style blended with their healing practices have got world wide attention. The Sitalsasthi Carnival is a must see for everyone who wants to see a glimpse of the art and culture of Odisha at one place.

PUDUCHERRY

The Union Territory of Puducherry comprises four coastal regions viz-Puducherry, Karaikal, Mahe and Yanam. Puducherry is the Capital of this Union Territory and one of the most popular tourist destinations in South India. Puducherry has been described by National Geographic as "a glowing highlight of subcontinental sojourn". The city has many beautiful colonial buildings, churches, temples, and statues, which, combined with the systematic town planning and the well planned French style avenues, still preserve much of the colonial ambience.

PUNJAB

The state of Punjab is renowned for its cuisine, culture and history. Punjab has a vast public transportation and communication network. Some of the main cities in Punjab are Amritsar, Chandigarh, and Ludhiana. Punjab also has a rich religious history incorporating Sikhism and Hinduism. Tourism in Punjab is principally suited for the tourists interested in culture, ancient civilization, spirituality and epic history. Some of the villages in Punjab are also a must see for the person who wants to see the true Punjab, with their beautiful traditional Indian homes, farms and temples, this is a must see for any visitor that goes to Punjab. India-Pakistan border at Wagha is also a popular tourist attraction.

RAJASTHAN

Rajasthan, literally meaning "Land of the Kings", is one of the most attractive tourist destinations in Northern India. The vast sand dunes of the Thar Desert attract millions of tourists from around the globe every year.

SIKKIM

Originally known as Suk-Heem, which in the local language means "peaceful home", Sikkim was an independent kingdom till the year 1974, when it became a part of the Republic of India. The capital of Sikkim is Gangtok, located approximately 105 kilometers from New Jalpaiguri, the nearest railway station to Sikkim. Although, an airport is under construction at Dekiling in East Sikkim, the nearest airport to Sikkim would be Bagdogra.

Sikkim is considered as the land of Orchids and mystic cultures and colourful traditions. Sikkim is well known among trekkers and adventure lovers, as West Sikkim has a lot to give them. Places near Sikkim include Darjeeling also known as the Queen of hills and Kalimpong. Darjeeling, other than its world famous "Darjeeling tea" is also famous for its refined "Prep schools" founded during the British Raj. Kalimpong is also famous for its flora cultivation and is home to many internationally known Nurseries.

TAMIL NADU

Tamil Nadu is the top state in attracting the maximum number of foreign tourists in India. Tamil Nadu. Marina Beach, Carnatic music, Bharata Natyam dance and country's largest Shopping locality. This city is also famous for Medical tourism and houses Asia's largest hospital. Archaeological sites with civilization dating back to 3800 years are found in Tamil Nadu. With more than 34000 temples this state also holds the credit of having maximum number of UNESCO heritage sites in India which includes Great Living Chola Temples and Mahabalipuram.

Country's largest temple srirangam and Pichavaram the world's Second largest Mangrove forest are located in this state. Tamilnadu has some great temples like Madurai Meenakshi Amman Temple, Tanjore Brihadeeswarar Temple, Srirangam Ranganathaswamy Temple and all the mentioned temples has world class architecture that really mesmerize everyone.

Kanyakumari is the southernmost tip of India provides sceneic view of sunset and sunshine over the Indian ocean.Hill stations like Yercaud, Kodaikanal, Ooty, Valparai, Yelagiri are widely visited. Velankanni Church and Nagoor Dharga are visited by people of all religion.Water Falls and Wildlife sanctuaries are located across the state.

UTTARAKHAND

Uttarakhand, the 27th state of the Republic of India, is called "the abode of the Gods". It contains glaciers, snow-clad mountains, valley of flowers, skiing slopes and dense forests, and many shrines and places of pilgrimage. Char-dhams, the four most sacred and revered Hindu temples: Badrinath, Kedarnath, Gangotri and Yamunotri are nestled in the Himalayas. Haridwar which means Gateway to God is the only place on the plains. It holds the watershed for

Gangetic River System spanning 300 km from Satluj in the west to Kali river in the east. Nanda Devi is the second highest peak in India after Kanchenjunga.

Dunagiri, Neelkanth, Chaukhamba, Panchachuli, Trisul are other peaks above 23000 Ft. It is considered the abode of Devtas, Yakashyas, Kinners, Fairies and Sages. It boasts of some old hill-stations developed during British era like Mussoorie, Almora and Nainital.

UTTAR PRADESH

Situated in the northern part of India, Uttar Pradesh is important with its wealth of monuments and religious fervour. Geographically, Uttar Pradesh is very diverse, with Himalayan foothills in the extreme north and the Gangetic Plain in the centre. It is also home of India's most visited site, the Taj Mahal, and Hinduism's holiest city, Varanasi. The most populous state of the Indian Union also has a rich cultural heritage, and at the heart of North India, Uttar Pradesh has much to offer. Places of interest include Varanasi, Agra, Kanpur, Lucknow, Mathura, Jhansi, Prayag, Sarnath, Ayodhya, Dudhwa National Park and Fatehpur Sikri.

WEST BENGAL

Kolkata, one of the many cities in the state of West Bengal has been nicknamed the City of Palaces. This comes from the numerous palatial mansions built all over the city. Unlike many north Indian cities, whose construction stresses minimalism, the layout of much of the architectural variety in Kolkata owes its origins to European styles and tastes imported by the British and, to a much lesser extent, the Portuguese and French. The buildings were designed and inspired by the tastes of the English gentleman around and the aspiring Bengali Babu. Today, many of these structures are in various stages of decay.

Some of the major buildings of this period are well maintained and several buildings have been declared as heritage structures. From historical point of view, the story of West Bengal begins from Gour and Pandua situated close to the present district town of Malda.

The twin medieval cities had been sacked at least once by changing powers in the 15th century. However, ruins from the period still remain, and several architectural specimens still retain the glory and shin of those times. The Hindu architecture of Bishnupur in terracotta and laterite sandstone are renowned world over. Towards the British colonial period came the architecture of Murshidabad and Coochbehar.

NATURE TOURISM

India has geographical diversity, which resulted in varieties of nature tourism.

- Water falls in Western Ghats including Jog falls.
- Western Ghats
- Hill Stations
- Wildlife reserves
- Deserts

WILDLIFE IN INDIA

India is home to several well known large mammals including the Asian Elephant, Bengal Tiger, Asiatic Lion, Leopard and Indian Rhinoceros, often engrained culturally and religiously often being associated with deities. Other well known large Indian mammals include ungulates such as the domestic Asian Water buffalo, wild Asian Water buffalo, Nilgai, Gaur and several species of deer and antelope. Some members of the dog family such as the Indian Wolf, Bengal Fox, Golden Jackal and the Dhole or Wild Dogs are also widely distributed. It is also home to the Striped Hyaena, Macaques, Langurs and Mongoose species.

India also has a large variety of protected wildlife. The country's protected forest consists of 75 National parks of India and 421 Sanctuaries, of which 19 fall under the purview of Project Tiger. Its climatic and geographic diversity makes it the home of over 350 mammals and 1200 bird species, many of which are unique to the subcontinent. Some well known national wildlife sanctuaries include Bharatpur, Corbett, Kanha, Kaziranga, Periyar, Ranthambore, Manas and Sariska.

The world's largest mangrove forest Sundarbans is located in southern West Bengal. The Kaziranga National Park,Manas National Park, Sundarbans and Keoladeo National Park is UNESCO World Heritage Site.

HILL STATIONS

Several hill stations served as summer capitals of Indian provinces, princely states, or, in the case of Shimla, of British India itself. Since Indian Independence, the role of these hill stations as summer capitals has largely ended, but many hill stations remain popular summer resorts.

Most famous hill stations are:

- Mount Abu, Rajasthan
- Pachmarhi, Madhya Pradesh-It is also known as The Queen of Satpura.
- Araku, Andhra Pradesh
- Gulmarg, Srinagar and Ladakh in Jammu and Kashmir
- Darjeeling in West Bengal
- Munnar in Kerala
- Ooty, Yercaud and Kodaikanal in Tamil Nadu
- Shillong in Meghalaya
- Shimla, Kullu in Himachal Pradesh

- Nainital in Uttarakhand
- Gangtok in Sikkim
- Mussoorie in Uttarakhand
- Manali in Himachal Pradesh
- Tawang in Arunachal Pradesh
- Mahabaleshwar in Maharashtra
- Haflong in Assam

In addition to the bustling hill stations and summer capitals of yore, there are several serene and peaceful nature retreats and places of interest to visit for a nature lover. These range from the stunning moonscapes of Leh and Ladhak, to small, exclusive nature retreats such as Dunagiri, Binsar, Mukteshwar in the Himalayas, to rolling vistas of Western Ghats to numerous private retreats in the rolling hills of Kerala.

BEACHES

India offers a wide range of tropical beaches with silver/golden sand to coral beaches of Lakshadweep. States like Kerala and Goa have exploited the potential of beaches to the fullest. However, there are a lot many unexploited beaches in the states of Andhra Pradesh, Gujarat, Maharastra, Tamil Nadu and Karnataka. These states have very high potential to be develop them as future destinations for prospective tourists.

ADVENTURE TOURISM IN INDIA

ANGLING IN INDIA

Today, in India, the sport of angling is combined with conservation. As per the existing Indian protection laws, the fish is allowed to be caught, but must be released within a stipulated time period.

The average time taken to land a Mahseer is in ratio to its weight—5 minutes to 5 lbs. With just enough time to record its weight, and preserve your moment of glory with the prize catch of film, before the fish is revived- you have to be really quick or else it could just end up as one of those fishy stories of, "the great one that got away."

CAMEL SAFARI IN INDIA

Thar Desert Camel Safaris of India are now one of Asia's fastest selling adventure holidays. These include camel treks ranging from short rides around Jaisalmer to extensive trips that remind you of Lawrence of Arabia on his epic journey across the Sahara, Marco Polo, on the historic silk route, a medieval trader leading his caravan through the hostile spice route or a royal caravan serai heading for one of the medieval kingdoms of the Thar desert- without many of the hardships of course! They are a great way to see the desert and to enjoy a novel and adventurous holiday. The Great Indian Desert may not have great expanses of sand dunes and incredible spaces of wilderness as large as those of the Sahara and Namibia, but more than makes up for it with some glorious citadels and extremely colourful and unspoilt villages. Its sand dunes are more easily accessible from airports and railway stations than those of many African countries.

CAMEL SAFARI CIRCUIT IN INDIA

The Camel Safari Circuit in India comprises of Jaisalmer, Jodhpur, and Bikaner, all in Rajasthan. They were the princely kingdoms in the desert belt of India Rajasthan. Each was comparable in size to many modern nations of Europe. All the former capitals prospered from trade with the camel caravans that traveled from West Asia and Europe to Mongolia, and were impressively fortified to protect these riches. The result was a wealth of palaces built for royalty, havelis or courtyard mansions built for merchants and nobility and intricately carved temples for the subjects.

Materials used were normally sandstone, which was easily available and provided a better medium to the silavats who specialized in making stone resemble lace. A camel safari is a great way to see the desert - visiting the villages, seeing wildlife, and riding across the open desert sands. Typical camel safaris organized around Jaisalmer take in the architectural ruins of Lodurva which was the former capital of the Bhatti Rajput desert kingdom before the founding of Jaisalmer, the Anasagar oasis, the sand dunes of Samm and the water source of Moolsagar where village women gather with pitchers at dusk. Night halts on basic safaris are at villages on the way or temporary bivouac camps in the desert scrub where camels are hobbled and let out to browse.

CAMEL SAFARI IN INDIA—TRAVEL KIT

The climate is extreme in the desert-afternoons may seem much hotter than the actual 26-30 degree temperature may suggest. Night temperatures may drop below zero on the dunes. It is essential to stock both woolen and cotton clothing. Shorts and skirts are comfortable wear for camel safaris but remember some of the off beat routes visit villages that have not seen many tourists and locals may look askance at ladies who do not wear ankle length clothing and men in shorts.

Sun hats with large rims or cotton caps that can be dipped in water when it gets too hot around midday, are essential preferably with a balaclava or scarf for covering the neck and forehead. At Jodhpur you can buy umbrellas that are quite convenient for camel safaris.

Sunscreen cream, moisturizers and lip salve area must. A water bottle can be comfortably slung on the camel saddle and it is practical also to carry tangerines as even on a deluxe safari it may not be practical to dismount each time to drink from the carted water supply. Bottled mineral water is available at Jodhpur and Jaisalmer. Find out if the baggage is being transferred by camel cart or vehicle. In case of the latter, a small handbag can carry the essentials you are likely to need on the way. If prone to sickness, carry suitable medication against the swaying gait of the camel. A torch, penknife an even cutlery will be required. Finally patience is an important piece of baggage on a camel safari as it takes time to get to grips with camel travel and to reach destinations that may be on your travel priorities.

MOUNTAINEERING IN INDIA

Mountaineering as a sport has a history as old as the history of the evolution of human race itself. Mountaineering started when the need was felt for people who could climb difficult heights and terrains to meet people across the border, to trade, or to conquer new territories. In the course of time, man developed new modes of transportation and communication and venturing out on these difficult routes were not needed. Nevertheless, what remained was his nature to take risks and getting pleasure in conquering something totally unknown and unexplored. This inner urge to take up challenges has led man to do things that are quite daring. In India, mountaineering as a sport came with the Europeans in the 18th century. That was a time when entire Europe was experiencing a new phase.

New regions were being explored, won, and native peoples were being made to become civilized. This zeal of adventurism found its ultimate fruition in the Himalayas-lofty, extremely difficult to conquer, and challenging enough to send a man back to his mother's womb. But, being men, these challenges were accepted and there began a tussle between men's ambitions and nature's reluctance. New heights were conquered, new routes were discovered, many lives lost, but the mission was accomplished.

Today, almost all the major peaks are conquered and even general people have started taking mountaineering as a serious hobby. For starters, India offers a wide spectrum of options for mountaineering as well as other related sports. Peaks and trekking routes are classified and maps are available for the interested travellers. Many institutes provide basic and advanced level courses in mountaineering and other related sports. All the equipment is locally available and other support resources can be found here.

PARAGLIDING IN INDIA

If you like Icarus ever wished to fly, as suggested, make your dream realise. The adventure of paragliding is something you just cannot miss. Soar over the hills, dip whenever you aspire to get a better view of the Earth, glide and sail, feel the freedom of the bird. The adventure of being at the altitude needs an attitude! No noise pollution, no smoke just plain fun. The thrill of have your own wings, the big wide sky with no traffic jams is a safe and easy aero adventure. Paragliding is fun for the people who constantly would love to reach new heights. Be amongst the stars during the day and count the constellations at night! Live life happily in the lap of Mother Nature. The package offers training for the novice too. Come fly, with us. The paraglider, harness, helmets, radios and ankle boots are equipments required for the adventure. Besides the monsoon season, the sky is your road for the escapade, come on touch the sky.

ELEPHANT SAFARI

How about a safari atop an elephant? Jeeps and other mechanical means of transportation may distract the fellow animals in the jungle. The Elephant is the best possible option available to admire the beauty of nature. The wildlife adventure in India is incomplete if an Elephant safari is not include in the itinerary. Come and explore the wild terrain of the Corbett National Park on the most majestic animal of all. Even horse safaris do well with the tourists in India. The strong and sturdy animal has since long been galloping across the terrific terrain in India.

ROCK CLIMBING IN INDIA

It is not quite easy to define rock climbing, but it is not difficult too. Anyone who claims to be a rock climber has his own version of the game. Rock climbing for some is to challenge their spirits and explore new heights, to give a fillip to their unbounded imaginations; for others, it is a way telling the world that he/she has finally arrived. For many of the professional rock climbers, it is not a sport.

Can you call a mission to moon a sport or pastime? If not, then why should rock climbing be called a sports is the argument. For them, rock climbing is an adventure of the greatest magnitude; it is a fight against self, against the elements, and the ultimate goal is to reach the summit and return back alive.

SCUBA DIVING IN INDIA

One of the greatest adventures in life can be to explore the totally unknown and unexplored world under sea. The joy of floating inside the sea like a fish where every creature is your friend and every new sight is a discovery can be immense. In addition, the sheer thrill of watching the rich flora and fauna of the sea in their natural habitat is unparalleled. The curiosity to know the underwater world of the sea is not a new phenomenon for human civilization. We have so many stories from the epic Ramayana describing the world beneath the sea when Hanuman was crossing the sea to reach Lanka. The origin of many mythical characters and objects are related to the sea.

There is a legend about Samudra Manthan that tells us that the sea was churned around a hill known as Meru with a snake around it. The gods pulled one end of the snake while the other end was pulled by the demons. Many amazing things came out of this exploration-an elephant called Airavata that became the property of Indra, a tree called Kalpavriksa that could grant anything, a cow known as Kamdhenu that gave milk everyday, the Goddess of wealth Lakshmi, the god of Ayurveda Dhanawantari, the Visha and Amrit.

Scuba diving and snorkeling as sports came with the Europeans who saw the vast expanse of the Indian coastline. Besides, many Indians who experienced this unique adventure also brought with them a new and exciting option for their fellow countrymen. Stretching many thousand kilometers, the Indian coastline spans the mighty waters of the Arabian Sea, the Indian Ocean and the Bay of Bengal. Dotted with the finest beaches, cliff promontories, mangroves, backwater, jewel-like island groups and marine life, there are wide diving possibilities. While there are many popular easily accessible sites, many more can be explored which are not at all known.

The sight of the smashing waves creating foaming breakers on the coral reef, which enclose azure lagoons whose crystal clear waters wash the fine grained white sands of the palm dotted low islands, is one of the few marvels of God's creations left untouched by the encroaching hands of industrialization and progress. The underwater city is a unique and diverse collection of colourful and weirdly patterned sea animals. Corals take pride of place in these reef cities.

Rich in variety and colour, the thousands of types of corals range from tall sea fans to small hydroids, from languidly waving sea anemones to glassy jellyfish. Danger there is, but only enough to add to the sense of adventure and thrill. This fun is multiplied many times over as you don the scuba gear. This gear has been especially devised for the deep sea diver and gives an opportunity for thrill and adventure unparalleled and unimagined by ones who think of the sea as nothing but a large saltwater lake.

India is fast becoming the adventure tourism destination of the world; and scuba diving and snorkeling as well as other water sports are going to be an integral part of this. If you have not had adventure in India, you do not know what adventure is all about.

SKIING IN INDIA

The sheer joie de vivre inspired by one's first successful slide down a ski slope defies description. Once limited to a privileged few, the adrenalin-producing pastime of skiing has been brought within the range of the common man now. For the purist, there is unsullied, powdery snow. For the accomplished and ego-conscious, there are punishing runs. For wobbly beginners and confident intermediates, there are easy slopes and understanding instructors who soon inspire dreams of Olympic glory.

With a first run to buoy one under the belt, there follows a succession of blissful days. Each day brings a fresh challenge to conquer and relish when you are at any skiing resort. Mastering the twists and turns and jumps of skiing, completing a longer ski run, and achieving faster speed are all part of this process. Every winter in the Indian Himalayas the slopes are warmed by the excited cries and laughter of entrants being introduced to the joys of winter sports: the magic of the wind rushing past as you whiz down a slope of skis, or the sheer pleasure of gliding gracefully, artistically cutting figures of eight in the snow.

Skiing, like any other high-altitude adventure sports in India, is a contribution of the Europeans. The summers in north India have always been unpleasant, more so for the Europeans who were mostly from the cold countries. To save themselves from this oppressive heat, they went to the Himalayas, not too far from major centres in north India. Many hill stations were established, the prominent among them being Shimla, Manali, Mussoorie, and Nainital. These places served not only as the home away from home for them but also as the centre where they could participate in recreational activities like skiing and trekking. Some of these places still have the best skiing slopes in the country. Affluent Indians started participating in this sport even before independence. After independence, with the efforts of adventure sport bodies, local youths were encouraged to participate in this sport.

They took to it enthusiastically and later helped in training hordes of tourists coming from other parts of the county and even abroad. Today, skiing is quite popular in the hill stations of North India and new facilities have added up to make it more popular among the masses.

TREKKING IN INDIA

Off late, trekking in India is becoming popular among the tourists all over the world. This might have been a new phenomenon for the travellers from abroad, for Indians, these mountains signify not only the natural beauty but also a source of spiritual guidance. Trekking has remained men's passion from the day he took his first step on the earth. He always ventured out of home and his natural surroundings to explore something new, a world that was unknown to him. It is astonishing to learn that the human race migrated from one continent to another when there were no means of communication, no helping hands, and most of them who left their home could never return back.

WHITE WATER RAFTING IN INDIA

If you want to get some kick, some change in life, or just to have some fun, river rafting can satisfy most of your desires. If you have the zeal, then go for the challenge and show others that you can do it. White-water rafting is not for fashionable thrill seekers, but for those who thrive on hair-soaking risks, which keep the adrenalin flowing overtime! The thrill of rushing down fast-flowing mountain streams a froth with huge waves, dashing against dangerous boulders and dizzy rapids, while you cling for dear life dependent on a fragile, inflatable rubber raft or dinghy.

Be swept along a rushing river in a rubber raft, tumble over rapids, plunge over waterfalls and feel the icy spray splash on your face, as your raft races along a mountain river in India. Experience the thrill of white water rafting in India along tumbling snow-fed Himalayan rivers in summer destinations in India. River rafting in India is an exhilarating experience that you can enjoy on your Indian Holiday. One of the best regions for river rafting in India is the stretch upto Rishikesh in Uttaranchal. White water rafting on Alaknanda, Bhagirathi and Ganga rivers is a popular adventure tourism activity in summer in India.

For the more adventurous traveller, white water rafting tours in India can also be organized on the Indus River in Ladakh and Brahmaputra River in Arunachal Pradesh White water rafting in India on the Alaknanda River is the most easily accessible white water river rafting stretch from Delhi. We drive from Delhi to Rishikesh and further north to Devprayag, where the Alaknanda River and Bhagirati River combine to form the Ganges, a river considered holy by Hindus in India. Further North is Rudraprayag, where the Alaknanda and Mandakini Rivers combine.

The white water rafting Alaknanda tour, consists of an approximately 130 Km long stretch from Rudraprayag to Shivpuri near Rishikesh in Uttaranchal, India. You will be given training by experienced river rafting instructors and guides. You will travel in groups in rafts, with an instructor at all times. Life jackets and other essential safety equipment are provided.

You can stay overnight in luxury tents, pitched on beaches alongside the river, as we halt each night. You can also enjoy campfires and bonfire nights on river rafting tours in India. As you swoop and tumble over the rapids with exotic names such as 'Roller Coaster;' 'Crossfire' and 'The Wall' you will feel the excitement and heart-racing thrill of white water rafting in India, on adventure tours to India this summer, with Indian Holiday.

ECO-TOURISM IN INDIA

Kerala Eco-Tourism

The naturally beautiful and exquisite Kerala landscape is one of the greenest destinations in India and is the perfect place to go on eco-tourism vacations. The clean and tranquil Kerala backwaters, the soothing velvety Kerala hills and a riotous explosion of greens in the intoxicating Kerala wilds offers countless opportunities for eco-tourism and nature vacations. The entire Kerala landscape is generously covered with coconut palms, pineapple groves, banana trees, Pandanus plants, thick leafy plants, dense forests and neatly clipped tea bushes. Acres of submerged paddy fields located in perfect harmony with the winding Kerala backwaters and the gentle rolling Kerala hills are heavenly paradisiacal eco-tourism vacation destinations. Regale the verdant Kerala beauty on your eco-tourism vacations to Kerala, South India with Kerala India Vacations. Visit the fascinating Kerala wildlife destinations and spot rare wild animals lazing in their natural habitat and enjoy the magic of nature. Eco-tourism in Kerala, South India is a fast developing sector and the state government is making extra efforts to promote eco-tourism. Among the manifold advantages of promoting eco-tourism in Kerala, South India one very important aspect is revenue generation and environment conservation at the same time. The concept of eco-tourism basically means that you get to visit the exotic nature rich tour destinations but at the same time you must take care not to soil the beauty of the region by not using polythene bags and other materials or things such as tin cans, wrappers etc that adversely affect the environment.

Kerala India Vacations guides you through the lush green paths within acres of rubber plantations so that you can experience first hand the incomparable natural beauty of green Kerala, South India on your eco-tourism vacations. Kerala, South India happens to be one of the leading producers of rubber in India though rubber is not a native Indian plant and was introduced by the Dutch colonialists, in fact Kerala accounts for 92 per cent of the rubber produced in India. Stay at a luxury resort or a farmhouse near a Kerala rubber plantation and enjoy the warm hospitality of the Kerala rubber plantations during your eco-tourism vacations to Kerala, South India and be fascinated by the rural Kerala lifestyle while you observe busy twittering birds, brightly coloured butterflies and squirrels scurrying here and there. Admire the thick shapely leaves on straight trunks that glisten in the bright sun.

Botanically known as Havea brasiliensis, a single rubber plant takes about 7 years to mature and can be harvested for latex (processed for natural rubber) for almost 20 years. The local rubber tappers who stay close to these lush rubber plantations harvest latex from these trees.

Pineapple is planted as an intercrop in most of the Kerala rubber plantations so you get to taste the juicy Mauritius pineapple variety while on your eco-tourism vacations to the scenic Kerala rubber plantations. Kottayam in Kerala, South India is an important Centre of commercial rubber plantations set on the picturesque banks of the serene palm fringed Kerala backwaters. Extensive rubber plantations cover the hillocks wrapped by silver ribbons of the fascinating Kerala backwaters, not a sight you would like to miss while on your eco-tourism tours to Kerala, South India.

Acres of tea plantations interspersed with shade fruit trees wrap the gentle Kerala hill slopes in a warm embrace and create soothing and striking vistas for you to visit on your Kerala eco-tourism vacations. Rows of neatly clipped tea bushes carpet the Kerala hills on the Western Ghats in Kerala, south India and offer you ample opportunity to gaze at the naturally enthralling Kerala beauty at its beatific best while on your Kerala India eco-tourism vacations.

The Britishers introduced the tradition of tea plantations in India. Tea bushes have the potential to grow to tree heights though they are kept neatly trimmed to waist height to make it feasible for the plantation workers to pluck tealeaves without much difficulty. Gaze at the lovely Kerala tea plantations while on your eco-tourism vacations and mark the fact that each tea bush is planted at a distance of 1 to 1.5 meter from each other along the contours of the landscape. Stay at the resorts and clean home-like accommodations on the Kerala tea plantations and spend your eco-tourism vacations in Kerala, South India in the midst of pure undulating greens. Watch the plantation workers plucking tealeaves and filling the baskets slung on their backs while you enjoy nature treks.

Usually it's the women who are employed for plucking tealeaves on these tea plantations in Kerala, South India. These women work in unison and sing peppy songs while plucking tealeaves and move along the rows of tea bushes in perfect rhythm. Kerala, South India has some of the highest tea estates located in India. Munnar is one of the most popular Kerala hill stations, which is known for its sweeping tea plantations. Some of the popular tea plantations in Kerala, South India are located at Peerumadu that is situated at a height of 914-meters above the sea level, Anayirankal that has acres of tea plantations located in the midst of dense evergreen forests and a few other Kerala hill stations that are definitely worth visiting on your Kerala eco-tourism tours to Kerala, South India.

Wander at leisure on the aromatic Kerala spice plantations during your Kerala India eco-tourism Vacations. Stay at the spice plantation farmhouses with the plantation owners and experience the magical charm of staying in the midst of luxuriant plantations laden heavily with a combination of scents of the various spices that are grown on these extensive plantations. Though you can visit spice plantations almost all over beautiful Kerala, Periyar is one of the most popular spice districts in Kerala, South India. This absolutely beautiful hill district is covered with a variety of spice plantations that lie close to the famous Periyar wildlife sanctuary.

Shop for rare spices at the local Kerala spice markets and inhale the intoxicating aroma of cinnamon, cardamom, pepper, ginger, turmeric, curry leaves and other spices. Besides the cultivation of these traditional Kerala spices the Kerala plantation owners have also taken to growing spices such as rosemary, oregano, mint, vanilla, bay leaves, basil, thyme and others. Discover the secret of the mouthwatering Kerala cuisine as you visit the acres of Kerala spice plantations on your eco-tourism vacations with Kerala India Vacations. Spices are basically fragrant substances of vegetable origin with distinct flavours used in selective combinations to give a special flavour to the exotic Indian cuisine.

Enjoy bird watching tours and nature treks to the lovely Kerala spice plantations with Kerala India Vacations and experience the Kerala natural beauty at its aromatic best. Watch the locals work on the extensive spice plantations and observe closely the way of life in these Kerala spice plantations and enjoy your eco-tourism vacations thoroughly.

Orissa Eco-tourism

Organized by Tourism of Orissa offers you the best seats in the house to attend what is essentially a spectacular show of competing colours, cacophony of voices, a jumble of animal instincts and raw emotions. No, we aren't talking about a Broadway show or a Hollywood musical production. Eco-tourism in Orissa is what concerns us at Tourism of Orissa. With Eco-tourism in Orissa tour package, offered by Tourism of Orissa, you get to see all the shades of the diverse ecological system that reside within the state of Orissa. Eco-tourism in Orissa may revolve around water bodies or beaches or national parks and wildlife sanctuaries alone or, it can be a combination of all these features that make Orissa such as enticing choice as a destination for eco travel and tours.

While hot springs (Atri and Tarabalo), lakes (Chilika), waterfalls (Badaghagra, Khandadhar) and reservoirs (Hirakud, Indravati) in Orissa have tourists lining up, the beaches of Orissa (Puri, Chandrabhaga, Gopalpur, Chandipur) have dazzled international and national tourist for centuries with their pristine beauty and positive vibes. Orissa's varying topography - from the wooded Eastern Ghats to the fertile river basin - has proven ideal for evolution of compact and unique ecosystems. Thereby creating such treasure troves of flora and fauna that even seem inviting to many migratory species of birds and reptiles.

Bhitar Kanika National Park is famous for its second largest mangrove ecosystem. The bird sanctuary in Chilika (Asia's biggest brackish water lake) and the tiger reserve and waterfalls in Simlipal National Park are integral part of any eco tours in Orissa, arranged by Tourism of Orissa. The Gharial Sanctuary at Tikarpada and the Olive Ridley Sea Turtles in Gahirmatha turtle sanctuary also feature on the list of avid nature watchers. The city wildlife sanctuaries of Chandaka and Nandan Kanan are a must visit for the lessons they teach is conservation and revitalization of species from the brink of extinction. Since Orissa is so rich in culture - history, traditions and people, Tourism of Orissa can even have your eco tour clubbed with other tours in Orissa so that you get the best of al te worlds at a single destination called Orissa.

Eco-tourism in Chhattisgarh

Chhattisgarh, the 26th state of the Indian Union, is located in the central part of India. The newly formed Indian state of Chhattisgarh is famous for its enchantingly beautiful natural landscapes, rich cultural heritage and unique tribal populations. With over 44 per cent of its total area under forests, Chhattisgarh is also amongst the greenest states of India. The Chhattisgarh region is known as a great repository of biological diversity. The unique combination of rich cultural heritage and biological diversity makes Chhattisgarh an ideal eco-tourism destination with immense potentials for the growth eco-tourism the region. The Indian Govt. is actively collaborating with the local officials of the state to realize the full potential of Eco-tourism growth of the region in order to make Chhattisgarh as one of the most important eco-tourism destinations in India.

Chhattisgarh is one of the greenest states of India with over 44 per cent of its total area under lush forests. The forests of Chhattisgarh are not only known for their diverse flora and fauna but also contain about 88 species of medicinal plants. In addition, Chhattisgarh has also formulated several ecological plans and working in the direction to become the country's first bio-fuel self-reliant state by 2015. And to achieve this goal the green state has devised a plan to plant over 100 million saplings of Jatropa Carcus. Chhattisgarh is also unique in its wildlife population and has 3 National Parks and 11 Wildlife Sanctuaries, housing some of the rare wildlife and bird species. With so much of variety for Eco-tourism, Chhattisgarh promises to be an ideal holiday destination for nature lovers, wildlife enthusiasts and also for those who want to discover the unique tribal life of the region.

Chhattisgarh has identified some regions with a very high potentiality for eco-tourism. The green state has launched an eco-tourism project covering three potential tourist tracks - Raipur-Turtiria-Sirpur, Bilaspur-Achanakmar and Jagdalpur-Kanger Valley National Park. In addition, a number of herbal gardens and natural health resorts have been created with increased local participation. The use of ethno-medicine, which has been practiced by aboriginal tribes since centuries, predating even Ayurveda, is also being promoted in Chhattisgarh. The major eco-tourism attractions, which are getting prime attention in Chhattisgarh, include the protection and development of the wildlife areas, camping grounds and trekking facilities. With so many initiatives, Chhattisgarh is destined to become the most Favourite eco-tourism destination in India and few among best in the world.

Rajasthan Eco-tourism

The Cultures of the Rajasthan Desert are some of the most well preserved in India. We, at Marwar Eco-Cultural Tours and Travels, are passionate about this land, its cultures and its people and we want to share this passion with you. The Desert and its people will captivate you.

Because we are able to provide you with in-depth cultural information that you would not receive on other Tours. If you have an adventurous spirit or a cultural thirst to quench, we have a Tour that should surpass all of your expectations. We also offer opportunities to get involved with the people and assist in ongoing, non-profit projects. As an NGO, we have assistance projects in most villages we will visit. All of our guides are from Rajasthan, and most are village natives or indigenous people.

They have a great knowledge of local and regional history and are great storytellers. They will keep your attention for hours next to a fire, counting tales of kings and warlords; castles, forts and Havelis (mansions); rituals and traditions. You will see the camel herds, observe villagers' craftsmanship, and gain insight into indigenous nomadic lifestyles. We will show you the best of Rajasthan, and we are very flexible and can modify our tours according to the group's needs. You can also design your own tour. You dream it up; we'll do the rest. We will organize the tour and guide you according to your wishes. Among other things, we can arrange a visit to a marriage ceremony, a farming or agricultural tour, Handicraft and Jewelry making, a stay in an Ayurvedic (traditional Indian Medicine) clinic, and more.

Madhya Pradesh Eco-tourism

Eco-tourism signifies to save the environment around us and preserving the natural luxuries and forest life. Whether it's about a nature camp or organizing trekking trips towards the unspoilt and inaccessible regions, one should always keep in mind not to create any mishap or disturbance in the life cycle of nature. A destination enveloped in magic, Madhya Pradesh is one of the most popular tourist destination in India. It's many tourist destinations are, by far, some of the most magical locales in the world.

With the highest mountains, beautiful wildlife, a cosmopolitan heritage from different civilizations, it is so rightly called tourist paradise. It has lot to offer from breathtaking natural vistas, amazing architecture, rich culture, and a warm hearted society of people living in virtual harmony.

Himachal Pradesh Eco-tourism

The majestic coniferous trees from an enchanting backdrop to the mountains with broad-leafed species like the Oaks, Maples, Birdcherry, Hazelnut, Walnut, Horsechestnut and Rhododendrons adding grandeur to the landscape. Whereas the ivies clinging to the trunks of stately Cedars appear to veil secrets of Nature, the vines flowing from atop the trees seem to invite the visitors with open arms. The violas popping up from under the forest floor and the riot of colours provided by the anemones, primulas, buttercups and many other herbs in the alpine meadows lay a colourful feast before eyes of the beholder.

Besides plants. the State also provides a very congenial habitat to a wide variety of Himalayan fauna. The Himalyan Tahar and the Ibex can be spotted as silhouettes on the high ridges in the trans-Himalayas. The Brown Bear and Musk Deer roam happily in the temperate forests, in the company of colourful pheasants including the Monal, the Western Hornes Tragopan, the Koklas and the Kalij. The lucky ones can even be traeted to rare sight of critically endangered species like the Snow Leopard and Snow Cock.

Also known as the 'Abode of Gods', the State conjures up visions of ancient temples, with exquisitely carved wooden panels, occupying almost every hilltop and the festivities associated with these religious places. Even a casual glimpse at the traditionally attired local deities being carried in meticulously decorated palanquins, devotees dancing to the rhythmic play of traditional drums and clarions, leaves a lasting imptint on one's mind.

This natural and cultural richness of the State coupled with its simple peace loving people and traditional hospitality makes the State a most favoured tourist destination. Anybody with a zest for life, a spirit of adventure and a love for nature will find all that his heart desires amongest the pristine environs of Himachal Pradesh.

Uttaranchal Eco-tourism

Uttaranchal blessed with magnificent glaciers, majestic snow-clad mountains, gigantic and ecstatic peaks, valley of flowers, skiing slopes and dense forests, this Abode of Gods includes many shrines and places of pilgrimage. Char-dhams, the four most sacred and revered Hindu temples: Badrinath, Kedarnath, Gangotri and Yamunotri are nestled in the Mighty Mountains. A picturesque state, with a breathtaking panoramic view of Himalayas, Uttaranchal promises its tourists a visit full of fun and unforgettable moments.

Ecosystem in India

The Himalayan region is a particularly fragile ecosystem. The interconnections between the different types of vegetation, between plant life and the soil, between the soil, vegetation and water are so close and so precariously balanced that the slightest change in one plunges the entire system into jeopardy. Ecosystems on seismic belts, for example, are literally 'at the mercy of the land'. Nature plays havoc in other ways too: the monsoon pattern often spells drought in the dry season, and terrible floods during rainfall.

Deforestation

Growing Population

Way back in 326 B.C., when Alexander the Great came to India, his advance was checked by almost impenetrable forests along the Indus. By the time Emperor Ashoka ascended the throne, stretches of forests had already been cleared to make roads. Ashoka realised the importance of conserving forests, and even appointed an officer for the purpose.

Sher Shah Suri was also farsighted, and planted trees all along the route from Delhi to his capital Patna. However, the Mughals' interest in forests was sadly limited to a rather hedonistic passion for big game. Under the British rule, deforestation became rampant in order to procure timber to build furniture, railway sleepers and ships for the British navy. However, the British soon realised that forests had to be spared the ordeal. After Independence, forests were cleared whenever wood was needed either for timber or agriculture, or for setting up townships. Forests were razed to the ground mindlessly till the eastern hill people decided to say a collective 'Stop'.

Forest Distructions Through Fire

Forest fires have largely contributed to deforestation. Forests in India are very susceptible to fires, especially in summer. All it takes is one little spark and a forest fire could reduce considerable green stretches to ashes in a matter of a few hours. Earlier the Bishnois of Jodhpur (Rajasthan) even laid down their lives to save trees. The Bishnois are a religious community, famous for their loyalty towards animals and trees. In fact, they are known to worship the blackbuck as a sacred animal. Various measures are being taken to curb the felling of trees. Clearing forests is now an offence under Indian law, unless approved by the concerned authorities. However, deforestation has acquired alarming proportions in India. The country's total forest cover today has fallen to a little more than approximately 10 per cent –a dismal situation for a country with a population of over a billion.

Land Degradation

Every year, valuable topsoil is swept away by floods in the rainy season. and deforestation contributes to the problem of soil erosion. Man may well have compounded the problem.

Chemical Farming

To sustain the country's enormous population, intensive chemical farming was introduced in the 1960s, ushering in the 'Green Revolution'. Chemical fertilizers and high yield grains were used on an unprecedented scale. Although production tripled, the quality of the land took a battering. Chemicals and toxic substances too have taken their own toll on the land. Desertification (cultivable land turning barren) is a serious problem in some parts of the country, especially in Rajasthan.

Water Conditions

Despite high rainfall, water levels have dropped alarmingly in many places in the country. Obviously this is due to the demands of a burgeoning population. In any case, the monsoon cannot always be relied upon; it is not uncommon for a region like Rajasthan to be stricken by drought once every two to three years. While hydroelectric projects are a partial solution to the problem, their overall 'efficiency' is not beyond interrogation.

The Narmada Valley Project – a vast project of several dams aimed at providing water and power for Gujarat, Rajasthan, Madhya Pradesh and Maharashtra – when completed, is projected to submerge an estimated 350,000 hectares of forest and 200,000 hectares of cultivated fields, and displace nearly 400,000 people. Spearheaded by the environmentalist Baba Amte, Medha Patkar, and more recently Arundhati Roy, a vigourous campaign is in progress against the building of the dams. Another controversial project is the Tehri Dam in Uttar Pradesh. Besides the displacement and loss it is projected to cause, another dread is that the dam may burst as it is being constructed on an earthquake-prone zone. The distinguished man in white, Sunderlal Bahuguna has once again spared no effort at raising public consciousness about the issue at hand.

Pollution

Despite having some of the strictest laws in the world against pollution, India is one of the most environmentally polluted countries in the world. Air pollution is so grave in cities like Delhi, Calcutta, Kanpur and some others, that simply breathing the air is equivalent to smoking 10-20 cigarettes a day! Recently, Delhi acquired the dubious distinction of being one of the five most polluted cities in the world. The rivers in the country have not been spared either. Industrial waste and a combination of other factors have contributed to the plight of these 'dying' rivers. In some places, safe drinking water, is a rare commodity. Lakes and river habitats too have been polluted. The Yamuna Action Plan was a project undertaken at a tentative cost of Rs 20,000 crore to cleanse the river of pollutants. A similar project was undertaken for the mighty Ganga River.

Conservation

Ancient texts including the epics, the Buddhist Jatakas, the Panchatantra or the more recent Jain scriptures, all preach non-violence towards even the lowest forms of animal and plant life, a philosophy that the Indian Maharajas and their British guests chose to overlooked for a while. The Indian Government has an uphill task to perform. It has been able to protect only about 4 per cent of the total forest cover in the form of National Parks and similar reserves. Underhand activities like poaching are not entirely unheard of even in these restricted areas. Currently there are about 80 National Parks and 441 sanctuaries in the country. Massive tree plantation Programmes are also being undertaken. The Vana Mahotsava, first started in 1950, is an annual tree-planting festival celebrated across the nation.

Individual Efforts

Vishweshwar Dutt Saklani of Garhwal, in Uttar Pradesh, is a small time farmer who started planting trees to seek solace after the death of his brother (who had initiated the practice) in 1948. In the last 50 years, Vishweshwar has overlaid 100 hectares of land with oak, cedar, walnut and rhododendron. People were dismissive of him until they saw the sea change that his work had brought about in the village. Denuded hills became green, land became more fertile and dry streambeds filled up. Fodder and fuel were in plenty and everyone was happy.Vishweshwar received the Indira Priyadarshini Vrikshamitra Award in 1986. Bikkalu Chikkaiah and Thimmakka were a childless couple who worked in a quarry close to Bangalore. They decided to raise banyan trees in lieu of the children they were unable to have. So they chose a barren piece of land en route to their quarry. The couple planted saplings and put protective barriers around them. In the evenings, they lugged water from a well a kilometre away. 40 years later, 284 banyan trees provided shade to a 3km stretch. Thimmakka received the National Citizen's Award in 1996. Abdul Karim of Kasargod, Kerala too did something similar. He turned a dry piece of land into a veritable forest after 19 years of hard labour. His deciduous trees brought water back into the soil. Karim went a step ahead and got some animals in this forest, to successfully replicate a healthy ecosystem.

Eco-tourism Policy

The Draft Tourism Policy 1997 states that "in the context of economic liberalisation and globalisation being pursued by the country, the development policies of no sector can remain static. "The policy further states that" the emergence of tourism as an important instrument for sustainable human development including poverty alleviation, employment generation, environmental regeneration and advancement of women and other disadvantaged groups in the country" requires support to realise these goals.

India's tourism resources have always been considered immense, in a tourism audit. The geographical features are diverse, colourful and varied. The coastline offers opportunities for developing the best beaches in the world. There are a wealth of eco-systems including bio-sphere reserves, mangroves, coral reefs, deserts, mountains and forests as well as an equally wide range of flora and fauna. The Policy further states that "international tourists visiting interiors of the country for reasons of purity of the environment and nature contributes to the development of these areas particularly backward regions". Thus Tourism "should also become a reason for better preservation and protection of our natural resources, environment and ecology".

The policy recognises that sustained growth of tourism can give rise to conflicts. To ensure that the growth of tourism takes place along desired lines, certain guidelines have been framed:

1. To remove the constraint of the information gap.
2. To create a tourist product that is desirable and supported by an integrated infrastructure.

3. To involve all agencies, public, private and government, in tourism development.
4. To create synergy between departments and agencies that have to deliver the composite tourist product.
5. To use both the circuit and scheme approach so that peoples participation through panchayats, local bodies, NGO's, and youth organisations will create a greater awareness of tourism. The Central Government can thus concentrate on larger investment oriented projects.
6. To create direct access for destinations off the beaten track.
7. To diversify the product with new options like beach tourism, forests, wild life, landscapes and adventure tourism, farm and health tourism.
8. To ensure that the development does not exceed sustainable levels.
9. To develop the seven north-eastern states, the Himalayan region and Islands for tourism.
10. To maintain a balance between the negative and positive impacts of tourism through planning restrictions and through education of the people for conservation and development.

Development Plan

The strategy for development should take into consideration the carrying capacity, local aspirations and benefits likely to accrue to the community. In particular specific policies and guidelines for eco-tourism development and adventure tourism are to be formulated, primarily through a regulatory framework. The Draft Guidelines have been approved at a State Ministers Conference and have been circulated to various trade and industry bodies. The guidelines draw a distinction between mass or resort tourism and nature or Eco-tourism, as the kind of tourism that has a lower impact on the environment and requires less infrastructural development. The Ministry hopes that the environment conscious international tourist will be made aware that India is taking steps to protect its ecology and environment.

Apart from the do's and don'ts, the guidelines are governed by a tourism management plan, the key elements of which are the protection of natural resources and a positive involvement of local communities, along with an optimum number of environmentally conscious visitors. The principles of management are scientific planning, effective control and continuous monitoring, development of physical infrastructure, zoning and a Management plan for public use of natural sites. The management plan should establish standards for resort development, style and location of structures, waste disposal, treatment of sewage, control of litter, use of public spaces and fragile areas. The operational guidelines rely on sensitisation of all the role players and this Programmes is based on a self-regulated environmental code.

Area specific rather than universal development plans keeping in mind the unique character of the location and its economic and social environment are important. This would help the State Government to coordinate with the industry in managing visitors and their activities. NGO's working on socio-economic Programmes in forest and remote areas could have a closer coordination with tourism service operators to transfer economic benefits, particularly the handicraft production and marketing sector. The guidelines are only a beginning, and it is hoped that with increasing awareness of the visitor the industry will regulate its practices.

Tourism Advisory Committee

There is an emphasis on the needs and perceptions of the international tourist running through the discussion on the guide lines although the data from the National Parks makes it evident that the domestic tourists outnumber international visitors, although they do not pay the same amount as the foreign visitor either in entry fees or for board and lodging and transport facilities. They do however demand a much higher per capita use of resources like water, fuel for heating and cooking and transport. They also make the same intensive use of time and try to maximize their stay by the number of animals and birds they can view in the 24-hour period.

It is interesting to note that no democratic participation has been called for in the policy formulation process, and all the amendments to the policy have come from trade associations and government think tanks. The tourism Advisory Committee also consists of eminent persons and community representation has been ignored.

The policy clearly recognises the debate on the tourism issue which has surfaced wherever tourism development, particularly in the case of tourism projects relating to the "gifts of nature" like beaches, rivers, mountains and forests, have already been developed. However, mere recognition of the hostility of people to tourism development is not enough to change the nature of tourism development or the resistance to tourism or what many have termed a poor tourism culture.

Perhaps to understand this in a better perspective, we should look at the issue of sustainable development in a critical way. Perhaps we can question the impact of sustainable development on the environment and sift through the jargon of development planners, international agencies, and environmental activists to see how sustainable development can be achieved without all the contradictions that are apparent as in the case of the tourism sector.

Development in Tourism

The concept of sustainability originated in the context of renewable resources like forests and fisheries and was subsequently adopted by the environmental movement. In most cases it is understood to mean "the existence of the ecological conditions necessary to support human life at a specific level of well being through future generations." However, in addition to ecological conditions there are social conditions that influence ecological sustainability in a nature-people interaction.

The social connotations have been described by Barbier (1987) who has defined social sustainability as "the ability to maintain desired social values, traditions, institutions, cultures or other social characteristics." The term sustainability came into usage in 1980 when the IUCN presented the World Conservation Strategy where sustainable development was linked to conservation of living resources. However, the fundamental goals have often been lost sight of because of operational goals (*e.g.* food, water, shelter, health are fundamental goals to be realised through self reliance, cost effectiveness, appropriate technology, people centred-ness etc.)

Consequently, the WCED made its definition brief: Social Development is development that meets the needs of the present without compromising the ability of future generations to meet their own needs. They did not make any assumptions on the direction in which changes in demand would take place. (*e.g.* equity, social justice, self-determination, or cultural diversity).

India's tourism policy follows the mainstream SD (Sustainable Development) thinking by adopting all the critical objectives: revive growth change the quality of growth meet essential needs for jobs, food, energy, water and sanitation ensure sustainable levels of population conserve and enhance the resource base reorient technology and management risk merge environment and economics in decision making reorient international economic relations make development more participatory.

These objectives are responsible for building a very broad consensus on the issue of sustainable development, yet the debate at the operational level continues. Most participants in the debate now accept that many human activities are reducing the long-term ability of the natural environment to provide goods and services, which will eventually affect human health and well being.

Enviromental Degradation

Many also accept that poverty is devastating the lives of millions in the Third World since there is no consensus between what is environmentally necessary and what is economically and developmentally feasible. The level of inter-dependence between the two insights is yet to be incorporated in the concept of Social Development. Some problem areas are: Environmental degradation, already affecting millions in the Third World, is likely to reduce human well being across the globe. Who is responsible for this rapid degeneration? Is it the poor or the rich? The poor have no option but to exploit resources for short-term survival. If we take the example of forests and their resources, which have been traditionally outside the market system and in the sphere of tribal or indigenous peoples rights, they are today seen as exploiters of the forests as against tourists, with all their demand for infrastructure and superstructure, who are seen to be conservationists. The inter-linked nature of the problem of sustainability is such that the impact of degradation will be quicker on the poor than on the rich.

Can Sustainable Development be the metafix it claims to be in reconciling increasing industrial, agricultural and resource use productivity with environmental needs. The weakness of the Social Development argument lies in the techno-economic approach to solutions with regard to common property resource management, through know how transfers, resource pricing, subsidy policies and building management capabilities. (World Bank, 1987) Deeper processes such as land reforms, industrial demands on raw materials, over consumption, changing legal and political structures are either ignored or looked at in a cursory manner.

For instance how can we claim a consensus between those who are concerned for the survival of future generations with those who are concerned with the survival of wild life, or human health and subsistence? Unless we can identify the trade-offs necessary for each specific objective of sustainability, we will not have clarity in the discussion. We will also fail to understand why, even when there is a broad consensus, projects on the ground result in conflicts. Suggested refinements could be:

1. A distinction between ecological and social sustainability and in the process an identification of the inter-linkages a distinction between renewable and non-renewable resources, between environmental processes crucial to human life and crucial to other forms of life dependent on the resources. a distinction between the techno-economic aspects of social sustainability (infrastructure, services, government) with political and cultural sustainability.
2. A distinction between equitable development and local participation, and decentralisation, what many have called NGOisation of sustainable development. This is because no rigourous testing of local participation leading to social equity or to sustainable resource use have been reported.

Environmental Impact

Case studies reflect personal, organisational or political preferences. Tourism is one of the activities which have caused concern because of the effects of increasing human traffic on fragile environments. Countries which are looking towards Tourism as a means of economic growth, like India, have limited resources and cultural restraints and they have the greatest need to pay heed to the possible negative impacts of tourism. The environmental impact of tourism is a basic issue, whether we are looking at a developed or an underdeveloped area, region or country.

The costs of tourism for a country like India include extensive investment in fixed assets with a low rate of return for infrastructure, transportation, accommodation, cultural institutions, exhibition centres, and park facilities. To this maybe added the social and cultural costs like additional demands on infrastructure like land, water, health services; the creation of new jobs for displaced people; the cost of positive community relationships; the disparity between the lifestyle of visitors and those who serve them; the possible friction between local residents and new users of valued local resources; the perception of local residents of the spending of scarce capital resources on what they consider low priority areas like tourism; cultural cost of alterations in local ceremonial or traditional values; loss of privacy for local communities as tourists come to gape at their living conditions and rituals.

Tourism also causes increasing congestion and pollution as thousands of visitors flock to parks and sanctuaries in motorised vehicles; there are changes in accessibility, landscape and the ecological balance between man and nature; there is the cost, both monetary and human, of creating conservation zones (core/buffer) with unforeseen or undesirable side effects; which have been observed in the Eco-tourism movement.

The benefit of revenue from tourism does not always redress these problems but goes towards the cost of administering the project. The tourism industry is generally self-centred and not given to educational, cultural or exchange Programmes on a philanthropic basis. The natural environment, with the best will in the world, cannot escape damage with the volume of visitors. As more and more tourists, both domestic and international seek the exotic and remote destinations around the world, the likelihood of the environment suffering as a result become greater.

Forests can suffer from trampling, fires, tree felling for facilities and waste. Wildlife, despite the protection in national parks, has suffered a loss of habitat, hunting and poaching, viewing and photographing, leading to an interruption of feeding and breeding patterns or hunting for food undisturbed. These are the prized moments for the viewer. The trade in wild life trophies or tourist souvenirs is the more deliberately destructive aspect of such tourism.

Sanctuaries

The building of tourist lodges in materials that are not integrated with the environment and the pressure they put on the land and water bodies is also wilfully destructive. Management techniques that include being less user friendly or control of numbers by closing access or by multiplying the number of attractions and areas or charging higher admission fees are generally not popular with the tourist or the tour operator and are also difficult to implement because of high administrative costs.

Equations, through its involvement in the field have had a variety of experiences relating to the debate on Eco-tourism and sustainable development. The major issues that have emerged after the policy of notification of wild life sanctuaries and their management by the Forest Departments are quite disturbing.

Wherever notification has led to displacement of people the experience of rehabilitation has not been successful and the conservation aims have not been met. Several sanctuaries have witnessed militant action by displaced communities against the developers of tourism. In many cases the tourism aims have also not been met in making the sanctuary accessible to viewers, naturalists, wild life photographers. Tourism has not been able to counteract poaching and the most extensive and the oldest conservation project, Project Tiger has not been able to save the tiger population.

The commercialisation of the experience, like the privileging of one species, for example the tiger, has led to congestion and noise pollution and this has put a pressure on the management of the sanctuary to organise tiger shows which are putting a pressure on the feeding and mating habits of the tiger. These are very invasive techniques of experiencing the wild. On the plus side, the concept of beneficiary led development has helped indigenous people to organise against their displacement and exploitation as well as to fight for the retention of their traditional rights and life styles.

Environmentalists have not only been involved in such organisations and movements but have done valuable documentation. This has influenced many urban visitors to be more sensitive to the wild and to follow the rules when participating in eco-tourism. This has also led to the development of a code of conduct for the tourist, the industry and the administrator. These attempts are in a very nascent stage. The kind of co-ordination that is required between the environmentalist and economist is just beginning to emerge and have still to counter the myths of neo-classical economists in the field of tourism. But a beginning has been made.

Coastal Issues

The Coastal Regulation Zone (CRZ) came into existence on February 19, 1991, with the gazetting of the notification by the Union Ministry of Environment and Forests (MoEF) under Sec. 3(1) and Sec. 3(2)(v) of the Environment Protection Act, 1986, and Rule 5(3)(d) of the Environment Protection Rules, 1986. Through the Notification the Central Government declared the coastal stretches of seas, bays, estuaries, creeks, rivers and backwaters, which are influenced by tidal action (in the land ward side), up to 500m. from the high tide line (HTL) and the land between the low tide line (LTL) and HTL as CRZ.

In the case of rivers, creeks and backwaters, the Notification stated that the CRZ could be modified on a case by case basis, on the basis of reasons to be recorded during the preparation of the coastal zone management plan (CZMP). However, the width of the CRZ from each bank could not be less than 100 m., or the width of the water body, whichever was less.

Activities Prohibited in the CRZ:

1. Setting up of new industries and expansion of existing ones, except those directly related to waterfront or requiring foreshore facilities.
2. Manufacture, handling, storage or disposal of hazardous substances.
3. Setting up and expansion of fish processing units including warehousing (excluding hatchery and natural fish drying in permitted areas).
4. · Discharge of untreated wastes and effluents from industries, cities, towns or other human settlements. The existing practices would have to be phased out by the concerned authorities within three years.
5. Dumping of ash or any waste from thermal power plants.
6. Land reclamation, bunding or disturbing the natural course of sea water with similar obstructions. Exceptions are made for activities required for the control of coastal erosion, the maintenance of water ways to ports; clearing sand bars; and for the construction of regulators, storm water drains and structures for the prevention of salinity ingress.
7. Mining of sand, rocks and other substrata materials, except those raw minerals not available outside the CRZ areas.
8. Drawing or harvesting of groundwater and construction of mechanism within 200 m. of the HTL. Between 200 and 500 m. it will be permissible only if done manually through ordinary wells for drinking, horticulture, agriculture and fisheries.
9. Construction activity in ecologically sensitive areas.
10. Any construction activity between LTL and HTL except facilities for carrying treated effluents and waste water discharge into the sea, facilities for carrying sea water for cooling purposes, oil, gas and similar pipelines and facilities essential for facilities permitted under the notification.
11. Dressing or altering of sand dunes, hill, natural features including landscape changes for beautification, recreation and other such purposes, except as permitted under the notification.

Regulated activities (requiring environmental clearance from MoEF):

1. Construction activities related to Defence requirements for which foreshore facilities are essential. Residential office, hospital, workshops will not normally be permitted in the CRZ, except in very special cases.

2. Operational construction for ports and harbours and light house.
3. Foreshore facilities of thermal power plants for transport of raw materials, in-take of cooling water and out fall for discharge of treated wastewater or cooling water.
4. All other activities with investment exceeding. 5 crores.

Coastal Zone Management Plan (CZMP)

All the coastal states have to prepare, within one year, CZMPs identifying and classifying CRZ areas as per the Notification guidelines. These plans have to be approved by MoEF All further development activities should be within the framework of these plans. In the interim period, before the approval of the plans, development activities should not violate the provisions of the Notification. Violations are punishable under the provisions of the Environment Protection Act of 1986. For regulating developmental activities, the coastal stretches within 500m of the HTL are classified into CRZ-1, CRZ-11 and CRZ-III.

CRZ-I — Areas that are ecologically sensitive and important (national parks, coral reefs, mangroves, areas close to the breeding and spawning grounds of fishes, areas of high natural beauty, historical heritage, high genetic diversity, and those likely to be inundated by global warming, 'etc.); and areas within the LTL and HTL.

Regulations in CRZ-I

1. No new construction shall be permitted within 500 m of the HTL.
2. No construction activity except for facility for carrying treated effluents and waste water into the sea or carrying sea water for cooling, oil, gas or similar pipelines will be permitted between the LTL and the HTL.

CRZ-II

Areas that have already been developed up to or close to the shoreline. 'Developed areas' that come within municipal limits or other legally designated urban areas which have been substantially built up and which have been provided with infrastructural facilities like drainage, approach road, water supply and sewage mains.

Regulations in CRZ-III

1. Buildings will not be permitted in the seaward side of existing roads (or those proposed in the CZMP) nor on the seaward side of the existing authorised structures.
2. Reconstruction of authorised buildings to be permitted subject to the existing floor space and without change in existing use CRZ III Areas that are relatively undisturbed and do not belong to either CRZ-I or CRZ-II. This will include coastal zones in the rural areas and also areas within municipal limits or urban areas that are not substantially built up.

3. Areas up to 200 m. from the HTL earmarked as no development zone (NDZ). No construction will be permitted within this zone except for repairs of existing authorised structures not exceeding the existing plinth area and covered apace. Raising of horticultural crops, gardens, pastures, parks, play fields, forestry and salt manufacture from sea water permitted in this zone.
4. Development of vacant plots between 200 m. 500 m. from the HTL, in designated areas with prior approval of MoEF, permitted for hotels and beach resorts.
5. Construction or reconstruction of dwellind units between the 200m and 500m of the HTL permitted so long as it is within the ambit of traditional rights and customary uses such as existing fishing villages and gouthans.

Building conditions would be based on the conditions that the total number of dwelling units does not increase more than double of the existing units; the total covered area is not more than 33 per cent of the plot area; the overall height is not more than two floors and 9 m. Guidelines for development of beach resorts in the designated areas of CRZ-III · No construction within 200 m. from the HTL and in the area between LTL and HTL.

6. The total plot size should not be less than 0.4 hectare and the covered area should not be more than 33 per cent. · The total height of the construction should not be more than 9 m. and the building should not be more than two floors.

Groundwater cannot be tapped within 200m of the HTL. Between 200 and 500 m. it can be tapped with the concurrence of the State or Central Groundwater Board.

7. Extraction of sand, leveling or digging of sandy stretches, except for the structural foundation will not be permitted within 500 M. of the HTL.
8. The quality of treated effluents, solid wastes, emissions and noise levels etc. must be within the standards laid down by the central or state pollution control boards. Untreated effluents and solid wastes should not be discharged into the water or beach.
9. To allow public access there should be a gap of 20m. width between two hotels. Two consecutive gaps should not be more than 500 m. apart.

The World Scenario of Tourism

In recent years tourism has emerged as a major economic activity that is employment oriented and earns foreign exchange. Its share in the worlds GDP in 1994-95 was 10 per cent which is more than the world military budgets put together. In global terms, the investment in tourism industry and travel trade accounts for 7 per cent of the total capital investment. Today 21.2 crore people around the globe are employed in travel trade and tourism. In future, this industry is likely to see unprecedented growth.

According to the World Tourism Council at Brussels, the revenues from travel and tourism in Asia Pacific region will grow at the rate of 7.8 per cent annually over the next decade. Amongst the economic sectors, the tourism sector is highly labour intensive. A survey by the Government of India notes that the rate of employment generation (direct and indirect) in tourism is 52 persons employed per Rs.10 lakh investment (based on 1992-93 Consumer Price Index). This is much higher than the rates of employment generation in most other economic sectors.

Indian tourism industry has also recorded phenomenal growth. The rate of international arrivals in India in recent years has been to the tune of about 19 lakh arrivals per year. The unprecedented growth in tourism in India has made it the third largest foreign exchange earner after gem and jewellery and ready-made garments.

This is not surprising since India possesses a whole range of attractive normally sought by tourists and which includes natural attractions like Iandscapes, scenic beauty, mountains, wildlife, beaches, major rivers and manmade attractions such as monuments, forts, palaces and havelis. However, in global terms, in spite of such attractions, tourist arrivals in India are a mere 0.30 per cent of the world arrivals. Receipts are similarly low, just a 0.50 per cent of the world receipts. We are still quite far from the target of 50 lakh tourist arrivals per year.

Travel and Tourism is the world's largest industry and creator of jobs across national and regional economies. WTTC/WEFA research show that in 2000, Travel and Tourism will generate, directly and indirectly, 11.7 per cent of GDP and nearly 200 million jobs in the world-wide economy. Jobs generated by Travel and Tourism are spread across the economy - in retail, construction, manufacturing and telecommunications, as well as directly in Travel and Tourism companies.

These jobs employ a large proportion of women, minorities and young people; are predominantly in small and medium sized companies; and offer good training and transferability. Tourism can also be one of the most effective drivers for the development of regional economies. These patterns apply to both developed and emerging economies.

Contributing to Sustainable Development

The 1992 United Nations Conference on Environment and Development (UNCED), the Rio Earth Summit, identified Travel and Tourism as one of the key sectors of the economy which could make a positive contribution to achieving sustainable development. The Earth Summit lead to the adoption of

Agenda 21, a comprehensive Programmes of action adopted by 182 governments to provide a global blueprint for achieving sustainable development. Travel and Tourism is the first industry sector to have launched an industry-specific action plan based on Agenda 21.

Travel and Tourism is able to contribute to development which is economically, ecologically and socially sustainable, because it:

1. Has less impact on natural resources and the environment than most other industries;
2. Is based on enjoyment and appreciation of local culture, built heritage, and natural environment, as such that the industry has a direct and powerful motivation to protect these assets;
3. Can play a positive part in increasing consumer commitment to sustainable development principles through its unparalleled consumer distribution channels; and
4. Provides an economic incentive to conserve natural environments and habitats which might otherwise be allocated to more environmentally damaging land uses, thereby, helping to maintain bio-diversity.

There are numerous good examples of where Travel and Tourism is acting as a catalyst for conservation and improvement of the environment and maintenance of local diversity and culture. (Some of these are set out in Section B of this paper and a fuller illustration of the range of industry action can be found on the World Travel and Tourism Council's Of course, there are also examples where development has not been sustainable. (Some of the lessons learnt from these poor practices are illustrated in Section C of this paper.)

Providing Infrastructure

To a greater degree than most activities, Travel and Tourism depends on a wide range of infrastructure services - airports, air navigation, roads, railheads and ports, as well as basic infrastructure services required by hotels, restaurants, shops, and recreation facilities (*e.g.* telecommunications and utilities).

It is the combination of tourism and good infrastructure that underpins the economic, environmental and social benefits. It is important to balance any decision to develop an area for tourism against the need to preserve fragile or threatened environments and cultures. However, once a decision has been taken where an area is appropriate for new tourism development, or that an existing tourist site should be developed further, then good infrastructure will be essential to sustain the quality, economic viability and growth of Travel and Tourism. Good infrastructure will also be a key factor in the industry's ability to manage visitor flows in ways that do not affect the natural or built heritage, nor counteract against local interests.

Challenge for the Future

Travel and Tourism creates jobs and wealth and has tremendous potential to contribute to economically, environmentally and socially sustainable development in both developed countries and emerging nations. It has a comparative advantage in that its start up and running costs can be low compared to many other forms of industry development. It is also often one of the few realistic options for development in many areas. Therefore, there is a strong likelihood that the Travel and Tourism industry will continue to grow globally over the short to medium term.

Of course, if Travel and Tourism is managed badly, it can have a detrimental effect - it can damage fragile environments and destroy local cultures. The challenge is to manage the future growth of the industry so as to minimise its negative impacts on the environment and host communities whilst maximising the benefits it brings in terms of jobs, wealth and support for local culture and industry, and protection of the built and natural environment.

8

Travel Operations and Consultancy

ORIGINS OF TRAVEL AGENCY

The British company Cox and Kings is sometimes said to be the oldest travel agency in the world, but this rests upon the services that the original bank, established in 1758, supplied to its wealthy clients. The modern travel agency first appeared in the second half of the 19th century. Thomas Cook, in addition to developing the package tour, established a chain of agencies in the last quarter of the 19th century, in association with the Midland Railway.

They not only sold their own tours to the public, but in addition, represented other tour companies. Other British pioneer travel agencies were Dean and Dawson, the Polytechnic Touring Association and the Co-operative Wholesale Society. The oldest travel agency in North America is Brownell Travel; on July 4, 1887, Walter T. Brownell led ten travellers on a European tour, setting sail from New York on the SS Devonia. Travel agencies became more commonplace with the development of commercial aviation, starting in the 1920s. Originally, travel agencies largely catered to middle and upper class customers, but the post-war boom in mass-market package holidays resulted in travel agencies on the main streets of most British towns, catering to a working class clientèle, looking for a convenient way to book overseas beach holidays.

SCOPE IN TRAVEL AGENCY

Travel and Tourism as one of the world's largest foreign exchange earner among industries, provides employment directly to millions of people worldwide and indirectly through many associated service industries. As a very large industry, it includes Government tourism departments, Immigration and customs services, travel agencies, airlines, tour operators, hotels etc. and many associated service industries such as airline catering or laundry services, guides, interpreters, tourism promotion and sales executives etc.

Travel and tourism enterprises include major internationals with thousands of workforce, though small private travel agent have handful of employees. Work in the travel and tourism industry is essentially concerned with providing services for people who are away from home, on business or holiday. Travel can be leisure travel involving package tours, pilgrim travel, adventure travel etc. or for purely business.

Work at every functional level in the industry involves dealing directly with people. Travel company personnel must be up-to-date on current rules and regulations and documentation required, in areas like cargo, ticketing and passports, visas etc. so as to correctly advise their clients, and to take care of the paperwork when necessary. Besides this, all tourism staff in marketing, counter sales, or guide services, should be knowledgeable about the places their clients visit, in terms of general background, how to get there, connections by air, rail and road and the facilities available. In India, Travel and tourism, as an industry, has been somewhat slower to take off than in many other places.

However, with increasing worldwide interest in travel, and with the Government's encouragement of its activities, it is undergoing massive expansion and improvement. This forecasts a bright future for all those who choose to make a career of travel and tourism.

Young people with drive and a capacity for hard work can rise to top positions very quickly in travel and tourism or even head their own agencies. A job in the industry gives good returns as well as perks including opportunity to see many locales at low prices. Now a days working in an airline, whether on the ground or in flight is an exciting option for many people. In the airlines, one can work as Traffic Assistance, Reservation and Counter Staff, Airhostess and flight pursers, Sales and Marketing staff and customer services. A course in travel and tourism or a qualification on Hotel management helps to get in. The jobs in airlines though challenging are glamorous and afford the possibility of travelling to exciting destinations.

Free tickets for the family offered by some airlines are an added advantage. Domestic and international Airlines such as Air India, Indian airlines, Jet airways, Air Sahara, Aeroflot, British Airways, Cathay Pacific, Emirates, Singapore Airlines etc. offer employment opportunities with attractive salaries and numerous benefits.

Opportunities are plenty in travel agency business. Many resorts, travel groups use travel agents to promote their tour packages to travellers. They deal with almost everything connected with travel including the shortest route to the destination, travel mode, obtaining important documents that are required like visa, passport, vaccination certificates etc., suitable places to stay, current exchange rates, tourist attractions to visit, climate and they will plan the trip keeping in mind the clients' preferences, budgets and special needs. In travel agencies there are openings for reservation and counter staff, Sales and Marketing staff, Tour escorts and tour operators, cargo and courier agencies etc. A short-term course or a diploma in travel and ticketing for few months duration will help gain entry into an agency. Several large travel agencies also offer short-term training programmes, and tend to absorb most of the candidates. Some agencies take in fresh graduates and train them on the job. Most travel agencies demand persons with a pleasing personality and the ability to deal with customers. A knowledge of destinations and procedures help a great deal. Now sky is the limit in the field of travel and tourism.

DEFINITION OF TOUR OPERATOR

A tour operator typically combines tour and travel components to create a holiday. The most common example of a tour operator's product would be a flight on a charter airline plus a transfer from the airport to a hotel and the services of a local representative, all for one price. Niche tour operators may specialise in destinations, *e.g.* Italy, activities and experiences, *e.g.* skiing, or a combination thereof. The original *raison d'etre* of tour operating was the difficulty of making arrangements in far-flung places, with problems of language, currency and communication.

The advent of the internet has led to a rapid increase in self-packaging of holidays. However, tour operators still have their competence in arranging tours for those who do not have time to do DIY holidays, and specialize in large group events and meetings such as conferences or seminars. Also, tour operators still exercise contracting power with suppliers (airlines, hotels, other land arrangements, cruises, etc.) and influence over other entities (tourism boards and other government authorities) in order to create packages and special departures for destinations otherwise difficult and expensive to visit. The three major tour operator associations in the U.S. are the National Tour Association (NTA), the United States Tour Operators Association (USTOA), and the American Tour Association (ATA). In Europe, it is the European Tour Operators Association (ETOA), and in the UK, it is the Association of British Travel Agents (ABTA) and the Association of Independent Tour Operators (AITO). The primary association for receptive North American inbound tour operators is the Receptive Services Association of America (RSAA).

DIFFERENCE BETWEEN TRAVEL AGENCY AND TOUR OPERATOR

Travel Agency is like a Retailer selling from all suppliers. He Can reserved a Hotel, rent a car for you or book your airport transfers. For tour packages he would use your choice and accordingly book a Coach tours are a Tour itinerary designed according to your wish with a Car Travel and Sightseeing + Hotel Reservation + Air Tickets/ Rail Tickets etc. directly from the respective suppliers or a Tour Operator.

Tour Operator is one who has already made some of his own itineraries and based on the category and budget choice of the Traveller (Who approaches him directly) or Travel agent (Indirect approach with respect to the Customer) make the full arrangement.

FUNCTIONS OF TOUR OPERATORS AND TRAVEL AGENTS

Sometimes there is confusion over the difference in functions of tour operators and travel agents. Tour operators are the organisers and providers of package holidays. They make contracts with hoteliers, airlines and ground transport companies then print brochures advertising the holidays that they have assembled. Travel agents give advice and sell and administer the bookings for a number of tour operators. It is estimated that there are some 7,000 travel agency shops ranging size from the multiples, with several hundred outlets each, to the individual shop.

Some travel agents also undertake tour operating - be it on a small scale, *e.g.* a local agent packaging a group holiday for a local club, or on a larger scale - most famously by the legendary Thomas Cook, who was the first tour operator, and Sir Henry Lunn (Lunn Poly) who is widely credited with "inventing" skiing as a leisure activity. Agents can also sell the 'components' (flights, ferry bookings, car hire etc.) for those who travel independently.

Although most package holidays are sold through travel agents a significant and growing percentage are sold direct to the consumer through advertising - Teletex, TV Travel Shops and the internet. ABTA - The Travel Association - represents both travel agents and tour operators. The Federation of Tour Operators represents only tour operators- its members have c.70 per cent of the market. All current FTO members are also members of ABTA, and the two organisations work closely together - with the FTO particularly active with overseas governments and suppliers.

OPERATIONS

As the name implies, a travel agency's main function is to act as an agent, that is to say, selling travel products and services on behalf of a supplier. Consequently, unlike other retail businesses, they do not keep a stock in hand. A package holiday or a ticket is not purchased from a supplier unless a customer requests that purchase.

The holiday or ticket is supplied to them at a discount. The profit is therefore the difference between the advertised price which the customer pays and the discounted price at which it is supplied to the agent. This is known as the commission. A British travel agent would consider a 10-12 per cent commission as a good arrangement. In Australia, all individuals or companies that sell tickets are required to be licensed as a travel agent. In some countries, airlines have stopped giving commission to travel agencies. Therefore, travel agencies are now forced to charge a percentage premium or a standard flat fee, per sale. However, some companies still give them a set percentage for selling their product. Major tour companies can afford to do this, because if they were to sell a thousand trips at a cheaper rate, they still come out better than if they sell a hundred trips at a higher rate.

This process benefits both parties. Other commercial operations are undertaken, especially by the larger chains. These can include the sale of in-house insurance, travel guide books and timetables, car rentals, and the services of an on-site Bureau de change, dealing in the most popular holiday currencies.

The majority of travel agents have felt the need to protect themselves and their clients against the possibilities of commercial failure, either their own or a supplier's. They will advertise the fact that they are surety bonded, meaning in the case of a failure, the customers are guaranteed either an equivalent holiday to that which they have lost or if they prefer, a refund.

Many British and American agencies and tour operators are bonded with the International Air Transport Association (IATA), for those who issue air tickets, Air Travel Organisers' Licensing (ATOL) for those who order tickets in, the Association of British Travel Agents (ABTA) or the American Society of Travel Agents (ASTA), for those who sell package holidays on behalf of a tour company.

A travel agent is supposed to offer impartial travel advice to the customer. However, this function almost disappeared with the mass-market package holiday and some agency chains seemed to develop a 'holiday supermarket' concept, in which customers choose their holiday from brochures on racks and then book it from a counter. Again, a variety of social and economic changes have now contrived to bring this aspect to the fore once more, particularly with the advent of multiple, no-frills, low-cost airlines.

COMMISSIONS

Most travel agencies operate on a commission-basis, meaning that the compensation from the airlines, car rentals, cruise lines, hotels, railways, sightseeing tours and tour operators, etc., is expected in form of a commission from their bookings. Most often, the commission consists of a set percentage of the sale. In the United States, most airlines pay no commission at all to travel agencies. In this case, an agency usually adds a service fee to the net price.

TYPES OF AGENCIES

There are three different types of agencies in the UK: Multiples, Miniples and Independent Agencies. The former comprises a number of national chains, often owned by international conglomerates, like Thomson Holidays, now a subsidiary of TUI AG, the German multinational. It is now quite common for the large mass-market tour companies to purchase a controlling interest in a chain of travel agencies, in order to control the distribution of their product. (This is an example of vertical integration.) The smaller chains are often based in particular regions or districts.

In the United States, there are four different types of agencies: Mega, Regional, Consortium and Independent Agencies. American Express and the

American Automobile Association (AAA) are examples of mega travel agencies. Independent Agencies usually cater to a special or niche market, such as the needs of residents in an upmarket commuter town or suburb or a particular group interested in a similar activity, such as sporting events, like football, golf or tennis. There are two approaches of travel agencies. One is the traditional, multi-destination, out-bound travel agency, based in the originating location of the traveller and the other is the destination focused, in-bound travel agency, that is based in the destination and delivers an expertise on that location. At present, the former is usually a larger operator like Thomas Cook, while the latter is often a smaller, independent operator.

CONSOLIDATORS

Airline consolidators and other types of travel consolidators and wholesalers are high volume sales companies that specialize in selling to niche markets. They may or may not offer various types of services, at a single point of access. These can be hotel reservations, flights or car-rentals, for example. Sometimes the services are combined into vacation packages, that include transfers to the location and lodging. These companies do not usually sell directly to the public, but act as wholesalers to retail travel agencies.

Commonly, the sole purpose of consolidators is to sell to ethnic niches in the travel industry. Usually, no consolidator offers everything, they may only have contracted rates to specific destinations. Today, there are no domestic consolidators, with some exceptions for business class contracts.

TYPES OF TRAVEL OPERATIONS

Now as suggested, review the different types of travel operations that are the main players in the travel trade.

TRAVEL AGENCIES

Travel agencies are perhaps the most visible companies in the travel trade. Their primary businesses is to resell accommodations, transportation services (including airplane and train tickets, car and bus transfers) individual services including guide and translator services, and package services such as sightseeing tours. Within each agency, there is often a focus on either inbound or outbound trade, with the outbound agencies focusing either on ticketing services and accommodation bookings, or on package holidays. Travel agencies generally serve a mix of long and short haul markets, although some specialize in long haul markets.

The majority of travel agencies seek to appeal to a large domestic market, so they focus mainly on products and services with a mass market appeal: beach and ski holidays, cruises, and package tours to well known and popular destinations. A small number may have a focus on specialty travel, and will offer products and services that cater to special markets. Examples would be agencies that specialize in custom travel arrangements, outdoor sports, or adventure holidays. Most travel agencies that focus on outbound travel resell the products of both outbound and inbound operators, but they can also find products to retail from other travel resellers or from travel portals. Most travel agencies offer ticketing services for international travel, and can assist their customers with obtaining information on travel requirements such as visas and vaccinations, as well as obtaining travel insurance.

Outbound Tour Operators

Outbound tour operators create and market travel products to customers in their own markets that are usually long haul travellers seeking a specific experience in a foreign destination. They may design and operate their own trips, working with partners in the destination, or they may choose trips already designed by inbound operators and simply market these to their own clients.

Outbound operators generally have an in depth knowledge of what their customers are looking for and what their travel requirements are, and are thus able to design travel products that meet those needs. In the past, most outbound operators focused on group travel arrangements, but increasingly they are offering package travel for independent travellers. Outbound operators usually offer trips to a variety of destinations, and many focus on a small number of specialty travel segments, leaving the mass market travel arrangements to travel agencies.

Inbound Tour Operators

Inbound tour operators create and market travel products and services to customers mainly in long haul markets. Customers in countries far away generally do not have in depth knowledge of a destination or the service providers in that destination, may not speak the language, and may not feel comfortable making their own arrangements. Inbound tour operators serve these customers by taking the guess work out of planning a holiday, and may offer experiences that would otherwise be inaccessible to independent travellers making their own arrangements.

For example, planning and organizing your own expedition to go trekking in Western Croatia would involve months of research to identify routes, find local guides, arrange transport and pack animals, and considerable expense to transport equipment and gear or purchase it locally. A local company can organize all this for you at much less cost and in less time than it would take for you to do it yourself.

Inbound operators usually specialize in package travel arrangements of this kind, and may have both group and independent travellers as clients. Inbound operators operate their own tours, although the services of many local companies may be packaged and resold as part of this tour. Inbound operator usually specialize in one country or region. They may offer tours catering to a broad range of interests if they are located in a country that is not well known to travellers, but if they are in a well known destination where it is easy for independent travellers to make their own arrangements they usually focus on specialty travel.

Ground Operators

These operations focus on providing travel services on the ground, including activities like horseback riding, boat trips or guided diving tours, cooking or wine tours, etc. that form part of a larger experience or packaged tour. Ground operators may sell their services directly to independent travellers that have already reached a foreign destination – this is common in more well known travel destinations. In lesser known destinations, where there are relatively fewer independent travellers, ground operators usually work mainly with tour operators (either inbound or outbound) to market their products or services.

KEY CONCEPT: PACKAGES AND TOUR OPERATORS

A 'package' can be defined as a pre-arranged combination, sold or offered for sale at an inclusive price, of not less than two of the following three elements:

- transport;
- accommodation;
- other tourist services not ancillary to transport or accommodation and accounting for a significant part of the package.

The growth of the package has been a major cause of the increase in the holiday market since the 1950s. The role of the package company goes beyond that of the wholesaler, in that they not only purchases or reserve the separate components in bulk but, in combining these components into an 'inclusive tour', they also become producers in the holiday market. The traditional appeal of the tour operators' product has been to offer a complete holiday package at the lowest price to a population often lacking the linguistic knowledge or the knowledge and confidence to organise independent travel. Consequently the tour operation has become the dominant feature of the holiday market in many tourist-generating countries.

INSEPARABILITY

The production and consumption of services are inseparable. To take advantage of an air flight or a bus service, for example, both you and the means of transport must make the journey at the same time. The implication of this inseparability is that the consumers have direct experience of the production of the service. They are, in effect, in the 'service factory' at the time of production. This has profound implications for the staff in service industries.

When a physical product is purchased, it comes packaged and the customer is likely to assess the product purely upon its product features (such as taste, size, specification, etc.). Managers have time to plan these aspects of product management to ensure that customer satisfaction is achieved. The circumstances under which the product is produced and how it is delivered are usually of little relevance to the customer.

In the case of a service product, however, customers are likely to be very concerned about the way in which the product is delivered, *i.e.* the level of customer service. At a hotel reception desk, for example, the customer is likely to notice if the receptionist is rude or unwelcoming. Similarly, the customer will also experience the production of the product if the receptionist is efficient, courteous and helpful.

The task of satisfying customers for the provider of a service is in many ways much more difficult than it is for the manufacturer of a product. In service industries everything has to be right first time, all the time and any mistake can prove very costly in terms of lost future custom. How service personnel conduct themselves in the customer's presence, what they say, what they don't say, how competent they are, how personable they are or how presentable they are, can determine whether the customer buys from the business again.

Perishability

Since production and consumption are simultaneous, services are instantly perishable if they have not been sold at the time of the production. The empty train seat, the empty hotel bed or the unsold holiday all represent lost opportunities. They are lost sales that can never be recovered (empty hotel rooms cannot be 'stored' for when demand increases). Unlike manufacturers of goods, they cannot just keep on producing services and store them for future sales and striking the correct balance between capacity and sales (supply and demand) is extremely difficult.

Consumer Capacity, Occupancy for accomodation

In travel and tourism, capacity refers to the number of people that can be accommodated in a hotel, aircraft, bus, resort, etc. It may be, for example, that a hotel has a capacity of 300 and an aircraft might be able to accommodate 130.

The important figure, however, is how much of the capacity is actually used at any time. This is the occupancy rate for accommodation or the load factor for transportation. If a hotel, for example, is only full on a quarter of the nights in a year, then it is paying the fixed costs on the empty rooms without any income from them. This is particularly important when considering seasonality and also explains why hotel prices fall in the low season—to maintain as high an occu-pancy rate as possible to help to cover the hotel's total costs.

The problems of perishability can be made even more acute by fluctuating demand but fixed supply. Demand can vary during the day, during the week or from season to season of the year. Many resort hotels, for instance, are full for only a few months of the year. Capacity may therefore be insufficient to meet demand at peak times, but in excess of what is required at slack times. Demand can fluctuate for all sorts of reasons, such as seasonal changes, changes due to the level of economic activity, and changes due to climatic conditions. Changes in demand can also occur very suddenly and can have a dramatic impact on service suppliers. For instance a single reported terrorist attack in a destination area could severely limit demand. Or more widespread instability such as the Gulf War of 1991 can also curtail demand. In the case of the Gulf War, the airline industry worldwide faced a major downturn in demand.

Supply, however is much more difficult to alter, at least in the short term. For example, a hotel has a fixed bedstock (number of beds) that it has to try to fill. A scheduled airline has an obligation to fly between advertised points regardless of the number of empty seats on the aircraft. A tour operator enters a contractual obligation, often months in advance of the date of travel, with the providers of accommodation to fill a certain specified number of rooms.

The management challenges, therefore, is to make sure that the company is operating at full capacity for a much of the time as possible. To be successful, the company will need carefully designed strategies to stimulate demand, lengthen seasons, or to offer appropriate pricing levels to manage and 'smooth out' occupancy levels.

Heterogeneity

Services, unlike mass-produced manufactured, goods, are never identical. One hotel in a chain of hotels, or one person's holiday, will never be identical to another. The human element and other factors in delivering services, ensures that services will be heterogeneous, *i.e.* varied.

Tourism products are 'people oriented', and the human factor plays a key role. The enjoyment gained from a holiday cannot be separated from the personalities who go to make up that holiday—the personnel employed in the travel agency, the airline crew, the hotel, staff, the tour operator's overseas representative, and of course, the holidaymaker. All of these have a role to play in ensuring that the holiday lives up to the customer's expectations.

Human behaviour, however, is highly variable and it is difficult for a company to ensure that its employees display good customer relation skills all of the time. Similarly, the company has no influence over the behaviour of the customer when on holiday. the customer's attitudes and behaviour will also contribute to the pleasure gained from the holiday. This means that there is an uncontrollable element inherent in the production of the travel or tourism product which can lead to the holidaymaker being satisfied or disappointed with the holiday.

To take account of this problem, it is important that as much information as possible is provided in advance to the potential customer, both by the tour operator and the travel agent. This will reduce the risk of the customer purchasing an unsuitable holiday at the outset. Special attention has also to be paid to the personnel who will deal with the client on a face-to-face basis to make certain that they have suitable personalities for dealing with the public.

In many cases in travel and tourism, the customer is actually attracted by the heterogeneity. Tourists would become bored if every tourist destination was identical, and hotel chains try hard to maintain a consistent brand image whilst at the same time trying to differentiate each hotel through varying design features. This heterogeneity is understandable, but it does make it very difficult for potential purchases to evaluate services and for managers to deliver products of a consistent quality.

SERVICES OF TRAVEL AGENCIES IN TOURISM

Tourism in India has registered significant growth in the recent years. In 1951, international tourist arrival stood at around 17 thousand only while the same has now gone up to 3.91 million in 2005. The upward trend is expected to remain firm in the coming years. Tourism is also one of the sectors, which employs the largest number of manpower. There has been a remarkable growth in the recent years, in foreign tourist arrivals to India due to various efforts made, including promoting India through the "incredible India" campaign in overseas markets.

According to the Ministry of Tourism, during January-June 2007, total tourist inflow stood at 23,86887 as against 21,32174 in the same period last year. The total foreign exchange earnings during January-June 2007 stood at US$ 3589.83 million against US$ 3037.04 million for the same period in 2006. Indian tourism is one of the most diverse products on the global scene. India has 26 world heritage sites. It is divided into 25 bio-geographic zones and has wide ranging eco tourism products. Apart from this, India has a 6,000 km coastline and dozens of beaches. India's great ethnic diversity translates into a wide variety of cuisine and culture. India also has a large number of villages, plantations and adventure locations. India is home to a great variety of wildlife and its reserves are well known throughout the world. It also has one of the world's biggest railway systems opening possibilities for those interested in rail tourism. India also has excellent hospitals offering affordable medicare and traditional health care systems like Ayurveda. In addition to this India organizes numerous fairs and festivals, which are quite attractive to foreigners.

Tourism sector holds immense potential for Indian economy. Tourism sector has the potential to stimulate other economic sectors through its backward and forward linkages and cross-sectional synergies with sectors like agriculture, horticulture, poultry, handicrafts, transport, construction, etc. Recogonising the importance of this sector, in the recent country budget, the provision for building tourist infrastructure has been increased from US$ 95.6 million in 2006-07 to US$ 117.5 million in 2007-08.

AN ENGINE OF ECONOMIC GROWTH

According to the World Travel and Tourism Council, India' s travel and tourism (T and T) industry is expected to contribute 2.1 per cent to Gross Domestic Product in 2006 (INR 713.8 billion or US$16.3 billion).

In the first half of the Annual Plan period of 2005-2006, the Ministry of Tourism has taken several initiatives in the field of infrastructure development and positioning Indian tourism as a major engine for economic growth.

These include:

- Emphasis for developing the existing and new destinations to world-class standards.
- Improvement of connectivity to important destinations
- Identification of 10-15 new destinations/circuits by each state/UT for development to world class standard with all the required infrastructure components.

A VERSATILE SECTOR

- *Medical Tourism*: The Ministry of Tourism has taken several initiatives, in partnership with the private sector, to promote India as a destination for medical tourism and make it a global health destination. Several promotional measures like road shows and developing publicity material have been undertaken for the same.Some of the main advantages that India has are as under:
  - It has world class doctors and hospitals
  - The cost of treatment is1/5th of costs in the west
  - Eastern health care wisdom along with the expertise of western medicine
- *Rural Tourism*: A concept of rural tourism has been developed for showcasing the art, crafts and culture of rural India and for creating gainful employment in villages with tourism potential. Rural tourism holds immense potential for India, where 74 per cent of the population resides in its 7 million villages.Thrust is being provided to rural tourism to spread tourism and its socio-economic benefits to rural regions.
- *Cruise Tourism*: India has a vast and beautiful coastline and hence the potential to develop cruise tourism.
- *Convention Tourism*: International convention Centres of the global standard is considered to be one of the important segments for promoting India as an attractive tourist destination in the global market. Ministry of finance has already identified New Delhi, Mumbai, Bangalore, Goa and Jaipur for opening of world-class convention centres. Several initiatives have been taken up by way of public-private partnership to develop small convention centres of high

standard. India is undoubtedly a unique Conference Destination as it offers cultural and heritage sites, the exotic and mystical, excellent facilities of beach and adventure holidays which can be combined as pre and post conference tours.

POLICIES AND SCHEMES OF TOURISM

In order to develop tourism in India in a systematic manner, position it as a major engine of economic growth and to harness its direct and multiplier effects for employment and poverty eradication in an environmentally sustainable manner, the National Tourism Policy was formulated in the year 2002.

Broadly, the "Policy" attempts to:

- Position tourism as a major engine of economic growth;
- Harness the direct and multiplier effects of tourism for employment generation, economic development and providing impetus to rural tourism;
- Focus on domestic tourism as a major driver of tourism growth.
- Position India as a global brand to take advantage of the burgeoning global travel trade and the vast untapped potential of India as a destination;
- Acknowledges the critical role of private sector with government working as a pro-active facilitator and catalyst;
- Create and develop integrated tourism circuits based on India's unique civilization, heritage, and culture in partnership with States, private sector and other agencies; and
- Ensure that the tourist to India gets physically invigourated, mentally rejuvenated, culturally enriched, spiritually elevated and "feel India from within".

SCHEME FOR PRODUCT DEEVELOPMENT

The focus under this scheme is on improving the existing products and developing new tourism products to world class standards. For infrastructure and product development, the Ministry of Tourism has been providing Central Financial Assistance to the State Governments during the 9th Five Year Plan which resulted in strengthening of the infrastructure and product development in the country. The scheme has been restructured during the 10th Five Year Plan to meet the present day infrastructure requirements. The past experience had been that a large number of small projects had been funded under the Scheme, spreading the resources very thinly, which at times had not created the desired impact. The focus in the Tenth Plan has been to fund large projects of infrastructure or product development in an integrated manner. Under the revised scheme, the Destinations are carefully selected based on the tourism potential. Master planning of these destinations is undertaken so as to develop them in an integrated holistic manner. The master plan is suppose to tie up all backward and forward linkages, including environmental considerations.

Realizing the importance of destination development, the total outlay for this sector has been increased substantially. Important tourist destinations in each State, in consultation with the State Governments, are taken up for development. This include activities ranging from preparation of master plans to implementation of the master plans.

The destinations are selected in consultation with the State/UT Governments:

1. *Definition of a Destination:* Destination is a place of tourist interest. For being eligible under this scheme the destination must be among the most visited sites in the State, or a recognized Heritage Monument. A group of attractions located in the same village, town or city would also qualify.
2. *Selection of the Destination:* The destinations will be selected in consultation with State Governments/UT Administrations.
3. *Finalisation of the Project:* The identification of the project, the implementing agency, and the mode of channelisation of funds would be done in consultation with the State Govt./UT Administration. The Ministry of Tourism would bear 100 per cent of the project cost (except refurbishment of monuments which would be funded on 66:33 basis, *i.e.* 66 per cent CFA) based on the project plan and estimates submitted, excluding the items which are the exclusive responsibility of the State Governments as listed in para 5. The maximum amount that could be sanctioned under this scheme would be ₹ 5.0 crores.

   The State Governments would have to bear the responsibility including for the items mentioned in para 5. However for projects in the 'Protected Areas' under ASI or the State Archaeology Deptt. The implementing agency would be CPWD or any other agency to be decided by the Ministry. of Tourism. In such cases funds would be directly released to such implementing agency.
4. *Monitoring Committee:* State level Monitoring Committees would be set up under the Chairmanship of the respective Secretary (Tourism). This Committee would comprise of a nominee of the Ministry of Tourism, Government. of India and a nominee of the executing agency.
5. *Funding Pattern:* All permissible activities will be fully funded by the Ministry of tourism, Government of India. However, the State/UT Governments will be fully responsible for the following components of the project:
   - Making the land available for development.
   - Implementation of rehabilitation package, where shifting of dwelling or commercial units is required. However, the

Government of India would provide assistance for construction of Tourist Reception Centres including shopping complexes to house the displaced shops.
- Maintenance and management of the assets created.
- Any other item decided by the High Power Committee.
- External infrastructure like Water Supply, Electricity and Roads

6. *Permissible Activities:* The following works may be taken up under the Scheme:
   - Improvement of the surroundings of the destination. This would include activities like landscaping, development of parks, fencing, compound wall etc.
   - Illumination of the Tourist destination and the area around/SEL Shows etc.
   - Providing for improvement in solid waste management and sewerage management.
   - Construction of Budget Accommodation, Wayside Amenities.
   - Procurement of equipment directly related to tourism, like Water Sports, Adventure Sports, Eco-friendly modes of transport for moving within the Tourism Zone.
   - Construction of public buildings which are required to be demolished because of implementation of the Master Plan.
   - Refurbishment of the Monuments. (66:33 basis, *i.e.* CFA of 66 per cent)
   - Tourist Arrival Centres/Reception Centres/Interpretation Centres
   - Other work/activities directly related to tourism.
7. *Release of Funds:* The funds would be released to the executing agency as indicated in Para 3 above.
8. *Installments of Release:* On sanction of a work, the first installment of 30 per cent of the approved CFA will be released. The second installment of 50 per cent will be released on receipt of the UC of the first installment. The balance would be released on the completion of the work.
9. *Following Codal Formalities:* The executing agency shall follow all codal formalities while awarding contracts and procurement of equipment and ensure complete transparency in its transactions.
10. *Management of Assets Created:* The infrastructure and assets created will be maintained and managed by the State/UT Governments or their agencies with no financial commitment to Govt. of India except those assets created in protected areas of ASI.
11. *Prescription of the Schedule of Rates:* While executing the works the executing agency shall follow the Schedule of rates prescribed by the CPWD or the State PWD.

12. *Submission of the Utilisation Certificates:* The executing agency shall furnish through the State Government the Utilisation Certificate for release of the second installment. A Completion Certificate has also to be furnished through the State Government before the release of the final installment. In case the works are executed by a Central Agency in a 'Protected Area' the UCs would be obtained from them directly.

AIR TRAVEL

RESERVATIONS

Air travel reservations are to be made through World Travel, either through direct communication with their agents or online via Concur Travel (which is strongly encouraged for straightforward itineraries). All air reservations are to be paid for with the traveller's corporate issued credit card, unless they have not yet been issued one. Requests should be submitted as early as possible in order to take advantage of significantly lower fares with fourteen or seven day minimum advance purchases. Airfare in excess of $750 requires VP pre-approval. Spectranetics has dictated that World Travel offer the lowest available fare at all times.

Travellers are expected to book the lowest available fare based on the following parameters:

- The flight's departure or arrival time is within two hours before or after the requested departure or arrival.
- One or more stops or connections may be required if a savings of $200 or more can be achieved.
- Alternate airports are to be used if within a 75 mile radius of the requested airport and a savings of $200 or more can be achieved.

Travellers' airline preferences will not be deciding factor in the flight selection. Reservations that are booked out of policy will require an explanation of why policy was not followed. You will be sent an e-mail from World Travel with travel details which will act as your receipt for travel expenses. The explanation for the airline expense is required and must be detailed (customer visited, project, etc.) Generic business purposes such as "sales" are not sufficient and are cause for reports to be rejected which delays processing time.

AIRLINE CLASS OF SERVICE

All Teammates are expected to travel coach class with the following exceptions:

- On international flights, the overseas portion of the trip may be booked in business class with prior VP approval
- Teammates of vice president rank or greater may select the class of service deemed appropriate to their itinerary.

- First Class service must be authorized by the CEO or CFO (with the exception of VP travel).
- The cost of upgrades is not reimbursable.

EXCEPTION

Teammates of vice president rank or greater may upgrade at their discretion.

- Cancellations/ Unused Tickets: Cancellations are to be handled through World Travel.
- If an electronic airline ticket is unused, the traveller is required to notify World Travel for refund processing.
- Delays/ Layovers: Delays and layovers are the responsibility of the carrier.
- Travellers are urged to enquire about vouchers for meals, lodging and alternate travel arrangements with the carrier at the carrier's expense.
- Airport Parking: Long-term parking should be used for travel exceeding 24-hours.

Frequent Flyer Programmes: Teammates may retain benefits resulting from frequent flyer programmes unless participation in these programmes result in incremental costs to the company beyond the "lowest available fare" as defined above.

- Airline Club Memberships: Airline club membership costs will not be paid by the company.
- Any exception to this policy requires vice president approval and in all cases is limited to one club per person.
- Risk Management: No more than 2 corporate officers may travel on the same flight.
- Policy Limits: Airline tickets in excess of $750 will be flagged for review.

OTHER TRANSPORTATION

Courtesy vans, taxis and all tips associated with ground transportation are considered reimbursable. Taxi service may be utilized when the cost is less than other sources available. Limousine or shuttle service for transportation to/from airport may be used when the cost of the service is less than the total expense for airport parking and mileage to/from airport. Policy Limits: Other Transportation in excess of $250 will be flagged for review.

LODGING

Lodging reservations are to be made through World Travel. Hotels in the range of $100-$150 per night for a single, standard room are to be used in all non-metropolitan areas. In larger cities (*i.e.* New York, Los Angeles, Honolulu, Chicago, Seattle, Boston, Miami) travellers should stay in safe, secure accommodations available in the range of $150-$250 per night, if located in the metropolitan area. Examples of comfortable, but moderately priced hotels, include Holiday Inn, Hampton Inn and Ramada Inn. Massage services, and sauna/spa facilities will not be reimbursed. Hotel gym expenses in excess of $25/day will not be reimbursed. Hotel laundry services are generally considered non-reimbursable expenses. However, hotel stays in excess of 3 days or stays that exceed the original planned duration may warrant the use of laundry services.

Exceptions must be approved by your immediate supervisor. Under no circumstances are laundry/dry cleaning services reimbursed when incurred in Teammate's home location. Non-lodging expenses included on the hotel bill such as meals, telephone, parking, etc. should be reported under the appropriate expense category and not included with lodging. Hotel folio detail is required documentation for reimbursement. If meals are charged to the hotel folio, the actual itemized meal receipt must be included as well. Policy Limits: Lodging in excess of $250 per night will be flagged for review.

CAR RENTAL

The Spectranetics Corporation will discipline any Teammate, up to and including discharge, who is found guilty of driving under the influence of alcohol and/or drugs while traveling on company business. Car rental reservations should be made through World Travel. Cars should be rented only when other means of transportation are unavailable, more costly or impractical.

Guidelines to follow when renting cars:

- All rentals should be for intermediate size cars or smaller, unless three or more people are traveling together.
- Private limousine service should be used only if cost is comparable or less than other alternatives (*e.g.* mileage and parking expenses).
- Travellers must decline all rental car insurance.

The Spectranetics Corporation insurance policy covers all rental car liabilities.

Travellers will not be reimbursed if they accept insurance coverage on a rental car:

- Travellers are responsible for canceling rental car reservations and must contact the travel agency or the rental car agency directly.
- Rental car is to be refueled prior to returning the car to avoid the high prices charged by rental agencies.
- In case of an accident, the police should always be contacted immediately.

Obtain the names and addresses of all parties involved, insurance companies and license numbers of all drivers involved. Also obtain names and phone numbers of any witnesses. Forward all information to company controller.

TOLL ROADS AND QUICK PASS EXPENSES

Several states offer an electronic billing of tolls used in a monthly billing cycle. They usually keep an "escrow" deposit on hand to fulfill the monthly tolls used. Once that cash reserve has been exhausted, the traveller is electronically billed for a new replenishment of their escrow. If a statement of the toll account activity is not available, a credit card statement showing the payment charged can be submitted as an acceptable receipt. The Teammate is responsible for noting and deducting any personal use from the total expense.

MILEAGE

The use of a Teammates' personal vehicle for company business will be reimbursed at the current company designated mileage rate. This rate will be adjusted periodically based on economic conditions. Mileage should be reported on a daily basis and must include both the origination point and destination point. If there are multiple destinations for one trip, the traveller can include all destinations or only the one furthest from the origination point. There must be sufficient information for an auditor to verify the mileage reported. The mileage allowance covers all auto costs (*e.g.* gasoline, repairs, insurance, car washes, etc.) other than parking and tolls.

Note: For Teammates who receive a monthly car allowance, the applicable mileage rate covers gasoline only. The monthly car allowance covers all other auto costs (*e.g.* depreciation, repairs, insurance, etc.) other than parking and tolls. For Teammates whose office is located in their home, all business mileage is reimbursable. For Teammates assigned to the Corporate office, mileage to and from home is not reimbursable. The destination and reason for all mileage claimed must be included on the expense report.

TELEPHONE/CELLULAR/FAX

Home internet and phone lines are not reimbursable expenses. A maximum of $20/month is allowable for a home fax line. Personal Communication Devices (PCDs) will be issued only to Spectranetics Corporation personnel with duties that require them to be in immediate and frequent contact when they are away from their normal work locations. PCDs are defined to include handheld wireless devices, cellular telephones, laptop wireless cards and pagers. The only type or style of PCDs that will be issued are those approved by the Spectranetics Corporation. Effective distribution of the various technological devices must be limited to persons for whom the productivity gained is appropriate in relation to the costs incurred. The company provided PCDs and service is issued solely for company use with minimal use for personal reasons. Should the company issued service not work in the business area that it is needed, the Teammate may obtain service elsewhere. The VP of Sales will be required to give pre-approval for this exception. This pre-approved PCD service expense is solely for company use with minimal use for personal reasons While traveling, Teammates must use their corporate cell phones for all business related calls. If traveller has a company issued cell phone, hotel phones are not to be used. In addition, use of air phones during air travel is prohibited. The Company will reimburse for reasonable calls during overnight travel if the Teammate does not have a company issued cell phone.

MEALS AND ENTERTAINMENT

When a business expense involves more than one Spectranetics Teammate, the bill is to be paid by the senior Teammate present. Personal Meal Expenses: Personal meals are defined as meal expenses incurred by the traveller when dining on an out-of-town business trip with an overnight stay. If a Teammate returns home the same day, then meals may not be expensed to the Company for that day. This does not apply to sharing a meal with a colleague for the business purposes mentioned in the Non-Travel Related Meals section below, or, for Entertainment where a meal is shared with a business contact outside of the company. Business travellers will be reimbursed for personal meal expenses. Total meal expense should be within reasonable and customary guidelines (no more than $60 per day). This is not a per diem. Traveller is required to submit actual meal expense up to the $60 threshold. When traveling with other Spectranetics Teammates, if one Teammate pays for another Teammate's meal, the person reporting the meal must report the total number of people paid for.

Restaurant receipts over $100 must include detail of the food items purchased and the tip amount. Tip amount should be written on receipt and included in total expense amount reported. If a meal is taken with a group and someone else in the group pays the meal, no separate meal expense for that meal may be claimed for reimbursement. Snacks, bottled water, etc. purchased while traveling should reported in the Meals-Travel category and should be within total daily meal guidelines. Policy Limits: Meals-Travel in excess of $60 per day/per person will be flagged for review.

NON-TRAVEL RELATED MEALS

Teammates will be reimbursed for business-related meals taken with other Teammates only in the following circumstances:

- Group meetings held during meal times
- When, for confidentiality reasons, business must be conducted off company premises
- For reward, recognition or other appropriate business purpose with prior manager approval

Note: Local meals with colleagues should be considered a personal expense unless the business being conducted is such that it cannot be done in the office.

An explanation of the reason as to why the meeting could not take place in the office must accompany the reimbursement request. Meals taken with individuals or groups other than Spectranetics Teammates should be reported in the Entertainment-non HCP category (if no HCP's are in attendance) or one of the HCP categories (if HCP's are in attendance). Policy Limits: Meals-Local in excess of $60 per person will be flagged for review.

TIPS

Gratuities for meals and entertainment should be in the 15 per cent - 20 per cent range and in no case should exceed 20 per cent.

HCP EXPENSES

The Advanced Medical Technology Association (AdvaMed) has adopted a Code of Ethics on Interactions with Health Care Professionals. Spectranetics has also adopted this code and all entertainment expenses involving Health Care Professionals should be conducted within the guidelines of the AdvaMed Code of Ethics. The Code is intended, in part, to avoid even the appearance that hospitality may be used an inducement to purchase or refer a product. Entertainment or other expenses paid on behalf of Health Care Professionals should follow the guidelines of being reasonable and modest.

The following categories are to be used to report any expenses that involve Health Care Providers:

- HCP – Education
- HCP – Meals
- HCP – Speaking Events
- HCP – Training
- HCP – HCP Travel
- Entertainment – Non HCP.

Entertainment expenses include any meals or events with non-HCP business associates whereby a business discussion takes place during, immediately before, or immediately after the event. The number of people in attendance must be reported for all entertainment expenses. Entertainment should only be used when there is a non-Spectranetics Teammate in attendance.

Documentation and IRS Requirements:

- Names of individuals present, their titles and company name
- Name and location of where the meal or event took place
- Exact amount and date of the expense
- Specific business topic discussed
- In the case of entertainment events (*e.g.* sporting event), the specific time the business discussion took place (*i.e.*, before, during or after the event)

Policy Limits: Entertainment in excess of $500 will be flagged for review.

MEETINGS

Meetings should be used for all expenses related to organized events such as regional training meetings. Business meals with colleagues should not be reported under meetings unless it is part of an organized event.

CREDENTIALING

Spectranetics has a master agreement with VendorMate that covers Teammate credentialing for access to most hospitals. If a customer location requires credentialing and does not accept VendorMate, then the Teammate can expense that fee under the Credentialing category in Concur.

OFFICE/ COMPUTER SUPPLIES

Spectranetics has negotiated discount rates with Office Depot for orders done on line through the home office access. Home office Teammates should submit their office supply orders to the designated office supply buyer in their department area. Your order request should include the Office Depot stock number, quantity, description and price. Supplies will be delivered the next business day in most cases. For Sales and Field Service Teammates, please purchase your company related office supplies at the location most convenient to you. Submit your expenses for reimbursement on line with the Concur Expense system. Please purchase your business related office supplies separate from other personal items to further aid in the receipt handling of your expense report processing. In all cases, Teammates should use good judgement and be cost conscious when ordering office and computer supplies. Policy Limits: Office supplies in excess of $250 will be flagged for review.

POSTAGE

Postage expense reimbursement is limited to company business only. Enter the purpose of your postage expense and/or the recipient of the delivery when entering that transaction in Concur. If it is simply for regular delivery stamps for business use, enter "stamps" in the remarks section. If the company FedEx account is used, the senders name must be included on the shipment form. Include your department number and project number (if applicable) on the reference line.

TEAMMATE REWARDS AND RECOGNITION

Gift cards, certificates or any type of recognition gifts may not be purchased by managers and reimbursed via expense reports. All recognition gifts must be processed through the payroll department to be included in the W-2 wages. Forward all requests to Payroll with the amount and type of the award, desired date of the award to be given, and the Teammate name clearly specified. Please allow one week for your request to be processed.

Non-reimbursable Expenses:

- Additional costs or charges for travel, meals and entertainment when a spouse or guest accompanies a Teammate (certain exceptions for P-Club and trips given for Teammate recognition)
- Airline, car rental or hotel membership fees (except with Vice President approval)
- Alcohol:

Individual consumption at non-meal times is non-reimbursable. Moderate consumption during business meals or in a group setting is allowable.

- Car repair
- Credit card interest and late charges
- Day care for children or pets
- Grooming, nail or hair salon expenses
- Headphones on airlines
- Meals, entertainment, hospitality, accommodations, transportation for employees of a federal government hospital
- Movie charges associated with lodging
- Parking and traffic fines
- Personal reading material
- Roadside service agreements (*e.g.* AAA)
- Spa/ massages unless specifically approved as part of a meeting or event (*e.g.* President's Club)
- Hotel fitness centers in excess of $25/day
- Toiletries, drugs and medicines
- Travel, collision and accident insurance purchased by employees for rental cars
- Other expenses that are not business or travel related
- Home phone and internet lines

9

Human Resource Management in Tourism Economics

Introduction

Human resources are now generally acknowledged to be the major determinant not only of successful health sector reforms and the performance of health systems in general, but also to achieve the Millennium Development Goals and effectively upscale anti-retroviral treatment programmes. However, in many countries, the health workforce is lingering in a permanent crisis with major problems regarding training and distribution of health personnel, motivation, performance and professional accountability. The impact of the HIV/AIDS pandemic and the brain drain are now compounding this chronic crisis in many countries in sub-Saharan Africa.

The "Health Care for All " Conference emphasised the need for strong health systems and highlighted as the critical factors affecting access to adequate health care the problems of financial affordability of care, deficient mechanisms to ensure quality of care, shortages of competent and motivated health personnel and the failure of disease control programmes to strengthen health care systems. These four issues are the basis of the policy supporting research programme *Health Care for All.* The study presented in this report has been carried out within the chapter on *Human resources.*

Regarding the health workforce, the Republic of Ghana currently presents a particularly interesting situation in that its health system has been undergoing important structural changes over the last decade. The far-reaching decentralisation allocated greater autonomy to hospitals, districts and regions. Ghana is also an important sending country in the global "brain drain", which reflects both the country's high medical education standards and a worldwide good reputation of its medical professionals and an inadequate retention capacity of the health system. While the health care delivery configuration may be different from neighbouring countries, the general situation regarding human resources is quite similar to that of other African countries and equally precarious. However, some health facilities appear to thrive or at least to do remarkably better than others. They seem to be able to attract and retain personnel and to be capable of maintaining good standards of performance in these adverse conditions. Among public health institutions in Ghana, the Cape Coast Central Regional Hospital seems to stand out in its management approaches his for many reasons. It has a well-maintained infrastructure, the staff displays a strong professional attitude and the management team exerts strong and effective leadership.

One hypothesis explaining this particular situation could be that the management team of C3RH manages to deal effectively with the internal and external constraints it faces and that its management practices are particularly appropriate, especially those pertaining to human resources, contributing eventually to the relatively high performance standards achieved by this hospital. As for any manager, hospital managers basically have two major roles that need to be mastered to make the hospital fulfil its roles. First, they need to manage the inner works of the complex organisation that is a hospital.

Second, they need to manage the boundary conditions, that is to manage the inter-organisational relationships and the influences and pressures within the environment in which it functions. In order to explore how at C3RH the hospital management team manages these two key dimensions of hospital management, we conducted a study on the management approach.

In a first part, this report spells out the background, the aim and objectives, the research questions the study seeks to respond to, the study design and the research methods. The second part presents a summary overview of Ghana and in particular the health sector reform process and the consequences for the planning and management of the health workforce. The third part describes the different aspects of the HR management practice at C3RH and a discussion of the decision spaces. Finally, the fourth part presents an analysis and discussion of some major emerging issues.

Rationale and Background of the Study

During a field visit for IMMPACT in April 2004, a visit to the Cape Coast Central Regional Hospital provided a short peek at a facility where the hospital management team apparently manages to retain and motivate its staff in a region with vacancy rates as high as 60 per cent for nursing posts. In Ghana, as in most African countries, the chronic crisis that has been affecting the human resources for health has been putting quite some pressure on the government in general and the health sector in particular. Burning issues such as HIV/AIDS, poverty and the internal and external brain drain are consistently exacerbating this lingering crisis. The public health literature regarding human resources for health reveals a recent flurry of reports that deal with the crisis of the human resources for health. One stream explores the human resource bottlenecks for the new global health initiatives and the rapid scaling up of ART and the effects of the pandemic on the health workforce. Another stream focuses on the brain drain, while a third stream presents global overviews of the factors that underlie the crisis. Often, authors of the latter two streams identify issues such as workplace conditions, remuneration and availability of drugs and equipment as factors affecting the attraction and retention of staff. But frustratingly few experiences of how to manage these problems effectively are documented. If anything, this 'new' attention being given to the health workforce shows that both the world of research and international development has taken up the issue of human resources once again, but it can be argued that the health workforce is again considered a constraint or an obstacle to successful programmes like the 3x5 initiative rather than an essential element of any health system that merits attention in its own right. In that aspect, this new wave of attention for human resources resembles the literature that focused on the health workforce in the light of the health sector reforms.

Initially, little attention was given to the consequences of health sector reforms for the health workforce, but gradually it became clear that reforms that do not consider the health workers would run into trouble. However, most stages remain at a general level of analysis and the 'messy' operational management aspect is conspicuously absent in the discussion. Indeed, in-depth documented knowledge on actual management practices taking place in developing countries is missing, l*et al*one studies on effective and efficient management practices. This study aims at exploring the issues of health workforce management from the operational level and more specifically from the point of view of a hospital management team of a regional hospital.

Our analytical framework is based on the model of management of tensions as proposed by Jaffee and holds that good management basically requires dealing with two 'domains'. The interorganisational domain includes the interface of the organisation with its environment; and the other organisations and the influences it needs to deal with. The intra-organisational domain covers all aspects of the hospital as an organisation in itself and especially the staff. This perspective is very similar to that presented by Glouberman and Mintzberg.

In this chapter, we will first briefly discuss the process of the health sector reform and its impact on human resource management in general, given the importance of the health sector reform and especially the decentralisation of the health system in Ghana for the inter-organisational domain. In a second part, we'll present the concept of decision spaces in the frame of decentralisation.

HEALTH SECTOR REFORM AND THE HEALTH WORKFORCE

The health sector reform in many industrialised countries as well as developing countries took the form of the introduction of concepts of new public management in public service management. This was generally based on the assumption that state-organised services are inherently inefficient and non-effective and often resulting in a low degree of responsiveness to patients and population. Evidently bureaucratic organisations, the template of organisational structure of many health services in developing countries, present several types of dysfunction.

First, organisations that are structured as bureaucracies may lead to a loss of individual freedom of the staff and impose limits to creativity. This leads to a tension between the pursuit of organisational effectiveness on one hand, the goal of any organisation, and the individual freedom and margin of creativity on the other hand. It can lead to high degrees of frustration, demotivation and alienation among staff. Merton similarly found that the obsession of any given well-functioning bureaucracy with compliance with formal rules could undermine the actual effectiveness and efficiency of the organisation through the mechanism of goal displacement.

Furthermore, despite its hierarchical and tiered structure that aims at achieving maximum control, the bureaucracy places its staff who work at the interface with the public, the street-level bureaucrats in a position that enables them to influence the execution of decisions, organisational strategies and policies to a great extent. Interactions at this interface indeed often shape how patients and citizens experience health care and service delivery. In short, it is not surprising that the very organisational configuration of health systems can inhibit and stifle innovation.

Without doubt, NPM addressed the right problems: low performance, poor quality of care and of service, limited responsiveness and low utilisation of services. Advocates of health sector reforms indeed argue that the traditional bureaucratic organisation of the health system and the rigid public service rules and procedures impose major hurdles to better manage the performance of both health workers and system. New public management's answer was to introduce performance management systems in which incentive systems were given an important role. It was characterised by a drive for attaining maximal efficiency and cost-effectiveness through down-sizing of the workforce and the introduction of short term contracts, internal competition and privatisation. However, NPM may itself have been the wrong answer in that it applied a market logic to public services that are essentially non-market activities.

Without entering in this complex issue, the emphasis on short-term and measurable results, the transformation of services to 'products', the diminishing commitment to social goals and the introduction of competition at the cost of trust relationships and collaboration has had a serious impact on the organisation and delivery of equitable health services. Not coincidentally, the NHS changed tack with the White Paper 'The New NHS: Modern, Dependable', moving away from the competitive internal market to more collaborative systems based on partnership, although this was at least in part an equally ideological decision of the newly elected Labour government.

Although some of the health sector reforms were thus directly aimed at improving the health workforce performance, the point of departure was the macro-level. Health sector reforms were framed in the concurrent administrative reforms of the governmental bureaucracies. In the initial wave of health sector reforms, some attention was given to assessing and strengthening the human resource planning and development capacity at central level, but the operational aspects of human resource management as experienced at the coal-face, or in this case at the health services itself, was completely overlooked. Often, elements of reforms that were likely to have an impact on human resource management, such as contracting, were introduced without strong evidence.

Also the effect of the decentralisation of the authority to hire and fire and the consequences for equity between regions with different socio-economic conditions and therefore different degrees of attraction to health workers has not been examined thoroughly. The few studies that did focus on the effects of health sector reforms for the health workforce concentrated on the consequences of decentralisation on the health workers performance and motivation. Kipp *et al.* indirectly explored HRM issues related to the introduction of user fees in Uganda and the use of part of the revenue for staff incentives, while Green and Collins explored the tensions that health managers at district level in many countries are facing. Somewhat unsurprisingly, Johnson showed that decentralisation of certain responsibilities requires sound management capacities at peripheral levels. This is confirmed by a series of case studies carried out by Ssengooba *et al.*

in Uganda in public and non-for profit hospitals showing that increasing autonomy of hospitals requires a strong management capacity and good reliability. In short, a review of the literature points out that human resource management has been neglected in the health sector reforms in many countries. In many instances little attention was given to assessing and strengthening the human resource management, planning and development capacity.

For Schick this should have deterred the introduction of NPM, since the preconditions for successful implementation of NPM requires a strong managerial capacity to manage for example the contractual approaches that were introduced in countries like New Zealand and the UK. But also the consequences of reform for the operational human resource management has often been overlooked. Only recently there has been some acknowledgement of the importance of the health workers and of a minimum management capability for the success of reforms.

It can be argued that in many cases of decentralisation, failure may be due to inappropriate design of the reforms due to inadequate consultation and insufficient capacity of both health service managers and health boards at district level.

DEFINING THE DECISION SPACES TO BETTER UNDERSTAND THE EFFECTS OF DECENTRALIZATION

One of the underlying assumptions of health sector reform was the low degree of responsiveness allowed to local health care managers in the bureaucratically organised public health systems in many developing countries. Bossert was the first to develop an analytical framework to assess the effectiveness of decentralisation for attaining the health system's objectives by introducing the decision space concept. The author defines the decision space as '*the range of effective choice that is allowed by the central authorities to be utilised by the local authorities* '. The decision space model covers the dimensions of finance, service organisation, human resources, access rules and governance rules. The model has been used to assess the degree of decentralisation in any of the dimensions and to compare processes among countries. The decision space of health care managers is formally defined through legislation and regulations.

In the case of Ghana, the cascade of contractual arrangements between the MOH and the GHS on one hand, and within the GHS on the other hand (between GHS and the regions and between the region and the health facilities) will additionally define the formal boundaries of the decision space. However, the *formal* decision space may differ significantly from the *actual* decision space.

Bossert mentions that the latter '*may be defined by the lack of enforcement of these formal definitions that allows lower level officials at each level to "bend the rules"* '. Indeed, the health care managers can be considered as street-level bureaucrats, who in a decentralised setting may wield even more powers to influence the actual degree and nature of the implementation of the new policies.

CALLING ATTENTION TO THE PROCESS ASPECTS

Mainly policy changes and structural approaches have been presented, usually based on macro-level analyses of the determinants of the health workforce crisis and this has led to changes in the structure of the health system and in the margins of decision spaces of decision makers at the different levels of the health system.

These changes introduced in isolation often miss the ball because the implementation capacity at the operational level has not been taken into account. At this point, it may be useful to introduce a definition of human resource management (HRM). Reflecting the changing perception of the HRM practice, we use the definition proposed by Johnson, which surpasses the traditional personnel administration role (staffing, workplace policies, compensation and benefits, training and regulatory issues) and includes the following domains.

First, HR managers play a support role to the senior management by translating the organisational strategy into appropriate HR policy and practice. Second, they should manage transformation and change.

Third, HR managers are responsible for management of the staff contribution, aiming not only at increased employee commitment and competence, but also being concerned about the staff's concerns and problems. In short, HR managers can play an important role in aligning their management practice with the goals and strategies of the organisation to optimise their staff's contribution to the organisational goals. Although in many hospitals in developing countries, including Ghana, there may be few specialist human resource managers, the same roles are to be taken up by the general managers or the hospital directors. In the implementation capacity for such an enlarged role, the management capability of the local teams evidently assumes an important role. This capability is determined by the quality of the management personnel (availability, qualifications and experience) and the management structure that is in place (composition and organisation of the team management, the information system and of the decision making process).

However, the less tangible process aspects pertaining to the input of the managers in terms of leadership, personal motivation and vision on one hand and to the actual management practice (the fit between management style and problem/type of staff, management of conflicts, introduction of change, dissemination of innovation) on the other hand is a key ingredient of successful management.

While in developing countries health worker motivation and morale has been studied, although not frequently documented, the motivation of the managers hasn't been documented yet, nor has the process aspects of the actual management practice. Factors that influence decision-makers at local level can be categorised in external motivators that include the pressure exerted by staff, the community and local politicians or by the incentives and sanctions defined by the institutional arrangements (Similar to the social capital approach, Putnam 1993) and in internal motivators (personal values and vision, including personal ideological conviction, religious beliefs, etc.). But also structural factors like the organisational configuration (the health system bureaucracy and organisational culture (including public service ethics, professionalism and organisational survival reflexes) may influence the actual practice of decision makers. These different dimensions are captured by the conceptual model we used to describe and analyse what shapes the actual behaviour of decision makers and/or managers at the regional hospital in Cape Coast.

TOURISM ECONOMICS

Most of the tourism activity also involves economic costs, including the direct costs incurred by tourism businesses, government costs for infrastructure to better serve tourists, as well as congestion and related costs borne by individuals in the community. Community decisions over tourism often involve debates between industry proponents touting tourism's economic impacts (benefits) and detractors emphasizing tourism's costs.

Sound decisions rest on a balanced and objective assessment of both benefits and costs and an understanding of who benefits from tourism and who pays for it. Businesses and public organizations are increasingly interested in the economic impacts of tourism at national, state, and local levels. One regularly hears claims that tourism supports X jobs in an area or that a festival or special event generated Y million dollars in sales or income in a community. "Multiplier effects" are often cited to capture secondary effects of tourism spending and show the wide range of sectors in a community that may benefit from tourism. Tourism's economic benefits are touted by the industry for a variety of reasons. Claims of tourism's economic significance give the industry greater respect among the business community, public officials, and the public in general. This often translates into decisions or public policies that are favourable to tourism.

Community support is important for tourism, as it is an activity that affects the entire community. Tourism businesses depend extensively on each other as well as on other businesses, government and residents of the local community. Economic benefits and costs of tourism reach virtually everyone in the region in one way or another. Economic impact analyses provide tangible estimates of these economic interdependencies and a better understanding of the role and importance of tourism in a region's economy.

Tourism's economic impacts are therefore an important consideration in state, regional and community planning and economic development. Economic impacts are also important factors in marketing and management decisions. Communities therefore need to understand the relative importance of tourism to their region, including tourism's contribution to economic activity in the area.

A variety of methods, ranging from pure guesswork to complex mathematical models, are used to estimate tourism's economic impacts. Studies vary extensively in quality and accuracy, as well as which aspects of tourism are included. Technical reports often are filled with economic terms and methods that non-economists do not understand. On the other hand, media coverage of these studies tend to oversimplify and frequently misinterpret the results, leaving decision makers and the general public with a sometimes distorted and incomplete understanding of tourism's economic effects.

How can the average person understand these studies sufficiently to separate good studies from bad ones and make informed choices? The purpose of this bulletin is to present a systematic introduction to economic impact concepts and methods. The presentation is written for tourism industry analysts and public officials, who would like to better understand, evaluate, or possibly conduct an economic impact assessment. The bulletin is organized around ten basic questions that either are asked or should be asked about the economic impacts of tourism.

Economic impact analysis

A variety of economic analyses are carried out to support tourism decisions. As these different kinds of economic analysis are frequently confused, let's begin by positioning economic impact studies within the broader set of economic problems and techniques relevant to tourism. These same techniques may be applied to any policy or action, but we will define them here in the context of tourism. Each type of analysis is identified by the basic question(s) it answers and the types of methods and models that are appropriate. Benefit cost analysis and economic impact analysis are frequently confused as both discuss economic "benefits". There are two clear distinctions between the two techniques. B/C analysis addresses the benefits from economic efficiency while economic impact analysis focuses on the regional distribution of economic activity. The income received from tourism by a destination region is largely off-set by corresponding losses in the origin regions, yielding only modest contributions to net social welfare and efficiency. B/C analysis includes market and non-market values (consumer surplus), while economic impact analysis is restricted to actual flows of money from market transactions.

While each type of economic analysis is somewhat distinct, a given problem often calls for several different kinds of economic analysis. An economic impact study will frequently involve a demand analysis to project levels of tourism activity. In other cases demand is treated as exogenous and the analysis simply estimates impacts if a given number of visitors are attracted to the area. A comprehensive impact assessment will also examine fiscal impacts, as well as social and environmental impacts. Be aware that an economic impact analysis, by itself, provides a rather narrow and often one-sided perspective on the impacts of tourism.

Studies of the economic impacts of tourism tend to emphasize the positive benefits of tourism. On the other hand environmental, social, cultural and fiscal impact studies tend to focus more on negative impacts of tourism. This is in spite of the fact that there are negative economic impacts of tourism (*e.g.*, seasonality and lower wage jobs) and in many cases positive environmental and social impacts (*e.g.*, protection of natural and cultural resources in the area and education of both tourists and local residents). An economic impact assessment (EIA) traces changes in economic activity resulting from some action.

An EIA will identify which economic sectors benefit from tourism and estimate resulting changes in income and employment in the region. Economic impact assessment procedures do not assess economic efficiency and also do not generally produce estimates of the fiscal costs of an action. For many problems economic impact analysis will be part of a broader analysis. Environmental, social, and fiscal impacts are often equally important concerns in a balanced assessment of impacts.

An economic impact analysis will assess the contribution of tourism activity to a region's economy. The basic questions an economic impact study usually addresses are:

- How many jobs in the area does tourism support?
- How much tax revenue is generated from tourism?
- How much do tourists spend in the area?
- What portion of sales by local businesses is due to tourism?
- How much income does tourism generate for households and businesses in the area?

An economic impact analysis also reveals the interrelationships among economic sectors and provides estimates of the changes that take place in an economy due to some existing or proposed action. The most common applications of economic impact analysis to tourism are:

1. To evaluate the economic impacts of changes in the supply of recreation and tourism opportunities. Supply changes may involve a change in quantity, such as the opening of new facilities, closing of existing ones, or expansions and contraction in capacity. Supply changes may also involve changes in quality, including changes in (a) the quality of the environment, (b) the local infrastructure and public services to support tourism, or (c) the nature of the tourism products and services that are provided in an area.
2. To evaluate the economic impacts of changes in tourism demand. Population changes, changes in the competitive position of the region, marketing activity or changing consumer tastes and preferences can alter levels of tourism activity, spending, and associated economic activity. An economic impact study can estimate the magnitude and nature of these impacts.
3. To evaluate the effects of policies and actions which affect tourism activity either directly or indirectly. Tourism depends on many factors at both origins and destinations that are frequently outside the direct control of the tourism industry itself. Economic impact studies provide information to help decision makers better understand the consequences of various actions on the tourism industry as well as on other sectors of the economy. For example, increased air pollution standards have been opposed in some regions due to the predicted economic consequences of the closing of plants that cannot meet the new standards. Tourism interests counter these arguments with estimates of the potential gains in income and jobs in tourism industries that depend on good air quality and visibility.

4. To understand the economic structure and interdependencies of different sectors of the economy. Economic studies help us better understand the size and structure of the tourism industry in a given region and its linkages to other sectors of the economy. Such understandings are helpful in identifying potential partners for the tourism industry as well as in targeting industries as part of regional economic development strategies. Issues such as economic growth, stability, and seasonality may be addressed as part of these studies.
5. To argue for favourable treatment in allocation of resources or local tax, zoning or other policy decisions. By showing that tourism has significant economic impacts, tourism interests can often convince decision-makers to allocate more resources for tourism or to establish policies that encourage tourism. Tax abatements and other incentives frequently given to manufacturing firms have also been granted to hotels, marinas and other tourism businesses based on demonstrated economic impacts in the local area.
6. To compare the economic impacts of alternative resource allocation, policy, management or development proposals. Economic impact analyses are commonly used to assess the relative merits of distinct alternatives. The economic contribution of expanded tourism offerings may be compared for example with alternatives such as resource extraction activities (mining, timber harvesting) or manufacturing. Impacts of alternative tourism development proposals may also be evaluated, *e.g.*, tourism strategies that emphasize outdoor recreation, camping development, a convention facility, or a factory outlet mall.

Tourism has a variety of economic impacts. Tourists contribute to sales, profits, jobs, tax revenues, and income in an area. The most direct effects occur within the primary tourism sectors —lodging, restaurants, transportation, amusements, and retail trade. Through secondary effects, tourism affects most sectors of the economy. An economic impact analysis of tourism activity normally focuses on changes in sales, income, and employment in a region resulting from tourism activity.

A simple tourism impact scenario illustrates. Let's say a region attracts an additional 100 tourists, each spending $100 per day. That's $10,000 in new spending per day in the area. If sustained over a 100 day season, the region would accumulate a million dollars in new sales. The million dollars in spending would be distributed to lodging, restaurant, amusement and retail trade sectors in proportion to how the visitor spends the $100. Perhaps 30 per cent of the million dollars would leak out of the region immediately to cover the costs of goods purchased by tourists that are not made in the local area (only the retail margins for such items should normally be included as direct sales effects). The remaining $700,000 in direct sales might yield $350,000 in income within tourism industries and support 20 direct tourism jobs. Tourism industries are labour and income intensive, translating a high proportion of sales into income and corresponding jobs. The tourism industry, in turn, buys goods and services from other businesses in the area, and pays out most of the $350,000 in income as wages and salaries to its employees. This creates secondary economic effects in the region. The study might use a sales multiplier of 2.0 to indicate that each dollar of direct sales generates another dollar in secondary sales in this region. Through multiplier effects, the $700,000 in direct sales produces $1.4 million in total sales. These secondary sales create additional income and employment, resulting in a total impact on the region of $1.4 million in sales, $650,000 in income and 35 jobs. While hypothetical, the numbers used here are fairly typical of what one might find in a tourism economic impact study. A more complete study might identify which sectors receive the direct and secondary effects and possibly identify differences in spending and impacts of distinct subgroups of tourists (market segments). One can also estimate the tax effects of this spending by applying local tax rates to the appropriate changes in sales or income. Instead of focusing on visitor spending, one could also estimate impacts of construction or government activity associated with tourism. There are several other categories of economic impacts that are not typically covered in economic impact assessments, at least not directly. For example:

Changes in prices — tourism can sometimes inflate the cost of housing and retail prices in the area, frequently on a seasonal basis.

Changes in the quality and quantity of goods and services — tourism may lead to a wider array of goods and services available in an area (of either higher or lower quality than without tourism).

Changes in property and other taxes — taxes to cover the cost of local services may be higher or lower in the presence of tourism activity. In some cases, taxes collected directly or indirectly from tourists may yield reduced local taxes for schools, roads, etc. In other cases, locals may be taxed more heavily to cover the added infrastructure and service costs. The impacts of tourism on local government costs and revenues are addressed more fully in a fiscal impact analysis.

Economic dimensions of "social" and "environmental" impacts — There are also economic consequences of most social and environmental impacts that are not usually addressed in an economic impact analysis. These can be positive or negative. For example, traffic congestion will increase costs of moving around for both households and businesses. Improved amenities that attract tourists may also encourage retirees or other kinds of businesses to locate in the area.

Induced Effects

A standard economic impact analysis traces flows of money from tourism spending, first to businesses and government agencies where tourists spend their money and then to: *Other businesses* — supplying goods and services to tourist businesses,

Households — earning income by working in tourism or supporting industries, and

Government — through various taxes and charges on tourists, businesses and households

Formally, regional economists distinguish direct, indirect, and induced economic effects. Indirect and induced effects are sometimes collectively called secondary effects. The total economic impact of tourism is the sum of direct, indirect, and induced effects within a region. Any of these impacts may be measured as gross output or sales, income, employment, or value added. Direct effects are production changes associated with the immediate effects of changes in tourism expenditures.

For example, an increase in the number of tourists staying overnight in hotels would directly yield increased sales in the hotel sector. The additional hotel sales and associated changes in hotel payments for wages and salaries, taxes, and supplies and services are direct effects of the tourist spending.

Indirect effects are the production changes resulting from various rounds of re-spending of the hotel industry's receipts in other backward-linked industries (*i.e.*, industries supplying products and services to hotels). Changes in sales, jobs, and income in the linen supply industry, for example, represent indirect effects of changes in hotel sales. Businesses supplying products and services to the linen supply industry represent another round of indirect effects, eventually linking hotels to varying degrees to many other economic sectors in the region. Induced effects are the changes in economic activity resulting from household spending of income earned directly or indirectly as a result of tourism spending. For example, hotel and linen supply employees supported directly or indirectly by tourism, spend their income in the local region for housing, food, transportation, and the usual array of household product and service needs. The sales, income, and jobs that result from household spending of added wage, salary, or proprietor's income are induced effects.

By means of indirect and induced effects, changes in tourist spending can impact virtually every sector of the economy in one way or another. The magnitude of secondary effects depends on the propensity of businesses and households in the region to purchase goods and services from local suppliers. Induced effects are particularly noticed when a large employer in a region closes a plant. Not only are supporting industries (indirect effects) hurt, but the entire local economy suffers due to the reduction in household income within the region. Retail stores close and leakages of money from the region increase as consumers go outside the region for more and more goods and services.

Similar effects in the opposite direction are observed when there is a significant increase in jobs and household income. Final demand is the term used by economists for sales to the final consumers of goods and services. In almost all cases, the final consumers of tourism goods and services are households. Government spending is also considered as final demand. The same methods for estimating impacts of visitor spending can be applied to estimate the economic impacts of government spending, for example, to operate and maintain a park or visitor center.

Regional Models

An input-output model (I-O model) is a mathematical model that describes the flows of money between sectors within a region's economy. Flows are predicted by knowing what each industry must buy from every other industry to produce a dollar's worth of output. Using each industry's production function, I-O models also determine the proportions of sales that go to wage and salary income, proprietor's income, and taxes. Multipliers can be estimated from input-output models based on the estimated re-circulation of spending within the region. Exports and imports are determined based upon estimates of the propensity of households and firms within the region to purchase goods and services from local sources (often called RPC's or regional purchase coefficients). The more a region is self-sufficient and purchases goods and services from within the region, the higher the multipliers for the region.

Input-output models make a number of assumptions. The basic ones are that:

- All firms in a given industry employ the same production technology (usually assumed to be the national average for that industry), and produce identical products.
- There are no economies or diseconomies of scale in production or factor substitution. I-O models are essentially linear — double the level of tourism activity/production and you double all of the inputs, the number of jobs, etc.
- The model doesn't explicitly keep track of time, but analysts generally report the impact estimates as if they represent activity within a single year.
- One must assume that the various model parameters are accurate and represent the current year.

I-O models are firmly grounded in the national system of accounts, which relies on a standard industrial classification system (SIC codes) and various federal government economic censuses, in which individual firms report sales, wage and salary payments and employment. I-O models will generally be at least a few years out-of-date, although this isn't usually a major problem unless the region's economy has changed significantly. An I-O model represents the region's economy at a particular point in time. Tourist spending estimates are generally price adjusted to the year of the model.

Multiplier computations for induced effects generally assume that jobs created by additional spending are new jobs, involving new households in the area. Induced effects are computed assuming linear changes in household spending with changes in income. Estimates of induced effects may be inflated due to the violation of these assumptions. Induced effects tend to account for the vast majority of the secondary effects of tourism, and therefore should be used with caution.

E-COMMERCE TOURISM

Tourism is growing fastest in the developing countries, where it is a major component of most economies. Tourism is one of the world's largest industries, and it is a natural partner for the Internet, where it is also the world's largest on-line industry. Community-based tourism (CBT) has been shown to foster local development in developing countries, particularly in the poorer rural areas. At the same time, Information and Communication Technologies are being deployed within poor communities in developing countries and are beginning to demonstrate their potential for inducing local development. This paper describes an action research initiative for introducing electronic commerce for community based tourism (e-CBT) in three Asian rural communities in order to reveal its potential for community development.

E-CBT targets an important and growing market segment in the developing world, consisting of individual travellers for whom travel is an essential component of their life-style and who seek new and authentic experiences that are not directed towards a mass market. The proposal describes strategic partnerships between a University in Hong Kong and three other Asian universities who will work with local communities and tourism authorities for the eventual propagation of the development benefits of e-CBT among wider rural populations in their countries.

The WTO forecasts that international arrivals are expected to reach over 1.56 billion by the year 2020. The total expected tourist arrivals by region shows that by 2020 the top three receiving regions will be Europe (717 million tourists), East Asia and the Pacific (397 million) and Americas (282 million). East Asia and the Pacific, South Asia, the Middle East and Africa are forecasted to record growth at rates of over 5 per cent per year, compared to the world average of 4.1 per cent. By 2010, WTO forecasts that the Americas will lose its number two position, behind Europe, to East Asia and the Pacific, which will receive 25 per cent of world arrivals.

Tourism offers huge opportunities for developing countries to increase incomes from the growing number of arrivals that land on their shores. However, it has been recognized that many tourism policies developed from central governments without local involvement fail to cater for the sensibilities and aspirations of the communities that tourists visit. The conference on

Community Based Ecotourism in Southeast Asia agreed that local communities should have the right to self-determination and to decide whether to accept or not accept the policies that affect their livelihood. As tourism is essentially a micro- enterprise, tourism lends itself to local entrepreneurial activity, and community-based tourism has emerged as a mechanism for fostering locally based tourism operations, as opposed to those whose financial interests are often located away from the tourist destination.

Moreover, as Information and Communication Technologies (ICTs) are beginning to be deployed in rural communities for the purpose of fostering local development, communities are able to implement electronic commerce in support of their CBT operations, and engage in e-CBT. Furthermore, it will be shown that the Internet is not only a natural partner for tourism, it also a natural partner for the market segment that e-CBT should target. With more than 600 million people on-line by September 2002, and more than 60 per cent of them residing in Europe or North America, even small and remote communities with an Internet connection can address huge global markets.

The purpose of this paper is to introduce the concept of electronic commerce for community based tourism, e-CBT, as a mechanism for local development. E-CBT involves the operation of local tourism activities which are promoted across the internet by a community using a community based telecentre, which provides community access to information and communication technologies. The concept is presented as a method for fostering rural development in developing countries.

Tourism is a principal export for developing countries and the least developed countries (LDCs). It is growing rapidly and is the most significant source of foreign exchange after petroleum (WTO, 2002). There is a general shift of tourism arrivals towards developing countries. Growth rates of international tourism receipts during the 1990s were, on average, 50 per cent higher in the major developing country destinations than in comparison with the major developed country destinations. By far the largest single developing country international tourism destination is China.

The People's Republic accounted for US$10 billion in international tourism receipts in 1996, receiving 22.7 million international visitors, experiencing 19 per cent annual growth rates of receipts since 1980. Together with earnings generated by the Hong Kong Special Administrative Region, China's 1996 receipts surpass US$20 billion. In 2001, China ranked fifth in the world's top tourism destinations, measured both by the number of international arrivals and by international tourism receipts. Yet in terms of Gross National Income per capita, China ranks 108 out of 173 countries in the World Bank's statistical indicators for 2001. China, Thailand and Indonesia together generated 40 per cent of all international tourism receipts accruing to developing countries in 1996.

The World Tourism Organisation says there is a strong economic case for promoting tourism in developing countries, suggesting that affirmative action and pro-poor policies are able to go beyond trickle down and multiplier affects by unlocking opportunities for the poor within tourism (WTO 2002). Success in poverty alleviation through tourism depends, says the WTO, partly on effective community-public-private partnerships that serve to reduce financial leakages and increase economic linkages to the local economy. Financial leakages occur where a disproportionately low percentage of tourism revenues stays in the local market, and they reduce the development impact of tourism. Linkages with the local economy foster revenue retention from tourism activities, and they depend on quality, reliability and competitiveness of local products.

WTO suggest various steps that can be taken to increase the benefits to the local economy in tourist destination areas, by;

- Facilitating local community access to the tourism market,
- Minimising the financial leakages from the local economy,
- Maximising the linkages of tourism to the local economy,
- Building on and complimenting existing livelihood strategies through employment and small enterprise development,
- Ensuring that tourism products contribute to local economic development not just to national revenue generation.
- Tourism is a principal export for 83 per cent of developing countries and it is the principal export for one third of them.
- Developing countries had 292.6 million arrivals in 2000, an increase since 1990 of nearly 95 per cent. The 40 least developed countries had 5.1 million international arrivals in 2000; they achieved an increase of 75 per cent in the decade.
- 80 per cent of the world's poor, those living on less than US$1 per day, live in 12countries. In 11 of these countries, tourism is significant and growing
- The developing countries are attracting an increasing share of global international tourist arrivals up from 20 per cent in 1973 to 42 per cent in 2000.

The developing countries and particularly the LDCs secured a larger increase in the income per international arrival between 1990 and 2000 than did the OECD or the European Union countries. The LDCs secured an increase of 45 per cent between1990 and 2000 and the developing countries nearly 20 per cent. This compares with18 per cent for the OECD countries and 7.8 per cent for the EU. In 2000, tourism ranked third among the major merchandise export sectors for both developing countries and LDCs. If petroleum industry exports are discounted (and they are significant in only three) tourism is the primary source of foreign exchange in the 49 LDCs.

Community Based Tourism

Community-based tourism provides alternative economic opportunities, which are in essence in rural areas. Community-based tourism is regarded as a tool for natural and cultural resource conservation and community development and it is closely associated with ecotourism, sometimes referred to as community-based ecotourism. It is a community-based practice that provides contributions and incentives for natural and cultural conservation as well as providing opportunities for improved community livelihood. It has the potential to create jobs and generate entrepreneurial opportunities for people from a variety of backgrounds, skills and experiences, including rural communities and especially women. Community-based tourism has been implemented in many developing countries, often in support of wildlife management, environmental protection and/or development for indigenous peoples.

Community tourism should;

- Be run with the involvement and consent of local communities. (Local people should participate in planning and managing the tour.)
- Give a fair share of profits back to the local community. (Ideally this will include community projects (health, schools, etc).)
- Involve communities rather than individuals. (Working with individuals can disrupt social structures.)
- Be environmentally sustainable. (Local people must be involved if conservation projects are to succeed.)
- Respect traditional culture and social structures.
- Have mechanisms to help communities cope with the impact of western tourists.
- Keep groups small to minimise cultural / environmental impact.
- Brief tourists before the trip on appropriate behaviour.
- Not make local people perform inappropriate ceremonies, etc.
- Leave communities alone if they don't want tourism. (People should have the right to say 'no' to tourism.)

Community based tourism occurs when decisions about tourism activity and development are driven by the host community. It usually involves some form of cultural exchange where tourists meet with local communities and witness aspects of their lifestyle. Eco-tourism also emphasises observation and learning by the tourist, alongside economic and cultural conservation, and the delivery of benefits that ensure long-term sustainability of communities and natural resources. In Nepal, the Tourism for Rural Poverty Alleviation Programme began in 2001, jointly funded by the United Nations Development Programme (UNDP), the UK Department for International Development (DFID) with advisory services from SNV (Stichting Nederlandse Vrijwilligers) a Dutch development organisation.

Operating in six remote locations, the programme employed social mobilisation and tourist awareness programmes in villages to empower local communities to manage their own tourism development. In Vietnam, the International Union for Conservation of Nature and Natural Resources (IUCN) or World Conservation Union, is operating a community based tourism pilot in Sa Pa, a highly visited area with colourful ethnic minorities. Funded mainly by the Ford Foundation, the goal of the project is to assist local stakeholders to achieve an environmentally, culturally and socio-economically sustainable form of tourism, establishing mechanisms that support the active participation of the community in tourism decision-making and implementation.

The Nam Ha ecotourism project in Lao PDR uses community-based tourism as a vehicle to integrate environmental and cultural conservation with sustainable socio and economic development. Working closely with local villagers, limits were set on the number of trekking tourists allowed each year so as not to overwhelm the communities and to ensure that tourist incomes supplement rather than replace other economic activities.

Typically, with community-based tourism, the community runs all of the activities that a tourist engages in; lodging, food, guiding and craft sales. Benefits include; economic growth in rural regions; the distribution of tourism revenue, which can foster improved welfare and equity in the industry; improved resource conservation by local people; and diversification of the regional and national tourism product.

Intertwined with community-based tourism in developing countries is the concept of pro-poor tourism. In most counties with high levels of poverty, tourism is a significant and/or growing component of the economy. Governments and aid agencies acknowledge that whilst economic growth is essential for poverty reduction, of itself, it is insufficient to ensure a significant reduction. Growth that is specifically pro-poor is a pre-requisite for significant progress towards agreed targets for poverty reduction. Tourism has many characteristics that make it potentially pro-poor;

- It is a diverse industry, which increases the scope for wide participation,
- The customer comes to the product, providing important opportunities for linkages(*e.g.*, souvenir sales),
- It is highly dependent on natural capital (wildlife, scenery) and culture, assets that some of the poor have in abundance, even if they have few financial resources,
- Tourism can be more labour intensive than manufacturing,
- A higher proportion of benefits (jobs, trade opportunities) go to women.

Pro-poor tourism is defined as tourism that generates net benefits for the poor. It maximises the potential for eradicating poverty by developing appropriate strategies in co-operation with all major groups, indigenous and local communities. Benefits may be economic, but they may also be social, environmental or cultural. Pro-poor tourism is not a specific product or sector of tourism, but an approach to the tourism industry. The core activity is to increase access of the poor to economic benefits. Pro-poor tourism strategies unlock opportunities for the poor; whether for economic gain, other livelihood benefits, or participation in decision- making.

Early experience shows that pro-poor tourifcsm strategies do appear able to 'tilt' the industry at the margin, to expand opportunities for the poor and have potentially wide application across the industry. Poverty reduction through pro-poor tourism can therefore be significant at a local or district level. Moreover, the poverty impact may be greater in remote areas, though the tourism itself may be on a limited scale. Most examples of community-based in tourism in developing countries qualify as pro-poor tourism as they are designed to foster development at grassroots levels.

WELFARE IMPLICATIONS OF TOURISM TAXATION

It is widely accepted in the literature that taxation should comply with three main principles: efficiency, equity and having a low disincentive to work effect. Tourism taxation may meet all three criteria or only some of them. The efficiency principle can be achieved because, unlike other taxes, tourism taxes can lead to an increase in welfare, thereby rendering tourism taxation more efficient than taxing other sectors. The main reason why this occurs is that the presence of tourists increases the tax base for commodity taxation and hence higher tax revenue is generated. However, the welfare loss corresponding to a tax increase is not reflected in domestic welfare since utility of tourists is not included in the social welfare function. This is explained in more detail below.

The equity principle can also be achieved as some tourism products are classified as luxuries. Following the redistributive effect of taxation literature, taxing such products entails positive equity effects because they are consumed mainly by individuals from the higher income brackets. The disincentive to work effect of taxation is also considered to be an important criterion for good taxation principles. It is believed that taxation leads to a disincentive to work because the more a person works, the more tax the person pays, so that to avoid paying high taxes, people work less and take more leisure. This effect is more notable with direct income taxation, but Corlette and Hague demonstrate how commodity taxation can be used to circumvent the problem. They argue that goods that complement leisure more can be taxed at a higher rate. The intuition is that by taxing goods that are complementary to leisure, the price of leisure will increase.

Hence, people will be less willing to undertake leisure activities, thereby reducing the disincentive to work effect of taxation. Taxing tourism products reinforces the above proposition because taxing tourism is equivalent to taxing commodities that are complementary to leisure, thereby not only reducing the disincentive effects inflicted by the commodity tax but also reducing those introduced by income taxation, hence making the overall taxation system more efficient. The latter two principles will not be considered further here but the focus of the analysis will be on the first principle and will concern the welfare implications of tourism taxation, based on the normative analysis of the taxation literature using demand and supply analysis.

A practical and common method of taxing the tourism sector is through consumption taxes. Consumption taxes can either take the form of special taxes designed specifically to tax the tourism sector, such as a hotel room tax, or can be levied through the general sales tax system. Tourism may be the only export sector that can be taxed using the domestic sales tax. This is because of the special nature of the tourism product as an exported commodity. In contrast to conventional commodity exports, foreign tourists who want to consume tourism travel to the exporting country; ie. rather than sending goods across boundaries, consumers move across boundaries to consume the product. Consumption of goods and services will thus have a non-tourism consumption and a tourism consumption component.

Therefore, in an economy where a sales tax already exists, the tourism sector is taxed even without any deliberate actions from the government. This is, of course, true unless there is price discrimination between local consumers and tourists in the sense that tourists are exempted from sales tax. However, this happens rarely, especially in developing countries, and if price discrimination is present, it is generally in favour of the domestic residents rather than the tourists. It is widely accepted in economics that there is a deadweight loss (a reduction in social welfare) attached to almost all taxes.

Sales tax may not always be welfare diminishing in the presence of tourists. Taxing tourists using the existing sales tax can be welfare improving. The presence of tourists means higher demand and, thus, a higher tax base that will generate more tax revenue. On the other hand, part of the burden of this additional tax revenue is borne by the tourists and is not accounted for in domestic welfare.

Therefore with higher tax revenue and a relatively lower reduction in domestic consumer surplus, the increase in the tax rate in the presence of tourists will have a lower deadweight loss, and in some cases a windfall gain may emerge. In this section, we examine this issue within a one commodity partial equilibrium framework.

Although, the latter does not take account of general equilibrium effects, it provides a range of interesting insights about the possible sources and directions of welfare gains or losses. We consider two cases, the fixed producer price and the variable producer price case.

Fixed Producer Price

In the fixed producer price case, prices are sticky over the short run, for example owing to contractual arrangements or costs of changing prices in the form of loss of goodwill or prohibitive marketing. In this case, the supply curve is perfectly elastic. The presence of tourists shifts the demand curve outwards and, with a perfectly elastic supply curve, price does not increase. DH is the domestic demand curve without the presence of tourists and DT is the tourism demand curve such that the post-tourism aggregate demand curve is DA, which is the horizontal aggregation of DH and DT. It is assumed that DH exceeds DT at any common price, and that DH is more elastic than DT. The latter assumption is realistic as, being foreigners in the destination country for a relatively short period of time, tourists have limited knowledge about the ways of bypassing taxes in terms of finding substitutes.

Without Tax Case

When there are tourists but no tax in the economy, the analysis of the introduction of tax is analogous to the analysis for the case where a country increases tax on tourism products when tourists were already present. These practices have been common in countries that are attempting to extract the maximum possible rent from the tourism sector to ease their budget deficit. The scenario is upward sloping to denote that increasing output is supplied at higher prices (the variable producer price case). The base position of the economy, with tourists and without tax, is illustrated by the initial price and quantity, given by p0 and Aq 0 respectively.

The introduction of the tax increases the price paid by consumers to pD and decreases the price received by producers to pS. Hence, the burden of the tax is borne by both consumers (domestic residents and tourists) and producers. Consequently, there is a decrease in the consumer surplus of domestic consumers given by area (since we are concerned with the welfare of domestic consumers), and also a decrease in producer surplus given by the shaded area [B+F]. The increase in government tax revenue is given by the square [E], which is equal to area [A+B+C]. Therefore, the change in domestic welfare is given by the area.

With Tax Case

In the case where tourists arrive at a destination in the context of an existing tourism tax, the analysis is similar to analysing the effect of an expansion in the tourism sector in the presence of tax in the domestic economy. Copeland (1991) has also investigated this issue using the duality framework of trade theory, and found that tourism expansion is welfare improving when tax is already in place. 'Back-to-back' demand and supply diagrams are a convenient way of representing the problem.

Tourism taxes have proliferated around the world as governments have viewed the expanding tourism sector as a ready source of tax revenue. The taxes are levied on both tourists and tourism businesses at rates that vary considerably from country to country and have often been introduced in an ad hoc fashion, without serious consideration of their economic and social effects. This is a serious limitation as the effects can be advantageous or adverse.

On the one hand, tourism taxes can help to generate revenue to finance the provision of public goods, to contribute towards the costs of using environmental assets and to decrease negative externalities such as congestion. Moreover, much or all or much of the tax burden can be paid by tourists who are not resident in the country in which the taxes are levied. On the other hand, the imposition of tourism taxes may generate retaliatory measures by other governments, significant costs may be involved in the collection of the taxes and an increase in the tax rate may even result in lower tax revenue. Thus, the case for or against imposing or changing tourism taxes is complex and each of the above issues requires further empirical investigation.

The major focus of attention in the paper concerned the effects of tourism taxation on the welfare of the residents of tourism destinations - an issue which has previously lacked attention in research, although it has often been assumed that taxation has the effect of decreasing welfare. This issue was considered in the context of fixed and variable prices, to illustrate the outcomes that would occur in different empirical contexts. The analysis showed that the excess burden associated with commodity taxation is reduced and can even be negative (welfare gain) in the presence of tourists. Welfare will increase more, the more inelastic tourism demand is relative to domestic demand. Welfare also increases more, the higher the share of tourism demand relative to total demand. In the case of variable prices, the value of the supply elasticity is also relevant.

The results of changes in the values of the demand and supply elasticities differ between the cases of fixed and variable prices and also according to the sequence in which the tax is introduced; *i.e.* before or after the presence of tourists in the economy. An increase in the price elasticity of tourism demand decreases welfare because foreign tourists bear a lower proportion of the tax burden. In contrast, an increase in the elasticity of domestic demand increases welfare as the proportion of the tax burden that is borne by domestic residents relative to foreign tourists decreases.

In the case of variable prices, an increase in the elasticity of supply increases welfare relative to the initial values of the parameters and an increase in the tourism ratio increases welfare in all cases. Changes in the rate of taxation on tourism give rise to different effects on welfare in the different contexts of fixed and variable producer prices. In the former case, the change in welfare peaks at a specific tax rate and the value of the total change in welfare is maximised at a higher tax rate, decreasing thereafter. In the latter case, the optimal tax rate can be indeterminate. The implications of the preceding results are that before introducing or changing tourism taxes, policy makers should pay explicit attention to the welfare effects that are likely to arise from them. Increases in taxes can give rise to adverse effects if the demand for tourism from non-residents is price elastic relative to domestic demand and/or if supply is inelastic. Under these circumstances, policy makers may wish to consider the alternative strategy of reducing taxes.

Conversely, an increase in tourism taxes in the context of inelastic demand for tourism by non-residents relative to domestic demand, in conjunction with elastic supply, can give rise to gains in domestic welfare. If policy makers wish to increase tourism taxes, they can also consider the longer term strategy of attempting to make tourism demand by non-residents more price inelastic, for example, by increasing the quality of the tourism product and/or differentiating the product such that it gains some type of monopolistic advantage.

EFFECTS OF TOURISM TAXATION

The analysis reveals that, unlike the traditional outcome of a deadweight loss associated with higher taxes, increasing taxes on tourism can be welfare improving. Tourism is being targeted as a growing source of tax revenue by governments across the world. However, tourism taxation can have significant effects on welfare, which should be taken into account when taxes are levied. Little research has been undertaken on the welfare effects of tourism taxation and, given the special characteristics of tourism as an export sector, direct application of the literature on commodity taxation and export taxation to tourism taxation is not appropriate. This paper examines the welfare effects of tourism taxation on residents of a tourist destination country within a partial equilibrium framework, in the context of fixed and variable prices.

It is also found that the higher the proportion of tourism demand in total demand, and the more inelastic tourism demand is relative to domestic demand, the higher will be the welfare gain. Tourism's role as one of the fastest growing economic activities in the world makes it a key target for taxation. As a major source of foreign currency receipts, tourism appears to be the salvation for governments faced with budgetary constraints and pressures to decrease their reliance on income tax and tariffs as sources of revenue. On the other hand, taxes on tourism have proliferated and there are now calls from international bodies and tourism businesses and consumers for reductions in the range and levels of taxes on tourism.

Although the revenue gained from tourism taxation can be used to benefit the public by such means as increasing the provision of public services, it may also reduce welfare and act as a disincentive to tourism demand. Given the increasing importance of tourism taxation in both developed and developing countries, greater understanding of the economic underpinnings of tourism taxation and its effects is necessary, so that modeling of tourism taxation can be undertaken and appropriate policies for tourism taxation can be formulated. Tourism taxes thus have a direct effect on domestic consumption and hence domestic welfare.

Moreover, trade policies such as import tariffs aimed at the tradable sector also affect the tourism sector, with the tourists paying the domestic price instead of the world price. Most importantly, the burden of a tax on the tourism sector falls on both domestic residents and foreigners (tourists). Therefore, the burden of a tourism tax is a combination of the burden of an export tax and a domestic tax. Formal analysis of the welfare effects of tourism taxation is undertaken in section 4, and the fifth section of the paper includes some parameter values in the equations for the welfare effects in order to determine the results of tourism taxation in alternative contexts

Taxing the tourism sector

In practice, the tourism sector can be taxed either by taxing the businesses in the tourism sector or by taxing the tourists directly. Both methods may be implemented either via the general tax system of the economy or through special tourism taxes. The World Tourism Organisation (WTO, 1998) has identified 40 different types of taxes applied to the tourism sector in both developed and developing countries. They are given in the tourism tax typology.

Additional taxes relating to tourists' use of the natural environment and general taxes that also fall on tourists have also been included. Of the 45 taxes, 30 are directly payable by the tourists and 15 are levied on tourism businesses. Five broad sectors involved in tourism taxation can be identified, namely airlines and airports, hotels and other accommodation, road transportation, food and beverages and provider of tourism services. The practicality of taxing each of these sectors is highlighted below.

Airlines and airports: In long haul destinations, international transport occupies a major part in the total cost of holiday packages and hence taxing this sector should, in principle, be lucrative. However, although this is an option for developed countries, this is beyond the reach of most developing countries because they normally do not own an airline company or if they do own one, it is often unprofitable. Revenue may, instead, be generated from airport-related taxes. Hotels and other accommodation: This is normally the most important revenue generator of the tourism industry and is also easier to tax. However, the practicality of taxing the accommodation sector also varies between developed and developing countries and tends to be more problematic in the latter. The hotel sector is often highly subsidised or receives investment and tax incentives from the government in developing countries, with the aim of attracting foreign and domestic investment to the sector. The motivation is twofold, first to expand the sector as a part of a policy to expand the tourism industry and second, to protect the sector because it is a relatively unstable one due to its highly seasonal nature. The contradicting implication is that the easiest and major target for tourism taxation is most likely to be freed from taxation.

Taxis, food and beverages and tourism services: These sectors are relatively easy to tax in industrialised countries but form part of fragmented small business sectors and do not normally contribute a major proportion of tourism revenue. They include such sectors as entertainments, handicrafts, jewellery and other souvenirs. In most developing countries, these activities form part of the informal sector or of the hard-to-tax formal sector and it is difficult to raise much revenue from this source. Ecotourism tax is a relatively new form of taxation that destinations such as the Balearics levy in an attempt to counter the environmental damage caused by mass tourism. Carbon tax and landfill tax are more general environmental taxes on the level of carbon emissions and wastes respectively, but are borne by tourists as well.

Although gambling (in-shop and racing) is not legal in some countries mainly due to religious opposition, casinos are socially accepted in several countries. Tourists are involved in gambling and casinos, and hence bear the tax associated with those activities. The tax can be levied on the suppliers rather than tourists as in the case of the UK where the betting tax that was initially levied on the gamblers is now levied on the gross profit of bookmakers.

Taxing Tourists

Since taxing tourism businesses is not always a lucrative way of raising tax revenue, much tax revenue from tourism is generated from consumption taxes and special tourism taxes applied directly to tourists' consumption. Consumption taxes take the form of general sales taxes or value added tax (VAT). Sales tax/VAT is levied in almost all countries, regardless of the tourism taxation policies.

Therefore, in the presence of this type of sales tax, tourists are being taxed without any deliberate tourism tax policy on the part of the government. In the spirit of optimal taxation, some countries discriminate between domestic and tourism consumption, such that the latter is taxed at a higher rate or an additional tourism tax is applied to tourists' consumption. However, this entails administration problems in enforcing and monitoring such taxes. Special tourism taxes are generally levied directly on tourists and they can take several forms.

Common forms include taxes on hotels and restaurants, passenger services, tourist transport, entry/exit taxes and hotel accommodation taxes. The last tax is the most common and, as the name suggests, hotel accommodation tax is simply a tax on the tourists' expenditure on accommodation. The rate levied usually depends on hotel class and the season. It is relatively easy to collect, although discrimination across hotel classes sometimes creates administrative problems. In countries such as Jamaica, it is levied at a flat rate amounting to around $4-12 per night, and in other countries it is an ad valorem tax, which differs across countries: for example, 13 per cent in South Africa, 12.5 per cent in Senegal and 7.5 per cent in Grenada. Entry/exit taxes include those on airport departures, which are fixed amounts that have to be paid when leaving the country, on airport embarkation, which is paid on entering the country, and the visa fee. These taxes are usually levied at a flat rate and are relatively small in amount: for example, the airport departure tax has been within the range $1-6 in Singapore, Indonesia, Malaysia, Philippines, and Thailand, and was set at $10 in Malawi, Tanzania and Zambia.

Controversy

The WTO (1998) posits that the nature of the tourism sector makes it a target for tax revenue not only because tourism taxes are easy to collect and easy to administer but also because international tourists are rarely voters in the destination country they visit. Most of the arguments in favour of taxing the tourism sector are based on the fact that tourism products are consumed jointly with unpriced natural amenities and public goods.

Unpriced natural amenities include the sun, sea and wildlife, while public goods can include security and health services. As Gray (1982) argues, "the question of public goods, their supply and their pricing, is relatively more important in tourism than in many other industries, in part, because of the needed role of the government in asset preservation and, in part, because of the greater role of the government in the normal routine when foreigners reside temporarily within its own borders."

The main reasons for tourism taxation can be considered under the following categories. Besides providing law and order, under which contracts can be enforced and property rights protected, so ensuring that the private sector is operating efficiently, one of the main roles of the government is to provide 'public goods'. The technical definition of public goods comprises the following: indivisibility, ie. commodities are not divisible into units that can be sold individually; non-excludability, ie. no one can be excluded from benefiting from the product; the free-rider problem, where it is difficult to charge users an appropriate fee.

Common examples of public goods include national defence and street lighting. The distinctive characteristics of public goods makes it difficult to provide them via the private sector because there is no price mechanism that controls the market. They can be provided only by the government, which uses its right to tax to generate the resources necessary to supply them. Domestic taxpayers usually finance the provision of such goods. The influx of tourists imposes an extra cost on the government relating to the provision of items such as greater security and an improved environment. As non-residents, tourists do not pay to finance these extra costs. A tourist tax will, therefore, serve to redress the balance and impose the burden on those who are responsible for them. There are often user charges for some attractions, such as parks and safaris, but in other cases, such as street lighting and public security, enforcing payment is difficult. In such circumstances, taxing the may be the only way of 'charging' them for the public goods they consume.

Higher government revenue can increase welfare by such means as financing improvements in public services. Furthermore, it may help to reduce the burden of income taxation on domestic residents, and it may also be an alternative policy for countries that want to reduce their dependency on trade taxes while, at the same time, not imposing an additional burden on domestic residents. The WTO (1988) estimates that 'tourist countries' obtain around 10-25 per cent of their tax revenue from the tourism sector. In some small specialised tourism countries such as the Bahamas, over 50 per cent of government revenue is generated from the tourism sector. In Mauritius, about 12-15 per cent of tax revenue is collected directly and indirectly from the tourism sector. The tourism sector is an unusual sector for revenue generation. Bird (1992) believes that developing countries tend to under tax their tourism sector, failing to exploiting fully the economic rent emerging from the sector.

Such rent results from less than perfectly elastic demand for their tourism products, due to the differentiated nature of their natural amenities. The degree of inelasticity of demand depends, in part, on the degree of differentiation of the destination and affects the ability to tax. The greater the degree of differentiation of the destination, the more inelastic demand will be and, hence, the greater the scope for taxation.

Tourism product differentiation generally occurs in terms of types and quality of attractions (endowments), types and quality of goods and services sold in the country, geographical location and distance. Examples of attractions with very inelastic demand are the pyramids of Egypt, the Taj Mahal and the Grand Canyon. Gray (1987) associates the demand for differentiated tourism products with 'wanderlust' tourism, involving seeing or doing something that is unique to the destination, as opposed to 'sunlust' tourism which refers to the sun, sea and sand destinations such as Mauritius and the Caribbean countries. 'Sunlust' destinations tend to have less inelastic demand because the tourism products tend to be less differentiated across countries.

Less than perfectly elastic demand implies that tourism gives rise to 'economic rents' which suppliers of tourism services may try to maximise and governments may attempt to tax. However, tourism is a composite product with multiple components, and each of the components can be taxed at a different rate. For example, Bonham et al. considered a room tax on hotel receipts in Hawaii and found that the tax resulted in an insignificant change in hotel revenue. Combs and Elledge found that a small ad-valorem tax room tax imposed on motels and other forms of tourist accommodation in the USA would have very little impact on the industry and would generate substantial revenue for the government. However, an increase in taxation on one component of tourism can result in lower expenditure on another. In one of the first systematic tourism taxation studies, Mak and Nishimura investigated the effect of a hotel room tax on the length of stay of tourists in Hawaii. The results were that visitors' length of stay was insensitive to price changes and that an increase in the room tax would not reduce tourist arrivals in Hawaii significantly. However, Mak and Nishimura also examined the effect of a hotel room tax on non-lodging consumption and find that tourists 'respond to marginal increases in price of lodging partly by reducing some of their non-lodging expenditures and partly by reducing their savings and/or spending at home'.

Exportability

Taxation on tourism may be exportable in the sense that tourists bear the major burden of the taxation. The issue of tax incidence is important in this respect, as discussed in the context of the UK by Durbarry and Sinclair. One of the first studies that examined the tax incidence of tourism taxes explicitly was by Fujii et al., who examined the incidence and the exportability of an ad valorem hotel room tax for Hawaii in a partial equilibrium framework.

Tax incidence refers to the distribution of the tax burden between the buyers and the hoteliers whereas tax exporting refers to the extent to which the burden of the tax is distributed between the residents and the non-residents. If the hotel industry is an enclave with a high proportion of foreign investment, then the distinction between tax incidence and tax exporting is minor because the incidence of the tax on the supplier is actually exported. Under a partial equilibrium framework, the incidence of a hotel room tax depends on the relative sizes of the elasticities of demand and of supply. Fujii et al. calculated the relative burden of the hotel tax on tourists and the tourism industry as the ratio of the supply and demand elasticities for accommodation.

They estimated the demand function for accommodation and found that the price elasticities of demand were negative and significant, and also found supply to be less than perfectly elastic. Their results suggested that one-third of the hotel room tax was borne by the tourism industry and the rest by the tourists. They also showed that the hotel room tax was more readily exported than similar taxes levied on meals, drinks and entertainment and the general sales tax. Hence the exportability of tourism taxes is liable to vary between different components of the tourism product.

Sustainability of the Environment

Many developing countries under balance of payments and foreign exchange pressure have targeted tourism as a means of development. In many cases, no proper management strategies have been formulated especially at the initial stage of the tourism development. Natural resources have been degraded to the point where environmental sustainability is threatened. Regulating the inflow of tourists and taxation are the two most popular tools used, or considered, to remedy the problem.

However, regulating the inflow of tourists may not be the ideal solution because it deliberately contracts the tourism sector and this may have negative repercussions on the economy. It should also be remembered that many countries are investing resources to expand the tourism sector, and therefore it would be contradictory to pursue these two policies simultaneously. Moreover, it is believed that unconstrained growth (not limiting tourist arrivals) is usually beneficial in the sense that it increases the level of per capita income, thus providing more funds for maintaining the environment and sustaining growth. On the other hand, regulation through taxation not only provides the government with revenue (if designed properly) but also targets only the activities and individuals involved in the environmental degradation process and is, therefore, an efficient way to tackle the problem.

Furthermore, with higher revenues, more resources will be available to sustain the development of the industry. The tourism sector does not only rely on the natural amenities in the country but also on public goods. A strong regulatory framework, such as maintaining high health and food preparation standards, is also important in the success of the tourism sector. Taxation can generate the necessary resources to provide these requirements. Of course, the tourism industry has no inherent right to have the taxes it pays ploughed back into the industry.

However, appropriate earmarking of tax revenue can help to sustain the tourism industry and also help to reduce and combat the associated degradation of the environment. The taxation issues involved in controlling environment degradation and sustaining tourism are similar. The basic method is to use the Pigouvian tax, whereby the tax rate should correct for the divergence between the market price and the social marginal cost. Such taxes should be applied to all users, including both domestic residents and tourists, and should as far as possible be directed to the goods and services that generate the externalities so as to avoid inefficiencies.

If resources are to be exploited only to the economically desirable limit, then the social marginal cost (hence tax rate) should be set sufficiently high to include not only the opportunity costs to local residents in terms of environmental damage and congestion costs, but also the maximum possible rent extractable. On the other hand the price, hence the tax rate, should not be set so high as to hinder consumption of the product and tourist arrivals in the country. Congestion is an important facet of sustainability. High congestion, often caused by tourists themselves, reduces the quality of tourism services, which can lead to a reduction in arrivals, especially of high class and high spending tourists. The presence of crowds may detract from the enjoyment of tourists seeking solitude and privacy.

Discomfort in crowds, long queues at popular places, traffic congestion and an untidy environment will not only affect the quality of tourism services but also the quality of life of domestic residents. Tourism taxation may be used both to reduce the inflow of tourists and to compensate the local residents. However, many tourism activities are not priced, for example, sun, sea and sand, and if some are priced, the associated transaction costs relating to monitoring and enforcement are generally very high.

Thus, they are supplied at a zero fee to all users and the problem of free riders is difficult to avoid. In this context, regulatory processes such as parking fees near crowded beaches and taxes on car rental can be applied. An entry/exit tax, which is a fixed amount of money that tourists pay when they enter and leave the destination country, can also be used. An entry/exit tax is an easy way of extracting economic rents from the tourism services the destination country is selling because it is often a tax included in the airfare, unnoticed by many travellers. Sometimes countries discriminate between domestic residents and tourists, so that only tourists pay the tax. However, an entry/exit tax has some disadvantages.

First, by capturing rents from tourists, an entry/exit tax does not provide any incentive for tourism to reduce their demand for the specific good that is causing the externalities, as should optimally be the case. The tax will reduce the number of tourist arrivals. Hence not only the demand of the externality generating commodity will fall but demand for other tourism services will also fall because of the complementary nature of tourism demand. The economic benefits normally attached to expanding the tourism sector may then be constrained. Second, a uniform entry/exit tax does not offer first degree price discrimination in the sense that both low and high income tourists or short and long stay tourists pay the same amount of tax. This may discourage short stay tourists. Third, since it is levied mainly on foreigners, or at a higher rate on foreigners, it may fail to take full account of the full contribution of residents to environmental degradation.

Despite the advantages of tourism taxation, governments have been cautious about the magnitude of the taxes levied on the tourism sector because there are also negative effects associated with tourism taxation. A range of arguments has been levelled against tourism taxation, and some of the key arguments can be included under the following headings.

Costs of Compliance

Taxes levied directly on the tourism sector are sometimes difficult to justify. The amount of tax collected may be small but the tax can still have a substantial negative impact on the tourism sector, with repercussions on the overall economy. This happens especially with taxes levied directly on tourists, such as visa fees. It is not only the high fees required; there is often unnecessary bureaucracy (indeed discrimination between tourists of different nationalities) that can greatly raise the compliance costs for the tax payer and act as a deterrent to visiting the country.

This may contract tourist arrivals and affect other sectors related to the tourism sector. For countries where tourism comprises a major part of the economy, this can adversely affect the employment level and the balance of payments resulting in an overall contraction of the level of economic activity of the economy. The fiscal effects are likely to differ from country to country and from time to time, for three main reasons.

First, the effects depend on the policy of the government. If the government wants to maximise revenue, the tax rates will tend to be high. On the other hand, if the government wants to promote the sector, tax rates can be very low. In some case the government goes further by providing subsidies, such as subsidies for airport and parking infrastructure, and investment incentives to businesses. Second, the effects also depend on how important tourism is to the economy. Obviously, the higher the contribution of tourism in the economy, the higher will be the effects of tourism taxes on the government budget.

Thirdly, the number and types of linkages with other sectors in the economy and leakages from the economy that the tourism sector brings about are also important. As a general rule, linkages tend to increase government revenue and leakages lead to a reduction in revenue. The amount of revenue that is obtained from tourism taxation depends, in part, upon the value of the price elasticity of demand for tourism. If the price elasticity of demand is high, the effect of an increase in tax may be to decrease revenue.

In the case of tourist accommodation, all obtained demand elasticities for accommodation that were significantly different from zero. Hiemstra and Ismail reported a significant price elasticity of demand for the lodging industry based on a survey of the properties owned and managed by the American Hotel and Motel Association.

Retaliation

Taxation generates revenue but, as in the case of trade taxes, it invites retaliation by other countries if they feel that the other government is unfairly treating their citizens. For example, Kenya and Tanzania introduced visa charges for UK citizens in retaliation to the application of visa fees by the UK on their citizens. Retaliation is always a threat and in most cases the eventual outcome is lower welfare for both countries. Tisdell (1983) showed how retaliation in the case of tourism taxes can lead to a lower economic surplus for both countries.

This is because the consumer surplus that the tourists from the leader country were enjoying in the retaliating country will disappear after the tax. The country with a more inelastic demand for tourism will lose less but, compared with the case without retaliation, both countries lose. However, if a developing country imposes, say, an entry tax on tourists who are mainly from developed countries, then retaliation will tend to affect the developing country to a lesser extent. This is because the number of tourists from the developing country visiting the developed is fewer than the number of tourists from the developed countries who visit developing country.

MOTIVATION AND COMMITMENT BETWEEN EMPLOYERS AND EMPLOYEES

Most knowledgeable observers in the field of human resource management (HRM) would agree that its major development as a profession came during the half century or so between the end of World War II and the early 1990s. As organizations employing as many as hundreds of thousands became dominant influences in the world of work and as questions about selection, training, work motivation, and compensation practices became more challenging in a growing, dynamic society, the need for professionally trained, skilled personnel became great.

Also, despite occasional downturns in the economy, the professional growth of HRM took place against a general culture of prosperity, a belief that such good patterns would continue and even improve, and an assumption that work organizations should and would share in such growth.

Important too as HRM developed during this era was that the policies and practices developed and implemented were based in large part on the assumption that a desire for personal growth was the most important motivational characteristic of the workforce, along with the belief that more of everything (particularly economic outcomes) is better. Korman (forthcoming) has referred to this pattern as self-enhancing motivation and has cited as illustrative of this type of motivation such actions as making choices that match and fulfill one's personal needs, engaging in activities that foster self-growth, attempting to attain high levels of work performance, and working for goals that legitimately enhance oneself in one's own eyes and those of others.

Given the cultural context and the assumption of the dominance of this type of motivational pattern, it was a relatively short step for HRM professionals during this era to develop a perspective that reflected them. Characteristic programmes of this type included job enrichment, career management and career development, self-appraisals and peer performance appraisals, and income incentives of various kinds.

Less significant as an influence on HRM during this era but still of some importance were programmes based on what Korman (forthcoming) has called self-protective motivation, defined as the desire to defend oneself from perceived threatening environmental and personal forces that might affect one's sense of identity. Korman suggests that it is this motivational force that underlies the need for personal and job security. Despite its importance, however, this need was generally viewed as less important than employee needs for growth, development, and achievement during the years of prosperity. There were several reasons for this difference in emphasis. One factor, certainly, was the prosperity and the continued expectations of same. It was not a climate that generated a sense of anxiety, whether warranted or not.

Second, the strength and membership of labour unions—organizations that have traditionally made job security a keystone of their efforts—were declining. With the assumption of continued prosperity and the weakness of labour unions, human resource (HR) managers and their allied professionals, such as industrial-organizational psychologists, worried less about providing job security than about providing the opportunity for growth, development, and achievement.

Third, theorists on motivation in work organizations generally had a low level of interest in such concepts as anxiety, even though important research findings were beginning to be reported on the significance of such related variables as fear of failure in performance settings. Instead, theories were popular if they saw people as growth-oriented, desiring meaningful work achievement, and interested in attaining both intrinsic and extrinsic goals.

Nevertheless, despite these influences, there was some concern even during these years about providing a greater sense of security for employees. Prominent among those expressing such interest was Frederick Herzberg, an important management writer who saw in the reduction of anxiety that came with job security a significant approach to reducing job dissatisfaction. In addition, although their membership continued to decrease, labour unions and their emphasis on job security did not totally disappear from the work scene. Far from it. Unions remained strong in some areas, particularly the federal, state, and local civil services, and their presence did much to ensure that job security remained on the table as an employee concern, at least in some instances.

There were, then, these two patterns of HR practice. One, the more influential, assumed that the more important motivational patterns were desires for growth, development, achievement, and self-enhancement. The second, less significant as an influence, assumed desires for job security and self-protection. Both were recognized, and both influenced HRM practices. Less recognized was that the disparity in influence of these patterns of practice encouraged another important underlying assumption. This assumption was that HRM policies and practices could be developed in a manner that would enable the attainment of two goals. The first of these goals was to help organizations obtain their objectives. The second was that HRM could help employees meet their most important needs because the employees' desire to attain positive outcomes (both intrinsic and extrinsic), that is, self-enhancement, and their willingness to work for them were congruent with organizational needs for effective performance. Furthermore, this congruence could be maintained and encouraged because of the continuing expected affluence. In contrast, rarely if ever discussed was that these practices and policies and the assumed congruence between employer and employee depended on these assumptions of continued prosperity and that other approaches would become necessary if the situation changed.

The New World of Work

Now that time has come. A new and different world of work has begun to emerge, one that exists alongside the traditional work setting and that may eventually come to supplant it. It is a world characterized by at least three major trends that have implications for HRM.

- First, downsizing is now a frequent key component of managerial decision making, with all the potential short- and long-term anxiety-inducing effects on employee motivation that we would expect.
- Second, the work-family conflict is an endemic part of the lives of both employers and employees.
- Third, we live in a world marked by the extensive use of temporary workers, part-time employees, and outsourcing.

Workforce Reduction

Downsizing has become so much a part of the world of work during the past decade that it is a term familiar to almost all who work or who wish to. Downsizing is a phenomenon that continues to this day. Some of the more recent downsizings announced in 1997 are Eastman Kodak (10,000), Fruit of the Loom (7,700), and Levi Strauss (6,400). Perhaps even more dramatic are the declines in some of the biggest companies. AT and T has shrunk in part as a function of court ordered divesting but also through downsizing, from 313,000 employees in 1993 to 128,000 in 1998. IBM has gone from about 410,000 employees in recent years to approximately 225,000. Downsizing is a fact of the world of work that influences the lives, attitudes, and emotions of millions. That other jobs are continually being created—and they are—may not significantly affect those concerned about their long- and short-term job prospects.

Work-Family Conflict

Also part of this new world of work is conflict with the family, an inevitable fact of life as our society is increasingly characterized by women in the workforce, dual-career couples, and single-parent families. The increasing presence of women in the workforce contributes to this conflict, a conflict that is among the most serious facing American families and work organizations as we approach the new millennium. It is a problem, both actual and potential, that is becoming increasingly widespread. It is also one of the characteristics of the new world of work that has had and continues to have a major impact on the motivational and attitudinal characteristics of people in the workforce, both men and women.

Noncore Workers

We now also have a work setting marked increasingly by outsourcing agreements between companies, relocation of companies from high- to low-wage areas, globalization, a desire for individuals to develop multiskill capability rather than job specialization, and explosive growth in the use of temporary and contingent employees.

Feelings of ambiguity and conflict have resulted from these changes. On the one hand, there are now new ways for individuals to seek self-enhancement in the world of work, paths that have important implications for the practices and policies HRM may adopt. But on the other hand, the resulting anxiety from these changes has led to a high level of self-protective motivation. The outcome has been a world of work where the two different motivations are assuming equal significance. In other words, it is a world in which the desire and need for security has become as relevant as the need for achievement, growth, and development. It is therefore a world in which both motivational patterns will need to be addressed by HRM, but in different ways than they have been previously. The remainder of this chapter focuses on meeting these challenges through a two-phase process. Phase 1 proposes new conceptual and attitudinal assumptions for HRM as a field. Phase 2 outlines the types of specific programmes that follow from Phase 1 and reflect the changes in the world of work already discussed.

Phase 1: The New Assumptions

HRM needs new and different assumptions on which to base policy and practice. One necessary change, I believe, is to assume no longer that there is a congruence of interests between employees and employers. Sometimes there may be, but sometimes there may not be. Second, we need to assume that the key interpersonal and intergroup relationships in a particular work setting are as likely to be among individuals from different organizations with different investments as they are to be among individuals within the same organization. The following paragraphs elaborate on these recommendations in greater detail.

Because self-enhancement was assumed to be the dominant work motivation during the years of the growth of the field, it is not surprising that HR professionals operated on the belief that it was both possible and desirable to design and implement policies and practices that could and would integrate the goals of both employees and organizations. In fact, one of the major books of this era, and one which served as a sort of conceptual guideline for many, was titled Integrating the Individual with the Organization.

In a similar vein and serving as further illustration of this assumption of congruence between employer and employee was the growth of job enrichment as a management tool, fueled by the belief that individuals would respond to the challenge of enriched jobs. According to this perspective, the enriched job provided a mechanism for self-enhancement and, in satisfying such desires, the individual would be more highly performance motivated and contribute more to the attainment of organizational goals.

Now, however, we need to change this assumption. More specifically, we need to view the individual and the organization as separate entities who will be able to integrate their efforts and cooperate with one another under certain conditions but not under others. Furthermore, determining what those conditions might be will be an important objective for HRM professionals in the coming years.

A second assumption about people and organizations during the years of growth and prosperity was that the interpersonal and inter group relationships HRM needed most to be concerned with were those that took place within the organization, that is, intra organizational relationships. In other words, the focus was on the relationships between people in different jobs, in different functions, and at different hierarchical levels, but all within the same organization. Although it was recognized that individuals often met with salespeople, suppliers, and others, such meetings with "outsiders" were generally limited to specifically designated occupational groups. Now, however, more attention will have to be paid to relationships between those with primary allegiance to a particular organization and those who may work in that organization but not have primary allegiance to it.

Today, individuals work full-time in an organization to which they have primary loyalty while next to them or with them are individuals on temporary assignments, part-time workers, and people working in joint venture settings and in outsourcing situations. The result may therefore be individuals working together whose allegiances and concerns may involve differences that are highly important to us. Relationships, views, and expectations among those who are all part of one group—or who view themselves as part of the same company or as "insiders"—are different from the types of relationships and communication patterns that develop among those who view themselves as belonging to different groups. For example, Korman (1988) has proposed that in situations in which we find insiders and outsiders, the former are more likely to discriminate and act in a prejudicial manner towards the latter.

The result may be unnecessary conflict and sometimes even "tribalistic" patterns, where each group cares only about itself and not about the other or joint goals. Although cases of severe conflict may be extreme—because there are usually some reasons for these different groups and individuals to at least try to work together— the potential for conflict between groups and individuals exists in this new work setting and there will be a need to take account of such possibilities in developing future HRM programmes. These new assumptions, which I believe to be more appropriate for the emerging work setting, suggest the need for new HRM approaches, techniques, policies, and practices that will allow satisfaction of both the self-enhancing and the self-protective motivational processes.

Phase 2: Some Programme Suggestions

Programmes consistent with the new assumptions need to be developed for HRM as it confronts this new world of work. The remainder of the chapter outlines four such programmes, with each discussed in greater detail in the following sections.

- Effective self-career management programmes based on the desire for self-enhancement
- Labour pool associations designed to meet needs for both self enhancement and self-protection
- Performance incentive programmes that are not based on organizational commitment, including financial rewards providing direct income as well as health, welfare, and pension benefits
- Insider-outsider training programmes

PROGRAMMES FOR SELF-CAREER MANAGEMENT

Self-career management programmes are designed primarily for those individuals who view themselves as relatively independent professionals or "businesses, " rather than as organizationally dependent job holders. These are individuals who can and do make their own decisions about their careers, know their capabilities, and understand where they can find the types of work opportunities where they can "sell" themselves as a business or service. Self-career management is a different way of looking at oneself and one's work capabilities.

It is a mechanism for declaring oneself independent of an organizational control system but at the same time being willing to negotiate mutual terms of acceptability concerning work contributions to that system. Self-career management—thus defined as the giving up of relatively permanent organizational relationships in favour of more self-controlled career decision making—has become increasingly recommended to and by HRM professionals as a possible approach to dealing with challenges presented by the emerging world of work, a world still dominated in great degree by the use of downsizing as a management strategy despite continuing questions about its outcomes.

Clearly, there are reasons for such positive evaluation. Self career management recognizes the tentative nature of a specific employment relationship while also emphasizing the need for employee skills and meaningful contributions and the opportunity to fulfill the desire for self-enhancement that is so important in the work setting. In addition, for the appropriate individual and the appropriate situation, self-career management also provides an approach to meeting the need for self-protection, because this can be negotiated by the individual involved. The key, however, is in the word appropriate. Self-career management is appropriate when the individual has or can develop both meaningful self-knowledge and the types of skills and abilities that are in demand. In addition, self-career management is appropriate when the individual has knowledge of the job market and the freedom to respond to the opportunities available.

A variety of techniques reflect self-career management when it is defined in this manner. Perhaps the most important and first question that needs an answer (for which the HRM professional must provide input) is whether a specific organization should provide financial and other resources for developing and implementing self-career programmes for its employees, particularly programmes emphasizing personal growth. This is not an easy question to answer. At first glance, there are clearly reasons for companies to undertake such programmes.

They provide recognition of the frequently temporary nature of contemporary work settings while at the same time encouraging positive relationships between individuals and organizations over the long run. Both of these outcomes may serve the individual and the organization in good stead at once or at some time in the future. In addition, these programmes may serve to illuminate and develop skills in the participants not previously realized and thus eventually prove beneficial to the individual and the organization. Finally, such programmes help the organization in situations where downsizing may become inevitable. Clearly, preparing individuals to deal with the loss of employment before it happens is to be preferred over sudden notices of termination.

Still, some negative aspects also need to be recognized before a corporate decision is made to undertake a personal growth programme encouraging self-career management. One obvious problem is the cost involved. The cost may be considerable, depending on the number of individuals involved and the type of programmes chosen. Second, there is the continuing reality that all the benefits the programmes may provide to employees may never be of value to the organization that pays for them (and, indeed, may turn out to be of value to competitors).

Third, it needs to be realized right from the beginning that such programmes are not for everyone. They should not be oversold as "the answer" to the problems of the new world of work. Rather, companies need to keep in mind that other programmes will be necessary regardless of what they decide about self-career management programmes. To be blunt, self-career management is not and cannot be appropriate for those who have neither the personality nor the technical skills, educational levels, or likelihood of developing the skills to the degree needed to make the approach fruitful. For these individuals, other alternatives will be necessary.

Assuming these pros and cons have been considered and the company decides to proceed with such programmes, how might they do so? One possible procedure is to make self-career management programmes a voluntary aspect of the HRM process. Such an approach would increase the probability of successful outcomes by making it likely that the individuals participating in the programmes possess the skills, abilities, interests, or personality that would enable them to benefit from the programmes.

In addition, once the decision to proceed is made, HRM can increase the effectiveness of self-career management programmes by generating and making available as much information as possible about the nature of potential and actual career possibilities in a particular job market for those participating in the programmes. Self career management programmes are much concerned with personal growth but are not aimed at personal growth alone. They also have career and work-oriented goals.

The more work opportunities available that the participant knows about and the more the participant has the time, knowledge, and personal characteristics to carry out a job or career search, the more self-management career programmes will be useful. A further advantage of providing job knowledge to those undergoing self-career management is that doing so will help identify those for whom such programmes might not be useful, that is, those who will not have job opportunities for the skills they have or are likely to develop. For this latter group, other types of programmes will be necessary, perhaps programmes of the type we now turn to.

Labour Pool Associations

HRM also needs to begin to develop mechanisms that are appropriate in assisting the adaptation of current and potential employees for whom the concept of self-career management is inapplicable. Among these are the unskilled and semiskilled, immigrant workers, single parents whose job freedom is limited, and people with little growth potential. Two factors concerning these individuals are crucial. First, there are great numbers of such employees and they may, in fact, be increasing relative to the population at large. Second, despite their numbers, economically they are falling farther and farther behind people with higher skill levels, as evidenced by the findings of an increasing disparity in income between those at the higher and lower levels of our population. Yet despite their numbers and this disparity, it is fair to say that little attention has been paid to how the new world of work can meet the needs of these people. For these individuals, basic educational training may have been insufficient, job training opportunities may not be available, and financial resources to keep up skill development may not be there. Also, the habit and encouragement of self-reliance in the occupational sphere may be more foreign to these individuals than those who are higher on the occupational hierarchy.

Rather, these individuals may have, perhaps, more of a tendency to rely on traditional employment relationships and organizational reward systems as sources of meeting self enhancement and self-protection needs. Because the characteristics of the emerging world of work makes this pattern increasingly unlikely, it is even more important to pay attention to helping these groups adapt to the new and different setting.

A new type of organization be developed with the aid of HR professionals in response to these considerations. Let's call them labour pool associations. Such associations can be conceived of as organizations based on cooperative relations among different companies (and perhaps government agencies) that focus on maximizing the human resources available to all of them. As cooperatively managed HR personnel from different organizations, labour pool associations would have several objectives. First, they would keep a continuing registry of individuals and their skills, thus ensuring a labour supply as needed by member organizations, large or small.

Second, they would serve as training-retraining-counseling centers for occupational entry and upgrading as desired and available. Third, and perhaps most uniquely, they would serve as "permanent employers" who, besides supplying and making available job and training opportunities, would also provide such "security type" benefits as health insurance and pension plans. These benefits would be paid into accounts maintained for each individual by the organizations. They would thus replace the security systems traditionally used by organizations, which are increasingly difficult to maintain in this era of downsizing and rapid corporate change.

One step towards this type of organization is the Talent Alliance (TA), an association of hotels that has been operating since spring 1997. One is to keep individuals employed in hotels and settings where they are most needed when they are needed. It is therefore an employee allocation system (or labour pool association) of the type we envision here. A second objective is to increase employee marketability; this is done in a number of ways, including through career growth counselors, training and retraining programmes for employees, and strategic planning seminars for corporate management aimed at adapting HR practices to the new world of work.

The TA is, therefore, a step towards the type of organization suggest here because it has some of the aspects recommend. However, it lacks at this time a focus on the necessity of meeting the needs underlying self-protective motivation, that is, the desire for the security of health and welfare benefits and pensions. A second possible limitation is that it is designed for the occupational spectrum of relatively big organizations employing large numbers of individuals, a considerable percentage of whom may be at a high technical level. Such organizations are, of course, crucial as major employers and these occupational groups are of legitimate concern. However, believe that labour pool associations need also be concerned with those individuals who, though working for small, sometimes marginal organizations, nevertheless have traditionally looked to organizations as the mechanisms through which they will meet their needs for both enhancement and protection.

One further note

Labour pool associations may be of value to those for whom self-career management programmes are appropriate as well as for those for whom it is not. This is because systems need to be developed to bring individuals and organizations at all levels together for their mutual benefit in this emerging world of short-range assignments as well as long-range jobs and rapidly changing skill and competency demands. Labour pool associations, as we have envisioned them, would satisfy this need.

In sum, we need organizations like the TA and others like it, such as Job Link in Louisville, Kentucky, to meet self-enhancement needs but also to meet the need for self-protection. (Job Link is a one-step career center established by the nonprofit Louisville Private Industry Council in 1989. It is basically a referral and counseling center that makes training available as a final resort.) We need organizations such as the TA and Job Link because the two major motivations in work settings—self-enhancement and self-protection—increasingly may not be met by individual companies. For some organizations, self-career management will be an appropriate alternative mechanism.

However, for others, cooperative efforts like labour pool associations will be needed to help them find qualified workers and to help workers find jobs that meet both self-enhancing and self-protective needs. Key here is the need for cooperative activity among different organizations, including accepting the principle of having these associations serving as an "employer" designed to meet self-protective concerns. This is perhaps a somewhat different perspective from that we are used to, but it is an idea that reflects the new world of work and the needs it has generated.

NONORGANIZATIONALLY LINKED INCENTIVE SYSTEMS

Financial incentive systems for performance have long been one of the staples of HRM and there is little reason to think they would or should lose their relevance in the new world of work. On the contrary, they may become even more relevant as other types of incentives—those that assume organizational links and commitment, such as promotion and transfer opportunities—will become less relevant to those who see their future as falling into the self-career management pattern or who are attaining employment through "labour pool associations."

Purely financial incentives, on the other hand, are not limited to any specific type of setting. Bonuses tied to individual or unit performance are innately transferable (or fungible) and do not have to be linked to any particular organization. That is, the value of financial incentives as mechanisms to self-enhancement are not limited to any particular context and will usually hold their meaning regardless of where they are offered. Financial incentives will, then, retain significance in the new world of work and may become even more significant as the ties of organizational loyalty become less common and less relevant. First, direct monetary income in this changing world of fewer commitments will gain increased significance.

Second, incentive programmes that enable individuals to meet their needs for self-protection will have increased value. Such needs might be met by developing and applying incentive payments directly into health, welfare, and pension programmes even though the employees involved may be temporary workers who frequently change employers. Consistent with the logic underlying the labour pool associations described earlier, HR professionals might well consider developing financial incentive programmes using individual "benefit" accounts into which employers (and employees) would contribute based on employment, no matter how temporary or varying that employment might be.

These would be financial incentives for performance designed to satisfy self-protection needs by paying into health, welfare, and pension accounts maintained by the labour pool association. In addition to being of value to the individuals involved, such contributions are likely to increase commitment and loyalty to an organization's needs. (One might note that the type of account we are referring to here is somewhat analogous to Social Security accounts. However, there are two major differences. First, these accounts are linked to individual work patterns and individual work behaviour in a more immediate manner. Second, these plans focus on health and welfare benefits as much as if not more than pay and pension concerns.)

Insider-Outsider Training Programmes

Training programmes designed to integrate individuals of diverse backgrounds and views into cohesive work teams are not new. They have been a standard part of HRM programmes in recent years as cultural and ethnic diversity has become a major challenge for organizations. Some of these training programmes have proved fruitful and some have not. However, the challenge to HRM here is somewhat different in that the programmes we refer to have generally made one major assumption that we cannot make in the new context: that the individuals and groups in these programmes, diverse though they may be, all wish to maximize the effectiveness of the same organization, that is, the organization to which they are all committed by reason of employment.

In the new world of work, group members may include permanent employees committed to the same organization and work unit as well as temporarily assigned employees who rotate from assignment to assignment within the same organization and are sent to different units with not always consistent goals.

Even more difficult, however, will be dealing with people who are individual contractors or temporary workers who go to different organizations once a specific job is finished. It is not just that there will be changing memberships and changing interaction patterns in these organizational settings. Rather, there are and will also be individuals working together who have different, perhaps even conflicting loyalties. How does one get these groups to work together for some super ordinate goal when some are truly insiders and some outsiders?

It is not clear how one proceeds here. Appeals to super ordinate goals may not be appropriate over the long run (although they may be for the short run). In addition, the need for emotional cohesion may not be great because the groups may not be conceived of as even quasi-permanent. It is also uncertain which type of development programme might be most appropriate and which type of incentive programme might be best. One possibility may be the extensive use of financial incentives to integrate such groups into a common effort because financial benefits are not tied to any particular organization or setting. These incentives may be performance based, perhaps even providing stock options keyed to the length, level, and quality of performance in a particular setting.

We really do not have any answers to these questions at this time, but the potential for conflict between insider-outsider groups within organizations is great, as is the potential for conflict among those with different perspectives who also need to work together, such as suppliers and vendors. Hence, it is in the development of appropriate training and performance incentive programmes to meet this need that HRM may make another significant contribution in the new world of work.

A work setting is beginning to emerge that is radically different from the one that has traditionally provided the context for HRM policies and practices. In this world downsizing is a tool of managerial decision making, work-family conflict is a fact of life for millions and, increasingly, contingent workers, part-time workers, and outsourcing are used. It is a work setting where opportunities to meet self-enhancement and growth needs exist for some individuals but not for all, and where opportunities for self-protection such as job and benefit security are increasingly difficult to come by.

These changes have made it necessary for HRM as a profession to re-evaluate its traditional practices and begin to develop and implement programmes that meet these needs for self-enhancement and self-protection in the new work setting.

This chapter offered illustrations of such programmes, including effective self-career management programmes based on personal growth principles; labour pool associations for those for whom self-career management is inappropriate; performance incentive programmes not based on organizational commitment, including financial rewards of both direct income and health, welfare, and pension benefits; and insider outsider training programmes.

Underlying these recommendations is my view that HRM professionals, regardless of specific training, need to take an active role in meeting the demands of the new world of work. Key to this process is recognizing that the opportunities for meeting and satisfying the primary motivational patterns of self-enhancement and self-protection are no longer what they used to be, whatever level of the occupational spectrum we are focusing on. For the benefit of both organizations and individuals, developing new mechanisms for responding to these changes is a major challenge facing HRM today.

MULTIPLIERS EFFECTS OF TOURISM

Multipliers capture the secondary economic effects (indirect and induced) of tourism activity. Multipliers have been frequently misused and misinterpreted in tourism studies (Archer 1984) and are a considerable source of confusion among non-economists. Multipliers represent the economic interdependencies between sectors within a particular region's economy. They vary considerably from region to region and sector to sector. There are many different kinds of multipliers reflecting which secondary effects are included and which measure of economic activity is used (sales, income, or employment).

For example,

- The Type I sales multiplier = direct sales + indirect sales direct sales.
- The Type II or III sales multiplier[1] = direct sales + indirect sales + induced sales direct sales.

Multiplying a Type I sales multiplier times the direct sales gives direct plus indirect sales. Multiplying a Type II or III sales multiplier times the direct sales gives total sales impacts including direct, indirect and induced effects. The multipliers defined above are called ratio type multipliers as they measure the ratio of a total impact measure to the corresponding direct impact. Comparable income and employment ratio type multipliers may be defined by replacing sales with measures of income or employment in the above equations. Ratio multipliers should be used with caution.

A common error is to multiply a sales multiplier times tourist spending to get total sales effects. This will generate an inflated estimate of tourism impacts.

The problem is that tourism spending or sales is not exactly the same as the "direct effects", appearing in the multiplier formula. Tourist purchases of goods (vs. services) are the primary source of the problem. To properly apply tourist purchases of goods to an input-output model (or corresponding multipliers), various margins (retail, wholesale and transportation) must be deducted from the "purchaser price" of the good to separate out the "producer price".

In an I-O model, retail margins accrue to the retail trade sector, wholesale margins to wholesale trade, transportation margins to transportation sectors (trucking, rail, air etc.) and the producer prices of goods are assigned to the sector that produces the good. In most cases the factory that produces the good bought by a tourist lies outside of the local region, creating an immediate "leakage" in the first round of spending and therefore no local impact from production of the good.

Before applying a multiplier to tourist spending, one must first deduct the producer prices of all imported goods that tourists buy (*i.e.* only include the local retail margins and possibly wholesale and transportation margins if these firms lie within the region).

Generally, only 60 to 70 per cent of tourist spending appears as final demand in a local region. While all tourist purchases of services will accrue to the local region as final demand, only the margins on goods purchased at retail stores should be counted as local final demand. The ratio of local final demand to tourist spending is called the capture rate.

Capture rate = local final demand / tourism spending in local area. Capture rates, like multipliers, will vary with the size and nature of the region as well as the kind of tourist spending included. One must therefore be cautious in taking a multiplier or capture rate cited in one study and using it in another.

Another way of calculating a multiplier (generally the preferred approach among economists) is as a ratio of income or employment to sales. This kind of multiplier is sometimes called a Keynesian multiplier or response coefficient.

- Type III Income multiplier = Total direct, indirect, and induced income direct sales
- Type III Employment multiplier = Total direct, indirect, and induced employment direct sales

This income (employment) multiplier produces total income (employment) impacts when multiplied by the direct sales. One must still be careful in distinguishing between tourism spending/sales and direct sales effects. Some studies may embed the capture rate in the multiplier, expressing the ratio in terms of tourism spending rather than direct sales.

The economic impacts of tourism are typically estimated by some variation of the following simple formula:

*Economic Impact of Tourism = Number of Tourists * Average Spending per Visitor * Multiplier*

The formula suggests three distinct steps and corresponding measurements or models:

1. Estimate the change in the number and types of tourists to the region due to the proposed policy or action. Estimates or projections of tourist activity generally come from a demand model or some system for measuring levels of tourism activity in an area. Economic impact estimates will rest heavily on good estimates of the numbers and types of visitors. These must come from carefully designed measurements of tourist activity, a good demand model, or good judgement. This step is usually the weakest link in most tourism impact studies, as few regions have accurate counts of tourists, let alone good models for predicting changes in tourism activity or separating local visitors from visitors from outside the region.
2. Estimate average levels of spending (often within specific market segments) of tourists in the local area. Spending averages come from sample surveys or are sometimes borrowed or adapted from other studies. Spending estimates must be based on a representative sample of the population of tourists taking into account variations across seasons, types of tourists, and locations within the study area. As spending can vary widely across different kinds of tourists, we recommend estimating average spending for a set of key tourist segments based on samples of at least 50-100 visitors within each tourism segment.
3. Segments should be defined to capture differences in spending between local residents vs. tourists, day users vs. overnight visitors, type of accommodation (motel, campground, seasonal home, with friends and relatives), and type of transportation (car, RV, air, rail, etc.). In broadly based tourism impact studies, it is useful to identify unique spending patterns of important activity segments such as downhill skiers, boaters, and convention and business travelers. Multiplying the number of tourists by the average spending per visitor (be careful the units are consistent) gives an estimate of total tourist spending in the area. Estimates of tourist spending will generally be more accurate if distinct spending profiles and use estimates are made for key tourism segments. The use and spending estimates are the two most important parts of an economic impact assessment. When combined, they capture the amount of money brought into the region by tourists. Multipliers are needed only if one is interested in the secondary effects of tourism spending.
4. Apply the change in spending to a regional economic model or set of multipliers to determine secondary effects. Secondary effects of tourism are estimated using multipliers or a model of the region's

economy. Multipliers generally come from an economic base or input-output model of the region's economy. In many cases multipliers are borrowed (often improperly) or adjusted from published multipliers or other studies. One should not take a multiplier estimated for one region and apply it in a region with a quite different economic structure. Generally, multipliers are higher for larger regions with more diversified economies and lower for smaller regions with more limited economic development. A common error is to apply a statewide multiplier (since these are more widely published) to a local region. This will yield inflated estimates of local multiplier effects.

5. Multipliers can also be used to convert estimates of spending or sales to income and employment. Simple ratios can be used to capture how much income or jobs are generated per dollar of sales. These ratios will vary from region to region and across individual economic sectors due to the relative importance of labour inputs in each industry and different wage and salary rates in different regions of the country. Be aware that job estimates are generally not full time equivalents, making them difficult to compare across industries with different proportions of seasonal and part time jobs. Income or value added are generally the preferred measures of the contribution of tourism to a region's economy.

The Typical Approaches for an Economic Assessment

At the simple, "quick and dirty" end of the spectrum are highly aggregate approaches that rely mostly on judgement to determine tourism activity, spending and multipliers. Such estimates can be completed in a couple hours at little cost and rest largely on the expertise and judgement of the analyst. At the other extreme are studies that gather primary data from visitor spending studies and apply the spending estimates to formal regional economic models for the area in question. In between are a wide range of options that employ varying degrees of judgement, secondary data, primary data, and formal models.

Different levels of detail and corresponding expense (time and money) and accuracy are possible for each of the three steps — estimating tourist volume, spending, and multiplier effects. Four typical approaches illustrate the levels of detail that are possible and the associated methods to sales estimates. With sound judgement in choosing the parameters, the MGM model can yield reasonable ballpark estimates of economic impacts at minimal cost. This approach, however, provides little detail on spending categories or which sectors of the economy benefit from either direct or secondary effects. The aggregate nature of the approach also makes it difficult to adjust recommended spending rates or multipliers to different applications.

The Bureau of Economic Analysis's (BEA) RIMS II user handbook illustrates how to apply published multipliers to estimate economic impacts. This approach starts with visitor spending (from survey or secondary sources) divided into a number of spending categories and makes use of sector specific multipliers to estimate the direct and total sales, income and employment effects. Multipliers from the BEA's RIMS II models are used to estimate secondary effects. Multipliers are reported for 39 sectors for each state in the second edition of their report (USDC 1992). This method uses margins to properly account for retail purchases of goods and makes use of disaggregate sector-specific multipliers for each state. Multipliers for sub-state regions are not as readily available, but can be acquired from BEA or other sources. Secondary effects cannot be disaggregated to individual sectors using the BEA approach.

The MI-REC/IMPLAN System: Stynes and Propst have developed a fairly complete micro-computer-based system for estimating economic impacts of recreation and tourism. The system combines spreadsheets for estimating spending with the IMPLAN input-output modeling system. IMPLAN uses county level data to estimate 528 sector input-output models for regions down to account level. IMPLAN generates a complete set of economic accounts for the region including multipliers and trade flows. MI-REC spreadsheets estimate visitor spending within up to 33categories based on the number and types of visitors attracted to an area. Spending is then bridged to the IMPLAN model sectors to estimate direct, indirect and induced effects in terms of sales, income and employment. Users may estimate spending via visitor surveys or use the MI-REC database of spending profiles, compiled from previous studies. The system also includes price indices to easily update spending data to a current year.

Two other systems for estimating economic impacts of tourism should be noted. The TEIM or Travel Economic Impact Model developed by the U.S. Travel Data Center (USTDC, 1997) has been widely used to estimate tourism and travel impacts at state and national levels. A more recent development is the satellite accounting approach developed by the World Travel and Tourism Council (WTTC 1996). Both of these systems are primarily designed for estimating the overall economic significance of tourism at national or state levels. They are not readily applied to estimate the impacts of particular policies and actions at the local level.

The TEIM relies on national travel surveys to estimate trip volume and spending on a state-by-state basis. Local estimates of impacts are obtained using simple allocation formulas to distribute statewide impacts to counties and cities within the state. These local estimates do not account very well for the distinct types of tourism activity or spending patterns in different sub-regions of a state. The WTTC effort also focuses on national and statewide accounting of tourism's economic significance. Their satellite tourism account identifies the contribution of travel and tourism to gross national product (GNP) or gross state product (GSP).

Using the standard national system of accounts, they identify the portion of sales, taxes and investment attributable directly to travel and tourism. The WTTC system does not use multipliers or attempt to estimate secondary effects. It does, however, capture a great deal of travel-related economic activity, not covered by visitor trip spending, such as durable goods purchases (boats and RV's), construction and investment in tourism, and government expenditures.

An economic impact study involves four basic:

1. Define the problem
2. Estimate the change in final demand (tourism spending).
3. Estimate the regional economic effects of this change
4. Interpret, apply, and communicate the results

The most important part of any study is the first step — clarifying the nature of the problem being addressed and intended uses of the results. Before launching an economic impact study, be sure this is the kind of study that is needed rather than one or more of the other kinds of economic analyses.

Stynes and Propst (1996) identify seven factors that should be specified as part of defining a problem for an economic impact assessment:

1. Define the action to be evaluated. Begin by clarifying the action or actions involved in the problem. Actions may include construction, government investment, changes in marketing, management, or policies, or changes in the quality or quantity of tourist facilities. If evaluating impacts of existing tourism activity, be sure to define what is to be included as "tourism".
2. Identify the change in the amount and kinds of recreation/tourism activity resulting from the action. The action must be defined precisely enough in step one to be able to estimate the changes in the number and types of visitors to the area and/or their spending patterns. As a general rule, the analysis should be with vs. without the action rather than simply before vs. after. Thus, if tourism has been growing by 5 per cent per year and a new promotional programme increases this to 10 per cent this year, only half of the 10 per cent growth can likely be attributed to the promotional programme. Identifying the net changes in activity that are attributable to an action can be a complex and difficult task.
3. Assessments of economic impact, however, rest firmly on such estimates, so attention to these details is very important. In situations of some uncertainty, we recommend evaluating impacts using a range of estimates in order to establish rough confidence intervals around

your estimates. Evaluating a range of alternatives also helps to evaluate the sensitivity of the results to your initial estimates of changes in activity levels.

3. Identify the kinds of spending to be included. Tourism may impact the local economy through visitor trip spending, durable goods purchases, government spending, or investment and construction. Which to include in a given analysis depends on how the problem is defined, and again, on attributing given spending changes to the proposed action.
4. Identify the study region. Perhaps the most important, yet often neglected part of a recreation and tourism impact assessment is the definition of a study region. The region defines the area for which impacts are desired, as well as the portions of visitor spending that are relevant. An impact assessment evaluates the impacts on households, businesses, and organizations within the given region. Spending that visitors make outside of a study region either at home or en route are not included in assessing impacts of spending on the designated region. For an economic impact analysis, the study region should be large enough to constitute a viable economic region. Since little economic data exists below the county level, the county is generally the smallest region one should consider for a tourism impact assessment.
5. Identify key economic sectors and desired sectoral detail. The proposed action and anticipated uses/users of the results should suggest the key sectors that will be impacted. Recreation and tourism activity typically impact the lodging, restaurant, amusements, retail, transportation and government sectors most directly. In the problem definition stage consideration of impacted sectors helps to identify relevant categories of spending. The desired sectoral detail plays an important role in structuring the presentation of results. In some cases only an aggregate measure of impacts may be desired. In other cases, clients may be interested in which particular sectors are most heavily affected and will want estimates of sales and jobs broken down by sector. If formal input-output models are used, impacts may be estimated in considerable sectoral detail. This is not possible if an aggregate spending estimate or multiplier is used.
6. Identify the most important measures of economic activity. Tourism impacts may be reported in terms of visitor spending, business receipts/sales/production, wage and salary income, proprietors income and profits, value added, and employment. The direct effects are the most important and are captured well by estimates of visitor spending. Simple ratios can be used to convert direct spending or sales to the

associated income and jobs. Input-output models and multipliers are needed only if one is interested in secondary effects.

7. Identify the tolerable levels of error in the results. Although confidence intervals and estimates of error are rare in economic impact studies, this doesn't mean they are not important. You should have at least a ballpark idea of how much error you can tolerate in the analysis, as this will dictate how much effort and expense you must put into it. The more accuracy you demand, the greater the requirements to gather up-to-date local data on visitation, spending and economic activity. These data allow you to fine tune the spending estimates and input-output models or multipliers. Such fine tuning will require time, knowledge, and money that must be weighed against the benefits of the improved estimates. Estimates of impacts are based on three components: visits, spending, and multipliers. You should try to balance the errors across these components.
9. What are some questions to ask when evaluating or interpreting a tourism economic impact study?

Evaluating, interpreting and applying an economic impact study requires a clear understanding of the findings and at least some knowledge of the underlying concepts and methods. Judging the accuracy or quality of a study can be based on the reputation of the author or the quality of presentation, although a careful evaluation of the methods that were used is the best approach. Here's some questions to ask when reading or evaluating a tourism economic impact study.

Impact of what? The report should identify the action being evaluated. An economic impact assessment is most useful when evaluating the effects of a particular action or policy. If so, the action and assumptions about alternatives should be spelled out in presenting a with vs. without scenario. If the study reports impacts of existing tourism activity, identify how tourism is defined (if at all). What kinds of tourism activity and spending are included? Which trip expenses are included? Does the study include all visitor spending or only spending of tourists who live outside the local region? Does the study address impacts of visitor trip spending, durable goods purchases, operational expenses of a programme, or construction and investment?

On what region? The study region should be defined (preferably with a map). It should be viable both economically and as a distinct tourism destination area. Spending that is included should be restricted to spending in this region and multipliers should represent the given region of interest. A short profile of tourism and economic activity in the region provides useful background for an economic impact study.

Sources and quality of the data: The report should identify the sources of the data for estimating visits, spending, and regional economic multipliers/

models. The methods that were used to estimate impacts should be clear. Judgements of the quality of the estimates must be based largely on an understanding of the data and methods that were used. A more disaggregate analysis reporting spending within at least six categories, visitors for two or more distinct segments, and multipliers and results broken down by sector will generally be more accurate and meaningful than a study that only uses aggregate data. Disaggregation is particularly helpful when adjusting secondary data taken from government reports or other studies to a new situation. The fundamental question is whether the visit estimates, spending profiles and multipliers adequately represent the intended population and study area.

Quality of methods: There are a number of issues to watch for in evaluating methods.

Visits: Has the study clearly defined which visits/visitors will be affected by the proposed action, separated local visitors from tourists, and identified which visitors would be lost or gained due to the action (with vs. without the action)? Are secondary sources of visitation reliable? If models are used, how good are they and do the assumptions hold for the intended application? Has the study handled potential double counting problems in estimating visits?

Spending: How accurate are the spending estimates? Do the spending averages or totals seem reasonable? If spending averages are taken from a secondary source, evaluate the source, as well as how well these averages may apply to the intended application. What year does the spending represent? Has the data been price adjusted to the current (or model) year? If spending data come from a visitor survey, evaluate the survey methods - how was spending measured, what was the sample size, the response rate, soundness of the analysis? Are variances and confidence intervals reported for the spending estimates? Are visitors divided into distinct segments to reduce variances? Also make sure the units for which spending is reported match the units for visits, *i.e.*, the study doesn't multiply a per party spending average times the number of person visits. If adjustments are made in units of analysis, evaluate the assumed or estimated average length of stay or party size assumptions.

Multipliers: If "off-the-shelf" or borrowed multipliers are used, investigate the source. Does the study clearly define what type of multiplier is being used (Type I, Type III, income, sales or employment, ratio or Keynesian) and use the multiplier appropriately?

In particular, watch for studies that multiply tourism spending by a multiplier taken from an input-output model. They should adjust for the capture rate either by reducing spending, only using retail margins on goods purchased by tourists, or using a "tourist spending" multiplier that takes the capture rate into account. If an input-output model is used, the report should summarize where it came from, what year it represents, the levels of sectoral aggregation, and the basic assumptions of the model.

Communication and reporting of results: The study should communicate the study results in terms that are understandable to the intended audience. For most audiences, a summary and glossary of economic terms is helpful. Most readers will not fully understand terms like indirect and induced effects, Type I and Type III multipliers, and input-output models. Formal definitions of the measures of sales, income, and jobs that are reported are also needed to clarify what each of these terms include and the measurement units. For example, is income only wage and salary income or does it also include proprietors income, rents and profits? Study limitations and errors should be indicated.

Study Cost

The costs of a tourism economic impact study can range from $500 to $50,000 and more. Costs will depend largely on the size and scope of tourism activity to be covered, the size and complexity of the study region, how much primary data are to be gathered and the level of accuracy and detail desired. The greatest and perhaps most significant cost will be the technical expertise of the analysts involved. Tourism economic impact studies require considerable technical judgement of specialists and a mix of corresponding skills:

- Knowledge of tourism
- Expertise in conducting tourism surveys, particularly spending studies
- Regional economic modeling skills, including knowledge and access to economic data bases, multipliers and input-output modeling systems
- Communication skills

The cost of conducting economic impact studies has dropped substantially in the past ten years due to improvements in microcomputer programmes for estimating spending and regional economic models. The three principal components of an economic impact estimate (visits, spending, and multipliers) each involve different costs and somewhat different skills. The costs and needed skills will vary considerably depending on whether primary or existing data are to be used. If levels and types of tourism activity are known and spending averages and multipliers may be taken from secondary sources, a complete economic impact assessment can be conducted in less than a month and in many cases for under $5,000.

You are paying primarily for the time, judgement and skills of the analyst. A small visitor spending survey may add another $5,000. For a more complete analysis of secondary effects using a formal input- output model, figure another $2,000- $5,000. Increase the cost estimate if several distinct alternatives are to be evaluated or multiple regions are involved. There will generally be scale economies in these situations with additional impact analyses costing less than half of the initial one. Costs will increase significantly if the number and types of visitors must be estimated using a general visitor survey or a demand model. Large scale spending surveys and custom input-output models based on primary data will also increase costs considerably. In many cases, the tourism activity and visitor spending data needed for an economic impact analysis can be gathered in a general visitor survey or market study. Spending averages for particular tourist segments can be estimated by having a portion of the general survey respondents complete an extra page of spending questions. Armed with good estimates of the number and types of visitors and their spending patterns, one can complete an economic impact study at little additional cost.

The principal motivations for a business or region to serve tourists are generally economic. An individual business is interested primarily in its own revenues and costs, while a community or region is concerned with tourism's overall contribution to the economy, as well as its social, fiscal and environmental impacts. A good understanding of tourism's economic impacts is therefore important for the tourism industry, government officials, and the community as a whole.

Tourism economics is unfortunately a technical area, involving concepts, methods, and models that are unfamiliar to most non-economists. In this bulletin I've attempted to define the key concepts and explain the basic methods for estimating the economic impacts of tourism, hopefully in as "non-technical" a way as the subject allows. Understanding the concepts and methods is critical to interpreting, evaluating, and applying economic impact results. This bulletin should be read along with one or more economic impact reports that can be used as examples and opportunities to test your grasp of the issues.

Thirdly, focus most of your effort on estimating the direct effects of tourism, usually as tourist spending in the area. Multiplier effects are not nearly as important in most cases, as their use in tourism would suggest and multipliers tend to introduce complexities that most users of the results do not fully understand. Even if multiplier effects are important to the study purpose, remember that any errors in estimates of the direct effects will also be multiplied by any multiplier. Fourth, if you must use multipliers be sure you understand them.

10

Computer Applications in Tourism

INTRODUCTION

The behavioural scientist—by definition—studies and evaluates the complex interactions of men as individuals, within societies, and within environments. Why then should he be concerned with computers, which belong to the realm of the physical sciences? The behavioural scientist studies man-machine relations in order to define the role of man in the control and use of the machine and thus to optimize system interactions.

In the growth of computer technology, man is assigning increasingly complex tasks to the machine and, in turn, is freeing himself to assume increasingly more complex tasks. From subjects as basic as perception, learning, and thinking, through analysis of specialized social organizations, man is harnessing the capabilities of the computer as a powerful research tool. The researcher in behavioural science must learn to use this tool or risk being left behind as his discipline advances. But the computer is more than a research device; it is a production tool. As such, it is being used to automate manufacturing processes, warehousing and office procedures. The applied behavioural scientist must be aware of the effects of this new technology upon industrial management, labour, and the other forces in our society.

As a research tool, the computer may contribute in three principal functions:

- Organization and reduction of statistical data
- Hypothesis seeking, by finding relationships
- Hypothesis testing, through modeling and simulation

Research involves the accumulation of data and their eventual analysis and reduction. As our research capabilities expand, more and more data are accumulated and analysis becomes increasingly complex and time consuming. The statistical techniques are themselves becoming more sophisticated. If behavioural science remains chained to the desk calculator, it will stagnate. High-speed electronic data processing provides a means for rigourously, analysing masses of data. While analysing and reducing these data, special computer programmes can search for patterns and relationships which, because of the number and quality of variables, might remain obscured and undiscovered. From these patterns, the researcher can develop new and significant hypotheses. Testing hypotheses can also be facilitated through the use of automatic data processing technology, by using a computer to simulate and study human behaviour. But why study simulation models rather than human beings? The physiological psychologist will immediately recognize the similarity of this question to the older, more common query: "Why do you study rats if you are primarily interested in human behaviour?" And the answer is very much the same: By simulating behaviour on a computer, and studying its operation in detail, we can, by analogy, make inferences about the more complex human activities. These inferences must then be validated before being applied. By way of illustration, consider the temperature control mechanism of warm blooded animals, or more specifically of man.

Normal temperature is 9.6°. The body temperature must remain constant within approximately five degrees. Yet the temperature of the environment changes from 110° or more in the heat of summer to below freezing in winter. The organism's life depends upon accurate control of heat production and heat loss. As scientists, we are interested in studying the homeostatic mechanisms in temperature control; as computer-oriented researchers, we consider simulating this process. In fact, such a model already exists, for a thermostat operates in a fashion analogous to the hypothalamus. In a low ambient temperature, the body temperature tends to fall.

The skin, which has in it receptors for heat and cold, responds to the change. Messages are sent along nerve fibres to the hypothalamus, and the organism takes action to conserve body heat—action such as shivering and/or the constriction of blood vessels near the skin.

Alternately, responding to a high ambient temperature, the message sent to the hypothalamus initiates action to dissipate body heat. The thermostat works analogously. A desired room temperature is set. A thermometer is the sensing device or receptor. Detecting that the room is too cold, the thermometer creates a message, sent along an electrical conductor that controls and starts the furnace. When the temperature exceeds the optimal limit, the furnace is stopped. The simulation model, *i.e.*, the thermostat, operates on a feedback principle. The similarity between the operation of the thermostat and the observable control of body heat leads to the conclusion that the human organism uses a similar principle.

The hypothesis is, at the very least, worthy of additional study and testing. In the course of these interactions, the computer specialist learns to design more sophisticated machines, and the behavioural scientist achieves greater understanding of the human organism—the most complex of all machines. Through the data organization capabilities of the computer, far more complicated relationships can be defined and enormous masses of information processed in terms of those relationships. Thus the computer becomes analogous to organizations such as those comprising another machine, a natural resource, an industry, or a social community. The computer programmed to model an industry, for example, responds to controlled fluctuations in variables such as production, sales, inventory, etc., and provides a basis for generalized conclusions about the parameters and their relationships.

The analogy of the organization of the computer itself to that of the human nervous system is even more pertinent to the behavioural scientist. It has been suggested that experience leaves a permanent mark on the brain—possibly by changing the configuration of protein molecules in the brain cells. The existing memory trace permits recall of the experience. Computer memory is somewhat similar. Information is recorded by magnetizing a certain small area of core memory. The computer can recall this information by checking to determine whether the part is or is not magnetized. During the past few year, much effort has gone into the development of a formal theory of thought and memory.

Cybernetics has this basic concept: the brain is a control and communication system which can be described mathematically in the form of logical nets composed of elements and connections. Although man-made communication nets may become extremely complex, then do not approach the magnitude of complexity existing in the human organism. Certainly, if we were able to describe thought, memory, and other human processes in mathematical terms—John von Neumann has pointed out that self-reproduction is also a mathematical problem—we could achieve a much better understanding of these functions. But the development of a theoretical model is not sufficient in itself. The model must be checked and verified under various operating conditions. For testing, the use of the computer is a necessity. Hand calculation would be infinitely laborious if not outright impossible.

In research, the computer can be used:

- To simulate a system of complex interacting variables, in order to facilitate control of the elements under investigation
- To simulate the environment in which the system must operate, again to permit a study of the system under various environmental conditions
- To record, reduce, and aid in the mathematical analysis of experimental observations

Yet, as versatile as it is, the computer is only a tool. By itself it can accomplish nothing, but in the hands of an imaginative scientist, its potentials are almost limitless. The computer has ushered in the age of self-regulating devices and automatic control. As more extensive use is made of the computer potentialities, man will receive new benefits and face new problems.

Whether the behavioural scientist is interested in pure or applied research, he will be using the electronic computer. In addition, the applied scientist will be concerned with automation and its effects. The trend or direction in which automation is leading us is obvious, for it is simply an extrapolation of our present practices.

Just as mechanization has been a continuing process, so one can predict that automation will find ever wider applications throughout the economy. Production, the gross national product, and our standard of living will all continue to rise. New products that are the result of automated manufacturing techniques will appear on the market. Fewer people will be employed in routine factory and office jobs, but employment will increase in those concerns manufacturing automated equipment.

This is the trend. It is obvious, definite and inescapable. Attempts to dismiss it or to counteract it may delay the process, but cannot change it. Automation is on its way. How rapidly it is adopted depends upon how profitable it proves. Many objects—the small table radio for example-are already being manufactured and assembled completely automatically. Airplanes and missiles are being guided to their destination by an "automatic pilot."

Soon it will be possible for a person to start his car, set the dials, lean back and read the newspaper or watch television while an "automatic chauffeur" drives him to the office. Since automation must be economical if it is to be adopted, its greatest benefit may be considered to be the virtual elimination of expensive and unpredictable human labour in the performance of routine jobs.

These economic advantages of automation were stated quite precisely and accurately by Frank K. Shallenberger, President of the Shalco Engineering Corporation of Palo Alto, California, and Professor of Industrial Management at Stanford University: Automation has given us devices which can see better, hear better, and measure better than human operators. They think and move infinitely faster than humans. They never get tired, they willingly work around the clock, they do not make mistakes, they do not talk back, they are obedient, consistent, and fully predictable. They will not go out on strike, they do not ask annually for higher wages, and they have few personal problems. The country's defence needs have provided another major impetus towards automation. The nations of the Communist bloc outnumber the Free World in population. To offset their numerical advantage, the free nations of the world must maintain a higher man-hour production rate or risk being overtaken in the Cold War struggle.

Our government recognizes this fact, and the country's tax structure and allowable depreciation encourage capital outlay for tools and automated equipment. Besides the many potential advantages of automation, certain deterrents and problem areas must also be recognized. Because automation means change, management must make the initial difficult decision as to why, where, and how much to automate. New equipment is expensive, and cost is a major consideration.

Retooling inevitably means a change in the product design, and this raises questions of consumer acceptance, an intensified sales campaign, etc. Production problems may arise, because maximum efficiency requires that automated equipment operate continuously. In a seasonal industry, continuous production may result in a large inventory with concomitant storage and cost problems. The impact of the new machinery on the labour force must also be considered, for management neither desires nor can afford to ride roughshod over its employees. The workers must be prepared, so that they accept the change, and trained, so that they can operate and maintain the equipment. Al though these are primarily problem areas for business management, they are also challenges to the industrial psychologist. To make reasonably intelligent decisions, management must have information on the anticipated effects of automation.

More and more, the behavioural scientist is being relied on to provide the necessary data:

- There is a need for market sampling to provide information on how new products, will be received.
- There is a need for improved selection of personnel to fill the newly created technical jobs.
- There is a need for improved techniques of labour-management communication.
- There is a need for improved training methods to develop the new skills required by automation.
- There is a need for improved techniques of retraining in order to equip the semiskilled worker to handle the more technically demanding jobs in the automated plant.

The behavioural scientist must be prepared to meet these needs. Automation thus is providing new impetus for basic research in the social sciences and is expanding the industrial opportunities for the applied scientist. Fortunately, the computer—the same general purpose computer that led to the current industrial revolution and all these new problems-is providing the tool to enable the social scientist to carry on the new research. No discussion of automation is complete without some reference to the problem of technological unemployment.

The phrase "technological unemployment" has a strong emotional connotation, which often distorts objective investigation. Indisputably, automation will displace some people from some jobs. Some people will therefore be unemployed, but this does not mean that there need be any mass technological unemployment.

The harness maker became unemployed when the horse and buggy was replaced by the horseless carriage, yet the over-all effect of the automobile was increased employment. History has shown that in the long run change, invention, and automation result in a higher standard of living and increased employment. "In the long run," however, the individual worker may suffer unless he receives help. Helping the displaced worker is the continual responsibility of government, industry, and organized labour.

These agencies can provide the will and the means to help. The behavioural scientist must provide knowledge about retraining, counseling, and other techniques designed to ease any suffering resulting from the new technology. Finally, one benefit that could result from automation is the shortening of the work week and increased leisure. But leisure is valuable only if it is used constructively. Misused, it can be injurious, and there is evidence that some people are misusing the shorter work week. Increased leisure has been blamed for the increase in crime in recent years. Boredom is said to be responsible for the rise in the number of people requiring psychiatric treatment. Evidently there is need for a special programme of education designed to teach people to make constructive use of their leisure time and to divert energy to healthful channels of activity. But what is meant by "constructive use of leisure" and "healthful channels of activity"? How is one to decide whether it is healthier to play baseball or watch the game on television? Can the behavioural scientist, the sociologist, psychologist, and educator develop programmes to help?

INTERNET AND TRAVEL BOOKINGS

The marketing of travel on the Internet is growing rapidly and with this so is travel e-commerce. Unfortunately, the research information to date on people searching for travel information online and booking travel through the Internet has lacked depth and sophistication. Therefore, this study developed and tested predictive models for the likelihood of booking travel online and for being a repeat booker of travel online. Using an interactive survey method, the respondents were asked to provide information on their sociodemographic characteristics, travel-related behaviours, Internet usage patterns, perceptions of the Internet, and last trips booked online. Stepwise logistic regression analysis was then applied to develop the two predictive models. A conceptual model was suggested depicting the process through which people become Internet travel bookers.

Internet marketing and e-commerce are irreversible trends. By using the Web and Internet as marketing tools, tourism organizations have gained some distinct advantages in cost reduction, revenue growth, marketing research and database development, and customer retention. All the leading hotel chains, car rental and airline companies now have their own Web sites. More smaller tourism organizations are also beginning to use the Internet as a marketing tool. It will be impossible to have successful marketing programmes in the future without having an Internet strategy. The number of Internet travellers is growing rapidly. Almost all Internet users in 1998 were also travellers. Half of them got information on travel products via the Internet ("Internet travel lookers"). More Internet travel lookers (hereafter referred as to "lookers") are booking online and becoming "Internet travel bookers" (hereafter referred as to "bookers"). In 1999, the number of Americans booking travel online increased by more than 80 per cent to 11 million. Some 31 per cent of the lookers who visited online airline sites in 1999 made reservations through the Web, compared with 21 per cent in 1998. The percentage that booked rooms through hotel Web sites grew from 21 per cent to 28 per cent from 1998 to 1999, according to The NPD Group, Inc., and the percentage that booked vehicles through car rental Web sites rose from 19 per cent to 28 per cent in the same time span. Furthermore, the potential for online travel is enormous. Eight million American travellers are poised to make their first online purchase. This rapidly growing population is the key target group for online travel retailers and the identification of possible customers (bookers) is crucial to their success.

Paying specific attention to the repeat booker segment has many advantages. Building repeat patronage is a means by which suppliers can increase revenues and decrease costs by reducing reliance on the much more difficult task of attracting new bookers. Repeat patrons also have the potential to be employed as a marketing resource, providing referrals and promoting positive images of online booking, which can expand the retailer's customer base. Identifying repeat bookers could be important because appealing to the repeat bookers may be the most practical and cost-effective way of developing a business. However, until now no research has been done to determine the characteristics of repeat bookers.

The primary purpose of this study was to model lookers' probability of being bookers in terms of demographic characteristics, travel-related behaviour, Internet usage patterns, Internet perception variables, and variables about the last trip booked online in the past 12 months. The second purpose was to model bookers' probability of being repeat bookers in terms of the same five categories of variables. It was expected that the results of this study would help online travel retailers to develop more effective marketing strategies. Online travel retailers can reduce marketing costs and increase their sales by efficiently are its speed, access to large numbers of people at identifying potential bookers and repeat bookers. Additionally, online travel retailers can increase their revenues by improving marketing strategies and pro- viding better service to attract and retain more bookers if they know which factors significantly increase or decrease the probability of booking online.

Internet Marketing in Tourism

Not until 1990 could organizations apply for Internet membership without providing valid reasons for connectivity. During the last 10 years, the Internet has revolutionized the whole business world and transformed corporate strategies, including marketing strategy. The Internet represents a potentially powerful communication and distribution tool for tourism organizations. It is becoming a major force in building new relationships between customers and organizations. Tourism organizations can eliminate the obstacles created by geography, time zones, and locations by utilizing the Internet because it enables them to communicate directly with customers. Internet marketing can significantly reduce distribution and reservation through lower agent commissions and savings on reservations staff time and costs.

Internet marketing mainly involves the use of the Web and e-mail. A Web site is a powerful medium offering unique marketing, advertising, product and service information, and communication opportunities between an organization and existing and potential customers. The contents of Web pages vary according to the type and size of organization, but usually a reservations function is available at the Web sites of larger organizations. For smaller organizations, Web pages mainly serve as an information dissemination tool, but they still can provide online reservations through Internet travel services such as Travelocity.com. E-mail is a feature of the Internet mostly used for communication. Its major advantages over other communication means, such as telephone and fax, the same time, and inexpensiveness. E-mail provides tourism organizations with enormous marketing power and is playing a more important role in tourism. It can be used to communicate with customers directly through personalized messages realizing one-to-one relation- ship marketing. Internet travel retailers use e-mail to inform potential customers about limited-time offers, as well as last-minute promotions. Previous buying behaviours are recorded in databases. Confirmations can be promptly sent to online bookers by e-mail after they have made online reservations.

From the travelers' perspective, the Internet is a tool for gathering information and making reservations. Based on the WWW user survey conducted by the Graphics, Visualization, and Usability (GVU) Centre in October 1997, Weber and Roehl (1999) stated that online information represented the most popular source for making travel arrangements. Moreover, the attraction of Internet marketing to businesses is the fact that people are making intensive use of the Internet and the numbers of Internet users and travel lookers are growing quickly. Travel is one of the most popular e-commerce purchase types, with 45 per cent of online buyers saying they had purchased travel online. Only books outpaced this, at 54 per cent.

Bibliography

A.S. Dileep and T. Rajesh.: *Ayurvedic Tourism*, Sonali Publications, Delhi, 2012.

Alan A. Lew, C. Michael Hall, and Allan M. Williams.: *A Companion to Tourism*, Rawat Publication, Delhi, 2005.

Alexandru Nedelea and Babu P. George.: *Comparative Tourism Marketing : Case Studies*, Abhijeet Publication, Delhi, 2010.

Anurag Kothari.: *A Textbook of Tourism Management*, Wisdom Press, Delhi, 2011.

Arvind Gautam.: *Critical Analysis of Hospitality and Tourism Industry*, Axis Publication, New Delhi, 2010.

Atul Saxena.: *New Trends in Tourism and Hotel Industry*, Navyug Publication, Delhi, 2008.

B S Badan and Harish Bhatt.: *Culture and Tourism*, Commonwealth Publication, Delhi, 2007.

B. K. Goswami and G. Raveendran.: *A Textbook of Indian Tourism*, Har-anand Publications, Delhi, 2010.

B. K. Goswami and G. Raveendran.: *A Textbook of Tourism*, Haranand Publications, Delhi, 2010.

Bimal Kumar Kapoor.: *Tourism and Hotel Industry*, Murari Lal and Sons, Delhi, 2007.

David Carr.: *Community Tourism and Natural Resource Conservation*, Discovery Publishing House, Delhi, 2011.

Debasish Mazumdar and Lavkush Mishra.: *Contemporary Tourism Development: Issues and Challenges*, Rajat Publication, Delhi, 2010.

Dileep Makan.: *Conceptualization of Tourism*, Adhyayan Publication, Delhi, 2006.

Dilip Das.: *Critical Issues in Tourism*, Murari Lal and Sons, Delhi, 2011.

Gagandeep Singh.: *Civil Aviation and Tourism Administration*, Aadi Publication, Jaipur, 2011.

Geetanjali.: *Career in Tourism*, Centrum Press, Delhi, 2010.

Gulshan Soni.: *Consumer Protection in Hospitality Travel and Tourism*, Aman Publication, Delhi, 2011.

Jitendra K. Sharma.: *Contemporary Tourism and Hospitality Management*, Kanishka Publication, Delhi, 2006.

Krishan K. Kamra and Mohinder Chand.: *Basics of Tourism: Theory, Operation and Practice*, Kanishka Publication, Delhi, 2002.

Manohar Puri and Gian Chand.: *Tourism and Hotel Industry*, Pragun Publication, Delhi, 2006.

Nirmal Dubey.: *Hospitality Tourism and Hotel Management*, Sonali Publications, Delhi, 2011.

P.K. Bal.: *A Textbook of Hospitality Tourism and Aviation*, Cyber Tech Publication, New Delhi, 2011.

Pragati Mohanty.: *Hotel Industry and Tourism in India*, APH Publication, Delhi, 2008.

Prem Nath Dhar.: *Cultural and Heritage Tourism: An Overview*, Kanishka Publication, Delhi, 2008.

R.M. Ahuja.: *A Handbook of Adventure Tourism*, Sumit Enterprises, Delhi, 2011.

Rattandeep Singh.: *Commonwealth Games and Sports Tourism: Global and National Perspectives*, Kanishka Publishers, Delhi, 2010.

Ravee Chauhan.: *Advanced Hotel Industry and Tourism*, Vista International Publishing House, Delhi, 2011.

Romila Chawla.: *Accommodation Management and Tourism*, Sonali Publication, Delhi, 2006.

Romila Chawla.: *Coastal Tourism and Development*, Sonali Publication, Delhi, 2004.

Rowe.: *Career Award Travel and Tourism: Standard Level*, Cambridge University Press, United Kingdom, 2001.

Suddhendu Narayan Misra and Sapan Kumar Sadual.: *Basics of Tourism Management*, Excel Books, London, 2001.

T.K. Sathyadev and P. Manjunath.: *Tourism and Hotel Management*, Pacific Books International, New Delhi, 2012.

Thomas Walsh.: *Creative Tourism*, Discovery Publishing House, Delhi, 2011.

V.Varija.: *Cultural Tourism in Andhra Pradesh*, Bharatiya Kala Prakashan, Delhi, 2011.

Vanaja Uday.: *Cultural Tourism and Performing Arts of Andhra Pradesh : Prospects and Perspectives*, Research India Press, 2012.

Index